D1573181

The Bisbee Massacre

*Robbery, Murder and
Retribution in the Arizona
Territory, 1883–1884*

DAVID GRASSÉ

Foreword by Marshall Trimble

McFarland & Company, Inc., Publishers
Jefferson, North Carolina

LIBRARY OF CONGRESS CATALOGUING-IN-PUBLICATION DATA

Names: Grassé, David, author.
Title: The Bisbee massacre : robbery, murder and retribution in the Arizona
Territory, 1883–1884 / David Grassé ; foreword by Marshall Trimble.
Description: Jefferson, North Carolina : McFarland & Company, Inc.,
Publishers, 2017. | Includes bibliographical references and index.
Identifiers: LCCN 2017001449 | ISBN 9781476667317
(softcover : alkaline paper) ∞
Subjects: LCSH: Massacres—Arizona—Bisbee—History—19th century. |
Outlaws—Arizona—Bisbee—History—19th century. | Cowboys—
Arizona—Bisbee—History—19th century. | Robbery—Arizona—
Bisbee—History—19th century. | Murder—Arizona—Bisbee—
History—19th century. | Revenge—Arizona—Bisbee—History—
19th century. | Bisbee (Ariz.)—History—19th century. |
Frontier and pioneer life—Arizona—Bisbee.
Classification: LCC F819.B6 G73 2017 | DDC 979.1/5302—dc23
LC record available at https://lccn.loc.gov/2017001449

BRITISH LIBRARY CATALOGUING DATA ARE AVAILABLE

ISBN (print) 978-1-4766-6731-7
ISBN (ebook) 978-1-4766-2735-9

Front cover: the lynching of John Heath (author's collection);
John Heath's gravestone in Boothill Cemetery
in Tombstone, Arizona (Library of Congress)

Printed in the United States of America

*McFarland & Company, Inc., Publishers
Box 611, Jefferson, North Carolina 28640
www.mcfarlandpub.com*

To my parents, Walter and Gerry Grassie.
"I don't have the words…"

Table of Contents

Foreword
by Marshall Trimble

On the evening of December 8th, 1883, five heavily-armed men rode boldly into Bisbee, tied their horses near Main Street and walked up the street to the Goldwater-Castaneda mercantile store which also served as the local bank. All but one were wearing kerchief masks. Two of them, armed with pistols and Winchester rifles positioned themselves at the front door while the other three entered with pistols drawn and ordered the patrons to raise their hands. One spotted one of the proprietors, Joseph Goldwater, and ordered him to open the safe. It was supposed to contain the payroll for the miners working for the Copper Queen Mining Company. However, the stagecoach carrying the big payroll hadn't arrived yet. Their take in the heist was small, about $800 and two gold watches.

Outside the store, shooting erupted as the two bandits posted at the front door began firing randomly up and down Main Street. In just a few moments three men, including a deputy sheriff and a woman, eight months pregnant, lay dead or dying in the street.

The five outlaws moved hurriedly back to their horses, mounted up and quickly rode out of town heading east towards the Sulphur Springs Valley.

The brutal and senseless killings would become known as the Bisbee Massacre.

Immediately after the gang made a hasty exit a posse was organized and went after the gang in hot pursuit. In the posse was a man who'd recently arrived in town named John Heath, who picked up the trail and about nine miles out of Bisbee, noted where the gang had split up.

The posse returned empty-handed having lost the trail but thanks to some good detective work on the part of Cochise County lawmen all five were quickly rounded up. The outlaws were identified as Omer "Red" Sample, James "Tex" Howard, Dan Dowd, Bill Delaney and Dan Kelly.

When the gang split up, Delaney and Dowd had headed for Sonora and Kelly for New Mexico. Sample and Howard returned to their stomping ground at Clifton where they stopped at Maud Elby's brothel and showed the girls the money and a couple of gold watches taken in the robbery. They also allegedly implicated a sixth man who'd lived in Clifton until recently. From there things began to unravel. The sixth man said to have planned the robbery and acted as inside man was John Heath. He was also arrested and charged with murder.

1

The wheels of justice was moving swiftly. Two months and a day after the massacre their trial began at the county courthouse in Tombstone.

Author David Grassé has done an excellent job of piecing together the story of one of Arizona's most sensational murder-robberies. Even more fascinating are the probing questions he raises. He dissects the testimony given by witnesses at the trial and takes what appears to be an open and shut case and turns it into a real page turner.

He also raises a number of questions. The citizens of Bisbee and Tombstone were outraged and wanted blood. So, why weren't they given a change of venue? And, why weren't they given separate trials instead of trying all five men together? Most of the testimony by the witnesses was hearsay and circumstantial. Could the court-appointed attorneys have done a better job defending their clients? Did they fear public retribution if they represented the defendants too well and planted seeds of doubt in the jury?

There was never any doubt about the outcome. The five men were convicted, found guilty and sentenced to hang on March 28th, a few weeks after the trial ended. Because he wasn't present at the scene of the crime, Heath was tried separately. His trial began immediately after the others were sentenced. All five testified that Heath had nothing to do with planning or participating in the Bisbee robbery-murder.

Heath was found guilty of murder but sentenced to life in the territorial prison. On the morning of February 22, an angry mob stormed the jail, ignoring the five condemned men, took Heath out and hanged him from a telegraph pole on Toughnut Street. John Heath was the only man in Tombstone's wild and wooly history to be lynched.

A few weeks later, on March 29, the five condemned men stood on the scaffold. Each proclaimed his innocence. It would be the largest mass hanging in Arizona history.

The Bisbee Massacre is much more than the story of the massacre and the trial that followed. There are biographies of key figures in the rich history of Cochise County from the movers and shakers to men on both sides of the law. Grassé tells us about the aftermath and what became of the principal figures in the story in the years that followed.

There is also a comprehensive history of the "Queen of the Copper Camps" early history including Army Scout Jack Dunn's discovery of the rich mineral deposits in Tombstone Canyon that led to the founding of what many have called the grandest city between San Francisco and New Orleans.

The Bisbee Massacre belongs on the bookshelf of anybody with an interest in frontier justice, Arizona and western history.

> Marshall Trimble
> Arizona State Historian

Preface and Acknowledgments

I would be hard-pressed to say exactly why I chose the subject of the Bisbee Massacre, what the impetus was for writing an entire book about it. The episode just intrigued me. Aside from the legendary feud between the Earps and the cowboys, the trial, conviction, and subsequent punishment of the Bisbee bandits was the most newsworthy event to happen in Cochise County in the late 1800s, yet no one, to my knowledge, has ever bothered to really delve into the event and produce a nuanced and in-depth study of this often overlooked, albeit darker, historical episode. Though events of the Bisbee Massacre have been recounted again and again, no previous writer had taken the time to gather together all the threads that so enhance the telling of this particular event. It was my ambition to collect all these different threads and weave them into a cohesive whole—a whole which would be both informative and entertaining.

When I first began this project, I very much thought I would simply be chronicling an event chronicled many times before, although with a little more detail than before. I wanted to include Deputy Sheriff William "Billy" Daniels and his pursuit and subsequent capture of the outlaws Dan "Big Dan" Dowd and William Delaney. The 1800s were an era completely devoid of the forensic science methods and sophisticated tools used in today's criminal investigations, such as mug shots, fingerprints, DNA evidence, computers, telephonic communication, digital surveillance, paper trails, etc. Yet here was a determined law enforcement officer, utilizing only a horse, an expert tracker and a single photograph, who was able to trail his quarry through the Arizona deserts—arguably some of the most inhospitable country ever created—across an international border, and into a foreign country and to capture both men without firing a single shot. This is a pretty impressive feat just in and of itself—a truly amazing and commendable piece of detective work.

However, it was not until midway through the episode that I realized there was something much more astounding about the Bisbee Massacre than Deputy Sheriff Daniels' heroic quest—something completely overlooked (or willfully ignored) by every previous researcher that would contest the accepted history: Mr. John Heath. I must admit I approached this project under the assumption that John Heath had been the mastermind behind the Bisbee Massacre—that it was he who had chosen the men, planned the caper, and would share in the spoils. This, after all, is the cherished legend. Every book, newspaper, and magazine article written thus far has testified to this version as being unimpeachable historical fact. I had heard about the Bisbee Massacre so many times, I had come to take it for granted as well. As far as my extensive research has taken me, there are no other versions of this episode extant. And so thinking, I commenced this manuscript with a presupposition of John Heath's guilt.

You know what they say about making assumptions ... the same goes for presupposition.

I am not going to make an assertion in regard to John Heath. I do have an opinion on the subject (as I do about most things) which you may well be able to discern from reading this book. But I have purposely stopped short of stating this is an absolute certainty, because, the truth is, I do not know it is an absolute certainty. And, unlike erstwhile writers of my acquaintance, I do not believe I am infallible. I am not going to attempt to pass my base-metal hypothesis off as 24-karat fact. Rather, I am going to leave it to you, the reader, to develop your own opinion as to Heath's guilt based on the evidence and arguments presented herein.

Additionally, I decided against analyzing the Bisbee Massacre in terms of its political and sociological implications. I considered arguing that the robbery and trials exemplified class struggles between the proletariat, as represented by the outlaws, and capital, as represented by the mine owners, which were common to the late 19th century, but thought better of it. Though the outlaws could be painted as working class insurgents rising up in opposition to an unjust system, the truth is this is not a Robin Hood–type occurrence. The perpetrators of the robbery of Goldwater & Castaneda's Mercantile were as much capitalists as the owners of the mines—both parties looking to fill their pockets at the expense of others.

I also considered comparing and contrasting the events surrounding the Bisbee Massacre with other crimes of the era, especially those committed by contemporary outlaw confederations such as the Sam Bass Gang and the "Black Jack" Ketchum Gang, but I felt that making such correlations would only diminish what is very much a unique occurrence in the Old West. Most of the significant outlaw gangs of the period consisted of either train and stagecoach robbers or livestock rustlers. There were a select few, such as the James-Younger Gang and the Hole-in-the-Wall Gang, which targeted banks also, but there are almost no instances of a gang of outlaws holding up an innocent mercantile on a bustling Saturday evening. The Bisbee robbery was a rather singular episode in the annals of crime in the Old West.

So, after due consideration, I chose to dispense with the idea of interpreting the Bisbee Massacre in terms of the political or sociological. In the end, I really just wanted to share an interesting event. I will leave the analysis of these events to others.

This said, I will beg your indulgence while I take a few moments to thank some of the people who helped to bring this book to fruition. First, I would like to extend my thanks to the staff at the Arizona State Library, Archives and Public Records, including Wendy Goen, Laura Palma-Blandford, Libby Coyner, and Ellen Greene, for being so generous with their time and assistance; the staff at the Arizona Historical Society, especially Ms. Laraine Daly Jones; and Ms. Amy Finston, Reference Desk Coordinator, Sharlott Hall Museum Library and Archives, and Sammie Townsend Lee, Library Associate, at the Texas and Dallas History Collection, Dallas Public Library, both of whom were instrumental in helping bring this manuscript to life.

I would also like to extend special thanks to genealogist Jean Ann Ables-Flatt for putting me on the right track with regards to the Heath family tree; Mr. Tony Black, Appraisal Archivist, Archives and Information Services Division, Texas State Library and Archives Commission, for his aid in finding the information in the first of the John Heath cases; and Ms. Mary Ann Igna and John Kyritsis of the Desert Caballeros Western Museum in Wickenburg for allowing me to photograph John Heath's revolver and being so very accommodating.

Closer to home, I would like to extend my gratitude to Ms. Amanda Hetro and Ms. Annie Larkin, present and past curators, as well as Stan A. Lehman and Don Healy, docents, at the Bisbee Mine Museum; Ms. Patricia Moreno of Tombstone for taking me on a guided tour of the old Cochise County courthouse; and Ms. Lizeth Zepeda at the Arizona Historical Society who tirelessly pulled folder after folder of photographs for my perusal. Further, I would like to thank Ms. Elaine Baca for her diligent work in editing and indexing this project.

I must also give mention to a few gentlemen who have been instrumental in my continued success as an author. First, I would like to thank Mr. Dakota Livesay, founder of *Chronicle of the Old West*, for hosting me on his show and helping to support my first published effort; Mr. Jeffery Millet of Graphic Publishers of Santa Ana for taking a gamble on an unknown author with a manuscript about an all-but-forgotten Arizona lawman; and last, but certainly not least, Dr. Bruce Dinges, editor of *The Journal of Arizona History*, who has been greatly supportive and encouraging of all my efforts in this field.

I would especially like to thank both Ms. Elizabeth "Lizzie" Mead, owner of Silver Sea Jewelry, and Ms. Margo Susco, the owner of Hydra, for always being true friends and supporting me in all my endeavors. Thank you for being there.

And I would be remiss [to say the least] in neglecting to mention my indebtedness to one of my dearest friends, Ms. Jennifer "Jenn" Wilfing. As she tends to get a bit flustered if you give her too many compliments, I will simply say, "I could not ask for a better friend," and leave it at that.

Lastly, a special, heart-felt thanks to all of you—friends, family, and those who are strangers to me—who put down their hard-earned money to buy a copy of my first book. I hope you will enjoy this one as much as you enjoyed the first one.

Prologue

The sonorous, cast-iron bell at the Tombstone Firehouse hung silently in the cool, dry air of a cloudless February morning. The bell was scheduled to have been rung earlier in the morning to announce the gathering at that location, and to summon the laborers back from the start of their shifts at the Grand Central, the Contention and the Toughnut silver mines. Still the bell remained ominously silent, and the workers had arrived at the mines only to find the elevator cages, which carried them down the shafts and deep into the earth's continental crust, were not running, and there was no one around to explain what had happened. Soon, the entire shift crews of all three of the mines found themselves standing about with their lanterns and tools in the chilly weather wondering at this unprecedented and unplanned-for occurrence.

The Tombstone Firehouse was plainly visible from all three of the mines. The workers could see a fair-sized group of townsmen had already assembled at that place, but still the fire-bell was not being sounded. There was restless and impatient discussion amongst the miners about what was going on up the hill and what course of action should be taken, mostly in hushed, urgent tones. Finally, one of the workers from the Contention mine secured a saddle horse and rode up the hill to the firehouse in the hope of obtaining some information. Upon arriving at his destination, the miner was met by a somber delegation of Tombstone citizens, led by a number of prominent mining men and civic figures from the nearby town of Bisbee. Most of the men present were armed.

It had been announced the previous day that all the mines in Bisbee, including the famed Copper Queen, would be temporarily closed on this day, so the miners and those employed within the mine management companies would be able to attend the gathering in Tombstone. Stanley C. Bagg, former editor of *The Tombstone Weekly Prospector* and eyewitness to the events of that day, recalled that the men of Bisbee, 100 strong, after securing horses and arms for themselves, rode through the night, across "a high pass and over the starlit deserts" in order to arrive at the firehouse in Tombstone early that next morning. Bagg also recalled the date, February 22, George Washington's birthday.[1]

A brief discussion ensued between the men gathered outside the firehouse and the lone miner. The miner was informed of the purpose of the gathering. When the miner inquired why no signal had been given, the men at the firehouse explained that they had not known about any prearranged signal nor that they had been expected to sound the bell once they had gathered. There had been some oversight or miscommunication somewhere along the line. It was there and then decided to forego the ringing of the firehouse bell altogether, as it might attract unwanted attention for all parties involved. Instead, the miner was ordered to ride back across the desert terrain to each of the three mines to deliver the dispatch from the firehouse that all was in readiness.

Upon receiving the news, the workers from the Grand Central mine proceeded up the hill to the Contention mine and, joining with the men from that locale, continued onward past the Toughnut mine, where they were joined by the workers there. The crowd of mining men, who were dressed similarly in work clothes, woolen jackets, and thick, heavy boots, were unusually quiet—almost funereal in aspect—as they made their way along Toughnut Street to the firehouse, on the block between 5th and 6th Streets, and the waiting clutch of townsmen. There was no shouting or other commotion among them.

Upon the miners' arrival, there were a few brief introductions and some conversation among the leaders. Every man, miners and townsfolk alike, was given the choice to either join the assemblage or return to their homes that morning. Tombstone resident George Parsons noted in his diary entry for February 22, 1884, that there were "no dissenters." Moments later, the entire body of men turned to the southwest and began the short walk toward the intersection of Toughnut and 4th Street where stood the Cochise County Courthouse. As they proceeded down the rock-strewn street, the courthouse, with its peaked roof, elegant white fascia, red brick chimney, and bell tower rose up majestically before them.[2]

The passage of the men down Toughnut Street was orderly and quiet. Though many of these citizens were armed with revolvers and rifles, none wore masks or sought to hide their faces. The men involved were all citizens of the county, residents of either Bisbee or Tombstone. The assemblage included both civic leaders and common-folk, and they were not afraid to be recognized or identified, as they felt their purpose was righteous. The men who led the march toward the courthouse this clear and brisk Friday morning believed a grave injustice had been perpetuated and they were resolved to give Lady Justice her due and proper. This was to be a reckoning.

The time was just after 8 a.m. In spite of the confusion over the failed signal from the firehouse bell and the slight delay this had caused, everything was proceeding just as it had been planned. Thus far, there had been no problems and no trouble. The crowd of men continued noiselessly along the wide, dusty street and on toward the County Courthouse, carrying with them a strong sense of resolve and a goodly length of rope with a noose tied into the end.[3]

CHAPTER ONE

The Town

The civilian scout and army tracker John Dunn, who was better known to most by the name of Jack, had ventured into the Mule Mountains in the southeastern Arizona Territory at the head of a detachment of 15 hard-tack soldiers from Company C, 6th Cavalry of the United States Army. The reconnaissance unit, under the command of Lieutenant John A. Rucker, had come to the scrub oak and prickly pear-covered slopes of these low hills in search of renegade Apache bands, that had been raiding settlements and ranches and attacking civilians throughout Northern Mexico and the Arizona Territory since the Anglos had first arrived in the area. The company had ridden out of Fort Bowie on May 9, 1877, and would spend the next three weeks afield, scouting for Indians. While Dunn was unable to find any sign of the Apache, the native of Ireland would inadvertently discover one of largest copper ore deposits in the United States.[1]

The Apache had long utilized the Mule Mountains as a way-station in their travels between the Mexican state of Sonora and their homeland in Arizona. Two natural springs occur within the hills forming Mule Gulch. The first spring, which would come to be christened Iron Springs, was located at the lower end of Mule Gulch. The second spring was located to the northwest in the upper portion of the same gulch (which would eventually come to be called Tombstone Canyon), gurgling forth near the base of a large rock formation known as Castle Rock. This spring would be after known as Apache. It was at the former spring that Dunn, Lt. Rucker, and the rest of the troop first bivouacked soon after entering the hills. However, the water from this first spring was somewhat brackish and, while potable, was not to the taste of the soldiers. The following morning, Lieutenant Rucker sent Dunn out to scout for a better source of water for his men and the animals.

Jack Dunn traversed the rocky, manzanita-covered slopes lining the gulch until he came upon the second spring at the base of Castle Rock, about half a mile up from the campsite. Always alert and observant of his surroundings, the scout also noticed a large limestone formation which, on further examination, showed signs of cerrusite and other minerals oft-times associated with silver ore deposits. On his way back to the original campsite, Dunn stopped and picked up a few choice ore samples from around the area of the outcropping. The erstwhile scout took the samples he had collected back to camp with him in order to present them to Lieutenant Rucker for the officer's consideration.

Upon his return, Dunn showed the ore samples to the Lieutenant and one T.D. Bryce, a civilian contractor who was also travelling with the troop. The following day, the soldiers moved the camp to the spring at the base of Castle Rock while Dunn, Rucker,

Left: John "Jack" Dunn, civilian scout for the U.S. 6th Cavalry, was the first to discover the ore deposits in the Mule Mountains. *Right:* Lieutenant John A. Rucker, 6th Cavalry, U.S. Army, and partner to John "Jack" Dunn, for whom the "Rucker Mine" was named (courtesy the Bisbee Mining & Historical Museum).

and Bryce further investigated the area surrounding the outcropping. The three men, believing they had made a discovery of some importance, staked off a rectangular section and marked the boundaries of their new claim with piles of rocks. They christened it the "Rucker Mine." The three men then gathered up some additional ore samples with the intention of taking them to an assayer upon their return to civilization. They also intended, as a matter of course, to register the claim with the County Recorder's Office in Tucson.

One can only imagine the latent feelings of excitation and expectation which the three men experienced as the troop broke camp and rode out of Mule Gulch the following day. Unfortunately, the demands of the U.S. Army took precedence over their personal concerns and ambitions. Their orders were to hunt for Apache renegades, not mineral deposits. The cavalry troop continued on with their assigned mission, proceeding northward through the cut that would come to be called Brewery Gulch, then travelling east through Dixie Canyon, and out across the plain of the Sulphur Springs Valley. Rucker's troop of cavalry remained in the field for 22 days, finally returning to Fort Bowie on May 31, 1877.[2]

Sometimes the fates cooperate with the best-laid plans of man and sometimes, it would seem, they do their best to thwart them. Dunn, Rucker, and Bryce were unable to file their claim upon their return to Fort Bowie as other duties demanded their attentions.

Castle Rock, Bisbee, Arizona Territory (author's collection).

It was almost three months later, on August 29, 1877, that Bryce was finally able to file notice of location with Pima County Recorder Sidney Carpenter. Oddly, the date of discovery was listed as being August 2 even though the troop had visited the site in May. The reason for this discrepancy is unknown. In the interim between the initial discovery and the filing of the Rucker Mine claim, a fourth man was brought into the partnership by Dunn. This man was George Warren, a part-time prospector, part-time teamster, part-time civilian scout for the army, and a full-time alcoholic.[3]

George Warren was born in Massachusetts in or about 1835. His mother died during his infancy and, as a child, he was sent to live with an aunt. At the age of 10, Warren was sent west to join his father Charles "Charley" Warren, a teamster for the U.S. Government, in the New Mexico Territory. One afternoon in 1859, George was out herding horses with his father when they were attacked by a band of Apache. The senior Warren was killed outright and George, just a boy, was wounded and taken captive. For the next 18 months, young George was virtually a slave to the Apache band which had captured him. His release was finally secured by a group of prospectors who, according to legend, traded 15 pounds of sugar for the young man. Orphaned and alone in the world, George was informally adopted by the prospectors and came to learn the fundamentals of geology, mining, and prospecting from these men who had rescued him. With time, Warren gained a mixed reputation both as a talented prospector and as a regular imbiber, a skill also learned from life amongst the prospectors.[4]

Warren was quite familiar with the Mule Mountains having prospected the area himself as early as 1869 with negligible results. This was probably the reason that Jack Dunn, who was busy with Army obligations, grubstaked and outfitted Warren, instructing him to further search the gulches and canyons around the mountains for indications of ore mineralization. Dunn and Warren agreed that they would equally divide all that Warren discovered between them, and that Warren would name Dunn on all claim notices he filed with the County Recorder in Tucson. However, instead proceeding directly towards the Mule Mountains as he had said he would, Warren chose to visit Camp Detachment, an outlying Army post that would eventually grow into Fort Huachuca. Once there, Warren began recruiting new partners in the venture. It is not known on what date Warren and his confederates finally reached the Mule Mountains, but on October 4, 1877, "at 49 minutes past 11 a.m.," Warren, in the company of his new partners, George Beat, M.M. Chapin, Harry McCoy, and Frank McKern, filed his first notice of location with the Pima County Recorder, Sidney Carpenter, on the Mercey Mine, which was staked on September 27, 1877. Jack Dunn's name did not appear anywhere on the document.[5]

There would be at least 12 claims located in Mule Gulch that first year after the filing of the Rucker Mine claim. The following year there would be 14 more and two relocations. Civil War veteran and early Bisbee pioneer, Judge James F. Duncan stated that there were actually more claims besides these, including the New York Mine which he personally staked out in November of 1879. For most though, the "scarcity of funds ... a disease at that time very prevalent" kept them from recording any claims rightfully staked. If such a "disease" did exist amongst the early claimants, George Warren seemed immune. In addition to the original Mercey Mine claim, which Duncan stated was never actually worked, Warren filed claims as the locator of the McKean, Rob, Neptune, Iron Springs, Wade Hampton, and Tar Heel mines. Warren also acted as witness to claims on a number of other mines, including the Silver Queen, Mohawk, Emmett, Halero, Virginia, and Excelsior. Again, Jack Dunn's name is absent from every document except the original Rucker Mine claim.[6]

However, what would become one of the most important claims in the Mule Mountains was not one of Warren's or his numerous associates, but a claim which was initially staked out by Messrs. Hugh J. Jones, Joseph Halero, and Harry (Henry?) McCoy. Recorded on December 14, 1877, and named for Halero, this particular claim was situated in Mule Gulch a mile and a half west of Iron Springs. More interested in silver, Jones bowed out of the venture when he discovered the mine was only producing copper stain, leaving Halero and McCoy as the sole owners.

The biggest obstacle confronting early prospectors in the Mule Mountains was finding a method to refine the ore they were unearthing so that it would be profitable to ship back east for further refining. To this end, David B. Rea, who had been brought in as a partner to Warren in the Mercey Mine venture, returned to Tucson to enlist the aid of Warner Buck for the construction of a furnace in which to smelt the ore which was being unearthed. Rea and Buck returned to the gulch with all the equipment necessary to the building of a charcoal-burning Catalonian furnace. Unfortunately for Halero and McCoy, the primitive smelter was only able to turn out copper matte and the return on the matte was inadequate to cover the transportation costs to refineries in the east.[7]

Disappointed by the returns on their investment, Halero and McCoy would eventually come to deed the Halero claim to George H. Eddleman and Tombstone attorney Col. William Herring. Eddleman and Herring would relocate the claim in December of

1878. Warren's Mercey Mine was also relocated in December of that year. George Eddleman shared a joint interest in the Mercey Mine along with Warren and his partner, David Rea. Eddleman and Herring eventually brought in Rea as a full partner, giving him one-third interest in the Halero venture. George Warren's Mercey Mine, which was just to the west of the Halero mine, would be renamed the Copper King and the Halero Mine would be re-christened the Copper Queen. And, while Eddleman kept his share of the Copper Queen mine intact, Herring and Rea divided their shares even further. Herring deeded one-third interests of his one-third interest to G.W. Anshurtz and George Klein in exchange for their help in assessing the Copper Queen claim. Rea divided his one-third interest equally with Warner Buck and the ubiquitous George Warren.[8]

For the briefest period, it seemed as if Warren's scheming and conniving would finally pay off, but this was not to be. A short time after being made a partner in the mines, Warren was visiting the saloons of Charleston, a rough frontier town just 20 miles distance from the Bisbee camp. Warren was deep in his cups when he decided to risk his interest in the Copper Queen venture on a rather unusual horserace—one between himself and a horse. In a moment of drunken bravado, Warren bet a man by the name of George W. Atkins that he could beat a man on horseback to a stake driven in the ground at a hundred yards distance, round it, and return to the starting point before the horseman could catch up with him. Warren optimistically reasoned that while the horse could easily outpace him on the straightaway, the animal was unable to take the turn around the stake as sharply as a man on foot could thus giving him the advantage and securing his victory.

George Atkins was not about to forgo the opportunity to separate a fool from his money (or in this case, his mining claim) and took the bet. Atkins put up his own mining claims and his saddle horse against Warren's interest in the Copper Queen venture and the race was on. To his credit, Warren was able to beat the horse up to and around the stake, but as would be expected, lost to the horseman on the straight run back to the finish line and, in losing the race,

George Warren, prospector, to whom Dunn and Rucker unwisely trusted their mining interests (author's collection).

lost the entirety of his 1/9th interest in the Copper Queen Mine. Additionally, Warren conveyed to Atkins his 1/9th interest in the Copper King and his 1/4 interest in the Neptune Mine. This would be the first of many misfortunes which would befall Warren over the remaining 15 years of life.[9]

By 1880, the mining camp in the Mule Mountains was beginning to resemble a substantial settlement. What began as a ramshackle collection of canvas tents and rough-hewn rock cabins was taking on the appearance of a proper townsite. While the burg still lacked a church, there were at least four saloons, army scout Albert B. "Al" Seiber's brewery (for which Brewery Gulch would later be named), a miner's mercantile, and General Allen's general store. Mail was delivered in from Charleston thrice weekly, at the rate of ten cents a letter, by John Watson, a private contractor. Watson also freighted passengers and supplies into Mule Gulch. On June 12, Manuel Simas opened the first restaurant in the camp, with his wife cooking and serving meals outdoors beneath a large tree.[10]

In their October 16 edition, the *Arizona Weekly Citizen* reported that the "lively little camp is having a 'boom' and no mistake. The [*sic*] are already 200 people in camp, and more coming daily, there being two buckboard lines from Charleston." Citing as their source an unnamed "gentleman just in from Bisbee City," the newspaper went on to report "that parties are now in this city [Tucson] negotiating the purchase of the Copper King mine, the western extension of the Copper Queen—which is proving such a bonanza—with a view to putting up extensive smelters thereon."

A month prior, *The Weekly Citizen* noted, "So deep an interest have the population of Arizona's brightest prospect [Tombstone] taken in Bisbee City that a subscription for direct communication has met with hearty approval" and that "Messrs. Chas. Ackley, Jas. Dickey, and H.M. Woods have surveyed the closest possible roadway this side of the San Pedro river, making an easy access to the Pass without passing through Charleston and avoiding a long circuitous route of about ten miles of unnecessary travel." The newspaper added that the new road had already been "flagged."[11]

James Duncan described his first sojourn to the fledgling camp thus:

> On my way that day I was more impressed with my surroundings than I ever was before in my life.... As I travelled up the Gulch its beauty, as it was unfolded to my sight made me feel indeed as if I had ceased to exist on earth. There was Mule Gulch almost in its virgin glory, scarcely disturbed by the hand of man, with its high hills on either side thickly covered with trees that had stood there for ages, festooned with mistletoe. It was indeed a grand sight. If I had been disgusted with what I had seen before of Arizona, I was more struck with its beauty in the Mule Mountains.... On my way up the road I came to a set of bars across the road, the first sign of the handiwork of man. The gulch was fenced with brush up the sides of the hills for some distance. The fence was where Col. Herring built his house in 1880. Afterward it was used as a Custom house.
>
> Proceeding on up, I came to the first cabin on the south side of the gulch, this cabin was occupied by two Union soldiers who had served in the Civil War—Marcus Herring [the brother of Colonel William Herring] ... and George Eddleman.... Next above was the tent of Charley Vincent.... Directly across from Vincent's tent was the cabin of Joe Dyer; it was just below the flood gates. Near the spring was the old rock cabin of D.B. Ray [*sic*] and Warren. About half way in the middle of the gulch, between the rock cabin and the Dyer cabin, stood the remains of the smelter used by Ray [*sic*], Buck, and Warren.... I never spent a more pleasing time than I did while there.[12]

As Bisbee historian Lynn R. Bailey observed, the early prospectors of the Mule Mountains did not have the necessary capital to properly develop their claims—to employ laborers, to construct smelters, to cover transportation costs, and the like. Hence, most of the original claimants, like Joseph Halero and Henry McCoy, either sold off their interests in the claims or simply abandoned them. This allowed the speculators to move in and snatch up the properties in order to bond them, option them, or secure the necessary capital to further develop them. One such man was Colonel William Herring, who together with some investors from Hartford, Connecticut, filed notice of location on the Neptune and Excelsior claims in December of 1879, and formed the Neptune Mining Company. Under the auspices of Colonel Herring, the company established a smelter 15 miles away on the San Pedro River (by this time, the Copper Queen had monopolized the natural springs in Mule Gulch) which began developing the mines further. Herring, brimming with confidence regarding the claims, built himself a grand home near the smelter known as "The Castle."[13]

Colonel William Herring was born in New Brunswick, New Jersey, on January 31, 1833, to Caleb and Mary (Fisher) Herring. The family moved to New York City, where young William received his primary and secondary education. In 1858, he married Mary M. Inslee. The couple would have seven children together, including a

Attorney Colonel William Herring, Manager of the Neptune Mining Company and future defense counsel for John Heath and the Bisbee bandits (Arizona Historical Society, 20658).

daughter named Sarah, who would become a prominent attorney in her own right. Herring graduated from the Columbia College Law School in 1866 and later that same year was admitted to the New York Bar Association. Herring served as the assistant district attorney of New York City and also on the state legislature in 1873, "where he introduced bills which started the creation of greater New York City." Herring was also responsible for authoring the law recognizing May 30 as Decoration Day.

Lured westward by the prospect of mineral wealth, William Herring moved his family to the Arizona Territory in 1879, taking a position as the general manager of the Neptune Mining Company of Bisbee. In addition to his mining interests, Herring opened a law office in the town of Tombstone, at the corner of Fremont and 6th Street. Among his first clients were the infamous Earp brothers and their associate John "Doc" Holliday, who had recently been indicted for murder in connection with the shooting of three "cowboys" in the vacant lot behind the O.K. Corral stable. Herring was able to successfully exonerate his clients, but victory came with a price. After receiving numerous death threats in connection with his representation of the Earps and Holliday in court, Herring began carrying on his person a pistol even when in the courtroom.

As a highly-regarded attorney, Herring would also represent William Claiborne, who had fled the street fight between the Earps and the "cowboys" just before the shooting

Department heads of the Copper Queen Mining Co. Standing: J. Wesley "Wes" Howell, Edward Reilly, Tom Devine, Steve Brandish, Lewis Williams. Seated: S.W. Clawson, Ben Williams, M.J. Brophy, W.H. Brophy, Edward Baker (courtesy the Bisbee Mining & Historical Museum).

began. Claiborne, who called himself "Billy the Kid," was indicted by grand jury for the killing of John Hickey during a brawl in the Queen's Saloon in Charleston. He was successfully defended in his second trial by Herring. In November 1882, after Claiborne was fatally wounded by "Buckskin" Frank Leslie, the young man requested that his pistol belt be given to Mr. Herring. The Earp and Claiborne cases were obviously difficult on Herring and may well have made him unpopular with some residents of Tombstone, but they were not as difficult as the case that he would take just two years later, defending a man who the entire county had come to believe was guilty of masterminding one of the most brutal crimes the territory had witnessed.[14]

On April 9, 1880, Herring, Eddleman, Anshurtz, and Klein conveyed their interests in the Copper Queen and Copper King mines to Mr. Edward Reilly for the sum of $9000. The following day, Rea, Atkins, and W.F. Bradley, who had bought up Warren Buck's interest, sold their stakes in the two mines to Reilly for the sum of $6000. Reilly, a lawyer and mining speculator hailing from Lancaster, Pennsylvania, had been told of the rich ore deposits being unearthed in the Mule Mountains by Tucson merchant, Louis Zeckendorf, while visiting that burg. Borrowing only enough money from Zeckendorf to cover the cost of travel, Reilly made his way to the mining camp. There he found the Copper Queen cut, which was assaying at 22 percent copper ore. Reilly, recognizing the potential of the claim, immediately approached the owners with an offer to buy them out. After giving the former owners a good-faith bonus payment in the amount of $800, Reilly posited the deed to the mines in escrow and took leave for San Francisco.

Left: **Louis Zeckendorf, Tucson merchant and one of the primary investors in the fledgling Copper Queen Mining Company (author's collection).** *Right:* **Ben Williams, the Superintendent of the Copper Queen Mining Company (courtesy the Bisbee Mining & Historical Museum).**

Upon arriving in San Francisco, Edward Reilly began negotiating with the engineering firm of Martin and Ballard through the mining firm of Bisbee, Williams, and Co. A week later, John Ballard, John Williams, Sr., and his son Ben Williams, accompanied Reilly back to Arizona and into the Mule Mountains to view the claims for themselves. Impressed by what they observed, Martin and Ballard agreed to put up a bond of $20,000. In early May, the firm of Martin and Ballard reached an agreement with the elder Williams and his partner Judge DeWitt Bisbee to finance the continued working of the claims and to construct a new smelter. In return, Martin and Ballard would receive seven-tenths interest in the Copper Queen and a two-thirds interest in the Copper King. Reilly would retain three-tenths interest in the Copper Queen and a one-third interest in the Copper King. Ben Williams and his brother Lewis would become the superintendent of the mines and the supervisor of the smelter, respectively. The partnership of John Ballard, W.H. Martin, and Edward Reilly would become the first Copper Queen Mining Company.[15]

In recognition of the financial aid they provided to Reilly, Louis Zeckendorf and his nephew Albert Steinfeld (who would go to become one of the leading merchants in Tucson, specializing in hardware and mining equipment) were given an exclusive contract for the freighting of materials and equipment into Mule Gulch from the railhead in Benson and freighting of ore and bullion for shipment to points back east. The contract also stipulated that Zeckendorf and Company would advance the Copper Queen Mining Company up to 80 percent of the market value of all copper matte that was transported. This arrangement would serve to keep the burgeoning corporation liquid during its early years.[16]

By August of 1880, Lewis Williams had the new Copper Queen smelter—a 36-inch Rankin and Brayton water-jacketed furnace—up and running. This first smelter was a rather primitive, wood-burning contraption which could only generate enough heat to produce blister copper which was only 85 to 90 percent pure (the later Copper Queen smelters would utilize charcoal and coke, materials which produced a higher heat index and allowed the company to refine a purer copper sample). Still, the ability of the company to ship out ingots of copper blister, as opposed to wholly unprocessed ore or copper matte, to markets in the east, made the operation much more profitable. As author and historian William C. Epler noted, the new smelter "immediately changed copper mining in Bisbee from a hand-to-mouth struggle to a viable, profit-making operation that provided money for further expansion and growth."[17]

By September of 1880, the population of the camp was nearing 500 souls. The first post office was opened that month in the newly christened town of Bisbee. The burgeoning settlement was named for Judge Dewitt F. Bisbee, the partner of John Williams, Sr., in the firm of Bisbee, Williams, and Co. Ironically, Judge Bisbee would never visit the town which was named for him, dying of heart failure in May of 1885. The post office was located in General Allen's store with Horace C. Stillman appointed first postmaster. At the behest of leading citizens of the town, the Pima County Board of Supervisors appointed James F. Duncan to the position of Justice of the Peace, with William Fenton as Town Constable. Preston Standifer, the first saloon owner in the gulch, was appointed to the position of Notary Public by John J. Cosper, the Secretary of the Territory. Pima County Sheriff Charles A. Shibell appointed Orrin House as the Deputy Sheriff for the region. James Duncan recalled, "The appointment[s] came in August and a copy of the [Territorial] statute of 1879 was sent along; and we were armed with the mighty powers of the laws of Arizona."[18]

When Canadian-born metallurgist and chemical geologist, Dr. James S. Douglas first arrived in Bisbee in December of 1880, he was less than impressed by the camp. Douglas later wrote, "The main street, with its few houses, constituted the whole town." Still, Bisbee was growing quickly. Dr. Douglas, who had been commissioned by some Philadelphia investors to evaluate two claims near the town of Jerome in Yavapai County, one of which would eventually become the United Verde Mine, had also been employed to evaluate the Copper Queen and some other properties in the Mule Mountains by owners Martin and Ballard. Martin and Ballard were concerned that the orebody they were mining might "pinch out" within a short period of time and were looking at other claims they might option. Douglas assured the owners that there were other orebodies in the vicinity and recommended the owners begin buying up neighboring claims including the Atlanta and the Copper King.[19]

Though George Warren would come to be known as "the Father of Bisbee," it could be argued that the title should belong to Dr. James Stuart Douglas, as it was Douglas who first realized the potential of the camp and worked to make it a reality. Douglas was born in Quebec on November 4, 1837, to Dr. James Douglas and his wife, Hannah Williams. In his youth, Douglas, his father, and the family, travelled extensively through Egypt, Palestine, and Italy. In 1855, he was accepted to the University of Edinburgh in Scotland, but later completed his studies at Queen's University, Kingston, Ontario. In 1860, he married Naomi Douglas, the daughter of Captain Walter Douglas (no relation). Douglas then returned to Edinburgh to study theology with an eye towards becoming a clergyman. After completing his studies, Douglas was admitted as a licentiate of the Church of Scotland. Unfortunately, his father's health began to fail and the younger James Douglas was obliged to return to Quebec. Upon his return to Canada, Douglas began to study medicine in order to aid his ailing father with his practice at the Quebec Lunatic Asylum.

The elder Douglas had invested in various mining ventures throughout Canada and the United States, most of which were unprofitable. In order to further aid his father, James Douglas, in addition to his pursuit of medicine, took up the study of chemistry, mining, and metallurgy. An intelligent and motivated young man, Douglas quickly mastered the subjects and soon found himself employed with Morrin College in Quebec as a Professor of Chemistry—a position he would hold for three years. His expertise in the field of mining operations, specifically in relation to the mining of copper ores—eventually garnered him a position as a manager with the Chemical Copper Company, which was involved in a copper mining venture near Phoenixville, Pennsylvania. Unfortunately, the company did not have the capital to sustain the operations. However, Douglas "gained valuable experience in the working out of metallurgic processes, and in further developing

Dr. James Stuart Douglas, metallurgist for the Phelps, Dodge & Co. and the Father of Bisbee (author's collection).

the well-known Hunt-Douglas patents for the wet-extraction of copper." Dr. James Douglas was becoming recognized as an expert in the field and was actively sought as a consultant by various large companies, including the firm of Phelps, Dodge & Co. of New York.[20]

The year 1880 was also the year the first recorded murder was committed in the town of Bisbee. In October of that year, a man identified only as Dodson went to the camp of an unnamed individual and "finding no one there but the daughter, a half–Mexican girl aged about 18, attempted to outrage her." The girl's father suddenly returned and "taking in the situation at a glance, jerked Dodson's revolver from its holster, struck him over the head with it, and drove him from the place." The father then returned to the smelter where he worked and turned the pistol over to the superintendent, Ben Williams, instructing Williams to return the revolver to Dodson "should he come around."

Meanwhile, the humiliated Dodson beat a retreat to Parshall and Reed's Saloon. Nursing his bruised head, Dodson told the bartender that he had been attacked and robbed of his pistol, which he claimed had cost him $80. Dodson stated that he meant to have his pistol back and avenge himself on the thief. Dodson then attempted to appropriate a shotgun belonging to Mr. Reed, but it was wrestled away from him by the owner and Dodson was unceremoniously ousted from the establishment. Now angry, humiliated, and bent on revenge, Dodson purchased a carbine and returned to the girl's residence under the cover of darkness. The family was enjoying their evening meal when Dodson began firing through the window of the home instantly killing the young woman's brother and wounding the girl in the arm. Dodson fled, leaving the town on horseback and heading out toward Tombstone. The saloon-keeper Reed was appointed to pursue Dodson, having been given a commission as a "special constable," but was unable to catch the murderer. Dodson was never found nor seen in southern Arizona again.[21]

The following year, on February 1, the County of Cochise was created by the Eleventh Territorial Legislature and named for the renowned Apache leader. The new county was carved out of the southeastern portion of what had been Pima County, with the town of Tombstone designated as the County Seat. No longer would residents of Bisbee have to travel the 95 miles to Tucson in Pima County to record official documents or seek redress with the courts. Governor John C. Frémont appointed the local officials, including County Sheriff John H. Behan, Probate Judge J.H. Lucas, County Recorder Arizona Territory Albert T. Jones, County Treasurer John Orlando Dunbar, and District Attorney Lyttleton Price. Milt E. Joyce, Joseph Tasker, and Joe Dyer comprised the first Cochise County Board of Supervisors.[22]

On April 2, 1881, on the advice of Zeckendorf and Steinfeld, the owners of the Copper Queen Mine incorporated as the Copper Queen Mining Company under the statutes of New York. Zeckendorf became the company Secretary and Treasurer, while A.A. Hayes, Jr., was appointed President of the new company. The executive committee consisted of Zeckendorf, Hayes, and Albert A. Levi. Zeckendorf also sat on the board of trustees along with Hayes, Levi, and owners Charles and William Martin, John Ballard, and Edward Reilly. The initial offering of stock was set at 250,000 shares and valued at $10 a share. The prospectus of the Copper Queen Mining Company, printed later that year, valued the company at $1,100,000, based primarily on the copper ore the company shipped the previous year. The mining company was overvalued, but the offering still excited the interest of other firms, including Phelps, Dodge & Co.[23]

Anson Phelps, together with his sons-in-law, William Dodge and Daniel Willis James, founded Phelps, Dodge & Co. in New York City in 1834 as an import-export company. The company exported cotton to England and imported metals such as tin, iron, and copper. Phelps also founded the Ansonia Brass and Battery Company and the Ansonia Manufacturing Company. By 1849, the company had realized over a million dollars in capital. With Anson Phelps' death in 1853, his son Anson Phelps, Jr., Dodge, and James took over the company. When Anson Phelps, Jr., suddenly died in 1859, Dodge and James took charge, though they retained the Phelps name. The company's capital was over $1.5 million. It was at this juncture, that Phelps, Dodge & Co. began to diversify. Though still primarily a mercantile company, the interests of Phelps, Dodge & Co. grew to include timber and mining. In 1881, Daniel James commissioned Dr. James Douglas to evaluate several mines out in the southwest. On the advice of Dr. Douglas, the company would come to purchase the controlling stock in the Morenci Copper Mine near the border of the Arizona and New Mexico Territories from the Detroit Copper Company for a loan of $30,000.[24]

In December of that year, the newly-incorporated Copper Queen Mining Company added a second Rankin and Brayton furnace directly beside the first one. The Copper Queen Mine, which began as a cut in the hill side measuring approximately four feet wide and going in about ten feet, was now an "open out"—60 feet in diameter and over 400 feet deep, dipping into the hill at about a 30-degree incline. Water was located at 300 foot level, and was soon being pumped out to run the steam engines and cool the furnaces. By this time, the mine was turning out half a million pounds of copper a month. Such was public interest in the continuing development of the mine, that the *Arizona Weekly*

The Copper Queen Mine in its infancy, Bisbee, circa 1883 (author's collection).

Citizen began running regular weekly updates chronicling its progress. In January, the newspaper reported that the owners of the Copper Queen had refused an offer of "a cool million for that marvelous property." In the March 13 edition, the Tucson-based paper reported that the Bisbee Miners' Union was 120 strong. Later that August, the *Weekly Citizen* reported that, after resolving some issues with the smelter, the "Copper Queen is working the usual force of men" and that "the mine is looking splendidly." Bisbee, the article stated, was in "prosperous condition."[25]

By contrast, *The Tombstone Epitaph* would deride the town of Bisbee as "lively," saying that "shooting can be heard at all times of the day and night." The newspaper reported "two men at Bisbee ... engaged in a quarrel, which resulted in one of them being shot in the neck, the wound being fatal." *The Epitaph* also reported "the body of a Mexican had just been found" implying the man was also a victim of foul-play. While neither of these reports can be substantiated, the town did witness three more murders that year. In February, saloon-keeper James Jordan killed Peter (possibly Ben) Hogan with a shotgun blast to the head in an argument over a trifling debt involving a third party. Eleven days later, at about half-past 11 in the evening, James Woods was gunned down by William Ham in William Roberts' saloon. The two men had a disagreement earlier in the evening during a card game. In yet another fatal confrontation, Samuel McFarland, a freighter, was killed while trying to intercede in a fist fight between his driver and Lewis Williams, the superintendent at the Copper Queen smelter. A fourth man, described only as "a Mexican" and thought to be in the employ of Williams, slipped up behind McFarland as the freighter tried to separate the combatants. The man pulled McFarland's pistol from his belt and shot him to death with it, then turned and fled into the hills. The killer was never apprehended.[26]

In spite of these episodes of violence, the town continued to flourish and the interests of business advanced at a steady pace. Phelps, Dodge & Co. had sent Dr. James Douglas back to the Arizona Territory to evaluate the mining claims of the Detroit Copper Company in Morenci. At the behest of owner Daniel James of Phelps, Dodge & Co., Dr. Douglas travelled to Bisbee in February 1882 and began scouting the Atlanta mining claim, which abutted the Copper Queen Mine, in earnest. The Atlanta claim was first deeded by George W. Atkins on October 15, 1879. Atkins eventually divided one-fourth interest in the claim between Samuel Shaw and Patrick Delaney, both of Tombstone. On April 25, 1881, Atkins and his partners sold out to James Mann, W.A. Pullman, and A.A. White of Pennsylvania for the sum of $40,000. Pullman and Man subsequently bequeathed one-quarter interest to John B. Smithman in consideration of the sum of $10,000. The partners' ownership of the mine would be rather short-lived.[27]

John H. Behan, first sheriff of Cochise County, appointed by Territorial Governor John Frémont, lost his re-election to challenger Jerome Ward mostly because of his involvement in the Earp/cowboy feud (author's collection).

When he first met with them in the winter of 1880, Dr. Douglas had recommended to Martin and Ballard and Reilly, the owners of the Copper Queen, and to their partner Louis Zeckendorf, that the company purchase the Atlanta claim. Unfortunately for the Copper Queen Company investors they did not heed Douglas' advice. In early spring with his report regarding the Atlanta mine in hand, Dr. Douglas returned to New York to meet with Mr. James. Impressed with Dr. Douglas' findings, Phelps, Dodge & Co. decided to purchase the Atlanta mine from owners, Smithman, Pullman, and Mann for the sum of $40,000—the very sum they had paid for it less than three months earlier. Where once there had been numerous small mining claims owned by multiple individuals or partnerships, by 1882 the majority of the claims within the Mule Mountains had fallen under the auspices of a small group of large mining corporations such as Phelps, Dodge & Co., the Holbrook and Cove Company, the Corbin brothers, Arizona Prince Copper Company, and the Copper Queen Mining Company. And so the rise of the corporations had begun.[28]

In November of 1882, in the first elections held in Cochise County, a number of Governor Frémont's appointees were swept from office. County treasurer John Dunbar was replaced by Benjamin Goodrich, district attorney Lyttleton Price was replaced by Democrat Marcus "Mark" Aurelius Smith, and John Behan, who earlier damaged his reputation as a lawman by becoming too deeply embroiled in the feud between the infamous Earp brothers and the cowboy faction in Tombstone, lost out to the Republican candidate, Jerome L. Ward. Additionally, E.H. Wiley was elected Territorial Council, Albert T. Jones to the office of County Recorder, and B.E. Peel to the position of Probate Judge. Theodore F. White, John Montgomery, and L.W. Blinn were elected to the Board of Supervisors and J.G. Barney to the office of County Coroner.[29]

Daniel James, owner of Phelps, Dodge & Co., which bought out the Copper Queen Mining Company (author's collection).

The town of Bisbee continued to grow at a remarkable rate, spurred on by the mining boom and the speculation which accompanied it. Aside from the assorted mining interests, many new, independent businesses were springing up in and along the gulch. In addition to the saloons and gambling houses, Florence Robinson Rundle recalled that Main Street included "a barber shop, a restaurant, two stores, a bakery, a jewelry store, Duffy's butcher shop, and Kate Sweeney's newsstand." *McKenney's Business Directory of 1883*, though mistakenly locating it in Pima County, described the burg as "[a] small town and post office, young in years but lively in business." The Directory made mention of the bakery owned by A.J. Kohner, a restaurant owned by Walker Harry, Tribolet's Brewery, several saloons and establishments selling spirits and liquors including Graff & McDougal and Reynolds & Stanley, the presence of a physician named H.W. Fenner, a hotel run by Miss Nellie Cashman, and, of course, the Copper Queen Mining Company, the town's foremost employer.[30]

In the newspaper's Saturday, October 6, 1883, issue, *The Tombstone Republican* stated, "The trip to Bisbee, as it can now be made in under 4 hours, is not nearly so arduous an undertaking as formerly. The ride is a pleasant one. And on entering Mule Pass you may come across a ranch owned by Robert Crouch, or Sandy Bob as he is best known." The article continued on, reporting that, "outside the Copper Queen at Bisbee much activity is being displayed. The Hendricks [mine] is daily shipping 10 to 12 tons of lead carbonate to the T.M.& M. Co.'s smelter in Charleston; whilst on the west end of the Atlanta, which enjoins the Hendricks, the Benson folks have secured a six month lease of 500 feet also, on account of the richness of the lead carbonate ore."

The Republican continued in this vein, reporting, "The Neptune company [*sic*] will, according to the statement of their resident manager, Mr. Jos. Dyer, soon start up work on more than one of their properties. Possibly the Uncle Sam and the Neptune, both of which are considered valuable, but in which work has been somewhat scattered. No doubt, however, they will now do further sinking, when this ground may turn out to far exceed the company's present ideas of their value. On the Black Jack steady work has been going on some months, and the developments are such as to gladden the owner's hearts at the enhanced value of the property." Unfortunately for Colonel Herring and the Neptune Mining Company, the claim quickly played out and, with their finances depleted, they were unable to continue with any further exploration. The company went in to receivership and was sold at a sheriff's auction in 1882 to the Holbrook and Cove Company.[31]

Eighteen eighty-three also saw the completion of town's first real school. The first schoolhouse, which opened in 1881 with Miss Clara Judson Stillman of Bridgeport, Connecticut, acting as the instructor, was a one room wooden structure in Brewery Gulch, which had previously served as a miner's cabin. It had neither a door nor windows. The students' desks were comprised of boards laid across packing boxes and their seats were nail kegs with wood planks set across them. The teacher's desk was a flour barrel turned upside down. The black board was just that—two large sheets of wood that had been nailed together and painted black. Miss Stillman's first class was comprised of three girls and two boys. The pupils had neither pen nor ink. The students worked with slate pencils (broken into several pieces in order to provide enough for everyone) on sheets of brown paper procured from the general store. Books were considered a luxury. While Miss Stillman did manage to lay in "a meager supply of books," the students would usually bring in whatever books their parents had in their homes.

Seeing the need for a proper schoolhouse, the Copper Queen Mining Company built and gifted to the community a large, one room adobe building. In comparison to the former schoolhouse, the new building was rather spacious with plastered interior and green shutters on the windows. The doors and windows were all framed in rosewood. The new building also had a working stove and a real desk (shipped in from Leavenworth, Kansas) and chair for the instructor. The student's benches and desks were also made of redwood and hewn by Copper Queen carpenters. By June of 1883, Miss Stillman had relinquished her teaching position to Miss Daisy Robinson, with the number of students in attendance climbing to 20. The new building also served as a community center, dance hall, theater, meeting place for the Ancient Order of United Workmen, and a church. Miss Stillman also organized the Protestant Sunday School.[32]

In spite of having some of the trappings of a larger town—a school house, church meetings, fraternal lodges, and a goodly number of shops and mercantile establishments, the town of Bisbee still had not evolved into a haven of civic virtue, benevolence, and propriety. The lure of precious ores had not only attracted legitimate business interests, but also the fraternity commonly referred to in the parlance of the time as the "sporting crowd"—the gamblers, the prostitutes, saloon-keepers, and others who made their living out past the edge of what was considered polite society by catering to the community's more base desires. They had in common with their more-principled neighbors the ambition to "strike it rich." Unlike their neighbors, they were willing to resort to illicit, iniquitous, and even illegal means to realize this ambition. The crowd brought with them a predilection towards criminality and a pension for violence as evidenced by the killing of John Connelly on the evening of January 15, 1883.

As reported by *The Arizona Daily Citizen*, Connelly had entered Charley Young's Saloon about 8:00 p.m., took a seat at Walter Rich's faro table, and began to play. After a time, Connelly decided he "wanted to bet beyond the limits of the game." When Rich refused him this request, Connelly became "incensed" and began verbally abusing the dealer. Connelly then picked up the case keeper and threw it at Rich, but missed him and injured a bystander. At this point others intervened in an attempt to calm Connelly but their efforts were for naught. His anger undiminished, he suddenly "arose from the table [and] said in threatening manner, "I'll be back directly" before storming out of the establishment. He returned a short time later armed with a loaded pistol.

Witnesses could not agree as to whether Connelly had the gun in his hand when he entered the saloon or drew down on Rich after he had come through the door. "At any rate, he and Rich began shooting at the same time." Connelly was only able to get off one shot to the four Rich fired from his revolver. The young man was shot twice in the chest, bullets perforating both his right and left lungs, once in the right arm, and once through the left thigh. Severely wounded, Connelly collapsed upon the wooden floor. He was conveyed back to his home where he later expired. Walter Rich was subsequently arrested and taken to Tucson and jailed. He would later be exonerated, the shooting deemed to be "self-defense." *The Weekly Citizen* described the saloon's resident faro dealer as "well and—although a sporting man—favorably known in the community as a quiet, well-behaved person."[33]

The mining boom in southern Arizona had also attracted a number of "cowboys"—an appellation which soon became synonymous with a loosely organized confederacy of rustlers, ruffians, and other criminals. "The cowboy," wrote the editor of *The Arizona Weekly Citizen*, "is a name which has ceased in this Territory to be a term applied to cattle herders." By 1881, the problem had become so noxious that the authorities in Cochise County appealed to the acting governor, John J. Gosper who, in turn, appealed to the federal authorities, stating frankly in an open letter, "At Galeyville, San Simon, and other points isolated from large places, the cowboy element at times very fully predominates, and the officers of the law are at times either unable or unwilling to control this class of outlaws, sometimes being governed by fear, at other times by hope of reward." The sheriff of Cochise said "he gave little hope of being able, in his department, to cope with the power of the cowboys." It was part of this confederation—men like "Curly" Bill Brocious, John Peters "Johnny" Ringo, and the McLaurey and Clanton brothers—whom the infamous Earp brothers battled in Tombstone through 1881 and 1882, before being obliged to flee the Territory.[34]

Communications from the Governor regarding the situation in Cochise County reached the highest levels of the federal government and, in his annual message, President Chester A. Arthur recommended the Committee of the Territories of the U.S. Senate modify the existing *posse comitatus* act to allow the U.S. Army to intervene "to assist the civil officers on Territories and border states in enforcing the law and maintaining order." With the killing of several of the cowboys and the subsequent departure of the Earp brothers, the situation in Cochise County was somewhat mitigated and the congress decided against sending in federal troops. Still the cowboy faction was not completely subjugated and tensions remained high. *The Arizona Weekly Citizen* reported in late July 1882 that there had been "a number of frontier cowboys in town [Tucson] Saturday night, and a vigilant watch was kept by our officials."[35]

In spite of the "vigilance of officials," depredations continued on throughout the territory, most of which were attributed to various cowboy gangs. Aside from the continuing theft of both horses and cattle from stockmen on both sides of the Arizona-Mexico border, there were incidents of stage robberies, train robberies, attempted jail deliveries, kidnappings, and assassinations. Especially troublesome was a gang of outlaws working out of the town of Clifton near the Arizona-New Mexico territorial border. "The cowboy element is causing much uneasiness in Clifton," reported *The Daily Citizen* in August of 1883. In his memoir, Edward Titcomb recalled meeting a "noted Character named Black Jack" in Clifton, who would go on to ride with "the Dan Dowd, Red Sample, and Tex Howard gang, which held up stages, payrolls, or anyone who was known to have money."

In November, *The Citizen* reported that "a party of outlaws ... before leaving Clifton created a row by shooting and cutting up. After leaving Clifton the next heard of them was at Sheldon, on the A. & N.M. narrow gauge road, where they obtained by force all they wanted to eat." However, by December, *The Clifton Clarion* reported that "the gang of cowboys and rustlers who infested our camp has been entirely broken up. Some of them are dead; others with prices on their heads, dare not come back." In fact, many of the so-called cowboys, including the aforementioned Dan Dowd, "Red" Sample, and "Tex" Howard, had simply moved on to other locales in the Territory.[36]

The town of Clifton had been slowly built along the banks of Chase Creek in the southeastern corner of the Arizona Territory, which flows into the San Francisco River, a tributary of the Gila River. The first Anglos to inhabit the area were fur trappers, who came to the area in the 1850s in search of beaver. It was not until 1870, when Robert "Bob" Metcalf and his brother, James, discovered evidence of copper ore in the vicinity, that pioneers began to converge on the area. In 1873, the first smelter—a primitive contraption built of adobe and fueled with charcoal made from native mesquite—was put in to operation by Lesinsky brothers and their nephew, Julius Freudenthal, who had partnered with Robert Metcalf. The partnership formed the nucleus of what would become the Longfellow Mining Company. The Lesinskys, Charles and Henry, also built the first general store, in what would in time become the town of Clifton, to supply the miners of the region. By 1877, a number of adobe and wood houses dotted the hillsides along Chase Creek, and a community was beginning to develop.

In 1882, a Kansas City mining speculator by the name of Frank Underwood, seeing the potential in the Longfellow Mining Company claims, offered the owners $1.5 million for the entire lot. With deeds in hand, Underwood travelled first to New York and then to Edinburgh, Scotland, where he sold the claims to a group of investors for $2 million. The investors named their new company The Arizona Copper Company, Ltd. And immediately began to improve on their investment by building a new copper-jacked smelter and laying track to Lordsburg in the New Mexico Territory to connect with the Southern Pacific line. When the company began to experience financial difficulties, the Scotsmen reorganized the board of directors, borrowed an additional $1.8 million, and sent their own metallurgist and mining experts to the wilds of Arizona, including engineer James Colquhoun, who would go on to serve as president of the company.

Historian James M. Patton described the burgeoning town thus: "Clifton at this time had a few saloons and restaurants and four stores. There were a few dwellings, mostly on the east side of the river. The offices of the company, the smelter, and a few adobe buildings were on the west side of the river. The courthouse, made of canvas, stood in what is now the river bed. Near it were ten or twelve adobe huts belonging to the Chinese laundrymen and vegetable men. All were washed away in a later flood." Patton continued,

Clifton, Arizona Territory, a notoriously wicked town on the New Mexico/Arizona territorial border (Arizona Historical Society, 14488).

"Clifton was a boom town. Small armies of railroad laborers, miners, drifters, and business men crowded the dusty streets. The moral tenor of the town was typical of the West at that time. Many had come here either to escape the law or to seek adventure and fortune. Most of them were not interested very much in a law-abiding town."[37]

Back in Bisbee, the year 1883 saw the opening of A.A. Castaneda's General Merchandise Emporium. This mercantile was located on the southeast side of Main Street, which for all intents and purposes, followed the route of the gulch running from the northwest to the southeast, and was situated directly across from Sima's Restaurant and betwixt two saloons—Joe May's and The Bon Ton. Owners Joseph Goldwater and Jose Miguel Castaneda stocked the latest goods and wares, which were brought in regularly over Mule Pass by freight wagon from the Southern Pacific railhead in Benson. Goldwater and Castaneda were the largest retailers in Bisbee, eclipsing the stores of J.C. Nichols, J.B. "Pie" Allen, and that of Louis Zeckendorf, which was located inside the Bisbee House.

Not only did the new mercantile carry a wide variety of merchandise and sundries, the owners also installed a safe. At the time, the town was without a bank, so Goldwater and Castaneda's sturdy iron box served the needs of those who required a convenient and secure place to cache their money and valuables, including the local mining corporations, who deposited their incoming payroll monies there at the store prior to payday distribution.[38]

Goldwater family historian, Dean Smith, said of Joseph Goldwater, "Here was one of

Upper Main Street Bisbee (before trees were cut down for fuel) (courtesy the Bisbee Mining & Historical Museum).

Arizona's most unlucky men ... he was repeatedly cheated, robbed, shot at, falsely accused of crime, and generally victimized by almost everyone." Born in 1830 in Konin, Poland, to Hirsh and Elizabeth Goldwasser (the brothers later anglicized the family name), Joseph had fled the family home just ahead of Russian conscription officers, following his brother Michel across Europe and, finally across the Atlantic. Joseph and Michel arrived in San Francisco in 1852. Finding San Francisco too competitive, the brothers ventured into Mexico and opened a saloon in the mining town of Sonora. The Goldwater ventures in Mexico were unsuccessful and the brothers eventually moved on to the fledgling community of Los Angeles, California. Once settled, Joseph opened a tobacco store across from the Bella Union Hotel and, later, a mercantile store. His brother Michel stayed only a short time in Los Angeles before proceeding on to Gila City in the Arizona Territory.

In 1862, Joseph Goldwater, at the age of 32, married Miss Ellen Blackman of San Francisco. Unfortunately, his various creditors called in his notes which resulted in the loss of his Los Angeles holdings. He then moved to San Francisco to work with his brother Abraham in his clothing store. By this time, Michel had relocated to La Paz, a mining camp on the Arizona side of the Colorado River, partnering with Bernard Cohn in a general store. Joseph soon joined him. Joseph would be personally involved in three different lawsuits during his tenure in La Paz, which cost him considerably. In 1869, the brothers moved to Ehrenberg, Arizona Territory, where Joseph made an unsuccessful bid for the office of Yuma County Treasurer. In June of 1872, while travelling the road back to Ehrenberg from Prescott, after trying unsuccessfully to secure a U.S. Army freighting contract, the brothers and their partner Dr. Wilson Jones were attacked by Mojave Apache. During the melee, Joseph Goldwater was shot twice in the back and seriously wounded.

Though he survived the ambush (he would have the bullet which Dr. Jones removed from his shoulder turned into a watch fob), Joseph was forced to return home to San Francisco and spent the next few months convalescing with his wife and children. By the fall of 1872, he was back in business, aiding his nephew Morris in opening the first Goldwater's store in Phoenix. Though the store was home to the town's first telegraph office, the venture was destine for failure. In April of 1875, J. Goldwater and Bro. liquidated their stock and closed their doors. Joseph returned to San Francisco to be with his family, while Michel and Morris made plans to open a new store (also under the name J. Goldwater and Bro.) in Prescott. Two years later, Joseph's wife Ellen died, leaving behind her husband and three children. The loss was difficult for Joseph to bear and it is rumored he began to drink. Joseph and his daughter Annie would later visit Michel in Prescott in early 1880. Under pressure from his wife Sarah, Michel dissolved the partnership of J. Goldwater and Bro. The Goldwater brothers would never again partner in another business venture.[39]

With nearly $60,000 in hand, Joseph travelled to Yuma and began investing heavily in the Castle Dome mining district. As a result, he was soon nearly broke. Determined to recoup his losses, Joseph ventured into the commission business, buying from wholesalers in San Francisco and selling to stores in Arizona. The business was a success, until one of Joseph's wholesale clients, after discovering Joseph had made an unannounced trip to Yuma, began spreading the rumor that he had skipped out on his creditors. *The San Francisco Examiner* picked up the story and soon a warrant was issued for his arrest. The unsuspecting Joseph was apprehended at the home of his old friend Isaac Lyons in Yuma and escorted back to San Francisco by U.S. Marshals. Joseph pled his innocence in court and the prosecutor, seeing no crime had been committed, dropped the charges. However, his numerous creditors began calling in their notes and Joseph, being cash strapped, could not meet these obligations. Once again, Joseph Goldwater found himself in bankruptcy court.

Broke, disheartened, and disillusioned, Joseph moved on to the boom town of Tombstone, arriving there in July of 1881. With the aid of one P.W. Smith, whom he had extended a loan to in the past, Joseph partnered with Paul B. Warnekros in a new mercantile business. After only a few months, for reasons unknown, Joseph sold his interest in the store to Warnekros and quit Tombstone. He relocated to Contention City, just 12 miles away. It was there he partnered with Jose Miguel Castaneda and a man by the name of Joseph Guindani in yet another mercantile venture. None of the three partners had good credit—Castaneda having been forced to close his business ventures in La Paz, Ehrenberg, and Phoenix, and Guindani still suffering financially from a failed enterprise in the town of Florence in Pinal County. So it was decided that the business would bear the name of Castaneda's wife, Ampara Arviso. The store of A.A. Castaneda was thereby able to purchase goods on credit and soon the partners were up and running. In fact, the partnership of Goldwater and Castaneda was becoming so successful they took a chance and opened a second store in the town of Bisbee.[40]

Prior to partnering with Joseph Goldwater in the mercantile business in Contention, Don Jose Miguel Castaneda had enjoyed some measure of success in the retail and freighting industries throughout the Arizona Territory. Born in 1836 in the state of Chiricahua,

Mexico, to J.M. and Reyo Castaneda, the boy was orphaned at an early age. He was sent to live with Ben Riddles, his uncle by marriage and a successful merchant. In 1855, the young Castaneda joined Riddles partner, John Able, in an expedition through the Arizona Territory and into California with 100 men and 10,000 sheep. Despite encounters with Apache warriors under the leadership of Mangas Coloradas, or Dasoda-hae, Mr. Able was successful in delivering the flocks to Los Angeles and San Francisco. While Able returned to Chiricahua, Castaneda chose to stay on in Los Angeles, finding employment with a large mercantile firm, in addition to working as a foreman for stockman Abel Stearns at the Alamitos Ranch.

Realizing he was more suited to the life of a merchant, Castaneda opened a mercantile business in San Juan Capistrano. In 1860, he moved his business to the boomtown of La Paz in the Arizona Territory. Unfortunately, his ill-health necessitated his closing the store and liquidating the inventory. From La Paz, Castaneda moved down to Tucson, where he partnered in a brewery with Henry Levine. Ill-health again forced Castaneda to abandon the enterprise. He returned to La Paz to open a new store. However, in 1870, the Colorado River flooded and changed course, leaving the town of La Paz without a landing. Commerce in the area dried up soon after the floodwaters did and Castaneda was forced to move on. He relocated to the town of Ehrenberg and re-established himself and his store in the burg.[41]

In 1873, Castaneda married Ampara Arviso, of Sonora, Mexico. *The Arizona Citizen* carried news of the wedding and said of the groom, "[He] was once a well known resident of Tucson and Tubac and for many years a prosperous merchant in La Paz and Ehrenberg. He is social and liberal." A year later, in November of 1874, Castaneda was elected to the Yuma County Board of Supervisors—a position he would hold for two years. It is quite likely that Castaneda first became acquainted with the Goldwater brothers in Ehrenberg during this period, as *The Arizona Sentinel* made mention of them in their May 27, 1876, edition: "J. Goldwater & Bro. and J.M. Castaneda are doing good and increasing business, amounting in the gross to about $16,000 per month." Additionally, Goldwater had been one of the candidates for the office of Council in the 1874 elections (subsequently losing to J.M. Redondo).[42]

By May 1878, Don Castaneda had moved to the boom town of Signal, Arizona, in Mohave County, where he established a well (which would serve both Signal and the town of McCrackin, 12 miles distant). There he began raising livestock and opened a brewery with partner William Goldkoffer. Castaneda also opened a general store with "one of the nicest and largest assortments of goods ever imported into Arizona." The excitement of the boom led the editor of *The Arizona Sentinel* to prophesize that the town of Signal would become the county seat. Unfortunately, the obstacles the editor of *The Sentinel* acknowledged—lack of mail service, lack of water, lack of timber to keep the mills running, scarcity of cash, and Signal's isolated location—would be the town's undoing. By August that same year, Castaneda was beginning the process of closing his stores in both McCrackin and Signal. Simply, Castaneda had overextended himself. By 1879, Castaneda had re-established in Phoenix. This venture was also short-lived. From Phoenix, Castaneda and his family moved to Contention City and into partnership with Goldwater and Guindani.[43]

In the waning days of November of 1883, a newly-arrived sporting-man and procurer by the name of John Heath, along with his partner, Nathan W. Waite, announced the grand opening of their combination dance hall and saloon. Heath and Waite's business was set to open two doors west of the A.A. Castaneda General Merchandise Emporium. The building in which the dance hall was to open had been built by W.B. Scott, and formerly served as a mercantile store, operated by brothers Edward and Ham Hardy. Forty-two-year-old Nathan W. Waite, a Massachusetts native and former saloon-keeper had been residing in Bisbee about a year, and had most recently worked for Frank Corey at the latter's saloon. John Heath, who was born in Texas and raised in Louisiana, had come to Bisbee by way of Dallas, Texas, and Clifton, Arizona Territory. This new establishment was slated to open to the public on the evening of December 8, 1883.[44]

CHAPTER TWO

The Robbery

Only half of the moon was visible in the sky on December 8, 1883, and the early evening mountain air held an implacable chill. Five horsemen rode slowly and purposefully down Bisbee's Main Street, cautious of their own presence and of their surroundings. To the average citizen they looked to be cowboys and were dressed in the habiliment of the profession with tall boots, wide-brimmed hats, and canvas trousers. They were protected against the cold and they were well-armed with revolvers and Winchesters at their disposal. They made their way along the primitive roadway past jerry-built wooden structures towards Preston's lumberyard on the south side of the street near the Hendricks Mine. They did not hurry. Upon arrival, the men dismounted and secured their horses. They then turned back down the street and, as a group, began to make their way towards the A.A. Castaneda's General Merchandise Emporium.[1]

The majority of the businesses along Bisbee's Main Street were open that particular Saturday evening; this being the custom of the time, with most enjoying "a brisk patronage." As the cowboys walked along the northwest side of the thoroughfare, they passed cobbler Pete Devo's place, Ms. Katherine Sweeney's Notions Shop, Dr. Barney's Drugstore, the town's post office, Duffy's Butcher Shop, and Gilroy's tent saloon. Further along Main Street, beside the tent saloon, stood the two-story Bisbee House, Sima's Restaurant (encapsulated now by four walls and a roof), William Roberts' saloon, Deputy Sheriff William "Billy" Daniels' saloon, the restaurant of Mr. and Mrs. Bob Roberts, and the Jordan saloon. Directly across from the Bisbee House was the Bon Ton Saloon. Abutting this establishment to the northwest was A.A. Castaneda's General Merchandise Emporium, along with Joe May's Saloon, Sol Piece's saloon and, just a few yards beyond, John Heath's new dance hall, which was delighting in boisterous grand opening.[2]

The cowboys, all but one of whom were disguising themselves behind 'kerchief masks, passed directly in front of the doors of the Bon Ton Saloon and paused for a moment outside Goldwater and Castaneda's mercantile. Inside, Joseph Goldwater and his clerk were assisting some customers with their purchases. Co-owner Jose Castaneda was convalescing in the back room having been recently taken ill with an attack of rheumatism. All five of the men ventured in. Then three of them stepped back outside with their guns in hand. The other two cowboys drew their revolvers and vociferously demanded the patrons and the staff "throw up" their hands.

Two residents, Richard Rundle and Harry M. Hartson, who had been walking towards the store, were forced inside by a man brandishing two pistols. Upon entering

Bisbee's Main Street, circa 1883, where the robbery and murders occurred (courtesy the Bisbee Mining & Historical Museum).

the establishment, they too were told to "throw up." The outlaw with the two pistols followed Rundle and Hartson back in to the store, saying as he passed the two who remained out on the sidewalk, "Kill them sons-of-bitches!" Rundle recalled seeing six or seven "men standing in a row with their hands up." One of the robbers told Rundle to "behave alright and no harm would come to [him]." The bandits then proceeded to fleece the customers taking from them their monies and other valuables.[3]

Two of the masked men stepped over to the clerk, Peter Doll, and pointed their revolvers at his head and ordered him to open the safe, "accompanying the demand with the remark to be 'Damned quick about it!'" The stalwart clerk replied that he could not open the safe as he did not know the combination, even though he had worked for Goldwater some time in both La Paz and Ehrenberg. The unmasked bandit then pointed towards Joe Goldwater, saying, "There is the son-of-a-bitch who can open the safe." Immediately, Goldwater became the focus of the bandits' attentions and three revolvers were aimed at his head. "Open the safe you one-eyed sheeney!" barked one of the outlaws. Goldwater would later say, "I did not anticipate any personal danger; my feelings were to get rid of them as soon as possible." With this singular thought in mind, Goldwater calmly complied with the bandits' demands, walked over to where the safe stood, dialed in the combination, and pulled open the door.[4]

Suddenly, the distinct report of a Winchester was heard coming from directly in front of the store. Startled, Rundle dropped his hands only to be brusquely instructed to keep them up. Meanwhile, Goldwater pulled the drawers and boxes from the safe and poured the contents into a large sack the robbers had produced. In among the contents of the safe was "a cigar box nearly filled with Mexican money" which fell short of the sack and spilled across the floor. One of the bandits, motioning towards Goldwater, was heard to say, "Why don't you shoot the old son-of-a-bitch?" As one of the bandits stooped down to scoop up the cash, his kerchief swung away from his face, giving Rundle the briefest glimpse at his profile. The bandit quickly pulled his mask back into place and continued grabbing the spilled cash, shoving it by the fistful in the bag. By this time the reports of gunfire outside had become general.

As the cash was being collected from the floor, one of the bandits stepped into the back room where Jose Castaneda lay prostrate on the bed. The bandit demanded the storekeeper get up out of bed and put his hands in the air. Castaneda replied meekly, "I can't get up. I am sick with rheumatism in my shoulders." The bandit raised his six-shooter to the ailing man's head and asked if Castaneda had any money about him. Castaneda nervously replied that he had "not a cent," that all the money was in the safe. The bandit was not so easily appeased. He jerked Castaneda roughly from where he lay and pulled away the pillow to find a buckskin sack full of gold coins. The thief grabbed it and as he turned to leave, he hissed back at the storekeeper, "There, damn you, lie quiet and you won't be hurt." He then passed back into the front room, saying to his confederates, "It's alright."[5]

Joseph "Joe" Goldwater, co-owner of A.A. Castaneda's General Merchandise Emporium, which was the target of the robbery (author's collection).

The Tombstone Republican reported that after emptying the valuables from the safe into the sack, Joe Goldwater "recovered his usual self-possession, which had been seriously disturbed by gazing into the depths of .45 caliber six-shooters" and said to the bandits in his thick Polish accent, "Can I do somedings more for you shentleman? We haf some very fine clodings, which I would be bleased to show you— some sblendit ofercoats, shust suitable for this vedder. In fact, shengleman, our stock can't be beat in." Goldwater's "eulogium" was interrupted by the muzzle of a pistol being pressed against his head. "Come, now, none of your guff!" said the revolver's owner. At this, Goldwater became "profoundly quiet."[6]

Suddenly, the front door swung open and one of the men who had been standing guard outside asked the others for more cartridges. To this request came the reply, "That's right! Pump out the old shells and put in the new! We'll teach these God-damned-sons-of-bitches that we are running this town for a few

Left: **Don Jose Miguel Castaneda, co-owner of A.A. Castaneda's General Merchandise Emporium. The business was named for his wife (author's collection).** *Right:* **John C. Tappenier, engineer for the Copper Queen Mining Company and the first person to be killed during the robbery (courtesy the Bisbee Mining & Historical Museum).**

minutes!" At this, the bandits began to make ready to depart. As the gang members made their exit, one inadvertently struck Mr. Rundle with his pistol. Rundle "turned quickly" as did the bandit which caused his kerchief to fly up from his face allowing Rundle a good, clear look at him. The man swiftly readjusted the mask over his visage and fled through the door with the other robbers to join the two bandits standing out on the porch. However, the street outside no longer resembled the peaceful thoroughfare it had been just minutes earlier.[7]

While the three outlaws were inside fleecing their hostages and cleaning out the store's safe, their two confederates had instigated a full-scale gun battle with the citizens of Bisbee. The shooting began when John C. Tappenier, an assayer for the Copper Queen Mining Company, and his friend, Joseph A. Bright of Wilcox, had the misfortune to exit the Bon Ton Saloon, just one door to the southeast of Goldwater and Castaneda's mercantile. One of the two bandits shouted at them, "Go back there!" Mr. Bright, sizing up the situation in a glance, turned away and began to run down the street. Tappenier, not understanding what exactly was happening, and possibly thinking it was a "friendly bluff" replied. "I won't do it!" The bandit immediately raised his gun and fired twice. His first shot missed Tappenier completely. The bandit's subsequent shot "took out the skull on the right side of the head." Reeling momentarily, Tappenier stumbled back a step or two and collapsed with his head just inside the doorway of the saloon he had formerly been coming from.[8]

D. Tom Smith arrived in Bisbee from the vicinity of Tombstone that very afternoon on business and was having dinner with his wife, Jennie, in Sima's Restaurant, which was located directly across the street from Goldwater and Castaneda's mercantile. Upon hearing the first shot, Smith, a rancher and newly deputized peace officer, promptly left the table where he was eating with his wife and ventured outside "to ascertain the cause." The larger of the two bandits standing outside the mercantile ordered him to throw up his hands, to which Smith replied, "I won't do it! I am a deputy-sheriff!" The bandit was heard to say, "Then you are just the son-of-a-bitch we want!" and both the bandits opened fire on him. Smith was shot once through the torso and once through the right arm. The wounded man cried out, "Oh, my God," as he began to collapse. A third bullet from the outlaws' guns pierced his forehead and Deputy Sheriff Smith fell backwards beneath the shafts of the delivery wagon belonging to Goldwater and Castenada.[9]

Having killed Deputy Sheriff Smith, the bandits turned their attention to a man known locally as "Indian Joe," who was standing across the street from the mercantile watching the tragedy play out. When the two gunmen began shooting at him, Indian Joe took to his heels and, though grazed across the leg by one of the bandits' rounds, was able to escape the fusillade. James A. "Tex" Nolly, a local lumberman and teamster, would become the murderers' next victim. Standing in the street with his team of mules and freight wagon, Nolly was struck in the chest by a single bullet, which may or may not have been intended for Indian Joe, causing a terrible wound. Nolly pitched into the street where he lay writhing in agony for several minutes as the gun battle continued.[10]

Cochise County Deputy Sheriff, William A. "Billy" Daniels, was playing billiards in his saloon, a few doors to the west of Sima's Restaurant, when he heard the first shot fired. Daniels went to the door to investigate and saw a man running up the street, away from the mercantile. Daniels, who was in his shirt sleeves despite the cold, ran across the street only to cross the path of yet another frightened citizen who was running from a saloon. Daniels grabbed the man and asked what the commotion was. The man told the Deputy Sheriff that there was "a large man standing in front of Castaneda's store shooting up and down the street." The outlaws spotted Daniels at the same time he saw them and ordered him to retreat. When the Deputy Sheriff did not immediately comply "they opened fire on him. After [hearing] the 'zip' of three or four bullets in close proximity to his head, he made a dash" toward his saloon to retrieve his revolver. Meanwhile, the bandits continued their reign of terror on the bustling Main Street of Bisbee.[11]

Inside the dance hall, just down the gulch from Goldwater and Castaneda's, there was "gambling, music, and dancing going on." John Heath was playing cards while his partner, Nathan Waite, tended bar. Everyone heard the first shots fired. Suddenly, a man came running in to the dance-house exclaiming there was trouble outside involving a man and his wife. Heath immediately stood up from the table, went over to the counter, and asked Waite for his pistol. Heath took up position at the far end of the bar, his revolver resting on his knee. It was a prime defensive position. Heath admonished his patrons as they moved towards the door to see what was going on in the street. "Better stand back," he warned them, "there is a Winchester going off."[12]

Miner James Krigbaum and his wife, Lina, kept a house on a low hill just to the north of Main Street. Krigbaum had been preparing to go out for the evening when he heard the first shots. Having already buckled on his gun belt, he grabbed his hat and headed off towards Main Street. Trotting the hill past Ben Williams' place and coming up behind the buildings on the north side of the street, he crossed the path of a man named Murray who was "hastening away from the town." Murray warned him of what

Olive Krigbaum, Lena Krigbaum, Lucien Krigbaum, Theodore Krigbaum, Fanny Lockling, James Krigbaum. Front row: Charlie Lockling, circa 1900–1910. James Krigbaum rode through the night to Tombstone with news of the robbery and murders (courtesy the Bisbee Mining & Historical Museum).

was happening in the street, but Krigbaum proceeded onward, albeit more cautiously. Krigbaum passed behind the shops and saloons, finally coming up through an alley between two of the buildings and shielded himself behind a low stone wall. This position afforded him a good view of Goldwater and Castaneda's store and of the two men who were standing in front of it.[13]

As Krigbaum was working his was up towards the alley, the door of Robert "Bob" Robert's restaurant opened on to the Main Street and a figure appeared silhouetted in the doorway by the lamp light coming from inside. One of the gunmen in front of the mercantile drew a bead on the figure in the doorway and fired. Mrs. Annie Roberts, lured to the door by the sound of the gunfire, was shot through and through, the ball entering one side of her abdomen, passing through her spinal column, fragmenting the vertebrae, and exiting out the other. In agony, Mrs. Roberts collapsed on the floor, just inside the doorway of the restaurant. On seeing his wife crumple to the floor, Mr. Roberts cried out and ran to her aid. Annie Roberts was eight months pregnant with the couple's first child.[14]

Having taken up a secure position behind the rock wall, Krigbaum commenced to firing at the bandits with his revolver. In the dim evening light he aimed at the larger of the bandits, who wore a light colored coat. Krigbaum would later claim one of his bullets grazed the outlaw, tearing across the back of his coat from shoulder to shoulder, leaving a seared mark on the fabric before lodging in the casing of the doorway of the mercantile. The bandits immediately returned fire, causing Krigbaum to duck down further behind the wall. But the bandits' bullets had no effect, as they passed overhead and tore through the cloth of the tent structure directly behind him. Suddenly, two bullets hit beside Krigbaum on the inside of the wall. It appeared someone was firing upon him from the lumberyard where the gang had tied up their horses. Krigbaum quickly deserted his position and sprinted back up the alley and on towards his home to retrieve his rifle.[15]

Meanwhile, Deputy Sheriff Daniels, having secured his revolver, slipped stealthily out the back door of his saloon and ran down the gulch behind the buildings on the northwest side of the street. The Deputy came back up a narrow alley beside the post office with his pistol in hand. By this juncture, the bandits were leaving the store. As the bandit who had inadvertently struck Richard Rundle with one of his pistols exited the store, he fired both his revolvers into the air. The bandits then started back up Main Street toward their horses, wantonly shooting as they made their escape along the avenue. Deputy Daniels, positioned not more than 40 feet from the men, fired upon them, but missed. The bandits returned fire, shooting as they fled toward their mounts. John Hiles, who worked for Mr. Lockwood in Lockwood's corral, was watching as the outlaws came running up the thoroughfare toward their horses. Even in the early evening darkness, Hiles was able to recognize a certain "dirty-colored gray horse" standing among the others.[16]

William Gerstenberg was in the butcher shop across from Preston's Lumberyard, where the outlaw's horses were tied when the five robbers ran past. One of the robbers, whom Gerstenberg would later describe as a "large man," passed through the light which served to illuminate the fruit stand in front of the shop. As the bandit had dropped his kerchief, Gerstenberg plainly saw his face. Judging by his size, this was the same man he had seen only a few minutes earlier standing in front of Goldwater and Castaneda's firing up and down the street. Now, the gunman was less than 20 feet from him. Seeing a man looking out at him, the outlaw raised his Winchester and fired a single shot in Gerstenberg's direction. "He shot right over my head and put out the light in the butcher shop." In fear for his life, Gerstenberg retreated to the cellar of the store where he remained hidden "until the trouble was over."[17]

Having gained their mounts, the five bandits charged back up Main Street, firing indiscriminately into the air and at bystanders. Deputy Daniels continued to fire upon the outlaws, emptying his Colt's revolver in the process. None of his five shots found their mark or had any perceptible effect. Mr. Krigbaum, who had since retrieved his rifle, and was now accompanied by his neighbor, H.C. Stillman, who was likewise armed, returned to the scene just in time to fire a few shots at the outlaws' backs as they galloped out of the gulch. Their shots were also ineffectual. The cowboy gang escaped into the Arizona night unscathed, leaving in their wake the bodies of four of the town's citizens. *The Tombstone Republican* would later attest that "the boldness with which the outrage was planned, and the audacity and reckless disregard for human life in its execution, find no parallel in the history of this county and probably not in that of the territory."[18]

Seeing it was safe to do so, Mr. Rundle immediately quit Goldwater and Castaneda's mercantile and ran over to the delivery wagon under which lay Deputy Sheriff Smith,

Bisbee's Main Street, winter 1883. The third building on the left with the wagon parked in front is A.A. Castaneda's General Merchandise Emporium. This photo was taken just a few weeks prior to the robbery (Arizona Historical Society, 20655).

only to find the man was dead. Close on Rundle's heels, Mr. Hartson also ran out of the mercantile and over to where John Tappenier was laying in the doorway of the Bon Ton Saloon, but he too was deceased, "his brains on the porch." James "Tex" Nolly was still alive, but his wound was quite grave. Nolly was taken in to Peirce's Saloon and given what medical attention was available, but the attempt was in vain. He would succumb to his wounds just 26 hours later. Mrs. Annie Roberts, in great pain and realizing her time was short, "begged for a priest to comfort her last hours." There being no Catholic clergymen residing in Bisbee and no way to call for one, her husband bid James Krigbaum to make the ride of 28 miles to Tombstone to summon one. In spite of the inherent danger of navigating the pass and freight road at night, Krigbaum agreed to undertake the journey. By 8:00 p.m., Krigbaum was mounted and en route to the county seat. Sadly, Mrs. Annie Roberts would expire before the priest could arrive at her bedside.[19]

As he rode out of town along the freight road, beneath the indifferent half moon, Krigbaum passed the stagecoach from Tombstone. In the conveyance, tucked securely under the bench seat on which the driver and coach guard sat, was a strongbox containing the monthly payroll for the employees of the Copper Queen Mining Company and other mining interests of the town. The payroll amounted to many thousands of dollars in cash. Though it was common knowledge among the citizenry of Bisbee that payday at the mines was on the tenth of each month, the exact date and time of the delivery of the strongbox to the mercantile was a closely-guarded secret. Being there was no bank in Bisbee, the payroll monies were kept in the safe at the Goldwater and Castaneda General Merchandise Emporium until they were distributed to the workers. It was these very monies, travelling along the road from Tombstone that evening, which had been the impetus for the robbery.[20]

Three days later, a Coroner's Jury was empanelled by J.S. Brittain, acting Cochise County Coroner, in Tombstone to establish how Annie Roberts, John C. Tappenier, D. Thomas Smith, and James A. "Tex" Nolly came to meet their respective deaths. Peter Doll, who gave his occupation as "bookkeeper" for A.A. Castaneda & Co., was the first to testify in Annie Roberts' inquest. Doll recalled he was "behind the desk, posting a letter" when the bandits entered the store. Two men, one masked and one unmasked, immediately covered him with their pistols and ordered him to raise his hands. "At first, I did not do so, being taken by surprise," the bookkeeper said. "They ordered me again, both of them pointing their pistols at my head. I held up my hands, and after collecting myself a little I noticed several more masked men in the store and at the door."

Doll stated all the patrons were instructed to raise their hands in like fashion. One of the robbers moved quickly off toward the back of the store. Meanwhile, several more citizens were herded into the store and they too were ordered to raise their hands. Then the masked man in the back said, "All right, Boys. Go ahead." The two other robbers again leveled their pistols at Doll and the one to his left—the taller of the two—ordered the bookkeeper to open the safe. "I told him I could not open the safe, that I did not know anything about the safe." The bandit again ordered Doll to open the safe, "or you are a dead man." Doll again stated he could not.

Then the unmasked bandit, whom Doll identified as "the leader of the gang," called out, "Hold on. Don't shoot him." Motioning toward Joe Goldwater, the bandit said, "This is the man that has charge of the store." Goldwater was subsequently "compelled" at gunpoint to open the safe. While this exchange was taking place, the bookkeeper heard one of the men outside the door order an unseen person inside. "The man outside the door refused, and immediately after that the man that ordered the man to come in fired the first shot." Doll was asked by the interrogator when the shooting took place to which he replied, "At the same time they were going through the safe." He was then asked if the men seemed to be shooting at any one particular person, to which Doll replied, "They were ordered to shoot anybody—the sons of bitches."

Doll was then asked by the coroner's jurors to describe the leader. He stated the unmasked man was "about 30 or 35 years of age, about five feet eight or nine inches high, full round face. Very light complexion, and I think he wore a light moustache and beard. He wore a light colored hat, and a brown overcoat. His voice was of a high key." In regards to Annie Roberts, Doll said, "I believe that Mrs. Roberts came to her death from the hands of those who fired in the street outside of the store of Castaneda and Co. as no other firing was done." From Peter Doll's testimony, the jurors concluded that "Mrs. Annie Roberts, age 33, native of New York, cane to her death the 9th day of Dec. 1883, from the effects of gunshot wounds afflicted [sic] by parties to this jury unknown."[21]

The inquest of John C. Tappenier was the next to be performed by the Coroner's Jury. Thomas Jones, a Bisbee resident, who gave his occupation as "clerk," was the first to give testimony. He stated that, upon hearing the initial shots, he had come from his house "to see what the trouble was." Jones stated he "could distinguish one man in front of Castaneda's store, shooting promiscuously." He watched as the gunman fired "five or six shots." Jones stated the gunman "called to myself and others that were standing near me to clear the street." Jones admitted he did not see the gunman shoot anyone nor did he see the body of John Tappenier until after the men rode off.

Miner Thomas Lawry took the stand after Mr. Jones. He stated he was in the Bon Ton Saloon when the shooting commenced. "I heard a shot fired," he said, "and I saw a man fall at the door of the saloon." Lawry then retreated to the back of the saloon. "After the shooting ceased, we went and found a man, which was Johnny Tappenier. He was dead when we found him." Lawry stated the deceased had "a single gunshot wound in the head" which he opined "produced death." It was also his opinion Tappenier "was shot in the back of the head, and also that the bullet that caused death passed through the head of the deceased, entering on the right rear of the head and continued over the right temple." Lawry said he had been with Tappenier just a few minutes before he was killed.

Harry M. Hartson, who had been one of the persons herded by the bandits in to the store before the shooting, recollected seeing two men with rifles outside the store. While in the store with his hands raised, he heard the order, "Come on in here," given to some person outside. He heard the reply, "No you don't," and identified the voice as being that of John Tappenier. There was no further conversation between the men, only the sound of two shots in quick succession. Hartson said he would not recognize the shooter, but would recognize again the unmasked man he had seen inside the store.

Hartson described the unmasked man—the same man Peter Doll thought to be the leader of the gang—as being "about five feet ten inches high, light complexioned, wore a gray coat, weighed probable in the neighborhood of 170 and 175 pounds." Hartson added, "I think he had a mustache of a light color [and] he appeared to be the leader." Hartson admitted he had never seen the man before. Upon exiting the store, Hartson recalled seeing the lifeless body of Johnny Tappenier, "lying on the stoop of the Bon Ton, his head lying toward the door."

The cook at the Bon Ton Saloon, Fred Gribi, testified that he was "standing at the door of the Bon Ton Saloon, along with Fred Tribolet" when the first shot was fired. "I saw a man fall against the door of the saloon." Gribi started out the door when he heard someone say, "Step back, you son-of-a-bitch, if you want to save your life." The cook was not sure if the party who said it was addressing him or someone else, but he retreated back inside the saloon. Gribi said he saw the body of John Tappenier afterwards, and admitted he had not seen "any of these men who did the shooting" and was unsure how many there actually were.

The verdict of the Coroner's Jury, after inspecting the body of John C. Tappenier and hearing the testimony, was the deceased, "aged about 25 years, native of Austria … came to his death from a gunshot wound inflicted by parties to the jury unknown. And that he was cruelly murdered while trying to warn people that the store of Castaneda & Co. was being robbed." The verdict in the examination of Deputy Sheriff D. Thomas Smith, age 48, a native of Danville, Illinois, was almost identical. Joseph Goldwater was the first witness to give testimony before the jury in Smith's inquest.[22]

Goldwater, after giving his place of residence and occupation, stated he was inside the store at the time of the killings, under the watchful eyes and guns of the other bandits. He stated he heard "a great many shots fired on the sidewalk of the store by the robbers." Goldwater also remembered, "Someone hallooed [sic] 'Johnny Tappenier is killed.'" The merchant stated the robbers kept him inside the office until they took their leave. Goldwater was then asked how many robbers there had been, to which he replied,

"There were five. They all came in, one after the other, in the store, between 7 and 8 o'clock p.m."

Goldwater was subsequently asked if he had heard any shooting before the men entered his store. Goldwater replied, "Of those five when they came in, two, possible three, went outside with their guns and pistols, ordering several people to go in to the store. One of the leaders was standing near to the door and gave orders, I heard him holler, 'Kill them sons-of-bitches.'" That was addressed to the part of the gang of robbers outside. One of the party outside walked back through the store, where Castaneda was in bed, sick, and demanded his money. He made Castaneda sit up and put his hand under the pillow and took a bag of gold coins. He then came back to the office, and told the (leader?) of the robbers, "The man inside is sick," and "It is all right."

Further questioning revealed that D.T. Smith had been in Castaneda's store about a half an hour before he was killed. Goldwater concluded his testimony, "According to my belief and knowledge, the killing of Mr. Smith was done by the robbers." M. Bayle, the owner of the Bisbee House, followed Goldwater on the stand. Moments before the Deputy Sheriff's murder, the "restauranteur" remembered seeing Smith and his wife, sitting at a table, eating. Bayle recalled Smith "heard the shooting and stepped out, and he got shot in the street." Bayle said he thought it was Smith's intention to go in to the store of Castaneda & Co. and that the officer had "an English bulldog pistol in his pocket when he went out."

By his own admission, Nicholas Kelly, who was employed as a miner, was standing inside the door of Bob Peirce's saloon when the firing commenced. He said he heard three shots in quick succession and passed through the door on to the porch to investigate. One of the men outside Castaneda's yelled at him, "Go back, go back, you son-of-a-bitch." Kelly stated, "I fell back and just then I felt a bullet whiz past my nose." Kelly remembered seeing Smith about three quarters of an hour before he was killed. He went on to say it was his opinion that "D.T. Smith came to his death from the effects of bullets fired by the robbers" though he did not actually see Smith shot.[23]

By his estimation, Edwin Phoenix believed James A. "Tex" Nolly (identified throughout the Coroner's Inquest documents as "James A. Nally") died from the effects of a wound to the left breast made by a "large calibre" rifle bullet. Phoenix, a carpenter by trade, recalled seeing Nolly immediately after he was shot. In his testimony, Phoenix stated Nolly lived another 26 hours after he was shot. R.P. Stevens, who testified immediately after Edwin Phoenix, stated he was in Evert's and Griffith's Saloon, in the company of several others, when the shooting began. "We talked the matter over and concluded it was a street fight, and we would stay where we were." However, when the shooting continued several minutes more, Stevens decided he would start for home to retrieve his own gun. As he crossed the street, he saw two men in front of Castaneda's firing up and down the thoroughfare. "Some of the shots went up in the air and some did not." By the time Stevens returned with his gun "the shooters were gone." Stevens stated he knew Nolly and "saw him after he was shot, lying in Bob Pierce's saloon."

Cobbler John M. Martin recalled he was working in his store on Bisbee's Main Street on the evening of the killing of "Tex" Nolly and the others. Martin testified, "I was in my shop and I heard the shooting. I did not think much of it—I heard a good deal of shooting—until a bullet struck the ground near the window and splashed dirt on the window." The shoemaker stated he put out the light in the store and went to the door to see what was happening. Martin said he "saw a man shooting up the street. He was standing straight in front of my door, just across the road." Martin believed the man was firing a Winchester rifle. "He shot a number of shots while I was standing there," stated Martin, "perhaps a dozen. He appeared to be shooting on a level" and was firing "up the street in a westward direction." Martin admitted he did not know where the shots went or if the gunman had hit anyone.

John Martin's testimony ended the Inquiry in to the death of James A. "Tex" Nolly and the Coroner's Jury concluded that Nolly, age 40, and a native of Mississippi, "came to his death on the 9th day of Dec. 1883, from the effects of a gunshot wound in the left breast inflicted by a band of robbers and murderers to this jury unknown, in Bisbee, A.T."[24]

The robbery of the A.A. Castaneda's General Merchandise Emporium can only be described as a terrible fiasco—poorly planned and poorly executed. It was far from professional. The robbers obviously knew, as did everyone else, the mine payroll would be in the store by the tenth of the month. Had they troubled to perform even the most simple of reconnaissance—watching the incoming stagecoaches and monitoring the store— they would have likely determined exactly when the monies arrived. The company would surely have put an extra guard or two on the stagecoach and there would likely have been an armed escort when the delivery was actually made. When the conveyance arrived in town, some men would have disembarked and gone directly from the coach to Goldwater and Castaneda's store. Even if they were not carrying a strong box, it would have been evident what they were about.

Author Scott Brown, in his article about the Bisbee robbery, suggests that the outlaws could have avoided the entire debacle by simply holding up the stage before it arrived in town. However, there was no way for the outlaws to be sure which stage was carrying the payroll and, if the outlaws stopped the wrong one, the company would have been alerted to their intentions, and would surely have increased security on subsequent runs. The fact was robbing the store was the better option, but the robbers should have ascertained the monies had actually arrived before commencing with their assault on the mercantile. Still, as Brown asserted, "had these men who were bent on the robbery taken the precaution, they could easily have done their work, and no lives of innocent people would have been taken, and they would have saved their own lives."[25]

Further supporting the certainty that this robbery was not the work of professional thieves was the fact that one of the robbers had not even bothered with a disguise, but brazenly walked in to the store bare-faced. There is absolutely no accounting for this oversight. There was no sense in it at all. As a result, every hostage in the store, including proprietor Joe Goldwater, would have easily been able to give a description of him and positively identify him as one of the robbers. The simple precaution of tying a 'kerchief over his features would have been enough to protect his identity and foil any witnesses in their attempts to later describe him to the authorities. To proceed unmasked was just plain foolhardy and would be one of the deciding factors in the undoing of the gang.

In addition to the thieves' incompetence at reconnaissance and disguise, was the completely unabashed and unnecessary violence associated with the robbery. The robbers had begun by corralling passersby into the store where they were told to take a place in line and throw up their hands. It was only when the robber standing in front of the store ordered Tappenier and Bright back inside the Bon Ton Saloon that the situation began to deteriorate. Had the bandit simply turned away and acted in a less conspicuous manner, Tappenier and Bright may not have even noticed what was going on as they exited the saloon. And if the two men had come towards the store, the bandits could have easily drawn down on them and forced them inside with the other hostages. By shouting orders at Tappenier and Bright, the bandit drew attention to himself and his accomplice. Even then, the bandit could have shot in the general direction of the two men—either over their heads or at the ground in front of them—rather than killing Tappenier.

It was only after these first two shots had been fired and Tappenier killed, that the town was alerted to the fact that something was amiss. Had it not been for the report of the Winchester on the street, Deputy Sheriffs Smith and Daniels would have been none the wiser to what was occurring on the main thoroughfare. Mr. Krigbaum would not have rushed down the hill from his cabin and Annie Roberts would not have come to the door of her restaurant. The bandits, by killing an unarmed man, who did not pose an immediate threat to them, simply because he would not comply with their demands, very much brought the subsequent events down upon themselves. Had the bandit not been so quick to bark orders at Tappenier and Bright and so quick to fire upon them when they did not comply, the robbery might have been pulled off without any violence at all. Of course, once the shooting had begun, the entire situation spun very quickly out of control.

It is known Deputy Sheriff Smith had a British "Bulldog" revolver on his person. Why he did not have it at the ready is a mystery, but he made three terrible and fatal mistakes. The first was rushing out on to the street without first assessing the situation. The second was going forward without having his weapon in his hand. Not taking what one would think would be an obvious precaution probably cost him his life. Smith's third mistake was identifying himself as a law officer to the two gunmen outside Goldwater and Castaneda's. If he had not been a target prior to this, identifying himself as "the enemy" immediately made him one. The moment after Smith made this declaration, one of the gunman reportedly said, "Then you are just the son-of-a-bitch we want!" and shot him.[26]

Did Smith misunderstand the situation? Did he think it was just a couple of cowboys "hurrahing" the town? Did he see the body of John C. Tappenier lying in the doorway of the Bon Ton Saloon? History can only speculate. Running out into the street as he did without first determining what was happening—which he could easily have done from inside the restaurant where he and his wife had been dining—can only be described as reckless. Why he did not retreat when ordered to do so by the gunman—a move which would have allowed him to go back inside, arm himself, and find a more defensible position from which to confront the outlaws—is also unknown. Smith's decision to stand his ground may well have been due to his inexperience or possibly bravado. Still, the fact remains, had Deputy Sheriff Smith approached more cautiously, with his weapon at the ready, he may well have been able to thwart the gunmen and prevent anyone else from being killed.

As with the killing of Tappenier, the murder of James A. "Tex" Nolly was completely unnecessary. Nolly was the very definition of an innocent by-stander and in no way posed an immediate threat to the gunmen. He was most likely not armed and was doing nothing to lead the gunmen to believe he was going to attempt to interfere in their business. For Nolly, it was simply a matter of being in the wrong place at the wrong time. By this point, the gunmen, fueled by adrenaline and attempting to exert control over a situation they tragically created, were shooting at anyone and everyone. Nolly was targeted because he was on the street and within range. It is curious that the freighter did not make an attempt to run or hide after hearing the shooting and seeing the gunmen. He may have even seen the lifeless bodies of Deputy Sheriff Smith and J. Tappenier. Perhaps the violence unnerved him and he simply froze where he was.

The killing of Annie Roberts and her unborn child was presumably unintentional. There has been speculation that the bullet which fatally wounded her had been intended for another—possible Deputy Sheriff Daniels or Indian Joe. Deputy Sheriff Daniels saloon was down the street past the Roberts' restaurant and, by Daniels' own account, the bandits had fired upon him when they saw him out in front of his place. It may well have been one of the bullets which were meant for the lawman which struck Mrs. Roberts. Certainly, the gunmen would not have purposely targeted an innocent woman. This would have gone against all the ingrained cultural mores and morality of the Victorian era, which made it incumbent on a man to protect women and children at all costs, no matter their proclivity for crime.

Then again, the robbers, with their adrenaline coursing and their nervous systems overloaded, may have developed what is commonly referred to as "tunnel vision." Modern studies have shown that during highly-stressful, violent encounters, human beings will experience a variety of symptoms, including narrowing of attention span and range of perceived alternatives, reduction in problem solving capabilities, and difficulties in maintaining attention to fine detail discrimination, all of which reduce their ability to make rational judgments and decisions. In short, the gunmen may not have been truly "seeing" the people they were shooting at. They may well have perceived anything that was moving as a potential threat and reacted accordingly. When the gunman saw the figure appear suddenly in the doorway of the restaurant, he may have not even registered it was a woman, in spite of the fact she was probably wearing a large dress, and simply fired at it.[27]

Not that it would matter. That these men had killed a woman—even if the killing was completely unintentional—was enough cause for general outrage among the populace of the burgeoning mining town. Notwithstanding the murders of two innocent unarmed civilians and a Deputy Sheriff, but the killing of Annie Roberts—a respectable married woman who was with child—made the crime that much more unconscionable and unforgivable. Arguably, it was also the killing of Annie Roberts which made the robbery national news. *The Chicago Tribune, The Milan Exchange* (Tennessee), *The Columbus Journal, The Abilene Reflector, The Omaha Daily Bee, The Sacramento Daily Union-Herald, The Honolulu Daily Bulletin* and *The New York Times*, in their coverage of the Bisbee raid, would all make mention of the fact that there had been a woman among the casualties.

As further evidence of the ineptitude of the gang, as they were making their escape up the street to their horses, at least one other member of the gang dropped his mask, adding yet one more mistake to a whole series which were committed by the hapless robbers. After dropping his disguise, the outlaw was seen by William Gerstenberg, who recognized him. The tally now rose to three of the robbers who could be positively identified by witnesses. Realizing he had been seen, the outlaw fired a single shot at Gerstenberg, but missed. The gunman did not stop to finish the job, but fled on with his confederates. Gerstenberg survived the encounter, hiding himself in the shop's cellar until he was certain it was safe.

Even in their choice of horses, the outlaws had made an error in judgment. Most outlaws, when committing crimes where anonymity would be paramount, would have chosen mounts devoid of any unusual markings or coloring, so as not to stand out. Indeed, four of the men were mounted on animals which were fairly non-descript and not easily identifiable in the darkness. However, one of the robbers—the same who had neglected to mask his visage during the robbery—was riding a very distinct grey-colored horse. The animal very much stood out even in the low light of the evening. John Hiles, the man working at Lockwood's corral on the evening of the robbery, was later able to give authorities a good description of both the horse and the man who was riding it.

These were not the only examples of carelessness, poor-planning, and short-sightedness on the part of the Bisbee outlaws. Even before the five men rode in to town that fateful December evening, they had all but doomed themselves to failure. If, as was later asserted, there was a master plan, it was neither well-formulated nor well-executed; it was a robbery devoid of professionalism. Simply put, the raid on A.A. Castaneda's mercantile was the work of rank amateurs—more specifically, cowboys, who may have been adept at stealing cattle and horses, but who had little or no experience in the business of armed robbery. Aside from the most rudimentary of sketches, there was minimal planning involved. The bombastic response made by the unmasked robber to his compatriots when they entered the store asking for more cartridges (yet another oversight on the part of the outlaws)—"That's right! Pump out the old shells and put in the new! We'll teach these God-damned, sons-of-bitches that we are running this town for a few minutes!"— would seem to belie any notion that these men knew what they were doing. A cooler, more-calculating head would have responded differently, namely, with restraint. These men were merely reacting to a situation they had created and then completely lost control of.[28]

CHAPTER THREE

The Manhunt

"About 11:30 o'clock last night," wrote the editor of *The Arizona Weekly Citizen*, "a couple of couriers reached Tombstone from Bisbee with news of an appalling and bloody tragedy enacted in that place a few hours previous. The names of the parties bringing news are Wm. Wallace and James Kregman [probably Krigbaum]. From the former was gathered the … details of the crime." Once news of the robbery reached the county seat in Tombstone, it was only a matter of hours before the telegraph wires were disseminating it across the country. *The New York Times*, *The Chicago Daily Tribune*, and *The San Francisco Examiner*, as well as smaller publications such as *The Abilene Reflector* of Kansas and *The Milan Exchange* of Tennessee, quickly picked up the story. Even *The Daily Bulletin* of Honolulu, Hawaii, printed news of the outrage in Arizona, albeit 19 days after the crime had occurred. As was the case just two years earlier, during the era of the Earps, the eyes of the nation were again focused on the doings in the wild and wooly Arizona Territory.[1]

Back in Bisbee, within an hour of the robbery, Deputy Sheriff Daniels had begun organizing and outfitting a posse of citizens "to go in pursuit, as soon as light would permit the following of the trail." When the news reached Tombstone an hour or so later, Under Sheriff Wallace, in the absence of Cochise County Sheriff Jerome Ward, dispatched Deputy Sheriff Robert "Bob" Hatch to the scene of the crime. Wallace then dispatched a second posse, under the command of Deputy Sheriff Si Bryant, consisting of Charley Smith, Andy Ames, Fred Dodge, and Joe Baker, with orders to ride to Bisbee to assist in tracking the outlaws. However, the first posse afield, was a small, heavily armed contingency from Bisbee, which left town immediately after the robbery. *The Tombstone Republican* identified the men of this posse as "Messrs." Waite and Heath, the dance hall owners, and Henry Frost.[2]

After the shooting had subsided, John Heath and Nathan Waite had ventured out of the dance hall, on to the street. Frost recalled seeing "several dead bodies." Waite would later testify to the fact that he and Heath had "offered our services to Deputy Sheriff Daniel [*sic*], to go after the robbers. Daniel [*sic*] picked out four of the men at the saloon; Heith and I were of the number." Conversely, John Heath recalled being "asked to go out with Deputy Sheriff Daniels after the robbers." Whether the partners approached Deputy Daniels or vice versa, Heath, Waite, and Henry Frost were immediately deputized, presumably by Daniels, and ordered to ready themselves to go in pursuit of the bandits. Within the hour, Heath, Waite, and Frost were riding out of Bisbee along the same route the outlaws had taken. Meanwhile, Deputy Sheriff Daniels continued organizing the larger posse of men which would take the field at daybreak the following day.[3]

Deputy Sheriff Bryant's posse arrived in Bisbee early Sunday morning only to find that Deputy Daniels had already ridden out with his five men. The Tombstone posse immediately set out after them. The trail of the outlaw gang was found to lead out of the gulch, up and over the pass, and down into the Sulpher Springs Valley. From there, the outlaws took to the Milk Ranch, about eight miles east of Bisbee. Witnesses at that locale later reported that the robbers had indeed stopped there and "watered their horses and were heard joking as to who should wear a couple of gold watches taken at Castaneda's store." Deputy Sheriff Daniels' posse pressed on.[4]

It wasn't long until Daniels' posse caught up with that of Frost, Waite, and John Heath. Together they followed the trail of the outlaws which led in the direction of Soldier's Hole, a watering stop along the original Butterfield Stage route about 25 miles north of the Mexican border. There, the two posses from Bisbee were joined by the contingency from Tombstone. Here the trail of the outlaws split off into two directions—one heading off to the east and the other south toward old Mexico. At John Heath's suggestion, it was decided the posse should also split to best follow the divergent trails of their quarry. Later, that same afternoon, Heath, Waite and Frost arrived in Tombstone, stating that the trail they had followed, that of two of the outlaw gang, had led them to that burg. Deputy Sheriff Hatch, when he returned from Bisbee later that evening, in the company of County Coroner Holland and Dr. Porter, was quick to discount the Heath party's report.

The Tombstone Republican reported that Undersheriff Wallace had sent out telegrams "to all the towns along the Southern Pacific [Railway] east of here, as far as Deming" describing the robbers and items stolen, more specifically the time pieces. Deputy Sheriff Hatch was of the opinion that the outlaw gang they were seeking in connection with the Bisbee outrage had been "during the past summer creating anarchy in Graham county" and were the same gang who had recently held up the Southern Pacific train near Gage Station, southwest of Deming in the New Mexico Territory. This rumor was repeated in the subsequent Associated Press reports. "Later advice state that the men are believed to the same who were engaged in the robbery of the Southern Pacific train at Gage Station of Nov. 17," reported *The New York Times* article of December 10. This story would be disseminated nationally through *The Chicago Daily Tribune*, *The St. Paul Daily Globe*, *The Columbus Journal* of Nebraska, and a host of other newspapers.[5]

Seven days prior to the Bisbee robbery, on November 30, 1883, *The Weekly Arizona Miner* reported that the "east-bound train on the Southern Pacific Railroad was robbed at Gage [Station], twenty miles west of Deming by six men at 7:30 p.m., on the 24th instant." The Prescott newspaper continued, "The robbers killed the engineer and robbed Wells, Fargo & Co.'s car. It was reported that the passengers were held up but the report is not confirmed. The railroad company and Wells, Fargo offer two thousand dollars for each robber captured and convicted." In a subsequent update, the newspaper branded the robbers as "cowboys" and stated that the robbers had fled toward the San Bernardino Mountains in Cochise County, A.T. Upon receiving a dispatch about the robbery, the famed Civil War veteran and Apache-fighter, General George R. Crook ordered a company of cavalry from Fort Bayard to go in pursuit of the villains.

Initially, reports described the Gage robbers as "thoroughly familiar with their business" and identified their leader as "noted desperado John Price, alias Johnny-Over-the-

Left: Cochise County Deputy Sheriff Robert "Bob" Hatch, who, was dispatched to Bisbee the morning after the robbery by Sheriff Jerome Ward. *Right:* General George R. Crook, U.S. Army, famous for leading the Geronimo Campaign, put federal troops in the field to aid in the search for the outlaw gang (author's collection).

Fence." Later, it was learned the robbers had taken $700 from the Wells Fargo car as well as a pocket watch and $100 from Mr. Vail, the conductor. The passengers were not molested by the bandits, as had first been reported, and they had probably killed engineer F.C. Webster through carelessness. In order to stop the train, the outlaws had removed the "fish plates, thereby spreading the rails" causing the engine and several cars to derail. Still, the newspaper insisted the robbers were "not common tramps, but quick, intelligent fearless men."[6]

The day after these reports appeared in *The Weekly Miner*, *The Arizona Sentinel* of Yuma, ran excerpts from an exclusive interview with conductor Vail. The train engineer had spotted the displaced rail as the locomotive entered a small gorge five miles east of Gage Station, but had not been able to stop the train in time to avoid the hazard. The engine left the track along with the two cars directly behind and slammed sidelong into the embankment. W.T. North, the locomotive's firemen, jumped from the engine only to be accosted by two gunmen. However, instead of holding North as a hostage, the gunmen began wantonly firing their revolvers at the engine and mail car, killing engineer Webster with a bullet through the heart. Seizing the opportunity presented to him, North proceeded to hide himself in the nearby sagebrush.

One of the passengers, described only as a "Chicago newspaperman" stepped off the train "to see what was the matter" and was quickly relieved of his timepiece and $155 by the robbers. At this point, Vail stepped from the sleeping car, and presented himself to the bandits. He too was robbed of his personal possessions. Vail then asked the robbers "what was their programme." The robbers replied, "Money was what they were after and money they proposed to have." The masked gunmen agreed not to harm the passengers, 19 in number, as long as no resistance was offered. They then escorted Vail and the newspaperman back to the express car and demanded the conductor open the door thereof. Vail explained that only the messenger could open the door, as the locks were on the inside. The outlaws instructed Vail to tell the messenger to open up, which he did immediately.

When the door to the express car was opened, the bandits proceeded to board and loot the car, breaking open the strong box and rifling through the contents therein. Disappointed at their take and suspecting there must be more money elsewhere on the train, the bandits proceeded with the conductor, the newspaperman, the messenger, and the baggage master down to the mail car, which was likewise ransacked. At one point, Vail, hearing the engine "poping [sic] off steam every few moments" and concerned the firebox would overheat, asked if he would be allowed to go forward and throw some water into the box. The bandits refused him this request.

While the bandits were busy looting and pilfering the mail car, the rear brakeman, one Thomas Scott, slipped off the train and started back afoot toward Gage Station to raise the alarm. The newspaper said of the brakeman's actions, "It was a desperate undertaking, but he got away with it." Having finished their business at hand, the bandits ushered Conductor Vail, the messenger, the baggage master, and the newspaperman into the express car, telling them to "not come out for five minutes." The robbers returned to their horses, which were tied just a few yards from the track, mounted up, and rode away. The robbery had taken nearly an hour to complete and netted the bandits less than $1000 in total. It was not until after the bandits left, that Conductor Vail discovered the lifeless body of engineer Webster laying beside the track with a single bullet wound in his chest. *The Sentinel* further reported that "Mr. Vail is positive there were only four men in the gang and they were evidently novices in the business as they took little precaution to protect themselves."[7]

On December 13, just four days after the Bisbee outrage, *The Sacramento Daily Record Union* newspaper reprinted an Associated Press report, under the headline "The Gage Station Train Robbers." The article was derived from a dispatch received the day before from San Simon Station, A.T. *The Arizona Weekly Citizen* would carry the same story the following day. According to the dispatch, United States Deputy Marshal C.B. Sanders and a posse from Deming, who were in search of the Gage Station bandits, received word that five men had put into the town of Galeyville the day after the train robbery. Sources said the men "applied to the miner's camp for provisions, but the foreman … refused to give them anything to eat. The suspects then left and made a camp about a mile from Galeyville." Upon his arrival in that town, Marshal Sanders rode out alone to ascertain where exactly the men were bivouacked. Having reconnoitered the area and located the outlaws' camp, the Marshal hastily returned to Galeyville to organize a posse.

The Marshal and a party of three men, returned to the suspects' camp to find the men saddling up to leave. Though the Marshal had ridden up near enough to take a few shots at the departing figures, the remainder of the posse was too far back to give chase and the suspects escaped. Marshal Sanders stated that there were only three men in the gang he pursued. The source in Galeyville identified one of the men as "York, alias Kelly" and another simply as "Red." One of the men was said to be wearing a "fine suit of clothes," sporting a seal ring, and a "fine gold watch." One of the others, described as "a small man, had a pair of pistols, one of which had an ivory handle and the other with pearl." The suspects were said to be riding "two claybank horses and a bay pony."[8]

In an addendum to their first report, *The Weekly Citizen* ran a second, more detailed description of the encounter between Marshal Sanders and the outlaws. Upon arriving in Galeyville, Marshal Sanders, in the company of H.L. Caples and J.M. Wilkins of Tucson, had visited G.B. Roberts. Roberts informed the Marshal that five men visited his cabin the "evening of the day succeeding the train robbery." He described them as "heavily armed" and stated their mounts looked "badly jaded." Roberts gave a full description of the men, which was very similar to the description of the robbers the Marshal had previously obtained. Roberts also stated that the men had ridden off in the direction of Cherry Creek, located in the mountains nearby, and said he had reason to believe the suspects were still in the vicinity. The following morning, Marshal Sanders, armed with a shotgun, set out alone in search of the men.

Two and half miles along the canyon through which ran Cherry Creek, the Marshal found the suspects' campsite, except there were no longer five men, only three. Noting this, the Marshal waited at a distance for the return of the other two. When the two missing men did not rejoin their comrades, he "made up his mind the others had separated." Marshal Sanders returned to Galeyville and hastily formed a posse, which included Caples, Wilkins, G.B. Roberts, Pony Dunean, a man named Bradley, and Dr. George E. Goodfellow of Tombstone and "in the face of a blinding snow storm started with the posse to affect the capture or death of the robbers." Upon reaching the canyon, the posse divided with the intention of attacking the camp from both sides. "They had proceeded but a short distance when Goodfellow, who was on a knoll a little above his party, discovered the men riding down the canyon" about 200 yards from his position. Goodfellow and his men immediately charged them.

Marshal Sanders, who had separated from the others, also spotted the outlaws, and he too gave chase. The lawman was within eight yards of the suspects when he opened fire. The suspect in the lead immediately swung off his horse and made towards a stand of sagebrush, closely followed by the other two suspects. It was then that Goodfellow and the rest of the posse arrived on the scene, but were forced to rein in their horses at a distance of about 80 yards, as there was too much open ground between them and the stand where the robbers had taken refuge, and they did not want to make easy targets of themselves. The Marshal and his posse fired several shots into the brush where the suspects were thought to be hiding but "met with no response." With the snow storm increasing in violence and the suspects having the tactical advantage, the posse decided to withdraw to the camp the outlaws had deserted.

The following morning, the posse revisited the site of the stand-off with the suspects only to find "the birds had flown." Dr. Goodfellow's party commenced their pursuit of the outlaws, while Marshal Sanders, Caples, and Wilkins returned to Bowie Station, "from whence Sanders notified every place south and east of the robbers having left the eyrie." The Marshal noted that the suspects had acquired new blankets and horses from "unknown parties." The suspects were now mounted on two duns and a "little bay mare with a large star in the forehead."[9]

While Marshal Sanders suspected he was on the trail of the Gage Station robbers, it is more likely he had crossed paths with three of the bandits who had robbed Castaneda's mercantile in Bisbee. *The Weekly Citizen*, in the same issue, reported that on Wednesday,

December 12, Omer W. "Red" Sample and James "Tex" Howard had arrived at Maud Elby's brothel house in Clifton telling "the girls they wanted something to eat in a hurry." As they dined, they related the story of their involvement in the "Bisbee affair and the arrangements to rob the town made by John Heath." The two fugitives showed the girls the money and gold watches acquired during the robbery. The newspaper named "Red" Sample, Billy Delaney, Big Dan, and Dowd Kelly as the perpetrators of the crime, solely based on what an unidentified woman of Elby's house had revealed.

"Red" Sample and "Tex" Howard explained how the gang had split up roughly nine miles out of Bisbee, just as Deputy Sheriff Daniels' posse later discovered, with Delaney and Dowd taking towards the Mexican border and the state of Sonora. Thirty miles on, Sample and Howard stopped at a ranch, where they retrieved their horses and took their leave of Kelly. The two outlaws went on to describe they made for Clifton, via the San Simon Valley. As Sample and Howard were leaving Maud Elby's, they ominously announced that they planned to "go north and get a crowd and serve Clifton the same as they had Bisbee." Nickolas Olguin (misidentified in the article as Nicolas Cleguins), who had been afield with his own posse tracking the Gage Station outlaws, later confirmed the unidentified woman's story. *The Weekly Citizen* reported that a posse of 19 men, under Deputy Sheriffs Hovey and Hill, had ridden out the following morning in pursuit of Sample and Howard. Olguin and his party also continued to dog the outlaws' trail.[10]

After a fruitless five day pursuit, Deputy Sheriff Daniels and his posse returned to Bisbee, arriving in that burg on Friday the 14th. *The Tombstone Republican* reported that Daniels and his posse had trailed the robbers to a point about 20 miles outside of Bisbee, where it appeared the suspects parted ways. "Owing to the rocky nature of the ground it was impossible to find any indications showing the directions in which any of them had gone." It was at this point, that Frost, Waite, and John Heath—who had been the one who first discovered that the robbers had split up—took their leave of the main body, following one of the trails in the direction of Tombstone. The remaining members of Daniels' posse spent the afternoon "cutting for sign" on the second trail before travelling on to the well at Soldier's Hole. It was here Deputy Sheriff Daniels and his men were met by Deputy Sheriff Bryant and the posse out of Tombstone.

After spending the night at Soldier's Hole, the combined force resumed the search for the outlaws' trail, but to no avail. As evening closed in on the luckless men, the party from Tombstone split off and headed back to town. Only Deputy Sheriff Si Bryant remained behind. Daniels' posse, accompanied by Bryant, trekked into the Chiricahua Mountains to a "certain ranch, [where] a full description of the five murderers was obtained." The newspaper did not immediately reveal the identities or descriptions of the outlaws "for prudential reasons." The Bisbee posse continued their pursuit, riding out to the Silver Creek and San Bernardino ranches and "other points" in a quest for some clue as to the direction the bandits had fled. Finally, after questioning "numerous cattlemen" in the area, Deputy Daniels and his posse gave up all hope of uncovering the outlaws' trail and decided to return to Bisbee.[11]

Deputy Sheriff William A. "Billy" Daniels was born March 22, 1842, in Iowa to John and Elizabeth Daniels. He was the second of five children born to the couple. Little is known about his life prior to his arrival in the Arizona Territory. A William B. Daniels appears on the U.S. Census of 1880, living in Babacomari Valley, near present day Sierra Vista, in what was then Pima County. His place of birth is listed as Iowa, his age as 37, and his occupation as "prospector." There is very little information about him otherwise.

It is unknown when Daniels took up residence in Bisbee, when he opened his saloon in that town, or when he was appointed as a Deputy Sheriff of Cochise County by Sheriff Ward. His name was not found in any of the local newspapers prior to the robbery and his official appointment documents appear to have been lost with the passing of time.[12]

The Tombstone Republican reported the rewards being offered for "the apprehension of the Bisbee murderers aggregate $7,500 or $1,500 for each participant in the dastardly deed." A notice on page two of the December 15 edition stated, in addition to the $2,500 being offered by Cochise County for the "apprehension and conviction" of the outlaws, County Treasurer Ben Goodrich, acting as the agent for the "responsible citizens of the county" had been authorized to offer an additional $5,000 for their "arrest and conviction," said sum to be "paid on the certificate of the Chairman of the Board of Supervisors and the District Attorney." The notice further explained that "a proportionate part of the sum" would be paid for the "production of the dead body of any one or more" of the Bisbee bandits.[13]

Cochise County Deputy Sheriff William A. "Billy" Daniels, County Sheriff Jerome Ward's right hand man in the manhunt for the Bisbee bandits (author's collection).

Anton Mazzanovich, a former private in Troop F, 6th Cavalry. U.S. Army, who kept a saloon in the town of Shakespeare, New Mexico Territory, was returning on the Southern Pacific line from a visit to Judge L.M. Wood of Monita, H.A. Morgan, and Colonel John Norton at Camp Grant. At Bowie Station, in the south-eastern portion of the Arizona Territory, about 60 miles south of Clifton, a young man boarded the train. Mazzanovich noticed the man acting queerly, which "aroused his suspicions." Surreptitiously, Mazzanovich inquired of the conductor how far the young man was going, to which the conductor replied that the young man had paid a fare through to El Paso, Texas. As the train approached San Simon, the young man left his seat and adjourned to the lavatory. After the train passed through the town, the young man reappeared. This same behavior was repeated as the train neared Lordsburg in the New Mexico Territory. When the train stopped in Lordsburg, Mazzanovich disembarked. Finding Deputy Marshal Bill Davenport on the platform, he told the lawman of the unusual antics of the young man and asked Davenport to go aboard with him. Davenport obliged and, as soon as the train left the station, witnessed for himself the odd behaviors of the young man.

Mazzanovich instructed Deputy Davenport to get off when the train reached Deming and search out Daniel "Dan" Tucker, a local peace officer of Mazzanovich's acquaintance.

As the train neared Deming, the young man again retreated to the lavatory. When the train pulled into the station, Davenport disembarked and went to find Tucker. Within a few minutes, Tucker was found and boarded the train with Davenport. Mazzanovich, Davenport and Tucker positioned themselves so as they would be occupying the seats to the front, to the rear, and directly across from the suspect when he returned to the car. A few miles out of Deming, the young man returned to his seat, unaware that he was now surrounded. Mazzanovich stated it was he who first pulled his weapon, getting the drop on the suspect. He ordered him to throw up his hands, and when the young man turned his head as if looking for a way out, he found the revolvers of Tucker and Davenport also pointed in his direction.

"Well boys, you sure got me," said the young man. While Mazzanovich and Tucker kept their pistols trained on him, Deputy Davenport relieved him "of his shooting irons and any other implements of war" he had on his person. Officer Tucker then handcuffed the suspect. Though they knew they had someone in custody, the three men were unsure who exactly they were detaining and why. Mazzanovich and Tucker began to question him and the suspect soon became "rattled and all twisted in his statements." Mazzanovich finally confronted him with his suspicion that he was one of the Bisbee robbers by the name of "York" Kelly. To this accusation, the man replied, "You hit it right, youngster. I am Kelly, the man you are looking for."

In his remembrance, Mazzanovich stated that when the train finally arrived in El Paso, he and the two lawmen escorted Kelly from the railcar to the local jail, where the young man was confined for the evening. Officer Tucker then proceeded to the local telegraph office to wire Cochise County Sheriff Jerome Ward with the news that Kelly had been apprehended and asked the Sheriff to send some men to retrieve the outlaw in Deming. The following morning, Mazzanovich, Davenport, and Tucker escorted Kelly back to the train station, where together they boarded a west-bound train for the town of Deming in the New Mexico Territory. Once arrived in that burg, Daniel "York" Kelly was promptly locked in the jailhouse to await extradition back to the Arizona Territory.[14]

Cochise County District Attorney Marcus A. Smith and Cochise County Treasurer Ben Goodrich (Arizona Historical Society, 3363 [cropped]).

The Arizona Weekly Citizen of December 15 noted that "Sheriff Ward left for New Mexico this morning to receive 'Yank' Kelly, recently arrested in Deming." The paper continued, "Sheriff Ward claims to have positive evidence that Kelly was one of the Bisbee raiders." Deputy Sheriff Daniels told the reporter from *The Tombstone*

Republican he was "confident the man apprehended in Deming, for whom Sheriff Ward departed this morning, is one of the murderers." *The Republican* went on to praise the law officers of the county: "The corps of deputies at the sheriff's office have all the business they can attend to now-a-days; but the business of the office has been so thoroughly systematized by Undersheriff Wallace that everything glides smoothly along, and without error or confusion a vast amount of work is accomplished."[15]

Anton Mazzanovich tells a compelling story. However, another account of the arrest of Daniel "York" Kelly exists. The latter, found in an unpublished manuscript by Harriet W. Harkin, details how Kelly made his way via train to Lordsburg in the New Mexico Territory, where he stopped in at a local tonsorial parlor for a shave. The barber recognized the outlaw from his description in the handbills the Cochise County Sheriff's office had circulated immediately after the robbery. Somehow, the barber got word to the local law enforcement officers, who descended in force upon the barber shop. Kelly was

Anton Mazzanovich, former cavalry soldier, who later asserted he had been instrumental in the capture of outlaw Daniel "York" Kelly, the first of the Bisbee bandits to be apprehended (Arizona Historical Society, 19589).

placed under arrest while still seated in the barber's chair. As with Mazzanovich's tale, there is no corroborating evidence to support this version of events. Unfortunately, none of the local newspapers reported any of the details of the young outlaw's apprehension, so we are left with these two somewhat dubious accounts.[16]

The Cochise County Sheriff's office had done a commendable job in dealing with the Bisbee outrage. Undersheriff Wallace responded immediately and forcefully to the crisis as soon as he was apprised of it. In less than seven days, the deputies discovered the names of all the perpetrators and more or less asserted where they had fled to. One of the suspects, Daniel "York" Kelly had already been apprehended and a posse was close on the trail of Omer "Red" Sample and James "Tex" Howard. The lawmen also brought in John Heath and Henry Frost for questioning in connection with the robbery. Heath had been a suspect in the Gage Train robbery, "but an alibi was clearly established for him in that case." However, Deputy Daniels suspected that Heath purposely tried to throw the posse off the trail of the bandits during the initial pursuit, even though it was Heath who pointed out the divergent trails of the outlaws indicating the gang had split up.[17]

A report from Lordsburg in the New Mexico Territory, dated December 12, subsequently published in the December 15 edition of *The Arizona Weekly Citizen*, revealed that "three rustlers with black masks" held up R.H. Porter's saloon and demanded he open the safe. When Porter refused to cooperate, the robbers fired their guns at him. Fearing for his life, the saloon owner reconsidered and the bandits made off with $550 in cash. On hearing of the robbery, Deputy Sheriff Haden and Deputy Marshal Davenport, the same man who Mazzanovich stated had been involved in the capture of "York" Kelly, immediately formed a posse and lit out after the bandits. The Lordsburg report identified the leader of the robbers as one "Joe Heath" and stated emphatically that he was "the leader in the late train wreck near Gage station on the 24th."

At the time of the train robbery, John Heath was seen at San Simon Station, "74 miles from Gage and en route to Bisbee." Further, at the time of the robbery of Porter's saloon, John Heath was being held in the Cochise County jail at the time of the robbery of Porter's Saloon. It is clear that Heath could not have been involved in either of these crimes and it is unknown why his name was mentioned in conjunction with either of them. Still, *The Republican* stated, "there is no doubt the [Bisbee] bandits had at least one accomplice in the town."[18]

During the second week of December, the posse came upon two men camped near Clifton. The posse was led by Nickolas Olguin, who had indirectly become involved in the search for "Red" Sample and "Tex" Howard. In their initial report, *The Weekly Citizen* stated that Olguin, believing the men to be Hispanic, ordered the men "in Spanish and English to throw up their hands." In response, the men drew their arms and fired upon the posse. In the ensuing gun battle, both "strangers" were killed. The county coroner was duly called to the scene and soon determined that the men were not outlaws at all but were, in fact, "were from the vicinity of Duncan" and "had located some land in the vicinity" on which to start a cattle ranch.

In a subsequent report from Lordsburg, it was revealed that the victims, L.M. Clements and his partner, William Wryscarber, both American citizens, were in the process of building a cabin on their land, when the party of Mexicans, led by Olguin, came upon them. The two victims were not armed at the time, having left their weapons at their campsite. After securing the men's rifles, Olguin and his posse wantonly attacked the defenseless two men. As the posse descended upon them, Clements and his partner began to run, first toward their camp and, when they were thwarted in this, into the neighboring hills. Clements was shot twice by the posse members, once through the breast and once through the body. Wryscarber fled almost a half mile before the Mexicans rode him down and shot him through the head.

Nickolas Olguin initially took to the trail with his posse of Mexicans after being attacked in his home by "a party of rustlers" earlier in the month. It seems Olguin had a vague idea of who his assailants might be, but had no conclusive evidence to support his assumptions. Whether the members of the Olguin posse truly believed they had just killed two wanted criminals or, after an otherwise fruitless pursuit, had simply vented their anger and frustration on these two convenient targets, two innocent men died at their hands. Subsequent actions of Olguin's posse were certainly not those of men seeking to advance the cause of law and order. Having killed Clements and his partner, the Mexicans robbed their bodies of a sum of $90 and helped themselves to their guns, horses, and camping gear. "They even took the boots from the dead man's feet." The Mexicans were subsequently arrested and held over in Clifton to await a hearing in the case of the murder of Clements and his partner. Though present at the time of the killings, the newspaper made no mention of Olguin in their subsequent report.

The Weekly Citizen described Clements as having "resided here about three years and has a reputation of having been an upright honorable man" and characterized the killings as "one of the most brutal murders ever perpetrated in [the] county." Trouble was certainly expected to come from the killing of the two "supposed American rustlers." The newspaper noted that a party of men "will leave here tomorrow and will be joined by about thirty more at Duncan to go to Clifton to attend the trial of the Mexicans, and probably by summary measures, avenge the death of the Americans." Though the hearing date was set for December 19, Olguin managed to have his men released, possibly by posting what must have been a significant bond, and was back in the field by Friday, December 14.[19]

"Red" Sample and "Tex" Howard made a foolish mistake in returning to their old haunts in Clifton. Early that Wednesday morning, December 12, Walter W. Bush, the night bartender at George Hill's saloon, was "aroused from his slumbers by hearing the tramp of horses at the rear of the house followed by a tap on the window." The woman Bush was with went to the window to inquire who the caller was. "Red!" came the answer, accompanied by a demand to be admitted immediately. When the woman hesitated, Sample repeated his demand, adding that he had been to Hill's saloon in search of Bush, and was informed by the night watchman the man he was seeking was staying at Maud Elby's house. "Bush bid the woman to open the door when "Red" and "Tex" entered." They quickly adjourned to the room where Bush was staying, where he asked what they were doing there and where they had been.

"Bisbee," said the outlaw.

"Do you know what you did in Bisbee, Red?" asked Bush.

"I think we must have killed someone." said Sample.

With that, "Red" and "Tex" went on to tell the bartender about the robbery. Bush later said the two men admitted to the shooting of Deputy Sheriff Tom Smith. Sample said he told the man to "turn back" and when he did not, he shot him. Sample also revealed that their take had been about $800 and a couple of gold pocket watches. Sample produced one of the watches, which was inscribed on the case the letters "W.C." Sample continued his tale implicating "Johnnie Heath" as the mastermind of the robbery. Heath "put up the job," said the outlaw, "and opened the dance hall as a guy [diversion]." After the robbery, about nine miles outside of Bisbee, William Delaney and Daniel "Big Dan" Dowd had broke off and headed off south toward Sonora. Twenty miles down the trail, the three remaining outlaws stopped in at the ranch of a "friend" who supplied them with fresh mounts. Sample did not say where they rode to after leaving the "friendly ranch," but it is presumed they took to the Chiricahua Mountains, where they later had a run-in with U.S. Deputy Marshal Sanders, Dr. Goodfellow, and that posse. Soon after this incident "York" Kelly took his leave and "Red" and Tex" then decided to return to Clifton.

After hearing their tale, Bush admonished the two robbers, telling them that it would have been bad enough to rob the town without killing anyone, but "you boys are reported to have killed three men and one woman in Bisbee." The bartender continued, "[A]s it stands, we will part now and hereafter be strangers." With this the pair departed Maud's and the town of Clifton, riding away into the pre-dawn darkness, and leaving their "friend" behind in his rooms. Bush, however, did not remain a-bed. He immediately went to the home of Graham County Deputy Sheriff John M. Hovey and, after awakening him from his "sweet slumbers," related to him the outlaws' tale. Deputy Sheriff Hovey promptly sent for Deputy Sheriff A.G. Hill and a "consultation" was held. The men decided that pursuit would be delayed until the strength of the outlaw gang could be determined. Bush added that as Sample and Howard were leaving they revealed they were headed for Happy Jack's, 35 miles to the north, where they were going to "get a crowd together" and "serve Clifton the same as they had Bisbee."

Later that morning, Deputy Sheriffs Hovey and Hill were waiting when the telegraph office opened and promptly sent cables out to Lordsburg and Deming instructing the officers there "to be on the lookout for Kelley [sic]." They also sent a telegraph to Tombstone instructing officers there to apprehend John Heath as an accessory to the crime. Hovey and Hill then began making preparations to ride out in pursuit of the bandits. The Deputy Sheriffs contacted Nickolas Olguin, who they found "ready for duty with his posse of thirteen men." By Friday morning, the posse was 19 strong and included Hovey, Hill, Henry Hill, George Bent, W.W. Bush, Olguin and his crew. "They expected, knowing the desperate character of the men they were after, desperate resistance, and went prepared for it."

By the end of the first day, the posse had reached the junction of the Blue and San Francisco Rivers. The following morning, they proceeded up the Blue, following the trail of three horsemen. Ten miles on, the posse came to Benton's ranch. "The deputies notified the man they found there that they would be obliged to accompany the posse, as they did not propose to leave anyone behind them to carry tidings by a circuitous route to the outlaws of their approach." Five miles further on, they came upon the Arnold ranch and there repeated their demands of the inhabitants. Later, the posse came to a halt and men were sent up into the adjacent mountains with field glasses "to view the surrounding country and report the approach of any riders." Soon after the men had arrived at their positions, a signal was given indicating a rider was approaching from behind. The posse hurriedly took cover.

"Utterly unconscious" of his surroundings, James "Tex" Howard rode directly into the ambush. The command to "throw up your hands" was accompanied by "the muzzles of 18 hostile rifles" being leveled at him. Howard recognized some familiar faces among his captors, including W.W. Bush, and remarked, "I don't intend to walk into anybody's graveyard." "Tex" was very quickly taken from his mount and shackled. The company then held a meeting. They now knew they were on the correct trail and that the outlaw's camp must be very near, although Howard had come from behind them. This meant Howard had "gone around the mountains either to the left or right of them so as not to make a fresh trail." With the evening's shadows deepening and knowing the robbers' camp was not too distant, it was decided the posse would camp for the night "in the vicinity, and continue the search the following day [Sunday]."

Though Howard was interrogated regarding to the whereabouts of his compatriot, he "was true to his amigo, and the few questions asked of him brought forth either no reply at all or very unsatisfactory ones." In the morning, the prisoner was put aboard a horse, and the posse continued on along the Blue River. After three miles, "the trail suddenly turned into a narrow box canyon … not wide enough for two men to ride abreast." Through the bottom of this steep ravine ran a swift stream which completely obliterated any sign of the trail the posse had been following. Nickolas Olguin volunteered to take his men and "ascend the gorge afoot," even though the waters of the stream "rose nearly to the tops of their boots." Olguin's contingency, described by *The Weekly Citizen* as a "brave band of Mexicans," traveled three miles upstream, to a point where the canyon widened to about 50 yards before opening out on to "an extensive mesa." It was here Olguin and his men found the outlaws' hideout.

Omer W. "Red" Sample was taken completely by surprise. The outlaw "was busy cleaning a revolver and two rifles" when the posse came upon him, and had "not a single cartridge" in any of the weapons at his disposal. Sample was ordered to throw up and, after securing the suspect, Olguin and his men searched his person. Sample was found to have $200 on him and "a valuable hunting case gold watch, with the name 'Wm. Clancey,' engraved on the inside of the lid and the initials 'W.C.' in monogram, on the outside." This watch matched the description of the pocket watch that was described in the fliers sent out across the territory to law enforcement officers immediately after the robbery. After placing Sample under arrest, Olguin and his men "proceeded to break up the robbers' camp" and returned downstream to where the remainder of the posse was waiting. The "homeward march" was then begun.[20]

The Arizona Weekly Citizen, in their December 22 edition, carried the complete story of the capture of "Red" Sample and "Tex" Howard by the Clifton posse, under the headline "The Robbers' Trail." The sub-heading below read, "A Complete and Connected Account of the Gage and Bisbee Train Robbers" even though there was no mention of the Gage Robbery in the article or the suspects' connection to it. Still, as evidenced by the headlines, it was commonly held that the gang which derailed and robbed the Southern Pacific train in the New Mexico Territory and held up the Goldwater and Castaneda General Merchandise Emporium in Bisbee were one and the same. The article did speak to the fact that on Thursday, November 22, two days before the robbery, the passengers on the stagecoach arriving in Clifton from the town of Solomonville had been "closely scrutinized by a gang of rustlers well know in Clifton."

It is unknown who in particular the gang was looking for, though the newspaper opined that it was "some persons who had made themselves obnoxious to them." Not finding the party or parties they were in search of, the five outlaws "mounted their horses and rode off in a southerly direction toward Duncan." The Weekly Citizen identified the men as Dan Dowd alias "Big Dan," O.W. Sample alias "Red," John C. Kelly alias "Yorkie," Willis alias "Tex," and John Heath. This would be the first time the press would make mention of Heath having direct association with the robbers. The newspaper defended its assertion that the Gage and Bisbee robbers were the same, stating, "there is much surmise about the portion of our account which related to the robbery of the train, the main facts, about who constituted the party, the number engaged in the robbery, and the course they took after the deed was committed, are in the main correct."[21]

As Deputy Sheriffs Hovey and Hill and Olguin were leaving Clifton in pursuit of Sample and Howard, Cochise County Sheriff Jerome L. Ward was arriving in Deming to take custody of "York" Kelly. In a December 14 dispatch, it was noted that the New Mexico Territory authorities would be turning the suspect over to Sheriff Ward "without waiting for a requisition from the Governor." The lawman revealed to the correspondent that he had three posses out in the field and "will not allow them to come in until every man engaged in the recent robberies has been killed or captured." When news of the Gage Station robbery first reached Cochise County in the latter days of November, Sheriff Ward responded by sending out a "large posse of men" to aid in the manhunt for the robbers. However, after the robbery and murders in Bisbee, a town well within his jurisdiction, his priority was changed and, like many others, Sheriff Ward was of the opinion that the outlaw gangs were one and the same.[22]

Sheriff Ward returned to Tombstone with Kelly the following evening. The reporter for *The Tombstone Epitaph* described the outlaw: "He is about 5 feet 10 inches in height, dark complexion and eyes, and apparently about 25 years of age. When brought in he had on a dark suit of clothes and a black hat." The newspaper went on to say that the local authorities "have convincing proof of his complicity in the Bisbee affair" but "very judiciously keep it to themselves." The following day, December 17, Sheriff Ward received a telegram from Graham County Deputy Sheriff John M. Hovey informing him that "Tex and Red" were captured and that a watch, answering the description of the one described in the circulars, had been recovered. The Deputy Sheriff added, "Have the men in prison." Sheriff Ward would be on a train the next day to Clifton.[23]

Two months in to his two-year term as Cochise County Sheriff, *The Arizona Weekly Citizen* had said Ward was winning "golden opinions" from the citizens. Despite his lack of law enforcement experience, Sheriff Ward, who had previously operated several businesses in Los Angeles and San Diego, was a competent administrator. Directly after his election, Ward appointed Judge Albert O. Wallace, a lawyer by profession, was known for "his knowledge of law, his integrity, his pluck, and his popularity," as his Undersheriff. Ward appointed men with experience and men he knew he could trust as his deputies, including Robert "Bob" Hatch, William Daniels and two of his own sons, Fred and William J. Ward.

Cochise County Sheriff Jerome Lemuel Ward, who was lauded as a hero for his efficient and speedy capture of the Bisbee bandits (Arizona Historical Society, 27037).

The second of six children, Jerome Lemuel Ward was born on May 6, 1830, in Vernon, New York, to Eliphalet and Effa (Taggart) Ward. In 1843, the Ward family moved on to Jefferson County, Wisconsin, and began farming. Ten years later, Ward married Miss Lydia Mary Christie in the town of Palmyra. The couple's first son, William J., was born August 15 of the following year. In 1856, the couple would have a second son, Fred. At the start of the Civil War, Jerome Ward joined the First Wisconsin Cavalry Volunteers, Company 1, as a Wagoner. He was discharged on February 9, 1863, as a result of a "disability arising from war service." In August of 1868, the couple's third son, Frank Christie was born. Two years later, Ward and the 16-year-old Will would put farming behind them and make their way to San Diego, California, where they would begin to invest in property and grow new businesses.[24]

Within two years, Jerome Ward and his son were running a cattle ranch in El Cajon, a livery stable, and a commercial mercantile commission firm in

San Diego. By 1874, when his wife Lydia and two younger sons came out to join him, Ward had expanded into the freighting business, moving goods between Los Angeles and Yuma, in an operation similar to that of Joe Goldwater. When the Southern Pacific Railroad reached Yuma in 1877, thus ending the need for wagon freighters, Ward moved the family to Yuma and began transporting supplies from the railhead in that burg into the interiors of the Arizona Territory. As the railway moved across the Arizona desert, Ward further modified his business "to accommodate short-haul operations from railhead points" to outlying communities. In 1878, Ward put his 20-year-old son Fred in charge of the freighting business and moved the family to the burgeoning boomtown that was Tombstone. What inspired Jerome L. Ward, a successful businessman and entrepreneur, to present himself two years later as a candidate for the position of Cochise County Sheriff remains a mystery, but this is exactly what he did, and was duly elected in November of 1882.

The new sheriff's first 11 months on the job were unremarkable. By April of 1882, the infamous blood feud between the Earp brothers and the cowboy faction had played itself out, with the surviving members of both gangs vacating the region in search of decidedly less sanguine locales. This left Ward to perform the typical duties of a county sheriff of the era—collecting tax revenues, subpoenaing witnesses for the district court, maintaining the county jail, and caring for the inmates thereof. The Sheriff had his share of criminals to contend with, including rustlers, murderers, an errant deputy, and two former county employees, Milt J. Joyce and John O. Dunbar, who he arrested for forgery and embezzlement (respectively). Until the evening of December 8, there had been little in the way of criminal activity that had not been quickly and efficiently dealt with by himself and his deputies.[25]

On Friday, December 14, Henry "Hank" Frost, who had been detained by the Cochise County authorities, along with John Heath, who had been suspected of complicity in the Bisbee raid, was released from custody. Deputy Sheriff Daniels and the Assistant County Attorney, Judge James S. Robinson, had "thoroughly investigated the case of Frost and it was on the motion of Judge Robinson that he was discharged from custody." Judge Robinson "took occasion to express his regret that circumstances made the arrest of Frost necessary" and stated that "careful scrutiny of all the evidence ... did not show even a suspicion of complicity on the part of Frost." Still, when Frost returned to Bisbee, he found himself shunned and ostracized by his "former acquaintances." A few days after arriving back, "he was handed a note, written in red ink" advising him to leave town and "never return." The missive was signed, "45–60s" and was "ornamented with a rude, but suggestive drawing of a gallows with a pendent noose." Mr. Frost, with "commendable discretion," took the next available stage back to Tombstone.[26]

Henry Frost was not the first to receive a threatening note in the wake of the robbery. *The Arizona Weekly Citizen* reported that immediately after the robbery, Joseph Goldwater, Copper Queen Superintendent Ben Williams, a man named Lowenberg, and "other prominent citizens" had all received threatening letters. The notes, "all addressed in a scrawling hand and evidently written by the same person," simply read, "Keep your mouth shut or you will be shot!" The missives were signed, "One of the Boys." Whether or not the threats were genuine, written by a confederate of the gang, or just some malicious prank was never determined. However, immediately after receiving the letter, Superintendent Williams offered an additional $1000 from the Copper Queen coffers as reward money for information about the author.[27]

Vigilante action was fairly commonplace in the western states and territories in North America during the 19th century. Often, with few law enforcement officers available and little or no access to courts of law in the territories, citizens felt their only recourse in dealing with criminals and outlaws was to form extra-legal protective bodies known commonly as "vigilance committees." These committees could be either anonymous, but very-structured organizations akin to legitimate fraternal organizations, such as the Oddfellows or the Masons, or they could be spontaneous, reactionary mobs formed to deal directly with a specific problem or issue as the occasion arose. Sometimes, these committees would take it upon themselves to avenge wrong-doing by hunting down criminals themselves, and meting out what was considered to be righteous justice, usually at the end of a rope. Other times, these committees "corrected" what they considered to be a miscarriage of justice or deficit in the existing legal system. Of course, the power of the vigilance committees was derived exclusively from their willingness to resort to violent means to enforce their will.

On December 27, *The Arizona Weekly Citizen* reported "[t]he examination of John Heath for complicity in the Bisbee murders closed this evening and resulted in defendant being held as an accessory." Heath allegedly admitted to "intimate associations" with the outlaws, most notably "Tex" Howard. According to the newspaper, his association with Howard and the others endured "up to within a few hours before the murders were committed." *The Weekly Citizen* also noted that all during his examination before the district court, which was reportedly "crowded with spectators," Heath had remained "very cool and self-possessed."

Heath was able to maintain his composure because he truly believed he had nothing to worry about. By all accounts, his association with the outlaws had been completely blameless. He had not tried to hide the fact that he knew the men, and had ridden in with them from Clifton. Heath been absolutely open with Deputy Sheriff Daniels and the posse about his acquaintance with "Tex" and the others, even warning the Deputy Sheriff that they would likely have to make a fight of it if they did catch up to Howard and his confederates. Considering how forthcoming he had been, Heath was probably rather surprised after the examination to find himself being held over as a accessory in connection with the robbery and murders.[28]

Sheriff Ward's highly anticipated return to Tombstone with "Red" Sample and "Tex" Howard caused a "feverish state of excitement" in that community. Such was the feeling of the citizenry that threats of vigilante action against the suspects were being made openly and by the time the regular evening stage arrived "there were fully 300 men in and about the jail." Soon after Ward departed Clifton, another group of men, mostly from Bisbee, invaded the town of Fairbanks, which was situated along the stagecoach route. "[T]heir only object," stated *The Citizen*, "could have been the lynching of the prisoners." *The Arizona Weekly Citizen* further reported that "most prominent citizens in the camp favored the summary disposal of the fiends as just and economical." However, Sheriff Ward had other ideas. No matter how unpopular it might make him with his constituents, he was not going to allow for the subversion of the law or the legal system of the county which he had been elected to uphold.[29]

Noon, the following day, Undersheriff Wallace received a telegram from Sheriff Ward informing him that the Sheriff had exited the train with the prisoners at Contention City, 14 miles from Tombstone and were en route. Undersheriff Wallace "quietly selected about fifteen men known for their bravery and coolness," armed them and "made ready for any attempted rescue." Fairbanks, where the vigilantes lay in wait, was the connecting city for the Tombstone stage. By leaving the train at Contention City, Sheriff Ward had avoided the mob and bought himself a little time. Unfortunately, the Sheriff's ruse was short-lived. Soon after Undersheriff Wallace had assembled his party in the Tombstone courthouse, Bisbee resident James Russell came galloping past on "an animal reeking with foam." On seeing the horseman, Charley Smith, one of the men selected by Wallace, said, "[W]e are in for it boys, that man can have only one object here; you know what it is."

What Russell's intent was is unknown. Perhaps Russell sought to wire Fairbanks to inform the vigilantes of the Sheriff's subterfuge, so they might intercept him before he arrived in Tombstone or, perhaps, he was coming to town "to raise a crowd ... in advance of the Sheriff's arrival." Fortunately for Sample and Howard, Russell was too late, as directly behind him "came a vehicle containing Sheriff Ward and deputies, and with them the prisoners, who, in the twinkle of an eye almost, were out of the wagon and safe behind bolts and bars." A correspondent from *The Tombstone Epitaph* had been on hand for the drama and named the men accompanying the Sheriff as "Deputy Sheriff John F. Crowley of Willcox, who went to Clifton with him; Deputy Sheriff John M. Hovey, who had captured the prisoners, and W.W. Bush of Graham County," the bartender from Clifton. Also among the posse were deputies Bob Hatch and Fred Ward, the sheriff's son.

The correspondent observed the suspects "looked haggard, but showed no signs of fear." Sample was reported to be suffering from a bullet wound "received at the hands of some Mexican in September and not yet healed"—a wound that would later become significant. Howard was described as "a splendid specimen of manhood and ... seemed to enjoy the attention." In anticipation of their arrival, efforts had been made "to have Judge [Daniel L.] Pinney call a special session of the grand jury to pass upon their cases." It was expected that the Associate Supreme Court Justice would accede. However, in common with the Fairbanks vigilantes, the journalist had already determined the guilt of the two prisoners. "Death is their certain portion," he wrote, "either by law or at the hands of Judge Lynch."[30]

The Arizona Weekly Citizen was very forthcoming in their praise of the law officers of both Graham and Cochise counties, stating they "have certainly done good work in hunting down and arresting the robbers, and are deserving of much more credit than they are ever likely to receive." The newspaper acknowledged that "it is no child's work to follow up canyons and track desperate men, who may fire upon you from ambush at any moment, and it is only the most sagacious and fearless men who dare to undertake to lead pursuing parties." Admittedly, large rewards had been offered for the capture of the Gage and Bisbee robbers, still the newspaper insisted the rewards were not the impetus for performing such "perilous duty. Being officers of the law, they had a pride—an ambition to succeed, rises above and beyond all other considerations." The editorial concluded, "Sitting back in our quiet and peaceful homes, we are to [sic] apt to underestimate the valuable services of these men. Though far away from us, they in reality not only protect our property and institutions, but our firesides as well."[31]

Conspicuously absent from mention in the glowing editorial, as well as from Sheriff Ward's escort, was Nickolas Olguin, the man who had actually captured "Red" Sample. *The Tombstone Republican* of December 29 divulged the reason for his absenteeism. In a dispatch received from Clifton, it was revealed that "Olguin and nine others of his posse were taken to Solomonville" to answer for the killings of Wryscarber and Clements.

However, efforts were being made on Olguin's behalf so he would not have to answer for the murders. A petition was circulated testifying to his "good character" and "exonerating him from criminality." Though the petition had been signed by numerous people, there was some dissention. *The Republican* stated that sentiment at the mines favored Olguin, "but on the Gila River the opposite is the case." Still, it was believed that Olguin and his men would be granted a writ of habeas corpus, allowing them to remain free indefinitely.[32]

Omer W. "Red" Sample was also facing charges in Graham County. The grand jury had two indictments against him—indictments that "were to have been kept secret until his arrest"—for the crimes of horse-theft and stagecoach robbery. *The Benson Herald* stated that the indictments had "turned up" immediately after Sample's apprehension and since he was facing indictment for "the graver offence of quadruple murder" there was no reason for "further secrecy." There would be no request for extradition from the Graham County authorities either, unless he was found not guilty in the Bisbee killings. *The Herald* stated, "Red and his confederates have committed numerous outrages in Graham County that have not found a record in the newspapers and the exposed settlers of that county are rejoicing over his arrest and the strong possibility he will meet with stern and speedy justice."[33]

Though *The Arizona Weekly Citizen* maintained they were "in the main correct," the newspaper finally conceded that the parties who committed the Gage Station robbery were not the same parties who committed the murders in Bisbee. Wells Fargo & Company detective J.B. Hume had visited the offices of *The Citizen* in Tucson on the morning of December 29, as the paper was going to press, in order to set the record straight. *The Clifton Clarion* had erroneously asserted that John Heath and the others were in that town casing the stagecoaches on Thursday, November 22, when in fact the men had been last seen in Clifton on Friday, November 23. Heath and his companions were seen later that day in Whitlocks Cienega, 35 miles away and it was at this place they spent the night. The following morning, November 24, Heath, Howard, and the others "took their departure in the direction of Galeyville." The group was next seen that afternoon at the San Simon Train Station, 78 miles from where the robbery took place. Hume stated that "it was impossible for them to have participated in the Gage robbery."

The detective also dispelled the rumor that Heath and his associates had known in advance of the Gage robbery, for on the morning of November 25, as they were about to leave San Simon, they met with the section boss of the Southern Pacific who told them of the robbery. They proceeded to inquire of the agent at the station if such a robbery had actually occurred. He confirmed the intelligence was correct. The gang then asked what kind of reward was being offered for the capture of the perpetrators of the crime. "In a joking way they said to the agent, 'We want you to bear witness that we had no hand in this robbery,' and made the remark that 'if the rewards were sufficient they might take a hand in capturing the robbers, as they were well fixed for that kind of business.'" The men then proceeded on toward Galeyville, arriving Sunday, November 25.

To prove beyond all doubt there was no connection between the Gage robbers and the Bisbee murders, after the capture of Sample and Howard, detective Hume and his partner Lee Harris brought the section boss and the agent from San Simon to Lordsburg to identify the suspects as the same men they had seen and spoke with on the 25th. The railroad men "at once positively identified 'Red' and 'Tex' as two of the parties ... they saw and talked with." Though Heath and the others were thereby cleared of complicity in the Gage Station robbery, *The Weekly Citizen* noted that "[t]he train robbers are still at large and the rewards offered by the railroad company and the express company still stand and hold good, and the amounts will be paid to any party or parties who may capture the robbers."[34]

Also, still at large were Daniel "Big Dan" Dowd and William "Billy" Delaney. On December 15, Deputy Sheriff Daniels expressed the belief that Dowd "made for the Sierra Madres by way of Cloverdale." By the 22nd, based upon information given the Clifton bartender W.W. Bush by Sample and Howard, it was being generally reported that Dowd and Delaney had fled into Mexico, specifically to the state of Sonora. *The Arizona Silver Belt* reported on January 5, that the previous Thursday, January 3, two masked men "were seen between La Noria and Yankee smelter, mounted and traveling toward Sonora." A man identified as "Mr. Harris, of the custom house" was traveling the opposite direction along the same road and fearing trouble, "attempted to avoid them, but they spread to the left and right and compelled him to pass between them." Harris reported that the suspects were at that point five miles west of the Washington camp and only two miles north of the Mexican border.[35]

While the news of the arrest of Sample and Howard commanded everyone's attention, Deputy Sheriff Daniels "quietly matured his plans for [an] expedition being accompanied by only one man, a Mexican from Bisbee" by the name of Cesario Lucero, an expert tracker. Deputy Daniels and Lucero left Tombstone for Bisbee on Christmas Eve and, on the morning of the 26th, took their leave for La Fronteras, Sonora. From La Fronteras the two men travelled on to the town of Bavispe, arriving there on the 30th. In Bavispe, Deputy Daniels learned that Delaney and Dowd had "parted company" and that Dowd had been forced to buy a new horse as his had been stolen by Indians "who had raided in that vicinity some days previous." The suspect had stayed only a few hours in Bavispe, purchasing a second horse, "which he had shod, and then struck across the mountains to Janos, which is on the east slope of the Sierra Madres, in the state of Chihuahua."

Deputy Daniels and Lucero hired two local guides to take them across the "rocky and precipitous" mountains to Janos by the most expedient route available. Dowd seemed to have been representing himself as an "American rancher who was visiting that section with the object of purchasing cattle." Deputy Daniels arrived in Janos at 3:00 p.m. on New Year's Day, only to find that his quarry had "just left" for the town of Corralitos, 27 miles to the southeast. Procuring fresh horses, Daniels and Lucero pushed on to Corralitos, arriving in that burg around 7:00 p.m. Once arrived, the lawman sought out A.B. Munzenberger, the superintendent of the Corralitos Mining Company. The Deputy Sheriff explained the object of his pursuit, described the suspect, and asked if the man he was searching for was in town. Munzenberger answered in the affirmative and, together, they came up with a plan to capture the outlaw.

"Big Dan" Dowd had stopped in at a "certain" house "occupied by some American employees of the company." When the superintendent entered the house he found Dowd sitting at a table near the fire with four or five other men sharing a bottle of mescal, "entirely oblivious of the fact his great crime had found him out." Superintendent Munzenberger, who entered the domicile ahead of Deputy Daniels, ordered Dowd to throw up his hands. On seeing the revolver in Daniels' hand, the outlaw immediately complied, was subsequently handcuffed, and then "safely secured for the night." The following morning, January 2, Deputy Daniels and the superintendent took Dowd to the blacksmith's shop "where fetters were riveted on his legs." The suspect "took his arrest very coolly, thinking it was for complicity in smuggling, as he had traveled part of the distance to Corralitos with a band of *contrabandistes*." On being informed of the real reason for his arrest, Dowd "visibly weakened" though he maintained his innocence.

As the Deputy Sheriff had come on horseback, Superintendent Munzenberger provided him with a wagon, team, and driver, so the prisoner might be more easily transported. Daniels' offer to pay for the use of the conveyance was steadfastly refused. The lawman loaded his prisoner aboard and began the 110-mile journey to San Jose, a station on the Mexican Central railway. The following day, they arrived at the San Domingo ranch. "J.B. Slocum, the superintendent, tendered them a hospitable reception." Slocum warned Daniels that the Mexican authorities "might impose obstacles to the transfer prisoner" back to the States and offered to assist with the process. Slocum rode with Daniels to San Jose station, where he "made arrangement with the conductor to lock the deputy sheriff and the prisoner in the express car" so they might travel through the country "secure from observation."

From San Jose, Deputy Daniels telegraphed Sheriff Ward informing him that he was en route to Tombstone with Dowd. The Deputy boarded the train and, confined safely within the railroad car, started out for El Paso, Texas. The town of El Paso was reached "without any noteworthy incident" and, once there, Deputy Daniels met with G.R. Puckett, superintendent of the San Simon Cattle Company, who escorted the lawman and his manacled charge on to San Simon Station on the Southern Pacific line. There the Deputy and his prisoner boarded another train for the 125-mile trip to the town of Bowie, where Sheriff Ward was waiting. The officers proceeded on to Contention, where they were met by deputies Bob Hatch and Fred Ward. Deputy Sheriff Daniels and the rest of the party rode in to town on Saturday evening with a fettered Daniel "Big Dan" Dowd to the "suprise [*sic*] of the majority" of the residents of Tombstone. The prisoner was immediately lodged in a cell in the courthouse with the rest of his "companions in crime."[36]

While *The Tombstone Republican* celebrated Deputy Daniels' return, stating emphatically, "No man has exhibited as much zeal and energy in the capture of the criminals," Dowd's reunion with his confederates was likely less cordial. In "evidence adduced in the preliminary examination" of Howard, Sample, and Kelly, it was learned it was Dowd who had gone into the backroom at Goldwater and Castaneda's and fleeced the owner as he "was lying sick in bed." According to the newspaper, Dowd secured almost $2000 in gold coins from beneath Castaneda's pillow, more than the $1200 initially reported stolen, whereas only about $800 had been taken from the safe. "From the sums found on the persons of [Howard, Sample, and Kelly]" it was deduced they had not shared in "Big Dan's" fortune. Dowd "was alone with his victim in the room at the time, and of course his accomplices were ignorant of the rich strike made."[37]

Back in the New Mexico Territory, there had been a break in the hunt for the Gage Station robbers. Sheriff Harvey Whitehill of Silver City, New Mexico, and Sheriff Simpson of Globe City captured "a large, ugly-looking negro named George Washington Cleveland" who was suspected of complicity in the robbery. Cleveland had been residing in the territory about two years and had worked on a ranch in Silver City for the Johnson brothers. *The Tombstone Republican* did not indicate why Simpson and Grant had detained Cleveland initially, but once he was in custody they "told him other members of the gang had been captured and given the entire affair away." Believing the ruse to be true, Cleveland made a full confession, which was recorded by the officers. He named his confederates as Frank Taggart, Mitch Lee and Christopher Carson "Kit" Joy. The newspaper described the men as "hard cases" and stated they had been "aimlessly knocking around in what was known as Duck Creek country, in Grant County, for several weeks previous to the train robbery."

After Cleveland made his confession, a posse was formed and rode out toward Duck Creek in search of the bandits. A week later, the posse returned empty-handed. There was speculation the outlaws were warned in advance and had since vacated that country. *The Republican* surmised "the entire cowboy element west of Silver City are in sympathy with the murderers and keep them fully informed of the movements of the officers." It was believed that Taggart had taken his leave of Mitch Lee and "Kit" Joy, who were said to be headed west toward the Blue country and possibly onward into the Arizona Territory. The newspaper noted that "Red" Sample and "Tex" Howard had been captured in the Blue country, which it described as a favorite haunt and refuge of "lawless characters who have endeavored for sometime to create anarchy in the Southwest." The aggregate reward for the Taggart, Lee, and Christopher "Kit" Joy was $2,200 a head and it was expected they would soon be apprehended. "Hunt them down!" admonished *The Silver City Enterprise*. "They are your enemies!"[38]

It had been nearly a month and a half since the Gage Station robbery and the New Mexico law officers had so far managed to apprehend only one suspect. In contrast, in less than a month, five of the men believed to have been involved in the Bisbee outrage—men who were basically career criminals—had been captured and incarcerated. Only William "Billy" Delaney was still at large and both Sheriff Ward and Deputy Sheriff Daniels were "confident" he would soon be captured. While on a sojourn to Hermosillo, Mexico, Pima County Sheriff Robert H. "Bob" Paul, who all along had been aiding his friend Sheriff Ward in the manhunt, "gave the governor of Sonora copies of *the Citizen, Clifton Clarion, the Tombstone Epitaph*, and *the Republican* containing full accounts of the Bisbee and Gage robberies ... and the governor had disseminated the information to all the state officials." The net was quickly closing up around Delaney. Daniels told a reporter from *The Republican* it was "quite probable the last of the Bisbee assassins is even now in custody."[39]

The five men in custody and being held in the Tombstone Courthouse had

Pima County Sheriff Robert H. "Bob" Paul, who lent his considerable expertise as a law officer to aid Cochise County Sheriff Jerome Ward in the apprehension of the outlaw gang (author's collection).

become objects of "morbid curiosity." By 10:00 a.m. on the morning of December 29—the day of the arraignment of Sample and Howard—"the district courtroom was crowded with citizens." A few minutes after the appointed hour, O.W. "Red" Sample, escorted by Sheriff Ward and his deputies, "made his appearance at the door. As he entered the crowded room, he hesitated a moment and appeared to shrink from the eager gaze of the crowd, while his eyes roamed furtively from face to face, never for a moment resting on any object." The prisoner was escorted to the bar and the warrant of arrest, charging him with murder was read by Justice of the Peace Swain. The prisoner was asked his name and he gave it as O.W. Sample. He was subsequently read his rights and remanded to the custody of Sheriff Ward, without bail, until his examination the following Wednesday, January 2, 1884, at 10:00 a.m. The Sheriff then escorted Sample from the courtroom.

Minutes later, the sound of chains could again be heard on the stairs as James "Tex" Howard was led up to the courtroom. As Howard "entered the room, he coolly surveyed the assembled crowd, returning with a defiant manner the piercing gazes bestowed upon him. He walked slowly up the aisle, with his head erect, his entire bearing indicating the utmost self-possession." As had Sample, Howard took his seat at the bar and "calmly faced the crowd." The warrant was read and he gave his name as James Howard. Whispered exclamations of "He's a good one" and "There's nerve for you," were reportedly heard from the courtroom gallery. After his rights were read to him, Howard stated he "desired to procure witnesses whose whereabouts he did not at present know." His examination was set for Thursday, January 3, 1884, at 10:00 a.m. The prisoner was then taken back downstairs to his cell.[40]

The examination of Daniel "Big Dan" Dowd was no different to that Sample and Howard had endured in terms of the attention it attracted from the populace. *The Tombstone Republican* reported that the district courtroom "was jammed full of curious humanity, all eager to obtain a glimpse of the redoubtable" outlaw. Soon, the "clanking of chains" was heard on the stairs leading up the courtroom and a hush fell over the gallery as Dowd entered, escorted by Deputy Sheriff Bob Hatch. Dowd "slowly edged his way through the dense crowd" toward the prisoner's dock, "his countenance wearing a look of easy indifference, occasionally changing to a smile as he recognized some familiar face in the crowd." The newspaper described the outlaw as "about 30 years of age, well built, light complexion, blonde mustache, the predominating expression of countenance when in repose being that of great good nature." Finally, after making his way through the multitude, Dowd was seated and the examination began.

Deputy Sheriff Daniels was called as the first witness and was sworn in before the court. The only real difference in the testimony given in Dowd's examination and the examinations of Kelly, Sample and Howard was the outlaw's insistence on the innocence of John Heath. After his arrest, Daniels stated that Dowd was told Heath had been implicated in the crime and this, the outlaw insisted, was not the case. Heath, Dowd emphatically stated, had not been in contact with the gang the morning of the robbery. *The Republican* stated that though Dowd's admissions "may be of some advantage to Heith [sic] … they assuredly seal his own doom." Otherwise, the testimony of the witnesses called before the court "was of the same import as in the examinations of 'Tex,' Sample, and Kelley [sic]." Afterwards, Dowd was led from the courtroom and back to his cell, "to await the action of the grand jury."[41]

Finally, the problem of curious citizens attempting to get a glimpse of the prisoners in their cells became so bad that Sheriff Ward had to ban visits to the county calaboose completely. *The Weekly Citizen* praised the Sheriff's decision to disallow all persons not having business with the Sheriff's office or at the Tombstone Courthouse. "In ninety-nine cases out of a hundred," the newspaper stated, "the visit is the result of morbid curiosity, and the sheriff does not propose that the county jail be turned into a menagerie for sight-seers."[42]

In addition to a curious populace, Sheriff Ward and his deputies also had to deal with the antics of the inmates. In his memoirs, former Deputy Sheriff William "Billy" Breakenridge recalled that Daniel Kelly and "Tex" Howard "were taking their exercise in the corridor when they became involved in a dispute which led to blows." Breakenridge did not reveal the source of contention between the two men, but stated that "Howard was getting the best of it when the officers separated them." As the two men were being led back to their cells, "Tex" allegedly turned to Kelly and said, "I hope they hang you first, you s__ of a b____; I want to see you kick!" If this confrontation did occur, the newspapers did not report on it and there are no other contemporary sources which make mention of such an altercation.[43]

Over the next week, there were several conflicting reports regarding William Delaney, the only one of the suspected Bisbee robbers who remained at liberty. Dr. Goodwin, the Wells Fargo & Co. agent in Nogales, appeared in Tucson declaring that Delaney had been captured in Minas Prietas. According to Goodwin, on Monday, January 7th, he met some "fellows" in Hermosillo who had been "shoving the queer [passing counterfeit money]" who had seen and recognized Delaney. Two days later, Goodwin went to Guaymas to "consult the authorities." Goodwin had discovered that the outlaw moved on to Minas Prietas and telegraphed Sheriff Ward in Tombstone with Delaney's whereabouts. The agent promptly wrote Covington Johnson, the superintendent at the Minas Prietas mine, and told him to give Delaney work "so as to detain him." The outlaw "fell into the job and immediately went to work."

On Sunday, January 13, Deputy Sheriff Robert "Bob" Hatch, who had been sent by Sheriff Ward, arrived in Minas Prietas, and placed Delaney under arrest. *The Arizona Weekly Citizen* printed the story citing as their source "G.S. Beard, the telegraph agent at Torres, a small town "midway between Guaymas and Hermosillo, and twelve miles from Mina Prietas." The Tucson-based newspaper also reported that, after fleeing Bisbee, Delaney crossed over into Mexico on December 15. In Batuca, Delaney had joined up with a Mexican cavalry unit under the command of Captain Kosterlitsky and traveled with the soldiers as far as Hermosillo. *The Weekly Citizen* stated that Dr. Goodwin had credited Captain Kosterlitsky with the capture of the errant outlaw.[44]

However, *The Tombstone Republican* questioned the reports coming out of Mexico about the outlaw, asking directly, "Is Delaney Captured?" The newspaper elucidated that the report of Delaney's apprehension "appears to lack confirmation." When questioned by a correspondent from the paper, a representative of the Tombstone Sheriff's office said "no news of the arrest has been received." The representative added that, contrary to recent hearsay, Sheriff Ward and District Attorney Smith were en route to San Francisco, not Sonora. *The Republican* stated that, after Dowd and Delaney parted ways in San Miguel, a small town outside of Bavispe on December 30, Delaney did indeed join up with Captain Emilio Kosterlitsky and his troop, who were riding to Oposura, where the Captain was stationed. "It appears that Delaney, who is a man of fine address and speaks Spanish fluently, ingratiated himself in the confidence of Captain Kosterlitsky." This gave rise to the report that the outlaw had enlisted in the Mexican army—a rumor that was quickly dispelled.

After the arrest of "Big Dan" Dowd had been affected, Deputy Sheriff Daniels had "dispatched the Mexican Lucero, who accompanied him from Bisbee, after Delaney." Lucero left Deputy Daniels at Corralitos on January 2 and traveled to the town of Oposura, "the same day Daniel [*sic*] started with his prisoner for Tombstone." How the Deputy determined that Delaney was destined toward said Oposura is unknown, but over the next nine days, there was no news from Cesario Lucero concerning his whereabouts or movements. Finally, on Friday, January 11, Deputy Sheriff Daniels received a telegram "presumably from Lucero." The contents of the telegram were unknown, but it caused Deputies Daniels and Bob Hatch to make ready for a trip to Sonora the following day. *The Republican* reported, "Nothing has been heard from Deputies Daniel and Hatch since their departure."[45]

Then in an addendum to the article, added just before the newspaper went to press, it was reported that Deputy Sheriff Daniels had returned from Mexico, with the news that William "Billy" Delaney had indeed been captured. Though the details were few, it was said the outlaw was captured in Minas Prietas on Sunday, January 13, and was subsequently jailed in Hermosillo. Daniels reported that "the Mexican authorities [were] refusing to surrender him without a requisition." After the capture of "Big Dan" Dowd, the Mexican consul had written a letter of protest to Territorial Governor Frederick A. Tritle, stating that the actions of Deputy Sheriff Daniel were completely "contrary to the treaty stipulations between the United States and Mexico" and asked for a formal federal investigation of the incident. The Mexican authorities were not going to allow this to happen again and were having Delaney held at the line pending "the necessary papers to have him turned over."[46]

Frederick Augustus Tritle, Arizona Territorial Governor, who arranged for the extradition of William Delaney from Mexico to the United States to stand trial (author's collection).

After entering Mexico, Delaney assumed the name of Rogers and it was under this alias he introduced himself to Captain Kosterlitsky. The fugitive traveled with the Mexican battalion to Oposura and "thence to Hermosillo, where the captain went on his business." From Hermosillo, Delaney rode to Minas Prietas, where he found employment with the Minas Prietas Mining Company. However, on Saturday, January 12, the outlaw "got full of mescal and became involved in a row with one of the shift bosses." Delaney was subsequently arrested and locked up. The following day, Deputy Sheriffs Daniels and Hatch arrived in town and contacted the mine superintendent. The superintendent took them to Delaney, who had been locked away and tied at the elbows with a heavy rope to prevent his escape. On seeing Daniels and Hatch, but not realizing their purpose, the outlaw exclaimed, "You are Americans? Can't you get me out of this? They have got me tied up like a dog."

After a moment of silence, Deputy Daniels replied, "When did you leave Buckles' ranch?"

Delaney "started as if he had been shot," but quickly regained his composure, saying, "'Buckles' ranch'? Where is that? I don't know such a place."

Deputy Sheriff Hatch then produced a photograph of the outlaw and "held it directly in front of the prisoner," and asked, "Do you recognize this picture?"

Delaney "made a feeble attempt to smile," and answered, "That's my photograph sure enough. Where did you get that?"

"It was given to me by one of your friends in Bisbee," was the Deputy's reply.

The prisoner "was for a moment disconcerted," but quickly responded, "Bisbee? Why, I was never there in my life. This picture was taken in Silver City, New Mexico."

Captain Emilio Kosterlitsky, Army of Mexico, who unwittingly played host to the outlaw William Delaney after the latter escaped in to Mexico (author's collection).

Deputy Daniels shot back, "Big Dan says you were there on the 8th of last December, and I saw you there myself on that date."

"Big Dan, whoever he is, is a damned liar, and you are mistaken."

The exchange between the officers and the outlaw continued a few moments more until Delaney finally asked, "Well, ain't you going to get me out of this—take the damned ropes off me?" To which one of the officers replied, "Oh yes, that is just what we are here to do." Then, presenting the outlaw with handcuffs and leg irons, quipped, "How would you like to try this jewelry for a change?"

Delaney lamented, "I guess I have jumped from the frying pan into the fire."

The following day, the suspect was taken to Hermosillo, where he was jailed, and remained under the close guard of Deputy Sheriff Hatch. Meanwhile Deputy Sheriff Daniels started north for Tombstone. Delaney continued to protest his innocence, saying "he had been in Sonora for the past three months, which he said he could prove by

Captain Kosterlitsky." However, Daniels told a correspondent from the *Republican* that he was prepared to swear he had seen Delaney in Bisbee on the night of the robbery. Not 20 minutes before the shooting began, while the Deputy was playing billiards in his saloon, "a stranger came in and stood by the stove some minutes, looking around carelessly, and then walked out." Daniels "noted his appearance particularly at the time," and when he saw Delaney again in Minas Prietas, "recognized him as the stranger who was in his saloon on the night of the tragedy."[47]

In an article dated January 15, *The Arizona Weekly Citizen* noted that Sheriff Ward and District Attorney Mark Smith had traveled down to Hermosillo to begin the extradition process necessary to bringing Delaney out of that country and back to the Arizona Territory. "If nothing unforeseen occurs he will by Sunday next be keeping company in jail … with Tex, Big Dan, York, Red, and John Heith, his confederates in the Bisbee butchery."[48]

On January 31, 1884, *The Tombstone Republican* received the following missive, which was reprinted in the February 2 edition of that newspaper:

> Bisbee, A.T.
> Jan 31, 1884
> Editor Republican
>
> Dear Sir,
>
> At a meeting of the citizens of Bisbee held at the Copper Queen Mining company's office, this evening; Mr. E. Baker, in behalf of the citizens, presented to W.A. Daniel, our efficient deputy sheriff, a purse of $600, as a mark of esteem and appreciation for his gallant and untiring exertions in effecting the arrest of the Bisbee murderers, Dowd and Delaney. By giving the above notice in your paper you will oblige the people of Bisbee.
>
> Yours respectfully,
> H.C. Stillman

Upon returning to Tombstone with Dowd in chains, *The Arizona Weekly Citizen* had dubbed Deputy Sheriff Daniels "the lion of the hour." Obviously, the citizens of Bisbee considered him worthy of greater esteem.[49]

The Clifton Clarion observed that Delaney, the last of the suspects to be apprehended, "must have greatly changed since leaving Clifton." Described by the Tombstone newspapers as "the hardest looking character of the entire number arrested for complicity in the Bisbee murders" the reporter for *The Clarion* stated that Delaney had appeared to him as "not only gentlemanly" but as "one who was an interesting companion, and who could converse in an intelligent manner on almost any subject that came up." *The Yuma Sentinel* revealed that Delaney was, in fact, the brother of Captain John C. Delaney, the Senate Librarian of the State of Pennsylvania. Prior to his arrival in the Arizona Territory, William Delaney had acquired an "unsavory reputation" in his hometown of Harrisburg and had been quietly sent west by relatives to escape an arrest for theft.

However, *The Clifton Clarion* would have the last word about William E. Delaney, saying, "One year ago, the man who would have made the prediction that in twelve-months, Delaney would be a felon standing under the shadow of the gallows would have been considered a lunatic. Yet such is the case. It ought to afford many a young man a topic for serious reflection, this downward career of W.E. Delaney. Avoid evil companions if you do not desire to be carried down the swift-flowing current which leads to dishonor and an unmourned grave."[50]

CHAPTER FOUR

The Trials (Part One)

Much in the same manner as were his alleged confederates, Kelly, Howard, Sample and Dowd, William Delaney was brought into court for an examination to determine his "complicity in the Bisbee murder [sic]." It was the decision of the court that Delaney should be held over without bail. On a more somber note, *The Arizona Weekly Citizen* reported that Cesario Lucero, "[t]he Mexican who accompanied Deputy Sheriff Daniels" in his pursuit of Dan Dowd and William Delaney, had been found hanging from a tree "his body riddled with bullets." The newspaper speculated it had been "the work of the rustler friends of Dowd." As it turned out, it was not Cesario Lucero, but some other unfortunate man who was left hanging in the trees. The newspaper did not make any further mention of the incident.[1]

Daniel H. Pinney had been nominated as Associate Justice of the Supreme Court for the Arizona Territory by President Chester Arthur and on June 19, 1882, having been given the approval of the United States Senate; Pinney was commissioned to a four-year term. The former Illinois legislator and Joliet city attorney was appointed court judge of the second judicial district which included Gila, Maricopa, and Yuma counties. However, Judge Pinney, in order "to facilitate the functioning of the judiciary" also presided over courts in other districts including the first district, which had come to include Cochise County.

Pinney was a native of New York, having been born in Albion on June 2, 1837, to Martin and Nancy (Johnson) Pinney. He was the seventh of nine children born to the couple. The future judge's early education was derived from "the common schools in his native town." As a young man he worked with the engineering corps on the enlargement of the Erie Canal. In 1856, he moved to Chicago and began to study the law. Soon after, Pinney relocated to Michigan City where he joined the firm of J.A. Thornton. He eventually moved on to Joliet, where he found a position with Snapp & Beckenridge. Pinney continued in his studies and, in 1861, he was "admitted to the Bar of the Supreme Court of the United States." The fledgling attorney first hung out his shingle in the town of Wilmington. Just two years later, Pinney returned to Joliet.

In 1865, Pinney married Miss Mary Lee. The couple had a son whom they christened William. The marriage lasted only seven years as Mary Lee Pinney died in 1872. Two years later, Daniel Pinney took a new wife, Mary E. Bowman of Shawneetown, Kentucky. The couple would have three children together. According to Pinney's biographer, through his dedication and hard work, he won the "confidence and esteem of the public." This is evidenced "by the fact that he was five times elected City Attorney of Joliet, and in 1876 he was the successful candidate ... for a seat in the General Assembly." Pinney remained in Joliet and at his practice until 1882, when the appointment was handed down to him from the president.[2]

November of 1883 had been the last term of the District Court and the next term was not scheduled until the first week in May of 1884. However, national interest in the Bisbee murders and pressures brought to bear by the local citizenry on the body politic and the judiciary for swift resolution of the case, made it advisable for Pinney to call for a special session of the court. *The New York Times* reported on December 27, "Judge Penny [*sic*] has called for a special term of his court to meet the last of January to try the cases of Red Sample, Texas Willis, York and Kelly, the Bisbee bandits." Accordingly, Cochise County District Attorney Marcus Aurelius "Mark" Smith began the process of impaneling a grand jury and subpoenaing witnesses in preparation for an indictment against the suspects.[3]

In accordance with Arizona Territorial statutes, Sheriff Ward was charged by the District Attorney "to summon twenty-four persons qualified to serve as grand jurors" which he did. John J. Bullis was named as foreman of said jury. The Sheriff was also charged with summoning witnesses to testify, including Richard Rundell, Lubian Pardee, William Daniels, Walter W. Bush, Joe Goldwater, Harry M. Hartson, and Frank H. Buckles. Also subpoenaed were "to appear before the District Court for the Second Judicial District, at the Court House in the City of Tombstone, on the 4th day of February, A.D. 1884 at 10:00 A.M. there to give evidence" were James McDonough, A. Riley, Daniel Inman, Henry A. Smith, Walter Myers, John Stiles, William Gerstenberg, Pat McLeane, Henry Forrest, Davenport, a man named Lindeman, and livery stable owner J.B. Lockwood. All but Davenport were named as witnesses for the Territory.

All but two of these subpoenas were returned by Sheriff Ward to the Clerk of the Court, W.H. Seamans, on February 11, 1884, with a notation stating the Sheriff and his deputies had "served the within subpoena on all the within named witnesses at Bisbee, Cochise County, Arizona, on or before" said date. The prosecution issued four more subpoenas on the 9th of the

Daniel H. Pinney, associate justice of the Supreme Court for the Territory of Arizona, declared a special session of the court in order to hear the case against John Heath and the Bisbee bandits (author's collection.

month, for George Pridham of Tombstone and Joshua Gilbert, which were
duly delivered by Sheriff Ward on the
same date. Pridham and Gilbert were
listed as defense witnesses. The Sheriff
was unable to locate William Luttley,
also named as a witness for the defense.
A.G. Hill of Clifton, A.T. was also subpoenaed by the court, as a witness for
the Territory. However, the subpoena
was not delivered by Graham County
Sheriff George H. Stevens until the
21st day of July 1884.[4]

On February 6, the grand jury
"found indictments against Dowd,
Kelly, Sample, Howard and Delaney."
The defendants were accused of the
crime of homicide—"to wit ... did
unlawfully, willfully, feloniously and
of their malice aforethought with guns
and pistols loaded with gunpowder and
leaden balls or other hard substances,
shoot, wound, and murder"—in the
death of Deputy Sheriff D.T. Smith.
Additionally, the defendants, including Heath, were found to have "with
force and arms and in and upon one
A.A. Castaneda feloniously, violently,
and by force and intimidation did make
an assault ... against the will of the

Marcus Aurelius "Mark" Smith, Cochise County
district attorney, who was charged with the prosecution of John Heath and the Bisbee bandits (Arizona Historical Society, 23608).

said A.A. Castaneda then and there feloniously, violently, and by force and intimidation
did rob, steal, take, and carry away" 800 in gold coin, 200 in silver coin, 1,000 in "green-
backs" and various "goods and chattels."[5]

The full report of the Grand Jury was published in *The Tombstone Republican* on
February 16:

Tombstone, A.T., Feb, 8, 1884.
To the Honorable D.H. Pinney, Judge of the Second Judicial District:
    Sir—We the members of the grand jury, impaneled for the present term of the district court, most
respectfully beg leave to submit to your honor the following report:
    There have been presented for our consideration eighteen criminal cases which we have carefully
examined into and disposed of as follows:
    Indictments found for murder, 7; grand larceny, 2; assault to murder, 3; robbery, 1; keeping an
opium den, 1.
    We have ignored five criminal charges as follows: For assault to kill, 2; murder, 1; keeping an
opium den, 2.
    As the affairs of the various officials of the county has been examined and reported upon by the
grand jury preceding us, and within the quarter, it is not necessary for us to do so at this time.
    At the invitation of Sheriff Ward we have visited the jail, and find everything in good order, the
cells and surroundings clean and well taken care of, the sanitary condition good, and everything

denoting that all possible means have been adopted for the comfort and welfare of the prisoners confined therein.

We have concluded our labors with the greatest dispatch possible, having been somewhat delayed by the absence of important witnesses, whom it was impossible to bring before us sooner.

Our duties have been very greatly lessened by the able manner in which District Attorney Smith has performed his duties, his thorough knowledge of the cases indicating careful study, and great appreciation of the duties and responsibilities of his office.

In closing our report we desire especially to return our sincere thanks to Sheriff Ward and his deputies for their many courtesies and prompt response to our necessities.

Respectfully submitted by the grand jury.
J.J. Bullis, Foreman.[6]

Unfortunately, this published letter is all the extant information that has been found concerning the special grand jury and the indictment found against the men accused of the Bisbee murders.

"Red" Sample still had several true bills against him waiting in Clifton. *The Clarion*, which called Sample the "most notorious" of the six defendants, stated that he had been indicted for the robbery of the Detroit Copper Company's offices the previous summer and that of an "old Mormon rancher" in August. "To sum up the matter, his record in [Graham] county has been one of crime." The newspaper continued in this vein, saying of Daniel Kelly, "he has not been considered a shining light in this community" though he was not known to have committed crimes in the vicinity. "Tex" Howard was "known as a cool-headed, desperate man" and Dowd as "a worthless fellow" who was suspected of being involved in the attack on a "wagon-load of Chinese" which left "two of the Mongolians" dead. William Delaney, *The Clarion* reported, turned outlaw after the killing of a man named Sawyer in Clifton in August.[7]

On the morning of February 7, Sheriff Ward and his deputies led the six defendants out of their cells on the first floor of the Tombstone courthouse, past the throngs of "curious citizens" who had crowded the hallways and up the wide winding staircase to the second-floor courtroom. At 9:35 a.m., the prisoners entered through the great double doors, with "Tex" Howard and Delaney in the lead. They were followed directly by Dan Dowd and John Heath. Behind them were "Red" Sample and "York" Kelly. Each pair of defendants was manacled to one another. The men were led by the Sheriff to the dock and there seated. The prisoners immediately fell into "earnest but whispered consultation" with the men appointed as their legal counsel, including James B. Southard, Colonel F. Stanford, Thomas J. Drum, Edward V. Price, and Colonel William Herring. Finally, Judge Pinney entered and the arraignment hearing for the six accused men began.[8]

"The defendants were arraigned and the indictment read to them and a copy of the same was handed to each of said defendants being asked if the name under which he was indicted and arraigned and as appeared in the copy of the indictment handed to him respectfully was his true name and severally answered that it was." The defendants "were each given until tomorrow [February 8] to plead." Colonel William Herring, attorney and the former superintendent of the Neptune Mining Company, had been appointed to represent William Delaney and John Heath. Herring asked the court to allow for separate trials for William Delaney and John Heath. "Counsel for the other prisoners announced that the right to separate trials would be waived by their clients." Col. Herring also "waived his request for a separate trial for Delaney and it was ordered by the Court that, as to John Heith, he be allowed a separate trial." The court then recessed until the afternoon.

Construction on the Cochise County Courthouse in Tombstone had begun in August

Cochise County Courthouse, Tombstone A.T. (prior to the addition) where the Bisbee bandits and John Heath were jailed and their trials took place (Arizona Historical Society, 9917).

of 1882, with the cornerstone being laid on the 10th of that month. The courthouse was built at the intersection of Third Street and Toughnut, over the site of the former Vizina mining claim, the land having been donated to the county for this purpose. The handsome red brick edifice, designed by Frank Walker, an architect and the superintendent of Tombstone's Sycamore Springs Water Company, cost the county nearly $50,000, a princely sum for the time. Walker also drew up the plans for the City Hall building. Construction was overseen by A.J. Ritter, undertaker, coffin and cabinet maker. The first floor of the building had been completed and was being occupied by December of 1882. Construction on the upper level was finally completed on March 3, 1883.

Originally built in the shape of a Roman cross (in 1903, an addition to both floors was added at the back of the building), the "territorial Victorian" courthouse had over 10,000 square feet of space and provided offices on the first floor for the County Recorder, the County Treasurer, and the County Sheriff. The County jail was also located on this floor. The second story housed the County Attorney's office, the Judge's quarters, the Jury Room, the Grand Jury Room (which was also utilized by the Board of Supervisors) and, of course, the wood-paneled courtroom. The imposing structure—one of the largest buildings in the Territory at the time it was built—featured redwood-framed windows, classical-style pediments, a "widow's walk," and a mansard-roofed cupola with eight windows for ventilation. The towering walls of the structure were nearly 16 inches thick, the bricks being hewn by Chinese laborers in Tucson.

The inside of the building was equally impressive, with 14-foot high ceilings on the first floor and 16-foot high ceilings on the second. The interior also boasted hand-painted wooden trim, and a spiral staircase leading up the second floor. The floors were made entirely of wood cut from the Huachuca and Chiricahua mountain ranges. The set of carved double doors at the entrance to the courthouse stood an imposing 12 feet in height. The building was lighted throughout with elegant brass gasoliers. The courtroom itself was 35 feet by 48 feet, with a ceiling 18 feet high. While the building would see much excitement over the years, little would compare to the drama which would unfold within its walls and in the adjoining courtyard over the next two months.[9]

On the afternoon of February 7, "[t]he defendants were brought into Court and, in the presence of their counsel and the District Attorney were asked by the Court how they plead to the indictment." Judge Pinney first "called the name of Dowd, who arose in his seat, and on being asked what plea he wished to enter to the indictment found against him, answered, in a firm voice, 'Not guilty.' Each one of the other five defendants, when queried as to their plea by the magistrate, answered in the same manner. 'The plea of not guilty was ordered to be entered.' After, W.B. Sample, being (*illegible*) asked his true name answered that it was Omer W. Sample, instead of W.B. Sample, as written in the indictment." The error was corrected by the clerk of the court. Colonel Herring then asked that he be excused as counsel for Delaney stating that he had been "retained to defend Heith [*sic*], and that his duties as counsel for defense in both cases would be conflicting and place him in an anomalous position."

Judge James B. Southard, who was assigned as co-counsel for Delaney, also asked to be excused saying that Col. Herring's assistance would be "invaluable to the defense" and if the court was to excuse Herring, he would also claim the right to be excused. Counsel for "Big Dan" Dowd and Howard, attorney George R. Williams, also asked to

be excused, giving as his reason "an aggravated carbuncle on the back of his neck" which Williams felt would hamper him in his ability to properly defend his clients. At this, Colonel F. Sanford, who was assigned as co-counsel for Howard and Dowd, asked to be excused, saying "pressing engagements" would require his being absent from Tombstone from the following evening on. Stanford magnanimously offered to assist in the defense of the two prisoners until that time. Judge Pinney listened patiently to the "ingenious excuses offered by counsel" and after a moment's consid-

James B. Southard, defense attorney and co-counsel for William Delaney (Arizona Historical Society, 1728 [cropped]).

eration, "smiled benignly, and said: 'Well, gentlemen, are you ready to proceed with the cases?'"[10]

While attorneys Williams and Stanford may well have been making excuses in order to have themselves dismissed as counsel for the defense in the case against Dowd, Sample, Howard, Kelly, and Delaney—a case they were probably convinced they could not win— Colonel Herring seems to have had good reason to believe he was facing a conflict of interest which would adversely affect his ability to defend his clients. Colonel Herring had been retained by Heath as his attorney. In an undated letter from Nathan W. Waite to John Heath, Waite explains that "those who are assisting you in obtaining proper counsel" had been able to raise $400, but were having difficulty raising the final $100 of the retainer.

In the letter, Waite writes to Heath, "if you could let me know where your people live, I could write them in such a way that they would not know of your troubles and perhaps obtain the remaining hundred from them." Waite also explains to Heath some of his friends were not to be relied upon, writing, "There is no use in your expecting Cronin to do anything for you." It is unknown what Herring was charging Heath for his services, but Waite states that "$25,000 of the $40,000 is in the Horse and Equipments." Still, the attorney must have been satisfied with what monies he had received, as Waite says, "Mr. Herring starts in at once on your case."[11]

Financially, John Heath was in a bind. In a letter dated January 14, 1884, his partner, Robert Austin, wrote Heath from Clifton explaining that "the Copper Co. [most likely the Arizona Copper Company] have taken our property from us without allowing anything for it." Austin laments the state of affairs: "It is a strange country where men are arrested for holding others up with a gun and put in jail [no reference to you] and on the other hand allowing Company [sic] to rob persons of money that they have worked hard for and say nothing about it." In what was likely a response to a request for a loan from Heath, Austin explained that he was paying rent on his home, and that the Exchange Saloon, which was owned by their friends Frank and Jim was to be "torn down in a few days." In other words, Heath would not be able to expect any financial help from those quarters.[12]

Heath received a second missive from Waite in which the latter wrote, "I believe you will come out alright." He tells Heath to "be patient—and don't be in such a hurry— You have good judgment and know yourself how bad things looked against you owing to your association with those men." Waite explains that Heath's belongings had not been sent from Clifton, though he had written two letters requesting them from Mr. Lepinver (a man Waite calls a "stinker"). Heath's friend also tells him his rifle "is in Bisbee—in the hands of a man named Duncan McGillis to whom it was given by Dave Lynch to satisfy some debt." Waite further tells Heath it will cost him $2,000 to reclaim the weapon from McGillis. As evidenced by the correspondence he was receiving in jail, Heath was in dire straits. Finally, in lieu of payment, Heath must have instructed Waite to turn over to Herring his saddle, saddlebags, and his engraved, mother-of-pearl handled Colt's revolver, in the expectation that, after the trial, he would be able to redeem these items.[13]

The preliminaries in the trial of the Bisbee bandits continued the following morning, Friday, February 8, 1884. Immediately after the courtroom was called to order, Thomas J. "Judge" Drum, the attorney appointed to represent Kelly and Sample, moved for a continuance, arguing that his "clients had since their arrest been incarcerated without money or friends and without being informed of the progress of proceedings against them." The defendants claimed to have witnesses in the New Mexico Territory that could provide them with an alibi. The attorney therefore asked "that time be granted so that the defendants could procure the attendance of their witness." Colonel Stanford immediately followed suit, asking the court for a postponement to a later date so that his clients, Howard and Dowd, might have the opportunity to contact those persons who might provide them with an alibi. Judge Pinney responded to the motion, saying that "the prisoners, although penniless, and friendless, should be treated as fairly and afforded the same means of defense as though they were wealthy men."

District Attorney Smith countered, explaining that during their preliminary examination the defendants "had been informed that all facilities would be afforded them to procure the attendance of witnesses, and that they had manifested no desire to do so." The prosecutor asked that the names and whereabouts of said witnesses be presented to the court in an affidavit. Attorney Drum asked for a continuance until Saturday, February 9, or possibly even Monday, February 11, in order to prepare said affidavit. Judge Pinney replied, saying that at 1:30 that afternoon would give the defense ample time to draft such a document. A recess until said hour was then declared by the court and the defendants were led back down to their cells by the sheriff and his deputies.[14]

The Arizona Weekly Citizen reported that District Attorney Smith and Deputy District Attorney Judge Robinson had "indisputable evidence that the prisoners at the bar [were] guilty as charged" and were confident in their ability to convict them of the crimes they were indicted for. However, the six defendants seemed "to have little realization of their position" and were reported to have been laughing and joking amongst themselves and with their lawyers throughout the proceedings. One can only wonder whether the display of mirth by the accused men was false bravado or fatalism.[15]

At 1:30 p.m. on the afternoon of February 8, with Dowd, Delaney, Howard, Kelly, and Sample sitting in the dock with their attorneys, the trial resumed. Once the court was called to order, the counsel for the defense submitted their affidavits "setting forth that material witnesses were in various points in New Mexico and Arizona," and then called for a continuance of proceedings "until their presence could be procured."[16]

John Heath's saddle, which he gave to his lawyer Colonel William Herring in lieu of payment (author's collection).

John Heath's engraved, pearl-handled Colt's revolver, which he gave to his lawyer Col. William Herring in lieu of payment (author's collection).

Specifically, the affidavit of Daniel Kelly stated that the defendant "cannot safely proceed to trial ... by reason of the absence from the County of Cochise of a necessary and material witness ... Joseph Mackey, whom the defendant believes to be in the Quiqota mining camp west of the city of Tucson." Kelly expected "to prove by the said Joseph Mackey that the defendant was at Rail Road Pass about sixty miles north of the Town of Bisbee on the night of the 8th December, AD [sic] 1883 at about 5 o'clock P.M. of that day." Drum, on behalf of his client, wrote, "This defendant has good reason to believe that if this cause is continued until the May AD 1884 Term of this Court he can secure the attendance of the said witness ... to testify on his behalf."[17]

The affidavit of O.W. Sample was not dissimilar in the wording, except that the defendant asked for a continuance so he might contact "John Myers and James Anderson, both of whom ... are now in the Black Range in the Territory of New Mexico, prospecting." Sample stated that Myers and Anderson would attest to the fact "on the night of the 8th day of December AD 1884 ... [he] went into camp about 7 o'clock in the evening about six miles [illegible] of Bowie and about sixty miles from the town of Bisbee [and] remained in said camp until nine oclock [sic] the following morning." The defendant also requested the presence of George Beuh, "a resident of Pima County," and Henry Hill, "a resident of Clifton" in Graham County, who would testify to the fact "that no watch was found on the person of the defendant or under his control at the time of his arrest in Graham County aforesaid." Sample stated "that he cannot prove the foregoing fact by any other witness."[18]

In his affidavit, Sample stated that he had "heard the affidavit of James Howard, his co-defendant herewith attached and knows the contents thereof [and] that the same is true of his own knowledge." This third affidavit, filed with the court on behalf of James "Tex" Howard, stated that "on the evening of December 8th, 1883, Howard was camped at a place about six miles southwest of Bowie Station and about sixty miles from the town of Bisbee ... with O.W. Sample, John Myers, and James Anderson." The affidavit described James Anderson as being "about thirty five years old, dark complexion, and getting a little gray—about five feet and four inches in height and weighs about one hundred and sixty pounds with dark whiskers all over his face but little gray." Anderson was further described as "a man of quiet and reserved manners and a man of high forehead and a thick head of hair." The affiant believed Anderson was residing in the "vicinity of Lake Valley, New Mexico, and to be employed as a "miner and prospector."

Howard's affidavit, which was referenced in the subsequent affidavit of O.W. Sample, described John Myers as "a man about thirty-five years of age, of sandy complexion without any whiskers except a moustache—about six feet in height, weighing about 170 pounds." Myers too was described as being "of quiet and reserved manners." In his affidavit, Howard swore he had known Myers "for the last twelve months" having initially net the man in Silver City, New Mexico Territory." It was Howard's assertion that he had camped with "said Meyers and Anderson," who were "then on their way to the Black Range north of Lake Valley" and that he had "not heard from said Myers or Anderson since said time but ... verily believes they are now in the vicinity of Lake Valley in the Black Range about twenty five miles north thereof."

As Howard stated in the affidavit, "Myers and Anderson can swear that affiant and Sample camped with them on the night of December 8th, 1883, as above stated" and asked therefore for the case to be "postponed until the next term on the court so [the defendant] can procure the attendance of said Myers and Anderson for said trial and procure their testimony. The affiant," the document read, "cannot prove the forgoing facts by any other witness and says he cannot safely proceed to trial without the testimony of said Myers and Anderson." The affidavit of James "Tex" Howard closed thus: "Wherefore affiant prays that the trial of this case be postponed until the next term of this court to enable defendant to procure the testimony above named." O.W. Sample's affidavit ended in a similar manner: "Wherefore the defendant prays that this cause be continued to the next term of the court ... that [he] may be enabled to procure the testimony of the within named witnesses."[19]

Defendants James Howard's and Omer Sample's praying was for naught, as Judge Pinney denied the defense's motion for a continuance "so far as the witnesses alleged to be residents of New Mexico were concerned." However, the judge was willing to grant a "temporary postponement" so the defendants could subpoena the witnesses residing within the Arizona Territory. District Attorney Smith, in the interest of expediting matters, "would admit that the witnesses, if present, would swear to the state of facts as set forth in the affidavits." Colonel Stanford, on behalf of his clients, refused the offer made by the prosecution unless the "same admission" was made in regards to the witnesses residing in the New Mexico Territory. The District Attorney refused this concession and the judge ordered the trial to proceed. Stanford acquiesced, but asked that the "exception be noted" by the clerk of the court in the transcript.[20]

The court then proceeded to the business of impaneling the trial jury, a process *The Tombstone Republican* expected would occupy the court for the remainder of the afternoon. By days end, 12 men had been chosen for service, including William Ross, T.P. Teal, J.D. Cummings, J.L. Moore, E.W. Layton, John Clifford, Joseph Bingham, H.L. Shack, Harry C. Reed, H.L. Kemp, and T.S. Merrill. The jury foreman was Herman Welisch. The following day, Saturday, February 9, 1884, at 9:00 a.m.—precisely two months and one day after the fatal robbery at the Goldwater and Castaneda Mercantile Emporium in Bisbee—the trial of Daniel "Big Dan" Dowd, Omer W. "Red" Sample, Daniel "York" Kelly, William E, Delaney, and James "Tex" Howard began in earnest.[21]

Five days prior to the arraignment of the suspects in the Bisbee outrage, *The Arizona Weekly Citizen* reported that the men who had robbed the train near Gage Station had been summarily apprehended and were languishing behind bars in Silver City, New Mexico. A week before, *The Arizona Champion* noted that Silver City Sheriff Harvey

Whitehill and John Gilmore had apprehended Frank Taggart. Unfortunately, the Mohave County newspaper provided no further particulars regarding how the capture was affected. It was revealed that "a writ of *habeas corpus* had been tried" but was rejected by the court. In contrast, the subsequent capture of Mitch Lee and "Kit" Joy was described by the press in some detail.[22]

According to *The Arizona Weekly Citizen*, Southern Pacific Railroad detective Lew Harris and detective Jim B. Hume of Wells Fargo & Company had been on the case since the beginning and had proved "equal to the difficult job" of running down the train robbers. "The clue of the tobacco bags and empty cans ... which had contained pickled pigs feet ... found on the desert" had helped the detectives to trace the movements of the robbers in the days and weeks following the robbery. "After determining [the robbers] point of departure, the place where the organization of the robbers was effected—Silver City— it was several weeks before a further clue was secured," wrote the correspondent. "The detectives groped their way in the dark" having to "ascertain who were not engaged in the robbery, before they could begin to search for those who were. Almost every suspicious character in western New Mexico and eastern Arizona was shadowed ... before the real work in hand began."

The newspaper went on to praise Hume and Harris: "the credit of working up the case and the execution of its details is almost wholly [theirs]. The first good hold was made on the negro Cleveland, who confessed to being in the robbery" and betrayed his companions to the law. Next, "French Tagart [*sic*] was captured at St. Johns, Apache county, and Kid Joy and Mich Lee in the Mogollon mountains near this place [Tucson]." The *Weekly Citizen* went on to explain how the bandits were at present secured safely behind bars in Silver City and said of Hume and Harris: "We owe much to ... the detectives above-named for the masterly and successful manner in which they have handled [this] case. No more daring and bloodthirsty robberies and murders have been committed in this section of the country, and none have been hunted down ... with more persistence and determination."[23]

However, *The Tombstone Republican*, in their coverage of the capture of "Kit" Joy and "Mich" Lee, made no mention of detective Hume and only scant mention of Harris. The Cochise County newspaper stated that Joy and Lee had been "captured by a party of ranchmen" in connection with the theft of some livestock. On or about December 29, the suspects "went down on the Gila river and stole, from Lyons and Campbell, two horses" leaving behind "one of their own, a worn-out animal." Upon discovering the animals missing, the "ranchmen banded together and went in pursuit." The five horsemen followed the thieves' trail into Apache County, "and to a ranch only ten miles from where Frank Taggart was captured and 165 miles west of Sorocco, New Mexico."

Upon arriving at the ranch, the pursuers introduced themselves, but "did not make known their business. Two of them sat down to dinner at that same table as the robbers, while three remained outside." Having put the suspects at ease, the ranchmen signaled their comrades, who immediately burst through the door with "guns cocked and told the robbers to surrender. Being taken by surprise, they readily complied" with the directive of the armed men. Joy and Lee were then disarmed and secured in bonds. "Although the country was flooded with circulars ... and they were in the immediate vicinity where Taggart had been captured, the ranchmen did not know they had succeeded in capturing the last two of the Gage train robbers." It was not until they had begun the journey homeward with the thieves that the men learned who their captives actually were.

The ranchmen turned their prisoners over to New Mexico law enforcement officers, and Joy and Lee were "taken to Silver City and lodged in jail." The four suspects were held without bail. *The Republican* reported that "strong pressure is being brought to bear upon Judge Bristol, of the Silver City district, to call a special grand jury for the purpose of disposing of the case as soon as possible." The newspaper, which cited its source as detective Len Harris of the Southern and Central Pacific railroads, went on to say that the "Santa Fe people and official of Wells Fargo & Co." would be joining Harris "in his efforts to have a special grand jury and a special term of the court called," just as in the Bisbee case. Harris went on to describe that suspects as "a hard-looking lot—regular cowboys … doubtlessly capable of doing all that is charged to them."[24]

So, what then was Detective Hume's involvement in the capture of the Gage robbers? The editor for *The Tombstone Epitaph* was of the opinion that Hume had been doing little more than duping reporters in an effort to make a name for himself. *The San Francisco Examiner* had published an interview with Hume in which he claimed to have been instrumental in the apprehension of the entire Gage robbery gang. *The Epitaph* responded saying it was "not the first time the Examiner had been fooled by a blowhard." *The Champion* backed this assertion stating that it was Silver City Marshal Harvey Whitehill who had actually arrested and exacted the confession of Cleveland and that "neither Hume nor Harris had anything whatever to do" in this. Neither had the two detectives been involved in the capture of Taggart or the apprehension of Joy and Lee. The editor then issued a challenge, saying, "If anyone can show anything that Hume did, except ride up and down the Southern Pacific railroad and look wise, the Epitaph would be pleased to make it known." In conclusion, the editor wrote, "To the officers of New Mexico alone is due the capture of the train robbers and the Epitaph don't [sic] propose that Jim Hume, or anyone else, shall wear their laurel, without entering a protest against it."[25]

At 9:00 a.m., on Saturday, February 9, the dissonant sound of the manacles which bound the ankles and wrists of the accused resounded throughout the Tombstone courthouse as the five inmates, accompanied by the sheriff and his deputies, laboriously ascended the 27 steps of the spiraling staircase toward the crowded courtroom. Ten minutes later, the five

Silver City Marshal Harvey Whitehall captured George W. Cleveland, who confessed to the Gage train robbery and subsequently informed on his partners (author's collection).

Staircase in the interior Cochise County Courthouse, up which John Heath and the Bisbee bandits ascended to the courtroom during the trials (author's collection).

fettered men had passed through the small gate in the railing which separated the well of the courtroom from the gallery and were seated in the dock. Typically, the defendant would be seated at the table with his attorneys during the proceedings. However, because there were five defendants in the case—more than could comfortably be accommodated at the defense table—the accused were probably seated to the left of the defense table against the east wall of the courtroom.

Directly in line with the main doors of the courtroom and the small gate through which the accused passed to enter the well of the courtroom and against the far wall, sat Judge Daniel Pinney, high above them on the bench. Just in front of the judge, at an elevated desk surrounded on three sides by a thick partition, sat the court stenographer and the clerk of the court. To the defendants' immediate left, seated at a long oak table, were their attorneys, T.J. Drum, James B. Southard, and Colonel William Herring. Across the center aisle, seated behind an almost identical table were District Attorney Marcus A. Smith and Deputy District Attorney Judge Robinson. Further on, past the table where sat the prosecuting attorneys and directly across from the defendants, stood a raised two-tiered platform enclosed by a solid, wood-paneled divider which could only be accessed by passing through a hinged gate in the front. Here sat the 12 members of the jury—the men who would ultimately decide the fate of the defendants—in high backed, wooden chairs.

Officers and attorneys inside the Cochise County Courtroom (from left to right) Judge Peal, James B. Southard, George R. Williams, Webster Street, John F. Lewis (standing), James Reilly (seated), unknown in light coat, George Berry, William H. Seamans, Judge Daniel H. Pinney, Casey Clum, Thomas Mitchell, Henry C. Dibble, Ben Goodrich, Marcus A. Smith (seated), unknown in light suit, John Hayes, and unknown with beard (it is likely this photo was taken during the trial of the Bisbee murderers) (Arizona Historical Society, 1728).

Even before the proceedings had commenced, *The Tombstone Republican* called it "The Most Important Trial in the Criminal History of Arizona" and continued on, stating, "Every move in the trial of the men charged with committing the Bisbee murders is noted with absorbing interest, not only by the people of Tombstone, but of the whole county, and in scarcely less degree by citizens of the territory at large. Upon the convening of court at 9 o'clock this morning the room was densely packed, and during the entire forenoon the crowd patiently kept their places, listening eagerly to every word uttered by counsel or witnesses, and watching intently each movement or change of countenance of the prisoners."[26]

With a sharp rap of the gavel, Judge Pinney called the court to order, and silence fell upon the courtroom. *The Tombstone Daily Epitaph* recorded that District Attorney Smith addressed the jury, "outlining to them, the theory of the prosecution." Unfortunately, his opening statement has been lost along with the minutes of the court stenographer, Mr. Risley. The only records of the proceedings extant are those which appeared in the local newspapers. It is also unknown whether the defense attorneys presented an opening statement before the court. The reporter for *The Daily Epitaph*, who utilized the stenographer's notes in writing the article which appeared in the Sunday issue dated February 10, made no mention of a defense rebuttal. The Minutes of the District Court record that the witnesses called by the prosecution that morning included William Daniels, Joseph Goldwater, Richard Rundle, John Hiles, and Walter Myers.

The first witness to be called by the prosecution was Deputy Sheriff Daniels. After being sworn in, Daniels testified as follows: "I was in Bisbee on the evening of the 8th of

December, 1883, when the killing of Smith, Tappenier, and others occurred. I was playing billiards in my own saloon; about 8 o'clock in the evening heard a shot fired; went to the door, and saw a man running up the street; ran across the street myself; met a man coming out of the door of a saloon; he looked very pale and excited; I caught hold of him and asked who fired the shot; [I] was told it was in Castaneda's store; saw a large man standing at the door of Castaneda's store, shooting up and down the street. I ran back to my saloon, got my pistol, went out the back way and came around on the street again in front of the post office, and as the man from the store started down street I fired at him; four or five men ran down the street firing at me as they ran. I fired five shots from a Colt's pistol, .45 calibre. The men, after going down the street below the Copper Queen smelter, mounted their horses and rode down the canyon, firing their pistols into the air."

Unfortunately, as mentioned previously, the original transcript of the trial has not been found. The testimony, as reprinted in *The Tombstone Daily Epitaph* does not include the questions asked by the prosecuting attorney which elicited the responses given by the witnesses [the newspaper ran the testimony of each individual witness altogether in their columns without any breaks]. It may be assumed that the prosecution began another line of questioning at this point, as Deputy Daniels abruptly changed subject and began speaking of the arrests of "Big Dan" Dowd and William Delaney. Deputy Daniels' testimony continued thus: "I arrested Mr. Dowd in the town of Coralitas, Mexico, about 150 miles from Bisbee. I got on his track at Ariape. Mr. Hatch and myself arrested Delaney at Minas Prietas; when arrested, he said he had never been to Bisbee. I saw him in my saloon about fifteen minutes before the shooting occurred. I only saw one man doing the shooting in the street; there were four or five men ran down the street and mounted. Soon after they left Bisbee, I took a horse and followed them; started with seven men besides myself; reached the [M]ilk [R]anch before day. As soon as it was light we went to look at the tracks of the horses; I measured the tracks—some of them; we followed this trail some eight miles; it led to Soldier Holes [*sic*]; There was only one white horse in the crowd."

Deputy Daniels was then cross-examined by the counsel for the defense. Again, the extant record does not provide the identity of the defense attorney or record what questions he asked of the law officer. Daniels stated he "was residing at Bisbee at the time of the shooting." He admitted he "didn't see the man who fired the first shot." Deputy Daniels went on to say, "I saw Delaney fifteen minutes before the shooting; Mr. Delaney, when arrested, said he was never in Bisbee. I do not know of my knowledge that the parties killed in Bisbee that night were shot by any of the prisoners; I do know that the parties were shot; I saw gunshot wounds on them. I pursued and captured Delaney because I thought him one of the parties who did the shooting. I never saw him from the time I saw him in Bisbee until I saw him in Minas Prietas; I did not recognize Delaney among the men who did the shooting."

Here the line of questioning must have changed again, as in the recorded testimony Deputy Daniels begins discussing the arrest of "Big Dan" Dowd. He states, "I arrested Mr. Dowd personally; I found Mr. Dowd in Chiricahua, Mexico; he offered no resistance when I arrested him. I had no acquaintance with Mr. Dowd prior to this time; in making my pursuit and capture of him I was governed chiefly by what I heard. There were four, five, or six men who rode away from Bisbee on the night of the shooting. One man passed me on the street; I shot at that man with a Colt's .45 calibre pistol; he ran to where the other men were standing, on a vacant lot; immediately after they mounted their horses and began firing into the air; I only saw one of them on the street. I knew a reward had been offered for the apprehension and arrest of these parties."

In answer to the further queries of the defense counsel, Daniels continued, saying, "Here I started in pursuit of Mr. Dowd; I found Mr. Dowd at a blacksmith shop at a mine; covered him with my rifle and told him to throw up his hands, which he did, and I approached him and took off his cartridge belt; he had no arms on him. One night, we got into Hot Springs very late, and I sat up with Dowd all the rest of the night. I told Dowd that on the morning before the robbery, Heith [*sic*] got on his horse at Bisbee, and rode down the canyon to where you fellows were camped below the slaughter house, and met you there. Dowd said, 'No he did not.' Then he got excited, and tried to fix it up; finally he said, 'I hope they will hang the d——d s—of a b——; he put on so much style with those ivory handled six shooters.'"[27]

Thus ended the initial witness testimony in the trial of the suspected Bisbee bandits. Of the five defendants, the prosecution had succeeded only in placing William Delaney in town at the time of the outrage, but they had not conclusively proved Delaney was directly involved in the robbery or the murders for which he had been indicted. While on the stand, Deputy Daniels had admitted he had not seen any of the other defendants in town on the evening of the robbery, including Dowd whom he had personally arrested. The ruse the lawman allegedly used on Dowd during their return trip from Mexico had been somewhat successful—it had served to illicit an acknowledgement from Dowd that he had been camped in Bisbee the morning of the robbery. Though Dowd allegedly said he hoped Heath would hang, his prior assertion implied that Heath was not directly involved in the robbery. Still, this part of the Deputy Sheriff's testimony amounted to little more than hearsay. Besides this, Heath was being tried separately from the others.

The next witness to be called to the stand was none other than Joseph "Joe" Goldwater. After swearing an oath upon the Bible to speak only the truth, Goldwater testified to the fact he "was keeping a store in Bisbee on the 8th day of December last." In response to the questions of the prosecuting attorney, the storekeeper stated, "Five men came into the store and robbed me of $700 or $800 and a gold watch with the name of William Clancy cut on the inside of the case. Four of them were masked, one of them was not masked; He is now here. They presented two six-shooters and demanded the bookkeeper to open the safe door; the bookkeeper could not open the safe. This is the man who wore no mask [pointing to Tex]. I was ordered to open the safe, which I did; one of them went into Mr. Castaneda's room and shortly afterwards came out and said it was 'all right.' J.C. Tappenier, D.T. Smith, Mrs. Roberts, and Mr. Nolly were killed that night in Bisbee."

Here the prosecution left off with the questioning of the witness and the defense counsel began with their cross-examination of Mr. Goldwater. Goldwater readily admitted he "was never robbed before" and "had never had any experience with such men before." The 54-year-old merchant continued on, saying, "I think I was a little more cool and collected at the time than I am now; when I saw two pistols pointed at my bookkeeper, I understood that something was wanted; I did not anticipate any personal danger; my feelings were to get rid of them as soon as possible." When asked about James Howard in particular, Goldwater responded, "There is nothing in particular on this man, Mr. Howard, that enables me to recognize him, save that I know the face and know him to be the man who held a pistol on my clerk."

At this point, the watch belonging to William Clancy was introduced as evidence.

Joe Goldwater recognized it immediately. He stated, "The name on the inside case of that watch is William Clancy; the watch went in a barley sack with the coin from the safe; I don't remember the number of the case; I recognize the watch as the one that was left in my safe for safekeeping." A quarter dollar piece was then introduced as evidence, which Goldwater was also able to recognize. "I identified that quarter of a dollar; it was my property; I don't know who put the letters 'M.E.S.' on the coin. I received the piece of money myself; it was taken out of my safe the night of December 8. It was exhibited to me first at the examination held in this courtroom; it was shown to me by the sheriff; it was handed to me, and I was asked if I recognized the coin; I said I did."

The defense attorney then returned to the question of Goldwater's identification of Thomas "Tex" Howard. The storekeeper reiterated, "The man without the mask is the one who presented the pistol; he was unmasked when he came in and left unmasked, and I know this is the man [pointing to Tex]. I know William Clancy, whose name appears on the inside of the case of the watch; it was left with me three or four months before the shooting occurred." With this statement, the defense ceased the cross-examination of the witness and Mr. Goldwater was allowed to step down from the stand. Goldwater's testimony was crucial to the building of the prosecution's case against the defendants. Where Deputy Daniels had only been able to put Delaney in town just prior to the robbery, Goldwater was able to positively identify the defendant James "Tex" Howard as being one of the men who had actually robbed him. Now, it was only a matter of connecting the other defendants to Howard.[28]

The next witness to be called to the stand was Richard Rundle, one of the men who had been pulled into the store during the course of the robbery. Mr. Rundle, being duly sworn in by the clerk of the court, testified that he too "was in Bisbee the night of the 8th of December, when the store of Castaneda and Co. was robbed." Rundle recalled "walking toward Castaneda's store about 7:30 p.m., when a man on the street with a pistol in each hand and a mask on ordered me inside. I went in. Some parties were taking money from the safe; a shot was fired outside; I started to drop my hands; was told to hold them up and do as I was told, and no harm would come to me; the man who was guarding with two pistols wore no mask, Mr. Howard, known as Tex, was this man; the man who was taking money from the safe dropped his mask and I saw his face; I think that is the man [pointing to Kelly]. Another man passed by me with a pistol in each hand; one of the pistols struck me, and I turned quickly; the man with the pistol turned also at the same time and his mask fell down perpendicularly and I saw him distinctly; the man called Sample is that man; one of the men who stood at the door was a large man and the other was small."

The defense seems to have begun their cross-examination of Mr. Rundle with questions about his identification of Howard, Sample, and Kelly. Rundle stated he recognized "Mr. Howard as the man who wore no mask and held the pistols." In answer to the defense attorney's questions concerning his identification of the defendants, Rundle said that "Red" Sample's "mask flew back and it remained back until he put up his hand and pulled it down" and that "Mr. Kelley stooped down to pick up some money dropped on the floor; as he stooped his mask flew from his face; I was standing about five feet from him and had a side view of his face." Rundle continued, saying, "I let my hands rest on top of my head; one pistol was pointed at me. Howard is the man who held that pistol—I am sure of that. I had seen him twice before, in Mr. Tribolet's saloon at Bisbee and recognized him readily; he wore a heavy overcoat; I recognized him from his features alone."

The defense must have then changed the line of questioning, asking Rundle if he knew anything about the shooting that occurred during the robbery. Rundle replied thus: "I did not see Mr. Howard fire any shots; the only man I recognize as doing any shooting that night is the man Sample; he fired his pistols in the air at the door of the store." Again the line of questioning must have changed and Rundle said in response, "Mr. Smith was killed by bullet wounds; I do not know who shot him. I saw five men—four masked and one unmasked; all carried arms on leaving the store. These five men went down to the Copper Queen smelter. I was about eight or ten feet within the store when I was told to throw up my hands by this man Howard, who had a pistol in each hand."[29]

With this statement the defense finished the cross-examination of Mr. Rundle and he was allowed to step down. Mr. Rundle was a key witness for the prosecution as he had been able to identify three of the bandits. He also had been able to corroborate Joe Goldwater's identification of James "Tex" Howard, definitively placing the man at the scene of the robbery. Further, he was able to identify Sample and Kelly and place them both inside the store on the night of the robbery, though his identification had not been verified by other witnesses. Rundle did say that he did not see any of the men inside the store fire any shots, except "Red" Sample, who discharged his revolvers into the air on exiting the building. One might then wonder why Howard, Sample, and Kelly had not asked for separate trials for their co-defendants, if they knew themselves to be innocent of the murders. It would seem to make sense that they would want to distance themselves from the members of the gang who had actually done the killing and been indicted for the crime of robbery, which was not a capital crime and not punishable by death.

Unfortunately for Sample, Howard, and Kelly, the law of the territory did not allow for such distinctions. An act to amend Section 21 of Chapter X of the Laws of the Territory of Arizona was passed by the Twelfth Legislative Assembly in 1883. The act decreed that "all murder which shall be perpetuated by means of poison or lying in wait, torture or by any other kind of willful, deliberate and premeditated killing, *or which shall be committed in the perpetration or attempt to perpetrate any arson, rape, robbery, or burglary shall be deemed murder of the first degree* … [and] in every case of a person or persons convicted of murder in the first degree the jury may in their verdict affix the penalty of death in their verdict; and if the jury do not affix the penalty of death in their verdict, every person or persons convicted of murder in the first degree shall suffer imprisonment in the Territorial Prison for life." This act modified the original statute, which was approved by the legislature in 1877, which prescribed the death penalty in all cases of first degree murder.[30]

Though not explicitly stated in the aforementioned statute, the law was commonly interpreted as meaning if a murder was committed during the commission of another crime—just as happened during the Bisbee robbery—then *all the parties* involved in the commission of said crime could also be charged with the murder. Still, an adept attorney could have challenged such an interpretation on behalf of his client, arguing that only the person or persons who had actually committed the murders during the perpetuation of the crime should be held accountable. In the case of the Bisbee defendants—especially James "Tex" Howard, who was known to have participated in the robbery but had not been directly involved in the murders—the defense attorney could have sought to have his case tried separately and, citing the equivocal and ambiguous wording of the statute, fought to have him indicted and tried only for the crime of robbery.

The same could have been done for Omer "Red" Sample and Daniel "York" Kelly,

FOUR. THE TRIALS (PART ONE)

91

who witnesses placed inside the store with Howard while the murders were taking place out on the street. Why these defendants, who knew they were not guilty of the murders that were committed that evening, did not ask for separate trials (as did John Heath) and why their attorneys did not pursue this angle—that of challenging the vagary of the statute—in defense of their clients are questions which remain open to conjecture and speculation. Instead, the five men elected to be tried together and as the evidence in the case mounted against each of them, it mounted against all of them.

The prosecution next called John Hiles, a resident of Bisbee and an employee at Lockwood's stable, to the stand. On the night of the robbery Hiles testified that he was in the corral tending to business, when he heard "ten or fifteen shots fired." He said he had "started up the street" toward the sound of the gunfire when he "saw a man coming down the street firing a pistol; five men ran down and mounted their horses behind the corral." Hiles stated he recognized one man and identified that man as the defendant James "Tex" Howard. Hiles went on to say that Howard "came to the corral some days before the affair, with John Heath; he had a dirty-colored gray horse; he mounted the same horse that evening. I saw the same horse in the stable on Allen street [in Tombstone] yesterday."

The cross-examination of Hiles by the defense counsel was equally brief. In answer to the attorney's queries, Hiles stated, "I have seen the man they call 'Tex' or Jim Howard, leading and riding this horse in Bisbee prior to December 8th; the last time I saw him riding the gray horse was on December 8th; I recognized him that night; he was riding down the canyon and passed within four or five feet of me; I saw him riding the same horse two different times before that in Bisbee; I was at work at the corral at the time and saw him take the horse out and exercise him." Hiles concluded his testimony, saying, "I did not see 'Tex' the night of the 8th of December until I saw him riding out of town."

As a witness for the prosecution, Hiles had been less than effective. He had indeed confirmed that James "Tex" Howard had been among the men who had fled from the direction of Castaneda's store on the night of the robbery, giving further credence to the testimony given by Joe Goldwater and Richard Rundle concerning Howard's involvement in the crime. Hiles statements also showed that John Heath was casually acquainted with at least one of the defendants, but Heath was not on trial at this time. Otherwise, Hiles' testimony had very little relevance and did not substantially enhance the prosecution's case against Howard's co-defendants.[31]

Following John Hiles on the witness stand for the prosecution was furrier Walter Myers. While under oath, Myers stated that on Wednesday, December 5, he had seen the five defendants together at the Buckles' ranch, and he had shod one of their horses. He stated after the shoe was affixed to the horse's hoof, Kelly "got on the horse and rode him around." The next time Myers said he saw the defendants was "on the night of December 8th, when I heard some men ride up to Buckles' ranch. I heard one of them say, 'We have raised hell,' I also heard one man say, 'I want a hat.'" Myers continued, saying, "I found a gray horse in an arroyo near Buckles' ranch the next morning; that horse is now in Montgomery and Benson's livery stable on Allen Street." Myers also admitted he "did not see any of the other horses except the one I shod for Kelley on Wednesday, Dec 5."

During the cross examination by the defense lawyers, Myers repeated his initial assertion: "I put one shoe on a horse for Kelley." Further, the furrier said, "I did not see the men come to Buckles' ranch, but I met them all there that day [December 5]. I knew Dowd and Delaney before; had known them some time." Returning to the subject of the horse, Myers said, "I do not know whether Kelley owned the horse or not, but the man who rode the horse was called Kelley by his companions." In response to the defense attorney's question, Myers admitted he "did not see the men who came back on the night of December 8th to the ranch" and that he had only heard their voices outside. "Mr. Buckles got up when they arrived that night. Buckles' ranch is, to the best of my knowledge, about 35 or 40 miles from Bisbee; it was well along toward the morning of the 9th that I heard the men come up to Buckles' ranch."[32]

Walter Myers' testimony, though circumstantial in nature, did prove the defendants were acquainted with one another and were riding together prior to the robbery. He was able to identify not only Kelly, but also Dowd and Delaney (though he did not say how he knew them). It was also ascertained that the Bisbee robbers had passed by the Buckles' ranch in their escape from the town. The gray horse found in the arroyo near the ranch gave credence to the assertion that the bandits had at the very least been in the immediate vicinity of the ranch that evening. While Myers admitted he did not actually see the men who rode on to the property that morning immediately following the robbery, he inferred that he was able to recognize their voices and implied that it was the same group of men who had visited the ranch three days prior when he shoed Kelly's horse.

In cross-examination, the defense attorney was very much lacking. The opportunity was given to discredit a portion of Myers' testimony, but it was not taken. Myers' identification of the men who arrived at the ranch the night of the robbery was not conclusive. Myers' said he had heard voices, but could not positively identify those he heard speaking. He was only superficially acquainted with Kelly—he only knew his name from hearing it spoken by others—and though he stated he knew Dowd and Delaney, he does not elaborate on the extent of their acquaintance. In fact, all Myers could say definitively was that the five defendants had been at Buckles' ranch on December 5, 1883. He could not even say for certain who the gray horse he found the morning after the robbery belonged to. As Myers admitted on the stand, he "did not see any of the other horses except the one [he] shod for Kelley."

At this point in the proceedings, Judge Pinney called for a recess—most likely for lunch. The defendants were taken from the courtroom and led back downstairs to their cells by Sheriff Ward and his deputies. Unfortunately, there is no record of what transpired during the break. Documented history is not always privy to the more mundane actions of the players—the meetings that may have been called, conversations that may have transpired, or even what was consumed at lunch. It is not even known how long the court was in recess—an hour, maybe two? All that is known for certain is that the court reconvened that afternoon at 1:00 p.m.

After the jury was brought back in, the defendants had been returned to the dock, the judge was seated at the bench, and the courtroom was again called to order. The next witness called to the stand for the prosecution was Lubien Pardee. "I live in the Chiricahua mountains, about ten miles from Buckles' ranch," he said.

> I saw the defendants, Dowd, Delaney, Red Sample, and Kelly at my camp. One day, I remarked to Kelly; "You must be going to hold up a stage?" Kelly say: "No, we don't hold up stages and we don't hold up anybody on the road. We are going down the country to rob a store, where I think we can make a pretty good stake." I was alone when Kelly told me this. Dan Dowd and Red Sample had gone out that day somewhere. Delaney was stopping at Buckles' ranch.
> After that, one day when I was cutting some posts, I went over to Dan Enmans' to get some wedges. When I came back I found Red Sample, Kelly, and Dan Dowd at my ranch. I told them I heard there was a train robbery at Clifton and that some men had passed down the canyon, and

Dan [Enmans] thought they were the train robbers. Dan Dowd got excited and said he was "going to get out of this." I asked him what he was afraid of. He said he was afraid of being arrested for the train robbery. He said they had concluded to go down there and rob a store, but they would let that go if everybody found out where they were. He said the two men in the canyon were Heith and "Tex," their friends. I told them, "If you are afraid of being arrested why don't you get out; I don't want you to be arrested here. There will be shooting, and I will be shot as well as you." Red said they were waiting until the 8th; that they could not leave before that time; that that was the time appointed to rob the store.

Dan Dowd saddled his horse, and in reply to Kelly, said he was going to Gila to look for a job. I asked Kelly if it was at Bisbee they were going to rob the store. He said yes. He said he was not afraid of having a hard job [and] that they had a man who had found out there would be plenty of money there then, and if they got there at the right time they would get plenty of it. Then Delaney came over and Kelly asked him if he knew how the thing was arranged. Delaney said he had an idea— that they would split the crowd; that Dan could go into the store, Red, Tex and himself would stop at the door and leave John Heith out altogether. We don't want any of those Bisbee folks to know he had anything to do with it.

When Sample came back he asked Kelly where was Dan. Kelly said he didn't know, but he thought he was gone back on the Gila. He said: "The g__ d___ fool; he thinks we cannot do business without him. We can very well get along without him. We are enough without Dan Dowd, and we can get the money all the same." Afterwards, Dowd came back and said he had been about forty-five miles up the country. I think that was on the 2d of December. In one of the conversations Dan told the boys, "We can get there, and get the money, and stay right there and smoke a cigar and play a game of billiards before we leave." And Red said: "When I get the money, if you think I will stay there and play a game of billiards you are badly mistaken." Dowd told me, December 2d, that he was going down to the country to rob a store. Red told me that Johnny Heith and Tex were at Bisbee, waiting for them, until the 8th, and they could not leave my place until then. It was at that time that they were going to Bisbee to rob the store, and the morning they left me, the 5th of December, they all told me they were going to camp near Bisbee. Red Sample, Kelly, and Dan Dowd stopped with me from the 28th of November to the 5th of December. I was at Frank Buckles' place the night some men came there; I heard their voices, but did not understand what they said. Frank Buckles went out to meet them.[33]

For the prosecution, the testimony given by Lubien Pardee was pure gold. By his account, he had been privileged to the most intimate discussions of the men accused of the Bisbee robbery. He had detailed knowledge of the defendants' plans to rob Castaneda's store in Bisbee. The outlaws confided in him, telling him how the robbery would be pulled off—"that they would split the crowd; that Dan could go into the store, Red, Tex and himself would stop at the door." He saw the interactions between the members, knew which of the gang was committed and which were hesitant. He knew Dowd had misgivings about the caper, that "Red" Sample was also a bit nervous, but that Delaney and Kelly were fully invested. Pardee also knew of Heath's involvement and Delaney's plan for keeping the saloon-keepers' involvement secret. By Delaney's comment about leaving Heath out, Pardee might have even concluded that the gang planned to double-cross him.

There is no indication that Lubien Pardee was cross-examined by the defense attorneys. His testimony, as presented, was very damaging to their case, but could have easily been called into question. First and foremost, there was no one who could collaborate anything he said—there were no other witnesses who were there who had come forth to verify the accuracy of his statements. What Pardee said transpired—the conversations between the parties and movements made by them—may well have, but there was absolutely no way to substantiate his claims. The prosecution had absolutely no proof that any of the defendants had actually made the statements which Pardee attributed to them. Basically, all the testimony given by Pardee while under oath was hearsay and should have been stricken from the record as hearsay and not given any consideration by the jury.

The testimony of the following witness, H.M. Hodson, only served to further implicate James Howard in the robbery. Hodson stated he was in "Bisbee on the night of the
8th of December," that he was "walking along the street and two parties in front of Castaneda [*sic*] ordered [him] to go in the store" and that, once inside, he had been "ordered
to throw up his hands and stand around in a circle." Hodson stated: "I was searched for
weapons in the store by one of the men at the order of James Howard, whom I recognize,
He had no mask. I saw a party taking money out of the safe; he was masked. He stooped
down once to pick something from the floor and his mask swung out from his face, but
I was not in a position so I could see his face. I heard 'Tex' give orders. At one time one
of the men on the outside came in and asked for more cartridges, 'Tex' said; that's right,
pump out the old shells and put in the new, we'll teach these G_d d____d s___ of b_____
that we are running this town for a few minutes." Hodson concluded, saying, "I saw five
men engaged in the robbery."[34]

Hodson's testimony agreed with that of Richard Rundle in the particulars. Hodson
had also seen the mask of one of the perpetrators fall away from his face, though this
did not help him to identify the man behind the disguise. Only Rundle had gotten a look
at the man's face, whom he identified during his testimony as Daniel "York" Kelly. Hodson's statements were particularly damaging to the defense of "Tex" Howard. He had not
only been able to identify him, due to the fact he had been unmasked, but he also indicated that it was Howard who had taken charge of the situation inside the store, giving
orders and directives to the other bandits. Worse, when the men outside had begun to
run low on ammunition and requested more, Howard had ordered them provided with
cartridges. While this in itself did not indicate Howard condoned the actions of his compatriots in the murdering of innocent by-standers, it did indicate that he was not opposed
to the use of violent means to suppress the population of the town.

"I recognize the quarter of a dollar marked 'M.E.S.,'" stated Sheriff Jerome Ward,
who followed Hodson on the stand as a witness for the prosecution. "It was given to me
by an officer in Deming with some other money; I showed Kelly the money in a bag with
the quarter lying conspicuously on top and he told me it was his money." The coin in
question was then presented to the jury and placed in evidence. His testimony concluded,
Sheriff Ward was dismissed by the judge and stepped down from the witness stand. There
is no record that he was cross-examined by the defense either. And, once again, the defense
team is found lacking. Though the Sheriff stated the marked coin was laid "conspicuously"
on top of the monies that were in the bag, this did not mean it was seen by the defendant.
The defense could have pursued other lines of questioning as well—was Kelly given more
than a cursory look inside the sack? Was he allowed to handle or count the money? Did
he identify that particular coin as belonging to him? The defense could have easily called
into doubt the testimony given by the Sheriff with very little effort, but did not.[35]

The next to be called to the stand on behalf of the prosecution was James McDonner.
Like Rundle and Hodson, McDonner had been passing the store when he was corralled
by the bandits and forced inside. In his statement, McDonner stated, "I met an unmasked
man at the door; he searched me; he said, 'Have you got a gun?' I said, 'No, nor anything
else.'" McDonner was then ordered to raise his hands and join the others who were standing inside in a row. "I recognize the defendant James Howard," said McDonner, "as the
man without the mask; there were two other men in the store that had masks on." McDonner also recalled, upon leaving the store, seeing the body of D.T. Smith, the deputy sheriff,
"lying under a wagon." McDonner, though able to identify Howard, had been unable to

identify the other two robbers. His brief and limited testimony did little to aid the case of the prosecution, nor was it particularly damaging to defense.[36]

J.B. Lockwood, the owner of the stable at which John Hiles was employed, took the stand after McDonner. Lockwood stated, "Mr. Howard put a white or dirty gray horse in my corral on the 30th of November, and it remained there until the 4th of December." Lockwood remembered that Howard had taken the horse out only once during this period and had kept him out about an hour. "That horse is now at Montgomery's stable in this town." Lockwood did state that when James Howard first brought the animal to him he was accompanied by John Heath. This was the extent of his testimony and while it served to further the case against Howard—who was by this point probably appearing quite guilty in the eyes of the jury—and implicated Heath by association—it did not really further incriminate the other four defendants. Again, one wonders why the defendants did not demand separate trials, if only to distance themselves from James "Tex" Howard.

Pat McCann took Lockwood's place on the witness stand after the livery owner was given permission to step down. McCann was sworn in and testified thus: "I was in Bisbee on the night of the robbery; on the night of December 7th, I saw Howard and Kelly in Lynch's saloon; I saw Howard there at different times from the first until this night; I noticed Kelly because he was a stranger; I was not present at the shooting." This was all the statement McCann made while on the stand. Though McCann's testimony did prove that Howard and Kelly were acquainted, it had very little bearing on the case otherwise. He had seen Howard about town prior to the hold-up, as had others, but McCann had not seen the actual robbery nor the shootings take place.[37]

The testimony of the following witness was probably the most damning of all for the defendants. Walter W. Bush, the bartender at George Hill's saloon in Clifton, was the next to take the stand for the prosecution. Bush readily admitted to being acquainted with all five of the defendants, stating "they had been living for some time in Clifton." He further said, "[T]hey were around my place some, and patronized the bar" where he worked, though "Delaney and Dowd had not been there for two months." Bush went on to say, "After the Bisbee murder, Howard and Sample came to Clifton and called for me at the saloon; they were directed to where I was, and came into my room; I was in bed. I asked them where they had been, and they said they had been to Bisbee and had held up the place for its money, and had had some trouble and had probably killed several; they had killed one man they knew of." Bush stated Sample had told him "that this man came down the street in the direction of where they were, and he ordered him to throw up his hands, and he replied that he was a deputy sheriff, and that he would die before he would do it; and he shot him, and he fell instantly near a wagon."

"Tex was sitting right by Sample when he said this," asserted Bush. The timepiece belonging to William Clancy was then presented to Bush. "I recognize this watch or one just like it was in the possession of Sample that night; Tex remarked that Red had beat him out of his portion of that, that he had got the watch out of the safe at Bisbee." Bush continued, saying, "Tex and Red were arrested on the Blue river in Graham county, some 40 or 50 miles from Clifton; I was with the party that arrested them; the watch was then in the possession of Red and he gave it to me himself."

Bush returned to the subject of the bandits' visit, probably in answer to a direct query from the prosecuting attorney: "When they were in my room that night they said they were satisfied they had killed somebody else besides the deputy sheriff; they did not know how many, and asked me what had been done there. I told them from press reports that there had been three men and a woman killed. They said after they left Bissbee [*sic*] they came out about 35 miles to the ranch of a friend of theirs where they got horses that were tied, waiting for them. The two horses they came to Clifton on were reclaimed by Linderman upon his making an affidavit that they were his property."

"Red said that he was the only man who had received a wound in the difficulty and he showed me the bullet holes in the back of his coat, between the shoulders," said Bush. "Red's head had been disabled for sometime. That night he had a white rag wrapped around it." When shown the bullet-creased overcoat by the prosecuting attorney, Bush stated: "I recognize this coat as the one Red had on." Bush ended his testimony before the court stating, "It was early on the morning of December 13th that they came to my place." The Clifton bartender was then allowed to step down. Walter W. Bush would be the final witness to be called on that, the first day of the trial of Dowd, Sample, Howard, Delaney, and Kelly.[38]

Aside from the fact that the majority of Walter Bush's testimony amounted to nothing more than hearsay—there being no collaborating witness who had overheard the conversation that the bartender claimed he had with Sample and Howard, nor even a witness to say the men had come to his place as he asserted—a glaring discrepancy is found between Bush's testimony and that of Richard Rundle. Rundle stated that he had recognized Sample as the man who had hit him with a revolver as he fled through the door and the outlaw's mask became momentarily dislodged. Yet, Bush stated that Sample told him he was the one who had shot Deputy Sheriff Smith. Bush also identified the coat that had been pierced through by a bullet as belonging to Sample. The wound Sample received was supposedly inflicted by James Krigbaum. Though not called to testify at the trial, Krigbaum later stated he had fired on a "large man" in a light coat standing in front of Castaneda's and had caused a wound similar to that described by Bush.

Either Sample was inside aiding in the robbery or he was outside shooting up the town, which means either Rundle's "eyewitness account" was faulty (which calls into question the rest of his testimony) or Walter Bush's recounting of his conversation with the outlaws was. Taking into consideration the evidence of the perforated coat and Sample's wound, as well as Krigbaum's account, it might be deduced that Omer "Red" Sample was one of the two gunmen who were standing in front of Castaneda's firing on the town residents on the night of the robbery. Sample's detailed description of the killing of Deputy Sheriff Smith—as related by Bush—would appear to bear out this conclusion. However, this illation raises two more questions: The first as to the reliability of Richard Rundle's "eyewitness" testimony and, the second, as to which of the other three defendants was in the store with "Tex" Howard?

It is more likely that Sample had been inside the store during the robbery and had been wounded, not by Krigbaum, but during the bandits' escape up Main Street to the horses. Sample may also have been wounded during the running gunfight with Deputy Marshal C.B. Sanders and his posse. It should be remembered that Krigbaum did not testify at the trial. His account of his participation in the efforts to thwart the robbery was recorded by author Harriet Hankin in 1927, some 40 years after the event took place. It is not inconceivable that Krigbaum had exaggerated his role in the affair in order to impress Ms. Hankin and make himself out to be one of the heroes of the story of the Bisbee Massacre (though Krigbaum did tell Hankin that in making his way back to his cabin to retrieve his Winchester, he had tripped over a large mesquite root in the dark and fell fully on his face—a less than heroic admission).[39]

Taking the testimony of all the previous witnesses as a whole, it appears that Howard,

Kelly, and Sample were inside the store perpetuating the robbery, while Dowd—the "big man" mentioned by Deputy Daniels—and William Delaney were outside shooting down the citizenry with their Winchesters. Of course, if Sample was inside the store as Rundle stated under oath, then this portion of the testimony of Walter Bush was perjury. And, if Bush lied about this (or remembered the conversation incorrectly) one must wonder what else in his testimony may have been a fabrication or falsehood. What of his testimony about the pocket watch and the overcoat? Were these inventions as well? And why did the defense attorneys not immediately jump on this inconsistency in the testimony between the two prosecution witnesses?

Not that it particularly mattered who had been inside the store and who had been outside committing the killings. Territorial law being interpreted as it was, if even one of the five defendants was convicted of first degree murder, they would all be convicted of first degree murder, whether they had actually pulled a trigger on another human being or not. While the existing statute did not speak directly to culpability of accessories— what is now termed "the common law felony murder rule" (which makes any participant in the commission of a felony criminally liable for any deaths that occur during or in furtherance of that felony)—the law plainly stated that a killing "which shall be committed in the perpetration or attempt to perpetrate any arson, rape, robbery, or burglary shall be deemed murder of the first degree." Because the law did not make distinctions between those who had actually committed the murders during the hold-up and their accomplices who were only involved in the robbery, if convicted, all of the defendants were facing either the death penalty or life imprisonment.[40]

The court was adjourned after the testimony of Walter Bush, the crowd of spectators cleared the courtroom, the jury "returned in the charge of a sworn officer," and the five defendants were led back downstairs to their cells by the Sheriff and his deputies. Judge Pinney's court was scheduled to reconvene on Monday, February 11, at 9:00 a.m. Meanwhile, the local press was acting the part of the harbinger of doom. The February 10 edition of *The Tombstone Daily Epitaph* ran a complete transcript of the witness testimony, as recorded by the court stenographer on Saturday, under the headline "DOOMED" and followed this with the pronouncements:

> "The Shadow of Death Envelopes the Bisbee Murders.
> NO HOPE FOR THEIR ESCAPE.
> The Evidence Direct, Positive, Overwhelming and Conclusive.
> FOOD FOR THE GALLOWS."[41]

And it may be safely assumed that the trial of the Bisbee banditti was a popular subject of conversation in the saloons, pool halls, and parlors in Tombstone that weekend.

"If such was possible," began *The Daily Epitaph*, "a larger crowd was present in the court room [on Monday] than on the opening days of the trial of the Bisbee bandits; several ladies being among the number." *The Tombstone Republican* further described the scene inside the Tombstone courthouse on February 11, 1884, recording that "[a]t an early hour this morning the courtroom was crowded with anxious spectators from all parts of the county, and when the bailiff announced the court was ready for business every available corner in the building was filled. At a quarter past nine the prisoners, accompanied by the sheriff and a large number of deputies, entered the room, and were conducted to their seats by their counsel. The clerk of the court called the jurors, and all being present, the court proceeded to business."[42]

The first witness to be called by the prosecution was Daniel Inman. He was immediately sworn in and seated. "I was living in Morse's canyon," he said, "in this county, on the 27th of [November] last; I lived about one mile and a half from Pardee's camp. On Tuesday, the 27th of November, Mr. Howard [Tex] and Heith came to my house about 12 o'clock; they said they came from Galeyville, had been lost and wanted something to eat; they said they just came in from Texas; one rode a gray horse and the other a dark one; I gave them something to eat." During the cross-examination, Inman stated he had asked the men if "they had drove the band of cattle that had just come through." They replied, saying "they had not, but that they had just came direct through Texas, and that there were a great many cattle on the road." Inman concluded his testimony, "I know that they were at my house on the 27th of November, because some bills came from Cadwell & Stanford that day and I noted the date on account of those bills."

Henry Smith was the next witness to be called by the prosecution to testify. He stated that he was at Pardee's camp when Dowd, Kelly, and Sample were there "some time last November." He also stated the Howard and Heath visited him at his residence about two miles from Pardee's place. Smith went on to say, "I hunted a horse for Red while they were at Pardee's camp; I have seen that horse since, here in Tombstone; I saw it in a stable on Allen street." Returning to the subject of the defendants, Smith said, "I saw Tex and Heith at my house one or two days before I saw Dowd, Kelly, and Red at Pardee's camp." However, while being interrogated by the defense, Smith admitted he could not remember the exact date he saw the men, saying it "was the 26th or 27th of November, 1883."

"I live about ten miles from Buckles' ranch," Smith asserted. "[I]n going from Pardee's to Buckles' we go up a trail through a canyon. I know the horse by a brand it is branded with—a small 'L'; Red told me the brand on the horse before I went to look for him. I think the brand belongs to Lake. The reason I think it was the 26th or the 27th is because Tex and Heath was at our house on the 24th, and it was two or three days after I found the horse for Dowd, Kelly, and Red." When questioned about the men, Smith said the defendants told him they were going to Tombstone to get some clothes and shoes. "I only saw the three men at Pardee's camp," said Smith. "I did not know any of them before, except Dan Dowd. I have known him for some time; He used to team on the road."[43]

The Daily Epitaph would later say of the witness testimony given before the court that Monday, February 11, "There was nothing of special interest to mark the day until Frank Buckles took the stand." In fact, the testimony of Daniel Inman and Henry Smith had done nothing to further the prosecution's case, except proving that the defendants had been in the territory since late November and were well-acquainted with one another. Unlike Pardee, Inman and Smith had not been privy to the nefarious designs and intentions of the men. They could not substantiate or refute any of Pardee's testimony as was given before the court on the previous Saturday. Smith was able to identify the horse that had been ridden by "Red" Sample but, in the end, this proved nothing, as none of the people who had seen the robbers ride out on the night of the robbery had identified this particular animal. Basically, all the first two witnesses of the day provided was circumstantial evidence.[44]

The testimony of William Gerstenberg, the next witness to take the stand for the prosecution, was more damning. "I was living in Bisbee on the 8th of December, said the witness. "I was out hunting on the morning of that day. About 10 o'clock I saw Dowd about three miles below Bisbee, about one-half mile below the slaughter house. I am sure that I saw Dan Dowd on that morning." When asked to point out the man he saw that morning, Gerstenberg pointed directly at Dowd and said, "That is the man." At the prosecution's urging, Gerstenberg continued with his testimony, saying, "I met Kelly again later, going down the canyon on foot; in the evening when the shooting began, I was in the butcher shop; as they passed by my place, the light from the fruit stand shown plainly on the large man, and I recognized him as the man I saw in the morning. Dan Dowd they call him."

During the cross-examination by the defense counsel, Gerstenberg stated he had never been formally introduced to Dowd. "I say it was Dan Dowd, because it was the man who sits there [pointing at Dowd] and they call him Dan Dowd." In response to a new line of questioning, the witness answered, "I am not sure whether I said anything to Mr. Daniels about this man or not; Mr. Robinson [the Deputy District Attorney] asked me something about it in the city hall when I was called here on examination; I told Daniels that I had seen men and a camp down the canyon in the morning." At this point, the defense must have redirected the witness, as he stated, "I saw a large man standing in front of Castaneda's store loading and firing a rifle; this man is the one who ran past me. The horses were standing right across the street. I looked this man Dowd right in the face just before he shot at me. He shot right over my head and put out the light in the butcher shop; he stood within twenty feet of me when he fired at me." When asked about "York" Kelly, Gerstenberg stated that he had seen "Kelly on horseback about five o'clock that evening and met him about one-half hour afterwards on foot." William Gerstenberg concluded his testimony, saying, "I know nearly everyone in Bisbee, and I naturally noticed these strange men closely."[45]

Gerstenberg did for the prosecution what no previous witness had done—he placed one of the defendants, specifically Dan Dowd, in front of Castaneda's store on the night of the robbery shooting at citizens. Unlike Richard Rundle, who had only caught a moment's glimpse of Kelly and Sample during the robbery when their masks failed, Gerstenberg had seen Dowd's full countenance, and he had seen it twice. The implication was because he had seen him earlier that morning under circumstances that allowed him to get a long and good look at the man, Gerstenberg and been more easily able to identify him that evening, even under duress. This fact alone, made his testimony invaluable to the prosecution.

The details concerning Gerstenberg's identification of Kelly are more problematic. He stated he had seen Kelly on horseback about 5 o'clock in the afternoon on December 8. He does not elaborate on this statement or say anything about the circumstances surrounding his meeting the defendant. Next, Gerstenberg states he saw Kelly afoot about a half-hour later. Again, he neglects to provide any further detail. The time frame he provides would have been about an hour and a half prior to the commencement of the robbery. This seems to indicate that Kelly had been in town at least two hours prior to the crime being committed. This statement also contradicts his earlier statement in which he says he saw the defendant "in the evening when the shooting began." Was Gerstenberg mistaken in his estimation of the time or was Kelly wandering about the town for at least two hours prior to the robbery?

Popular accounts of the robbery have the five bandits riding into town as the sun was sinking in the west, travelling up to the stable, dismounting their horses, and then heading back up the street, *as a group*, to Castaneda's store. But, according to Deputy Daniel's testimony, Delaney had stopped in his saloon prior to the robbery to warm himself near the stove. Perhaps, Kelly too had arrived in town beforehand in order to do some reconnaissance. If Gerstenberg was not mistaken in his estimation of the time of day, it means that Kelly had been in town at least two hours prior to the robbery. If so, did he then mount up again and ride out to meet up with the others or did he remain in town and wait for them to arrive? And what of Delaney? Had he been in town prior to his being seen in Daniel's saloon? Had he come in with Kelly to reconnoiter the town as well? Unfortunately, due to the lack of documentation, an accurate accounting of the movements of the bandits in those few hours just prior to the robbery may never be known.

The testimony of William Gerstenberg also calls into question a statement made in *The Tombstone Republican* after the capture of Dan Dowd. According to the newspaper, during the robbery, Dowd had gone into the backroom at Goldwater and Castaneda's and fleeced Jose Castaneda as he "was lying sick in bed." Supposedly, Dowd had secured almost $2000 in gold coin from beneath Castaneda's pillow and had kept it for himself. Joe Goldwater confirmed that one of the robbers had gone in to Castaneda's room, but could not identify the man as he was masked. It is positively known that James "Tex" Howard was one of the robbers inside the store. Richard Rundle (if his testimony is to be credited) identified Sample and Kelly as the other two robbers in the store. This suggests it was Delaney and Dowd who remained outside, standing guard while the robbery was taking place. Gerstenberg then positively identified Dowd as one of the two men who were standing outside shooting up the town.

If Dan Dowd was outside, as Gerstenberg asserts, how could he have possibly fleeced Castaneda? And, if as seems most likely, it was not Dowd who molested the storeowner, which of the robbers was it who ventured into Castaneda's backroom and relieved him of his monies? And where did the story in *The Republican* come from? The newspaper stated that the story they ran was derived from "evidence adduced in the preliminary examination[s]" of Howard, Sample and Kelly. It seems the monies found on the three bandits were not as much as what had later been found on Dowd when he was arrested. This could have led to the summation that it was Dowd who had taken Castaneda's bag of coins. However, if as the combined testimony of Richard Rundle and William Gerstenberg indicates—that Dan Dowd had not been in the store at any point during the robbery—how would he have robbed Don Castaneda and obtained this supposed surplus of money? Again, the historical record is lacking and we are left with another minor mystery.[46]

The defense attorneys missed a grand opportunity to discredit at least one of the prosecution's witnesses. Richard Rundle had stated he saw Howard, Kelly, and Sample inside the store. Walter Bush stated that Sample told him he was one of the men who had been standing outside and had personally shot Deputy Sheriff Smith. Bush also said Sample had told him he had been wounded during the melee, though he did not provide details. Gerstenberg, in his testimony, placed Dan Dowd in front of the store. If Rundle and Gerstenberg, the eyewitnesses, are to be believed, Howard, Kelly, and Sample were inside and Dowd was outside. Only Delaney remains unaccounted for. If Walter Bush is to be believed, and Sample was outside, it follows that Delaney would have to have been inside. The problem is, if Sample was outside, then Rundle was mistaken in his identification of the man, which calls the remainder of his testimony in to question. On the other hand, if Sample, as Rundle asserted, was inside, Walter Bush's testimony must have been wrong in his recollections, and his testimony must be questioned.

At this point in the proceedings, the prosecution re-called Sheriff Jerome Ward to the stand to answer questions about the coat, which was said to belong to "Red" Sample and which had been entered into evidence, along with his hat. Still under oath from his previous appearance before the court, Sheriff Ward stated, "That coat was delivered to me by Messrs. Hill, Bush, and Hoovey [sic]; it was brought here by Messrs. Hoovey [sic] and Bush; it was brought from where Red was captured in Clifton." As to the hat that was presented to him, the Sheriff said, "That hat, I should say, is the hat that I found with Mr. Kelly; I had it in Deming." During cross-examination, the Sheriff stated that he had taken the hat from Mr. Kelly at the time he was first incarcerated in Tombstone. "I then turned it over to District Attorney Smith; from the time of Kelly's arrest to the time of the examination, the hat was in the charge of the jailer, under lock and key." In answer to a query from the defense, Sheriff Ward replied, "I don't know whether Mr. Kelly had another hat or not." This concluded the County Sheriff's testimony before the court and he was subsequently excused.

Deputy Sheriff Robert "Bob" Hatch followed Sheriff Ward on the stand. The Deputy stated for the record that he was in the company of Deputy Sheriff Daniels when he arrested Delaney in Sonora, Mexico. "[W]hen he was arrested, he said his name was not Delaney; I asked him if he would know his picture if he saw it; I showed him a photograph and he said it was his picture and asked me where the hell I got it; I told him never to mind that—I got it. I asked him if he had been to Buckle's ranch; at first he said he had not, afterwards [Delaney] said he had been there and that he and Dowd went directly from Buckles' ranch to Mexico; said he had never been in Bisbee." At this point the prosecution retired and the defense attorney began to question the Deputy. To the defense attorney's queries, Deputy Hatch replied, "I am one of the officers that arrested Delaney; when I arrested him he said, 'I expect you want me for the Clifton business; I had some trouble in Clifton and had to kill a man there.' I said, 'I will let you know later what I want you for.'"[47]

The Sheriff's testimony served to establish the chain of custody for Sample's perforated coat and Kelly's hat, presumably the same hat Kelly had procured at Buckles' ranch after the robbery. On the stand, Walter Bush stated that when Sample and Howard came to visit him, Sample had on a bandage. According to Bush, Sample stated he had been wounded and had showed Bush the bullet holes in his coat. Still this amounted to little more than circumstantial evidence, especially since there was no one who could say for certain that they had wounded the outlaw during the heist. Bush testified that Sample said he "received a wound in the difficulty," but was not anymore specific than this. As previously noted, Sample may well have received the wound during the firefight with Deputy Marshal Sanders and his posse. Kelly's hat was equally suspect. It proved he was at Buckles' ranch the night of the robbery, but nothing more.

Deputy Sheriff Hatch's testimony was almost as pointless. All it proved conclusively was that Delaney was a liar. He lied to the officer about who he was and about visiting Buckles' ranch. Delaney maintained that he had never been to Bisbee and, aside from Deputy Daniels' identification of him as the man who had come in to his saloon just prior to the robbery, there was no evidence presented to prove he had been. Certainly, Delaney had been seen in the company of the other defendants and, if Pardee's testimony was to be believed, was heard discussing plans for the robbery with the others, but this only amounted to guilt by association at best. There was no one who could definitively place him in Bisbee at the time of the robbery. Conversely, when he was arrested by Deputies Daniels and Hatch in Minas Prietas, Delaney had thought it was for the killing of a man

their involvement in the affair. They revealed to him that they had netted about $1,200 from the heist and had killed "two persons, if not four." Buckles was able to positively identify the hat he said he had given to Kelly that evening and thought he recognized the canvas coat which "Red" Sample had been wearing. He also reported that Sample had threatened his life, presumably on the morning after the robbery (though the witness was not clear on this point), if he spoke to the sheriff's posse of their whereabouts.

Still, the entirety of Frank Buckles' testimony amounted to nothing more than hearsay. There were no witnesses to collaborate anything which he said occurred or to any of the conversations he claimed he had had with the defendants. Walter Myers had testified that he had heard "some men ride up to Buckles ranch" the morning after the robbery and stated he had heard one of the men say they had "raised hell" and heard another demand a hat from the owner, but had not been able to hear any more of the exchange between Buckles and the riders and had not been able to positively identify the men. The evidence of the hat would indicate that "York" Kelly had been among the riders who stopped over at Buckles on the morning of the 9th of December, but conclusively proved little more than this.

After the trial, *The Daily Epitaph* would say of William Delaney, "in his connection with the Bisbee murders and since, proved himself the shrewdest ruffian of them all." The truth of the matter is, except for his continued acquaintance with the other four defendants prior to the robbery, there had been nothing in the testimony given or evidence found that proved beyond a reasonable doubt that Delaney was involved in the heist. Buckles had stated that Delaney had rode out of his place with Dowd and Sample the day before the robbery and Deputy Daniels had identified Delaney as the man who had visited his saloon just prior to the robbery, but no one had been able to place him either inside the store or on the porch outside at the time of the robbery. Buckles had also stated that Delaney had not been among the men who visited his house the morning after the robbery.[49]

In fact, no one had been able to positively identify his horse, or any specific item of clothing he was wearing, nor were any of the monies or artifacts from the robbery found about his person when he was arrested. Delaney had lied to Deputy Hatch at the time of his arrest, identifying himself as another, and stating he had never been to Buckles' ranch or to Bisbee. His photograph had been obtained by Deputy Hatch from some unknown source (possibly Buckles, Pardee, or one of his co-defendants—this remains a mystery), but this proved nothing more than an acquaintance with the person who had formerly been in possession of it. Delaney later claimed he lied as he believed the deputies were from Clifton and had come to arrest him in connection with the killing of a man in that locale. William Delaney maintained throughout his questioning and throughout the trial—even though his assertion was in direct disagreement with the testimony given by Daniels—that he had never been to the town of Bisbee.

J. Wesley "Wes" Howell, a foreman for the Copper Queen Mine, was the next to be called to the stand by the prosecution. After being sworn in, Howell was questioned about the shooting of Deputy Smith. "I was in Bisbee on the evening of December 8th," he said. "[I] was at the post office at the time the shooting occurred; I was about 110 feet from Castaneda's store; two men stood at the door of the store, one was a large man, the other a small one; I saw the large man shooting at D.T. Smith; [I] heard Mr. Smith say, 'Oh, my God.' And saw him fall; he fell under a wagon; I saw him after the shooting; he was dead; a bullet hole through the head. I saw his dead body the next morning."

Howell's testimony, given during the cross-examination did not vary much from his initial statements to the prosecution. The mine foreman stated, "There was but two men at the door; the large man fired up the street [and] the small man fired down the street, toward the Queen smelter; the large man must have killed Smith, and the small man killed Johnny Tappenier. I ran to my cabin to get a gun." Howell continued, saying, "[W]hen the first shot was fired, I stepped to the door of the post office; the small man was firing down the street; Mr. Smith came out of a house across the street, and the large man turned his gun toward him and began firing; I heard Smith cry, 'Oh, my God,' and saw him fall; I saw horses tied up near the lumber yard as I went up to my cabin to get my gun; [I] saw no one else doing any shooting except the two men that stood at the door of the store."[50]

This concluded Mr. Howell's testimony. In essence, Howell had witnessed the murder of Deputy Sheriff Smith, but was unable to identify the killer except to say that he was a large man. He said he believed the small man had killed Mr. Tappenier, but he had not actually seen the murder take place. His conjecture was based solely

J. Wesley "Wes" Howell, foreman, Copper Queen Mine, testified to having seen the murder of Deputy Sheriff D.T. Smith on the evening of the robbery, though he was unable to identify the killers (courtesy the Bisbee Mine Museum).

on the directions in which the two men in front of the mercantile had been shooting when he saw Deputy Smith felled. As he stated, after seeing the shooting, he had proceeded to his cabin to retrieve his gun and, though he had seen what he assumed were the bandits' horses tied up at the stable, he had not seen the men escape or anything else of consequence relating to the robbery.

After Howell's testimony was completed the prosecution rested their case and Judge Pinney called for a recess until 1:00 p.m. The Minutes for the Distinct Court on February 11, 1884, state, "At the coming in of the Court after the recess, the above entitled cause was resumed and W.W. Bush was re-called for the prosecution." However, *The Tombstone Republican* reported that, before the recess, Sheriff Ward had been re-called by the prosecution. The Sheriff simply confirmed that D.T. Smith was a law officer and in his employment at the time of the robbery, saying, "I had sent a copy of the appointment of D.T. Smith as a deputy sheriff to him at Bisbee a few days before the shooting occurred." The sheriff was not cross-examined. *The Tombstone Daily Epitaph* reported that it was only after the testimony of Sheriff Ward that the court recessed for lunch. Why the official minutes did not include these particulars of the trial is not known.[51]

As noted, after the recess, the court reconvened and bartender Walter W. Bush was recalled by the prosecution. Having previously been sworn, W.W. Bush resumed the witness stand for a re-direct from the prosecution. Unfortunately, the only extant copy of his testimony, as published in *The Tombstone Daily Epitaph*, is incomplete. What portion of the testimony that does exist reads thus: "Re-direct—At the time Tex and Red spoke to me in Clifton concerning the Bisbee matter, Tex said that he had been in Bisbee two or three times prior to the robbery, and on the night of the robbery was in the store unmasked. At the time of his arrest, Red gave me." At this point, the article becomes illegible for several lines. The column resumes just below, reading, "jury to the fact that a reward aggregating $8,500 in all had been offered for the defendants."[52]

With the testimony of W.W. Bush, the prosecution again rested its case against the defendants. Though the majority of the evidence presented had been circumstantial and based on hearsay, the prosecution had presented eyewitnesses who were able to place four of the five defendants at the scene of the crime. James "Tex" Howard, who had neglected to wear a mask during the robbery, was identified by numerous witnesses including Joe Goldwater, H.M. Hodson and Richard Rundle. Richard Rundle also claimed to have recognized both Daniel "York" Kelly and Omer W. "Red" Sample as being among the three men inside the store during the hold-up when their masks slipped away from their faces as they went about their business. William Gerstenberg claimed to have recognized "Big" Dan Dowd as he fled from the store after the robbery. Gerstenberg also claimed to have recognized Kelly, though he was somewhat vague in describing the circumstances surrounding his identification of the defendant.

Overall, between the eyewitness accounts and the testimony given by Walter Bush, Frank Buckles and Lubien Pardee, prosecuting attorney Marcus Smith had presented a compelling argument on behalf of the territory for the conviction of the five defendants. Of course, public opinion, as evidenced by the articles appearing in the various newspapers throughout the territory, was strongly set against the accused.

This is probably the reason the attorneys for the defense, James B. Southard, Col. Stanford, T.J. Drum, F.V. Price, and Col. William Herring had been so reluctant to take the case. They must have realized from the beginning that their chances of obtaining a verdict of "not guilty" for their clients as slim at best. It could be argued that their cross-examination of the prosecution witnesses had been seriously lacking as though they had already conceded to what must have seemed inevitable.

Where the case for the prosecution had taken two days to present, the case for the defense would take less than three hours on the afternoon of February 11, 1884. The first witness called to the stand was Deputy William Daniels, who had also been the first to be called on by the prosecution. During the re-cross, Daniels stated that he and Deputy Sheriff Hatch had gone together to Minas Prietas in pursuit of William Delaney. "We had a conversation after getting there with him," stated Daniels. "[I] don't remember all the conversation. There was considerable said. When Hatch and I first went to see him he had his hands tied. He was drunk, but got up to his feet and said; 'You are Americans; get me out of here.' He said that he had come to Minas Prietas from Oposura with a captain in the Mexican army."

Deputy Daniels went on with the interview, saying, "[We] asked him when he left

Buckles' ranch. He answered he knew no such place. [We] asked him who he went to Sonora with. He answered, alone. [We] told him that Dan Dowd said he and Delaney had travelled into Sonora together. He said Dowd lied. Showed him a photograph of himself, and told him I had secured it at Silver City. Finally, [we] notified him that he was under arrest for the Bisbee murders." This seems to have been the extent of Daniels' testimony or, at least, this was all that was reported by *The Tombstone Daily Epitaph* in their coverage of the defense's case. The newspaper did not record if the witness had anything more to say or if he was cross-examined by the prosecution before he was allowed to step down.[53]

At this point in the trial, defense attorney Thomas J. Drum, who had formerly represented the Earp brothers and John Holliday when they were indicted for murder after the infamous gunfight at the O.K. Corral, presented the court with the affidavits of O.W. Sample, Daniel Kelly and James Howard, asking they be read and entered as evidence in the case. According to the affidavits, "John Myers and James Ardison, two very material witnesses for the defense, were in the Black Range, New Mexico, prospecting, and without their testimony the defendants could not get a fair trial, as by them they could prove that on the night of the 8th of December they and the defendants camped six miles southwest of Bowie, and 60 miles from Bisbee, where the murders and the robbery were committed. Defendant Sample further states that he can prove by Deputy Sheriff" (here again there is a flaw in the original microfilm which makes the passage illegible for several lines) "prove by said witnesses that on the night of 8th he was with him at a place called railroad station." The newspaper continued on to say that the prosecution "admitted if the witnesses were present they would testify as the defendants stated."

The next to take the stand for the defense was William E. Delaney, who was sworn in as a matter of course and testified as follows: "Prior to the 8th of December [I] was stopping at Buckles' ranch; had been working there for several weeks; had made efforts to get work as an engineer without success. When I left Buckles' ranch to go to Sonora, I left in the interest of Buckles to hunt for lost horses. If Dowd and I found the horses he was to pay us for our trouble. Had known Dowd but a few months before meeting him at Buckles; first knew him in Clifton; [I] never made any arrangement with anyone; [I] never knew of any arrangement at any time between any parties to go to Bisbee and rob a store. I was never in Bisbee in my life; I told the officer so when he arrested me in Minas Prietas."

Delaney continued in his testimony giving the following account of his movements: "I left Buckles' ranch on the 5th of December with Dowd for the state of Sonora; went on horseback; that is Buckles' old ranch; left Buckles' new ranch on the morning of the 6th, camped the night at Silver Creek, next night camped at San Bernardino. On the night of the 8th of December camped near the foothills of the Sierra Madres; camped on the 9th near Bavispe; next day went into Bavispe. [I] told Kelly at Buckles' ranch that I was going to Bavispe, and not Bisbee; never made any division of plunder with anyone, nor anyone with me; [I] went to Sonora to look for work."

At this point, the defense left off with their questioning of the defendant Delaney and the prosecuting attorney began his cross-examination. Unfortunately, the record here is incomplete as well. Delaney states, "Came to Buckles ranch from Clifton; [I] left Clifton because" (here the document becomes illegible and resumes several lines below as follows) "rode a horse I got from Dan Dowd and I went alone from Buckles' old ranch to his new ranch; had $5 when I got to Bavispe; had been at Bavispe but once before. The last time

I was at Buckles' ranch was on the evening of the 5th of December; never saw Tex, Red, or Kelly after that time; [I] was not there on December 7th as testified to by Frank Buckles."[54]

Delaney's alibi might well have been sufficient to raise a reasonable doubt in the collective mind of the jury, had he and the man he claimed to have been travelling with, Dan Dowd, not been seen in Bisbee on the day of the robbery. Frank Buckles' testimony was easy enough to dismiss as it was hearsay—basically, it was his word against Delaney's. The testimony of William Gerstenberg and Deputy Daniels was a different manner. Gerstenberg stated he had seen Dowd twice in Bisbee on the 8th of December, once in the morning, while he was out hunting, and again in the evening, as the bandits were fleeing the store towards their horses. Daniels had stated he saw Delaney himself in his saloon just minutes before the robbery occurred. It might have been possible for the jury to believe a case of mistaken identity in one of the two witnesses' statements, but not both. Additionally, the fact he had lied to Deputies Daniels and Hatch when they caught up to him in Mina Prietas likely made his testimony seem all the more suspect in the eyes of the jury.

Daniel Dowd, who followed Delaney on the stand for the defense, told almost the same story. After being sworn, Dowd stated, "On the morning of December 5th, [I] was at Pardee's ranch; had been there eight or nine days. On the evening of the 5th was at Buckles' ranch; pulled out the same night with Delaney. On the night of the 6th, we camped about five miles from Silver Creek; on the night of the 7th we camped fifteen miles below San Bernardino creek; on the 8th we camped in the Sierra Madres. The last time I was in Bisbee was about a year ago. When I started for Sonora I intended going to Bavispe; [I] drove a lumber team into Bisbee from the Chiricahuas when last there; [I] heard Buckles' testimony; I never told him or anyone else I was going to Bisbee to rob a store. Delaney and I were together from the 5th of December until about the 20th. We separated at Bavispe, he going away with a Mexican officer. I arrived at Cerralitos, Chiricahua seventy five miles from Bavispe; when arrested I had $51 and some small change."

Under cross-examination by the defense, Dowd did not waiver, but elaborated on the details of his story. "Don't know that I told Buckles or Pardee I was going to Bavispe, said I was going to Sonora. Delaney and I separated because the Mexican officer said he could get me work as an engineer by going with him. Delaney said I could not get work and we split." When asked again about the money he had on his person, Dowd stated, "Got the money I had at Clifton, most of it. [I] last worked in Globe four or five months ago; worked for Ludly driving team. It was May or June. Didn't get the fifty-one dollars there. The reason Delaney and I left Buckles' old ranch was because the feed was all eaten off there and there was none on the new ranch. Tex, Kelly, and Red struck out about the same time we did for the Swisshelms. [I] don't know the name of the ranch on Silver Creek where we camped; Silver Creek is due east. Have been there about five times. An American lives at the ranch where I stopped. It is about 35 miles from Buckles' ranch to Silver Creek. [I] am not certain of day of the month or day of the week I left Buckles' ranch."[55]

Why Dowd and Delaney and their counsel were so concerned with discrediting the testimony of Frank Buckles when there were two eyewitnesses whose statements were more damaging to their case is unknown. As noted previously, the testimony of Frank Buckles was little more than hearsay and had not been substantiated by any other witness. Again, it seems that the defense attorneys were not being as diligent as they could have been on behalf of their clients. The fact that Dowd and Delaney had not been in possession of large amounts of monies when they were arrested, made their story a little more plausible but, in Dowd's case, the testimony that most needed to be impugned and refuted was that of William Gerstenberg. The jury needed to be made to believe that the man whom Gerstenberg saw in Bisbee the morning of the robbery, while he was out hunting and the man who fired a shot at him in the butcher shop later in the evening were not one and the same man and were not Daniel Dowd.

The witnesses following Dan Dowd on the stand spoke almost exclusively to the character of the defendants in the case. Though the extant record of his testimony is incomplete, rancher J.D. Gilbert spoke favorably of Dowd, saying, "[I] am a rancher. Have lived in Cochise county about 4 years. Know Dan Dowd. [I] have known him three years. Met him first in Tombstone. He worked for me at times. First time about four" (here the document become illegible for several lines. It resumes legibility, in the midst of the cross-examination, thus) "from Tombstone. The last time I saw Dowd at work was about a year [I] have heard he worked since that time in Globe. The men whom I have heard speak of Dowd's reputation were teamsters. [I] heard Humphery speak of it. Never heard Dowd was a quarrelsome man. Heard Mr. Stout say he was quiet, peaceable man."

The defense attorney, obviously wanting to drive home the point that Dowd was not generally perceived as the type of man who was prone to criminality and murderous rampage, redirected the witness, who answered his query, stating, "Never heard any of the neighbors say anything against [Dowd]." The prosecution also felt a need for clarity on some point of Mr. Gilbert's testimony, for there was a second redirect. Judging by the answer, one might surmise that the question put to the witness concerned whether Dowd had been a law-abiding man or, at least, given to habits which reflected a certain morality and respect for the law. The witness answered the prosecutions question, stating, "[I] never heard any Tombstone people speak of his reputation for peace and good order." This ended Mr. J.D. Gilbert's testimony.[56]

The next to take the stand on Dowd's behalf was George Fridman, who was sworn and testified, "[I] am merchant and reside in Tombstone. Know Dan Dowd. [I] have known him between two and three years. First knew him as a teamster between Tombstone and the Chiricahuas, He was often in my store, as were the other teamsters, we doing a good deal of business with them. Have not seen Dowd for about 18 months." At this point, the witness, by his admissions, became less than helpful to the defense's case as Fridman stated for the record, "Don't know anything about his character. [I] never heard a word said against the man in my life, that is, not until the Bisbee matter." During the cross-examination, the prosecution played up the fact the witness was only acquainted with Dowd in the most superficial of terms. "[I] have heard nothing of [Dowd] for about two years," Fridman said. "There was no difference in his coming into, or being about my store, than in lots of other men." Mr. Fridman concluded with his impressions of Dowd, saying, "He always seemed very quiet."[57]

The defense team then called F.E. Davenport to the stand, where he was sworn and seated. Davenport was to provide a rebuttal to the testimony of Sheriff Ward on behalf of Daniel Kelly and Omer Sample. In answer to the questions put to him by the defense attorney, Davenport stated, "I live in Lordsburg. I am an official of the S.P.R.R.; have lived there about five months; know Kelly: [I] saw him at Deming on December 11th; he had on a black hat; [I] also saw Mr. Ward. Mr. Gilpin turned him over to Mr. Ward" (here the document becomes illegible again). The testimony of the witness resumes several lines below, with Davenport saying that Sample had "nothing on him but some Mexican silver and a pocket knife." Under cross-examination, Davenport replied to the prosecution inquiries thus: "Red had been in [the] charge of Bush fully five minutes when I made the search." This ended the witness' testimony and the case for the defense.[58]

"This closed the testimony in the case," wrote the reporter for *The Daily Epitaph*, "and Judge Southland notified the court that the defense under the circumstances were willing to submit the case without argument. To which the prosecution agreed." Judge Pinney then gave the jury a "very elaborate charge" which is recorded here in its entirety:

> Gentlemen of the jury, the court instructs you, that murder in the unlawful killing of a human being, with malice aforethought either express or implied. The unlawful killing may be affected by any of the various means by which death may be occasioned.
>
> Express malice is that deliberate intention unlawfully to take away the life of a fellow creature which is manifested by external circumstances capable of proof.
>
> Malice may be implied when no considerable provocation appears, or when all the circumstances of the killing show an abandoned and malignant heart. All murder which shall be perpetrated by means of poison or lying in wait, torture, or by any other kind of willful, deliberate and premeditated killing, or which shall be committed in the perpetration *or* attempt to perpetrate any arson, rape, robbery, or burglary (emphasis Judge Pinney's) shall be deemed murder in the first degree. And all other kinds of murder shall be deemed murder in the second degree.
>
> The jury are instructed that if the killing of the person mentioned in the indictment is satisfactorily shown by the evidence, beyond all reasonable doubt, to have been the act of the defendants or either of them, then the law pronounces such killing murder, unless it appears from the evidence that circumstances existed excusing or justifying the act.
>
> The court instructs the jury that when an unlawful unintentional killing of a human being happens in the commission of an unlawful act, which in its consequences tends to destroy the life of a human being, the offence will be murder.
>
> If the jury believe from the evidence beyond a reasonable doubt that at the time of the alleged killing the defendants had entered the store of the witness Goldwater and Castaneda for the common purpose of stealing and carrying away any article of personal property therein, and in the prosecution [sic] of that purpose or in their efforts to escape with such property the defendants, either of them, shot and killed the deceased, as charged in the indictment, then such killing would be murder and it would be wholly immaterial whether such killing was intentional or not.
>
> If you believe, from the evidence beyond a reasonable doubt, that the defendants [sic] or either of them, at the time of the alleged killing, made an attack upon the witness Goldwater or other parties in the store or on the street in front of the store for the purpose or with the intent of feloniously taking from Goldwater or other parties, by force and against his or their will, his money, watch, or other article of personal property, and in the prosecution [sic] of that purpose either one of the defendants shot and killed the deceased, as charged in the indictment, then such killing would be murder, not only on the part of the one who fired the fatal shot, but also on the part of one or more of the defendants, who were present aiding or assisting in the original attempt to take property of Goldwater or other parties, by force, or against his or their will. If the jury find from the evidence, beyond a reasonable doubt, that either of the other defendants was so present, aiding, or abetting. And in such case it would be immaterial whether the shot was fired with the intention of taking the life of the deceased or only disabling him.
>
> The court instructs the jury that before a conviction can be rightfully claimed by the people in this case, the truth of every material (*illegible*) contained in the indictment, must be proved to the satisfaction of the jury beyond a reasonable doubt. That as a matter of law, the defendants are presumed to be innocent of the crime charged until such time as the guilt of the parties is proved as alleged by competent evidence and beyond a reasonable doubt.
>
> That in order to fairly determine whether the defendants are proved guilty of the crime as charged in the indictment, beyond a reasonable doubt, as the law requires, the jury should take into consideration all the evidence and circumstances as proof in the case, and after a full and dispassionate consideration of all the evidence before you, you still entertain any reasonable doubt as to whether the defendants or either of them committed or aided and abetted (as already defined to you) in the commission of of [sic] the crime as charged in the indictment, then you should acquit the person or persons as to whose guilt you entertain such reasonable doubt.

The court instructs the jury that circumstantial evidence is legal and competent and, if it is of such a character as to exclude every reasonable hypothesis, other than the defendants are guilty, it is entitled to the same weight as (*illegible*)-proof. That what is meant by circumstantial evidence in criminal cases is the proof of such facts and circumstances connected with or surrounding the commission of the crime charged tends to show the guilt of the parties charged, and if these facts and circumstances are sufficient to satisfy the jury of the guilt of the defendants, or either of them, beyond a reasonable doubt, then such evidence is sufficient to authorize the jury in finding a verdict of guilty as to such defendants as the jury (*illegible*) so satisfy beyond a reasonable doubt, from the evidence are guilty.

The court instructs the jury that a reasonable doubt within the meaning of the law is such a doubt as would cause a reasonable, prudent, and considerate man, in the graven and more important affairs of life, to pause and hesitate before acting upon the truth of the matter charged or alleged. If after a careful and impartial consideration of all the evidence and circumstances in proof in the case, you can say and feel that you have an abiding conviction of the guilt of the defendants or either of them, and are fully satisfied of the truth of the charge, then you are satisfied beyond a reasonable doubt.

The jury are instructed that when evidence is given tending to show admissions made by the defendants in a criminal case, the whole of the admission must be taken together as well that part which makes for the accused as that which makes against him. The whole statement must be considered by the jury, but the jury are [*sic*] not obliged to believe or disbelieve all of such statement, they may disagree such parts of it, if any, as are inconsistent with the other testimony, or which the jury believe from the facts and circumstances proven on the trial are untrue.

If the jury believe from the evidence that one or more of the defendants made the confessions as alleged, and attempted to be proved in this case the jury should treat and consider such confessions precisely as they would any other testimony, and hence if the jury believe the whole confession to be true they should act upon the whole as true. The jury are [*sic*] at liberty to judge of it like other evidence in view of all the circumstances of the case as disclosed by the evidence.

The court instructs the jury that generally the confessions of a prisoner out of the court are of a doubtful species of evidence and to be received with caution, and the credit and weight given to them depend very much upon what the confessions are, if the crime itself, as charged is proven by other testimony, and it is also proven the defendants, or persons making the confession was so situated that he had an opportunity to commit the crime, and his or their confessions are consistent with such proof, and corroborative of it, and the witness or witnesses who swear to the confession is apparently truthful, honest, and intelligent, then such confessions so made may be entitled to great weight with the jury.

The defense of an alibi that is—that the defendant was at another place at the time of the commission of the crime is a proper defense in this case and the court instructs the jury that such a defense is proper and is legitimate, if proved as any other defense (illegible) all the (illegible) bearing upon that point should be carefully considered by the jury, and in view of all the evidence, the jury have any other reasonable doubt as to whether the defendant or either of them were in some other place when the crime was committed, they should give such defendants or defendant the benefit of the doubt and find them or him not guilty.

The court instructs the jury that the law makes the defendants in this case competent witnesses. Still the jury are the judges of the weight which ought to be attached to their testimony and in considering what weights hold be given it the jury should take into consideration all the facts and circumstances surrounding the case, as disclosed by the evidence and give the defendant's testimony such weight as they believe it entitled to in view of all the facts and circumstances proves in the trial. The jury are further instructed that the fact that one or more of the defendants have not testified in this case must not be construed by the jury as raising any presumption against them.

The court instructs the jury that evidence of previous good character is competent evidence in favor of a party accused as tending to show that he would not be likely to commit the crime alleged against him. Still, if the jury believe from the evidence, beyond a reasonable doubt, that the defendant Dowd committed the crime as charged in the indictment or that he aided in such crime as defined by the instructions of the court, then it will be your sworn duty as jurors to find the defendant guilty, even though the evidence may satisfy your minds that the defendant previous to the commission of the crime, had sustained a good reputation and character (*illegible*) and quietness."[59]

A portion of this charge was derived from a motion submitted by the prosecution to the judge asking for the inclusion of certain points for consideration by the jury during deliberations. The motion was included in the official record of the trial and is included below for the edification of the reader:

Territory of Ariz.
vs.
Daniel Dowd
Wm. Delaney
Daniel Kelly
James Howard
O.W. Sample
Instructions asked by Prosecution
1.

If the Jury believe from the evidence that the defendants, in this county and before the finding of this indictment were associated together for the purpose of, & were engaged in, the robbery of the store of A. A, Castaneda & Co., or in the robbery of any one in the town of Bisbee; and that while so engaged. And in furtherance of a common purpose between them, to there 9 (and) then commit such robbery; D.J. Smith was slain by any one of the defendants, then under the law, the act of one associate is the act of each of the others; and each one of the defendants is just as accountable, as though his own hand had intentionally fired the fatal shot; and each of the defendants so engaged, and associated together is guilty of murder in the First degree. (49 Cal 562).
2.

And you are further instructed that it is no defense to a party associated with others in, and engaged in, a robbery; that he did not propose or intend to take life in its perpetration, or that he forbade his associates to kill, or that he dispproved [sic] or regretted that any person was thus slain by his associates. If the homicide in question was committed in furtherance of a common purpose to rob, each associate is equally guilty.
3.

Whether there was an agreement or conspiracy between these defendants to commit robbery or not and whether they were all engaged in the robbery at the time of the killing is a question of fact for the jury to determine from the facts and circumstances in proof before you."

After Judge Pinney had instructed the jury concerning the nuances of evidence and the law, the jury "retired in charge of an officer." *The Tombstone Daily Epitaph* reported that "prevalent opinions had been that not more than five minutes would be required by the jury, the evidence being so plain; but time rolled by until fully half an hour had elapsed, and still no verdict. The countenances of the prisoners, which had been cast down in gloom as the jury slowly filed past them, lightened up, as the lengthening time seemed a chance for a disagreement."[60]

Judge Pinney seemed somewhat surprised also, and finally remanded the prisoners into the custody of the sheriff. Hardly however, had they been removed, when the jury came in with the announcement of an agreement. The defendants were ordered back. "The defendants with their attorneys and the District Attorney being in Court, the jury was asked by the Court if they had agreed upon a verdict. They answered through their foreman that they had, and being directed by the Court to declare the same, returned a verdict in the words following, to wit: 'We the jurymen find the above defendants guilty of murder in the first degree, as charged in the indictment.'"

On hearing the verdict, Daniel Kelly was reported to have remarked, "Well boys, hemp seems to be trumps." The judge stated that he would "pass sentence, or, hear a motion for a new trial on Wednesday next, and again remanded the prisoners." *The Epitaph* reporter then opined, "This closed the most remarkable trial in the history of criminal jurisprudence."[61]

News and opinions about the verdict in the trial came quickly, beginning with *The Tombstone Daily Epitaph*, which ran a series of "notes" directly beneath the final column in the continuing coverage of the proceedings against Dowd, Delaney, Kelly, Howard, and Sample. "Yesterday was the grandest day Cochise County has ever seen," the newspaper stated. It continued on in this vein, saying, "Who would have thought, two years ago, that five men could be hung [sic] in Cochise county at one time?; How much better it was to let the law take its course; The counsel appointed to defend the prisoners did all in their power, but the task was hopeless; Murder and robbery in Cochise county is played out; All honor to the brave Bisbee men who listened to reason, and allowed the majesty of the law to be maintained."

"Judge Pinney presided in the most dignified and impartial manner," stated *The Daily Epitaph*. Of Sheriff Ward, the newspaper said, "his conduct of the case, from the night of the murder, has shown him to be not only a good executive officer, but a detective as well. In the selection of men and the plan of the operation his was the directing hand, and to him more than any other man rests the success of the capture of the entire band. Sheriff Ward and his deputies have made a record in the case they may be proud of." The reporter had high praise for Deputy Sheriff Daniels as well, saying "his pursuit of Dan Dowd through the heart of the Sierra Madres and his capture at Corralitos, Chiricahua, was the bravest act of the affair, too much credit cannot be given him."[62]

News of the trial in the Arizona Territory had been followed all across the nation with dispatches being sent out by telegraph regularly. The citizens of Chicago received the news of the conviction of the Bisbee robbers the following day via *The Chicago Tribune*. The city of Sacramento, California, was treated to a complete transcription of the testimony of Frank Buckles in *The Daily Record-Union*. Closer to home, the citizens of Las Vegas, New Mexico, received the news of the verdict on February 12 from *The Las Vegas Daily Gazette*. Of course, the territorial newspapers had much more to say on the subject.[63]

The Arizona Silver Belt informed its readers of the verdict on February 16, laying credit for the conviction to the testimony of Frank Buckles, saying his evidence "was sufficient to hang them, even had it not been corroborated by other witnesses." The article went on to recount the highlights of his statements for its readers. Of the defendants, *The Silver Belt* said, "Kelley [sic] remarked after he and his pals were remanded to jail, 'Well, boys, hemp seems to be trumps.' He, Delaney, and Dowd seem to take things very coolly. Tex Howard, with all his bravado, was the first one who offered to squeal, but was not listened to by the prosecuting attorney." In a separate column, the Globe newspaper further spoke of Dan Dowd, who was known to some of the residents having been a teamster with the Buffalo Company in that burg.

In the column, *The Silver Belt* took *The Tombstone Republican* to task for "eulogizing" the outlaw. "[*The Republican*] says that sympathy is expressed for him because he was always such a free-hearted, liberal fellow," wrote the editor. "We did not expect to see such sickly sentimentalism displayed for a cold-blooded murderer in an Arizona community." In their analysis, *The Silver Belt* touched on what must have been the opinion of the members of the jury and many citizens of the territory: "It makes not a particle of difference what his former record was; the fact that he was one of the parties in that hellish affair is sufficient reason that he should stretch hemp, and we have no doubt that we shall shortly record his permanent removal from this mundane sphere."[64]

On the same date, *The Arizona Weekly Citizen*, the local newspaper based in Tucson, erroneously announced that "Dan Dowd, John Heath, Red Sample, William Delaney and Tex, the Bisbee murders and desperadoes, have all been convicted of murder in the first degree," when, in fact, John Heath's trial would not begin until the following day, Tuesday, February 12. The newspaper declared the trial to be "the most important ever held in the county" and noted that "the result was watched with intense interest by all. The announcement of the result," it stated, "was received by applause and much excitement and interest was manifested."

In common with *The Silver Belt* and *the Daily Epitaph*, *The Weekly Citizen* believed that it was Frank Buckles' testimony that had convicted the defendants and included a verbatim transcript. There was also some editorializing within the columns dedicated to coverage of the verdict. To wit: "The feeling is that Cochise county will put down crime of every character and especially that committed by the element that prefers to consider that a six-shooter, a good horse and a pair of spurs are the model marks of a desirable citizen." As to the defendants, *The Weekly Citizen* remarked that they "had received the result with perfect calmness, not showing in the least way that they felt the halter slowly but surely gathering around their necks."[65]

Chapter Five

The Trials (Part Two)

On Tuesday, February 12, 1884, the day after Daniel "Big Dan" Dowd, William Delaney, Omer W. "Red" Sample, Daniel "York" Kelly, and James "Tex" Howard were found guilty of first degree murder, the trial of John Heath, the sixth suspect in the Bisbee Massacre commenced. The trial began with the dismissal of a juror named H.J. Heorne, who "for good cause shown [was] excused for the term." The minutes do not elaborate. This was the only action taken in regards to the case that day. The actual trial would commence on Friday, February 15. It began late that morning as the court had been occupied with other business since convening at 9:00 a.m., with Judge Pinney presiding over the proceedings. "Despite the drizzling rain," reported *The Tombstone Republican*, "a large crowd was in the courthouse when John Heith was brought before Judge Pinney." *The Epitaph* reminded its readers that Heath had been indicted by the grand jury for complicity in the robbery and murders. The newspaper noted, "The prisoner is much changed in appearance, not presenting the nonchalant and careless appearance noticeable at his examination."[1]

John Heath was born in 1855 in the state of Texas to John Heath, whom he was named for, John Heath, Sr., a carpenter by trade, was born December 28, 1815, in Ireland and his wife, Sarah, was born in Maryland on November 30, 1825. The younger Heath had no siblings. In 1850, the husband and wife were residing in the town of Marshall, Harrison County, Texas. It was here John Jr., was likely born. By 1860, just prior to the start of the War Between the States, the Heath family had taken up residence in Keatchie, DeSoto, Louisiana. Ten years later, the family was still residing in Louisiana, but had moved to the town of Shreveport. John Jr., was 14 years of age. Not much is known of John Heath's upbringing and youth. It may be assumed was not altogether different from the lives of other children growing up in the latter half of the 19th century.

Five years later, on February 7, 1875, John Heath married a young lady from Marion County, Texas, by the name of Virginia Tennessee "Jennie" Ferrell, the daughter of John Ferrell of North Carolina and Jane Elizabeth Gilmore of Tennessee. "Jennie" Ferrell was 18 years of age at the time of her marriage, having been born July 27, 1857. One can only speculate as to why the Ferrell family chose to name her for the state in which her mother was born. One can also only speculate about how the young woman felt when her husband of three years was arrested, tried, found guilty, and sentenced to two years in the state penitentiary for cattle theft. What must she have thought when her husband subsequently absconded to Arkansas, one step ahead of the authorities, leaving her behind with his parents?[2]

Officers and attorneys in the Cochise County Courtroom, Tombstone, A.T.: 1. Charles Clark 2. George R. Williams 3. Colonel William Herring 4. James Reilly 5. Thomas Mitchell 6. Judge Peel 7. unknown 8. John F. Lewis 9. Henry B. Dibble 10. unknown 11. unknown 12. Marcus A. Smith 13. John Haynes 14. unknown 15. Webster Street 16. unknown 17. Ben Goodrich 18. George Berry 19. William H. Seamans 20. Casey Clum 21. Associate Justice Daniel H. Pinney (it is likely this photo was taken during the trial of the Bisbee murderers) (Arizona Historical Society, 1728).

John Heath appealed his conviction in the District Court of Kaufman. He had been tried separately from D.C. Moore, B.B. Kaufman, and Buck Smith, his alleged accomplices in the theft of a steer from Mr. H.T. Nash. In his defense, Heath claimed he bought the steer, though there was not a signature on the bill of sale. Heath also produced J.W. Baker as a witness to the transaction. Kaufman and Smith, during their examination by the state, "implicated themselves at least as clearly" as they did Heath and it was on the strength of their testimony that Heath was "found guilty by the jury and his punishment was assessed at two years in the penitentiary." In his appeal, Heath's attorney argued that "conviction cannot be had on the uncorroborated testimony of two accomplices" and "the testimony of one could not be invoked to aid the other" and that the jury should have been instructed accordingly.

The appeals court sided with Heath, stating, "The instructions asked by the defendant to the effect that a conviction cannot be had on the uncorroborated testimony of two accomplices ... should have been given by the court with proper corrections and additions." Furthermore, the court found, "as the evidence introduced by the State might lead to establish the theory that the defendant had in good faith bought the animal alleged to have been stolen, it was also incumbent on the court ... to have submitted that issue to the jury, as a part of the law applicable in that case. The charge [to the jury] should embody instructions applicable to every legitimate deduction the jury might draw from the evidence." Based on these findings, the Court of Appeals reversed judgment in the case and remanded the cause. However, John Heath was not inclined to stick around for a second trial.[3]

Kaufman County Courthouse, Texas, where John Heath stood trial for cattle rustling (author's collection).

On April 7, 1880, *The Dallas Daily Herald* reported that John Heath had been re-captured and was being held in Hot Springs, Arkansas. Heath, "so celebrated in this section for his inordinate love of hooking horses, and who was supposed to be the head of a gang of horse-thieves that infested this country some time since, had been heard from through the Sheriff at Hot Springs, where his is durance vile." Heath was remanded by the court after his appeal and once again lodged in jail, "but afterwards succeeded in giving bond for his appearance before the District court." The defendant then "skipped the country and was not heard of by the authorities ... until Sheriff [William W.] Moon received information that he was in Hot Springs." At the time the article appeared, Sheriff Moon was en route to retrieve the suspect.[4]

Sheriff Moon returned with Heath in custody on April 9. *The Daily Herald* expounded on Heath's crimes and flight from justice, stating that three years prior, Heath had been indicted in three cases for stock theft. "Last summer, he was convicted of stealing cattle, but was granted a new trial. When his case came up, he failed to appear." The authorities were not about to make the same mistake twice, and as of April 23, 1880, Heath was still being held in the city jail in Dallas awaiting trial in the District Court of Dallas County. *The Daily Herald* reminded its readers that the defendant was charged with having "stolen cattle from parties in Kaufman county in 1878, and disposed of them to parties in Dallas." The newspaper also stated that "there are several more charges similar to this one, pending against Heath in Dallas and Kaufman counties." But indictments do not guarantee convictions. *The Daily Herald* reported on April 24 that Heath was found not guilty and acquitted of the charges against him. Still, he was not a free man. Heath was remanded by the court to the custody of the Dallas County sheriff to await trial for other misdeeds he was suspected of committing.[5]

The Dallas Daily Herald recorded that on May 8 that Kaufman County Sheriff Alexander Taylor Wilson had been subpoenaed as a witness in the case of the *State vs. John Heath*, "who is being tried in the District Court of that county on the charge of cattle-stealing." The Texas newspaper went on to explain that Heath "figured extensively in a number of crooked cattle transactions, there being several indictments in that and this county against him." Three days later, *The Daily Herald* reported that Heath had been acquitted of the charges brought against him. The reporter noted that Heath "was tried on a similar charge in District Court here some two weeks since and came clear." The article went on to say, though he had been found not guilty in this case, there existed "two more indictments of a like character in this county against him, and he is still held by the authorities to answer to those charges." In conclusion, it was noted that "Heath's friends claim the prosecution is malicious."[6]

John Heath was able to beat the remaining indictments against him, and for nearly a year kept his name out of the newspapers, though not necessarily out of trouble. Then, on June 1, 1881, *The Dallas Daily Herald* carried the story of a strong-arm robbery which had been committed at the Long Branch Saloon and Dance Hall the previous evening. According to the newspaper an unidentified man had entered the Long Branch and "began to participate in the proceedings in a gentlemanly sort of way." *The Daily Herald* continued, "It was not long until it was apparent that he was possessed of some money—a thing in great request by the fellows who loaf about such places—and it was not a great while longer until several of these fellows had made up their minds to transfer his money to their pockets. A plan was accordingly concerted by which to accomplish the transfer." Two of the young women who worked in the dance hall invited the man out into the yard and "while they were talking to him, the roughs came up to attend their part in the play."

The man was summarily seized by the throat and backed up against a fence. While he was held thus, a second man "rifled his pockets" while a third stood back as a look out. The thieves relieved the man of his watch and all the money he was carrying before making good their escape. The man reportedly yelled for the police, "but raised nobody." The entire incident was witnessed by John Hathaway and Henry Wilson, "who gave such a description of the robbers" that when the police went to the Long Branch the following morning, they were able to quickly identify the culprits. Dan Kearns and John Heath, described by *The Daily Herald* as "very notorious and suspicious characters" were promptly arrested and taken off in irons to the city calaboose. "Later in the day, the third robber was apprehended by the authorities." This man was identified only as "Canada Bill." However, as of the time the article appeared, "the robbed man had not been found" and it was unknown how much money the thieves had actually taken from him.[7]

Three days later, the Dallas newspaper reported that "Bessie Wells swore out a warrant in Justice Edwards' court" for the arrest of Annie Heath. Ms. Heath, who was neither the wife nor a blood-relative of the suspect, was to be charged with "threatening to take her [Bessie's] life if she testified against John Heath, the hackman, charged with being implicated in the Long Branch robbery." The following day, *The Daily Herald* reported that Anna Heath was arrested on the warrant which had been sworn out by Bessie Wells. Ms. Heath subsequently appeared before Justice Edwards, "who put her under a $100 bond to keep the peace." Then, on June 8, the newspaper reported that A.K. Johnson, "the man who was robbed at the Long Branch, a house of ill repute, who made it his business to hide out after the arrest of the parties" responsible, had himself been apprehended. Johnson was able to positively identify John Heath and Kearns as his assailants.[8]

By the end of the month, Heath had posted bond in the amount of $700 and was given his freedom. However, the Grand Jury had found a true bill against him, and he was obliged to appear in District Court to answer for the robbery. The day after the news of his release appeared in *The Daily Herald*, it was noted that "the case of the State vs. Dan Kearns and John Heath, charged with robbing one Johnson, was called in the district court ... and continued until the next term of that court." The newspaper also noted that "Kearns, who so far has been unable to give bond, is still in durance vile." Heath and Kearns were still under indictment for the robbery of A.K. Johnson nine months later when *The Dallas Weekly Herald* printed the following story about the 37-year-old part-time hack-driver and would-be desperado[9]:

> Barnum had his ancient woman, Joyce Heath [*sic*], about whom volumes were written, but Joyce Heath was a humbug. Texas has John Heath, but John is not a humbug. He is a live, shrewd, quick-witted young man, who can get into more trouble and get out of it slicker than any other man of equal years in all the state. He has been charged with so many violations of the law, been arrested, imprisoned, bonded, tried, acquitted, etc. etc. that he has achieved the reputation of being either the slyest, smartest rogue extant or the worst used, most unfortunate man living. He was arrested and jailed Saturday night on suspicion of having burglarized Dr. A.A. Johnson's residence a week or so ago. It seems that Mrs. Johnson was awakened by the breeze blowing on her face from the door left open by the burglar, and as the lamp was burning in her bedroom, she saw the burglar distinctly. She did not know him, but a few hours afterwards she described him accurately to Detective Jack Duncan and he "spotted" John Heath as the guilty party. He would have been arrested at once, but just then burglaries were being committed every night and City Marshal [Jim] Arnold and his police had several suspicious characters [illegible] and desired to await further developments with the hope of securing evidence against Heath and the other suspected parties, sufficient to convict them of other burglaries. It was known that Heath was under bond for his attendance upon the present session of the district court, and therefore it was not deemed necessary to be in a hurry about his capture.
>
> The grand jury yesterday found a true bill against him, charging him with the burglary of Dr. Johnson's residence and the capias was served on him in jail.
>
> Heath lived in Kaufman county about seven years and when he first went there stood very well well [*sic*] with all who knew him. He stood so well, indeed, that he courted, won the love, and married a most excellent young lady. After a while his name began to be whispered about in connection with horse and cattle-stealing, and finally he was charged with the theft of cattle and he was indicted. This was the opening of the ball. And for the past four or five years he has vibrated back and forward between Dallas and Kaufman counties, answering indictments for horse and cattle-stealing in these two counties. He beat every charge made against him and but for an indictment pending against him for highway robbery, alleged to have been committed by him and one Kearns, some time last year in this city, and for which he was under bond, he would have been entirely loose-footed when charged with this burglary of Dr. Johnson's residence. It said that because of the many accusations against him, Heath and his wife have separated.
>
> For most of the time past, Heath has been driving a hack in this city and he has been regarded with suspicion by both city and county officers all the time, and whenever any burglary or robbery has been committed during his presence in Dallas, John Heath has been suspected by these officers. He has been in jail a number of times, but has in all his cases been fortunate in securing bail eventually. Whether or not there are grounds for looking upon John Heath as a bad man, it is not the province of our reporter to say. He knows not whether he is guilty or innocent, and has no opinion to express on the subject. It is said that Mrs. Johnson recognizes Heath as the man who was in her house on the night in question.[10]

On April 6, 1882, less than three weeks after this article appeared, the District Attorney of Dallas County decided not to further prosecute Heath in two different cases (one of which involved John Heath, Sr.) as long as the defendant paid the court costs accrued. Nevertheless, John Heath was arrested once again in Dallas along with Georgia Morgan, proprietress of the Long Branch. The couple were brought before the court in June of 1882

Dallas, Texas, 1879, as it looked when John Heath resided in that city (author's collection).

and charged with running a house of ill-repute. Still, Dame Fortune continued to smile upon John Heath. In November of that year, the burglary charge against Heath was dismissed and on May 10 of the following year, Heath was acquitted of another of the numerous rustling charges against him. Still, Heath must have realized his luck was not going to hold out indefinitely and decided it was high time to vacate Texas. Why he chose to move on to the Arizona Territory is unknown, but his activities there soon became a matter of public record as his trial proceeded.[11]

Ironically, according to the records of the Fourteenth District Court, on Saturday, December 8, 1883, the very day of the robbery in Bisbee, the District Attorney of Dallas County dismissed the case of the *State of Texas vs. John Heath and D.C. Moore*, for the theft of a steer; the case of the *State of Texas vs. John Heath*, for forgery; and the case of the *State of Texas vs. John Heath*, for robbery in connection with the mugging of A.K. Johnson. At the time of the Bisbee robbery, John Heath had been acquitted of all charges brought against him in Texas. This is significant in light of some of the accusations and allegations that would later be made by the regional newspapers against the man.[12]

After Judge Pinney called the court to order on Friday, February 15, the trial of John Heath began in earnest. The first order of business was the empanelling of the jury. "The following named persons were called, sworn, and accepted to try the case, viz: Wm. Whitaker, H.H. Allen, F. Ruez, G.W. Chapman, J. Ellichson, J.S. Bogart, J.D. McDougall, S. Curtis, O.L. Bashford, John Henck, E. Dees, and J.M. Stump. The indictment was then read to the jury along with the plea of the defendant. Whereupon, the following witnesses were called, sworn, and testified in behalf of the prosecution: W.W. Bush, Richard Rundle, M.M. Hartson, W. Gerstenberg, Dan'l. Inman, Henry Smith, Frank Buckles, Lubien Pardee, and L.D. Lockwood." Unfortunately, the original court transcript has been lost in the dark

Clifton, Arizona Territory, where John Heath settled and opened a saloon after leaving Texas, and where Heath became acquainted with the men who were later accused of committing the robbery in Bisbee (author's collection).

oubliette of history, therefore, coverage of the trial as described herein is sourced primarily from the pages of *The Daily Epitaph,* published two days later, on Sunday, February 17, 1884: "The District Court room again yesterday held its full compliment of humanity eager to hear every incident connected with the Heith murder trial. It has long been the prevailing opinion that Heith was the prime mover in the diablerie which resulted in the Bisbee murders and it was generally feared that he had so covered his tracks that conviction and execution under the law would not reach him. The evidence on the first day's trial, while tending in a strong manner to show complicity in the matter, was not as conclusive as wished for, and a look at the jury showed that they so considered it."[13]

The first witness to testify for the prosecution at John Heath's trial was bartender Walter W. Bush of Clifton. His testimony was succinct. "I know Heith, Dowd, Sample, Kelly, and Delaney," he said. "I saw Heith in Clifton with Tex Howard in November last; they were on horses and rode out of town together; [I] saw Tex and Red Sample on the 12th of December at Clifton; did not see Heith again until I saw him here in Tombstone." During his cross-examination by the defense, Bush stated he assisted in the arrest of James Howard and Omer Sample and expected to share in the reward. In response to questions about his sighting of Heath and Howard, he explained how he was standing in front of Hill's Saloon early in the morning, when they rode past him on their way out of town.

"The street," the bartender described, "is 150 to 200 yards long; [I] did not see them get on their horses; [I] am not sure it was Heith and Tex separately that morning; don't remember anyone else riding out of town that morning except Heith and Tex." He went on to say he had known Heath "about five months" and that he "kept a saloon in Clifton; at the time I tended bar for George Hill; I am now a partner at Hill's." Returning to the subject at hand, Bush said, "[I] saw Heith and Tex riding by for about 50 yards; I think they were leaving Clifton, because they were riding out together, and I have not seen Heith in Clifton since."[14]

Walter Bush's was the only testimony heard that morning, as Judge Pinney called for a recess until 1:30 that afternoon. When the court reconvened, the prosecution called its second witness, Richard Rundle, the same man who identified James Howard, Omer Sample and Daniel Kelly as the perpetrators of the robbery inside Castaneda's mercantile. After being sworn, Rundle stated he lived in Bisbee and was in town on the night of the robbery. "[I] saw John Heith in Bisbee several days before the 8th; don't know what he was doing there." Rundle said he was present at the killing of D.T. Smith then admitted he was in Castaneda's store when the killing occurred. Rundle then recounted his experiences from the night of the robbery.

"About 7:30 o'clock, as I was walking up the street," the witness said, " [I] was accosted by a man and told to go into Castaneda's store; went in and found men standing in a row with their hands up; was told to behave alright and no harm would come to me; saw five men engaged in the robbery; identified the three men in the store; there were two men outside, one tall the other short; of the three men inside, two were masked and one unmasked; the men I saw in the store were Tex, Red, and Kelly; saw Red's face when his mask flew up in passing me; Tex had no mask on; saw side of Kelly's face when he stooped to pick up some money which had dropped on the floor; Tex and Red were armed; saw no arms on Kelly; heard shooting outside; a great number of shots were fired; saw D.T. Smith after he was killed; he was shot in the forehead. I was the first man to him after the firing; he laid [sic] ten or twelve feet from the store under a wagon."[15]

This was the extent of Rundle's testimony. He was not cross-examined by the defense. There was no need, as his testimony was not damaging to their case. Walter Bush had seen Heath with Tex, which proved that the defendant was at least acquainted with one of the bandits. Rundle saw Heath in Bisbee, but he was not in the company of any of the convicted men and it was several days before the robbery occurred. By his own admission, the witness had no knowledge of Heath's purpose for being in town nor of his subsequent actions while there. In point if fact, Rundle's testimony had absolutely no bearing on the case at all (except to inflame the prejudices of the jury in favor of the prosecution) and the defense lawyer, Colonel Herring was remiss in not calling this to the attention of the jury.

The prosecution pushed ahead with their case, calling as their next witness Mr. M.M. Hartson, an engineer for the Copper Queen Mining Company. Here again was a witness who had no information in regards to John Heath. The defendant was not even mentioned in the testimony Hartson gave while on the stand. Once sworn, Hartson stated he was in Bisbee, in Castaneda's store, on the night of the robbery, having been ordered in off the street by "a large man with a rifle, who was masked." He explained that a second masked man, smaller in stature, reiterated the order, and that he complied with their demands. Once inside, he recalled being told to throw up his hands. "I saw two masked men step up to the clerk and tell him to open the safe," continued Hartson. "[T]he unmasked man said, pointing to Joe Goldwater, 'There is the man who can open the safe.' Goldwater then opened the safe as directed, and poured the contents of drawer into a sack held by the robbers. Some of the money fell on the floor and one of the masked men stooped to pick it up, and in doing so his mask flew up, but I could not recognize him. The unmasked man I recognized in this court as Tex Howard."

Hartson continued, "I heard a good deal of shooting outside and a masked man came in and asked for more cartridges. Tex said, 'That's right—pump out the old shells, and put in new. We'll show these s—ns of b——s that we're running this town for about ten minutes.' I heard at least one hundred shots fired; heard some party on the outside order another to go in the store. The party ordered said, 'No, you don't.' This remark was followed by a shot, and I recognized the voice as that of Johnny Tappenier. Also heard a man say, 'Go back in there,' and the answer 'I won't do it—I'm a deputy sheriff.' This remark was followed by shots. The men outside doing the shooting were not alike in size—one quite large, the other quite small. I distinctly heard Tappenier's voice; [I] was the first man to him after the murders; he was lying about ten or twelve feet from the store, with his head inside the Bon Ton saloon."[16]

This concluded Hartson's testimony. There was no cross-examination by John Heath's defense attorney. William Gerstenberg was the next witness to be called for the Territory. Gerstenberg testified previously at the trial of Dowd, Delaney and the others, and at Heath's trial, he basically reiterated his statements from the first, though in a somewhat confused manner: "[I] lived in Bisbee on December 7th; was also living there on the night of December 8th; on the morning of the 8th saw Dan Dowd about a quarter of a mile from his camp, going toward Bisbee; saw four horses and two men in the camp mentioned. Recognized Dowd plainly; was about sixty feet from him; saw him since in this courtroom. The camp I mean is about half a mile from the Bisbee slaughterhouse. Saw Dowd first in the morning, and again in the evening. The last time he had a rifle in his hands."

In answer to further questions posed by the prosecution, Gerstenberg continued in his recollection, saying, "I was there in the butcher shop in Bisbee between 6:30 and 8 o'clock p.m. At the time I saw him there had been a great deal of shooting; was in the shop when the shooting began; looked out and saw a large man loading a rifle; Dowd was the man I saw in the street shooting with the rifle. I called the butcher's attention to Dowd as he passed the shop, saying, 'That is the man.' Dowd took a shot at me; it put out the lights, and I went down into the cellar and remained there until the trouble was over." At this point, the prosecution re-directed Gerstenberg in his testimony, questioning him specifically about John Heath. The witness acknowledged the fact he had known Heath "before this difficulty." He explained further, "[I] saw him and Tex come to Bisbee eight or ten days before the shooting. Saw Heith also on the day of the shooting. Saw Kelley on the evening of the shooting, near Joe Dyer's house; he passed me riding on a gray pony, and going to town; he met me again as he was coming out—on foot. Heith opened a dance hall that night. The dance hall was about fifty feet above Castaneda's store, on the same side."

Defense attorney Herring cross-examined Gerstenberg after the prosecution concluded their questioning, and asked him to elaborate on his testimony regarding the occasion he saw Heath the night of the robbery. In answer to the attorney's queries, the witness stated, "[I] saw Heith come up the main road leading into town. I was at Indian Joe's corral; he passed between 4 and 5 o'clock; [I] did not see him below Joe's; this was on Friday afternoon—am sure of it; the shooting was done on the evening of the 8th." This was the full extent of Herring's cross-examination. Like the witnesses before him, the testimony of Gerstenberg in no way tied John Heath to the robbery. Heath had been seen about town by both Rundle and Gerstenberg but, as the latter noted, Heath had just opened a new dance hall on Main Street and his presence in town was easily explained by this fact.[17]

Daniel Inman was the next to take the stand, having been subpoenaed by the prosecution to testify. The testimony he gave was short and to the point. Inman began by saying, "I know Heith by sight; I first saw him in Morse's canyon in the Chiricahua mountains, on the 27th of November." He went on to say, "He came to my house between 11 and 12 o'clock with a man whom I since know to be Tex Howard. They came from the direction of Galeyville, distant about 10 miles. They ate at my house; said they had been lost. They rode a white horse and a bay horse. [I] have since seen the white horse in Montgomery's corral in this city. The date was Tuesday the 27th. They said they had come directly through from Texas on horseback. They were both armed. They took their horses to Smith's because I had no feed for them. Mr. Pardee came to my place on December 1st for tobacco. Bisbee is about 50 miles from my place. Tex and Heith told me they were going to Tombstone." The defense did not choose to cross-examine Daniel Inman or, if he was cross-examined, the testimony he gave was not recorded by the newspapers.

Inman was followed on the witness stand by Henry Smith, who was duly sworn and questioned by the prosecutor. Smith stated that in "the latter part of November" he was living in Chiricahua Mountains. He continued, "[I] saw Heith at the house; know he is the man; he and a man called Tex got their horses fed at the ranch with barley; Heith offered to pay for it; they rode a sorrel horse and a gray horse. Our place is 1½ miles from Inman's. The day of the week was Tuesday." The remainder of his testimony was irrelevant to the case against Heath. Smith said, "I went to Pardee's camp on the following Sunday; found Kelly, Dowd and Sample there; talked to them awhile. The only one I knew was Dan Dowd. I hunted up Sample's horse for him while I was there. Kelley asked me to do it and he paid me. I delivered the horse to Kelly. Have since seen the same horse at Montgomery's stable; know it by the brand and the color."[18]

This concluded Henry Smith's testimony. The defense declined to cross-examine the witness. While it was not necessary, it would have been advisable, if only to remind the jury that Heath had so far only been connected to one of the robbers, James "Tex" Howard, and that as far as could be factually proved, the two men had simply been travelling together. In spite of all the testimony heretofore given, there was no proof Heath conspired in the planning of the robbery. Inman had stated that both Heath and Tex were armed, but that was to be expected in that they had been travelling through unfamiliar country. At Smith's, the men had asked for feed for their mounts and Heath even offered to pay. They had not attempted to strong-arm the rancher. There was nothing in the defendant's demeanor or his actions, as described by witnesses, that would make him suspect. However, the next witness would serve to call his culpability into question.

Frank Buckles, who the newspapers felt had been the key witness for the prosecution during the trial of Dowd, Delaney, Kelly, Sample, and Howard, had been called back to testify against Heath. Buckles began by stating he lived on the White River, near the west end of the Swisshelm Mountains and that he was personally acquainted with John Heath as well as the men who Heath was suspected of having conspired with in the planning of the Bisbee hold-up. Buckles said he first met Heath, who was traveling with James Howard, on either the 26th or 27th of November 1883, when they arrived at his ranch approximately an hour before sundown. The travelers told him they had ridden in from Clifton. Buckles recalled that William Delaney, "a man named Hall and some teamsters were there at the time" and later that "same evening, Dan Dowd and Red came to the ranch." He said the five men stayed the night at his place and that Heath bunked with Delaney that evening. "Red and Dowd left the next morning," explained the rancher, "saying they were going to Bisbee; this was the 28th or 29th." Heath, he said, "bought some barley from the teamsters while he was there and left some when he went away. Dowd returned the day Heith left and got the barley; Dowd was alone at the time."

Buckles said the next time he saw Dowd, Red and Tex was on the 5th of December, and that they were accompanied by Kelly. "Delaney had been at my place five or six weeks; he went by the name of Johnson then. Tex got to my place on the night of the 4th of December; he staid [sic] all night and left the next morning, returning in about five hours with Dowd, Kelly, and Red. They said they had come from Pardee's camp." Buckles remembered the men staying about an hour and then leaving all together. "[They] said they were going to an old mine [in] back of my place. Dowd told me they were going to Bisbee to rob a store; no one was present when he made this statement; it was in my cellar."

In response to a question from the prosecuting attorney, the rancher said, "Kelly got a shoe put on his horse at the ranch." He then returned to the subject of the conversation with Dowd, saying it occurred on the 5th and that he did not remember any of the other men speaking of it. "Delaney," he recalled, "came back to my house and remained all night; saw Dowd, Delaney, and Red on the night of the 7th of December; they came and turned loose a horse that I had given to Delaney to go to the old mine on; they told me they were going to Bisbee to rob a store and they would return the night of the 8th, and wanted me to have horses staked out for them." As promised, Buckles said, Sample, Howard and Kelly appeared again on the night of the 8th. Delaney and Dowd were not with them, as they had skinned out toward Sonora, Mexico. "Red said they had had a fight and had killed two to four people," stated Buckles. The outlaw also told him that both he and Delaney had been shot and "he and his party were going to Clifton."

In response to a new line of questioning from the prosecutor, Buckles began to speak of John Heath, saying, "Since Heith's arrest, I had an interview with him in the jail; he said he understood Pardee was giving the boys away, and wanted me to get him out of the way.; he said he expected to get his trial first, and if he got clear he would get Pardee out of the way. The interview occurred the evening Dowd was lodged in jail." This concluded Buckles' testimony on behalf of the prosecution. However, the defense chose to cross-examine the witness, asking more pointed questions in regards to Buckles' alleged interview with Heath. Buckles responded,

[I] went to the jail with Deputy Sheriff Ward [the Sheriff's son] to see the prisoners; did not go at anyone's suggestion; went about 6 or 7 o'clock in the evening; went to see the prisoners and the jail; had not seen it since first built.

[I] saw Tex, Red, Kelly, Dowd, Heith, and other prisoners; they all talked to me about the case; the conversation between me and Heith was very low; Ward had gone into the jailor's room to get a newspaper at the time. I was a witness against the other prisoners at their trials; have not previously stated this conversation on the stand; was not asked about it; told Fred Ward about it the morning after it occurred, and also my partner, Hall. [I] have not been arrested or menaced with arrest; have heard the street talk that Linderman, Lake, myself and others would be implicated in the Bisbee matter; don't remember whether I heard the remarks before or after my conversation with Heith; did not supply any of the party that came from Bisbee on the night of the 8th with horses; they got two horses from Linderman's ranch. Meyers was at my house on the night of the 8th.

Linderman's place is four miles from mine; the horses gotten by the party never were at my place; never heard they were at my ranch.

Buckles then returned to the subject of Heath, saying, "When Heith came to my place he said he felt bad; said he would lay up on the day if I did not object; he said he was going to Bisbee to start a dance hall, and asked me about the place." In response to the defense attorney's inquiry, Buckles returned to the subject of the horses describing the animals outlaws obtained from Linderman as "dun-colored mares." There was then a short re-direct from the prosecution. Buckles stated he had testified at "both the examinations and trials" of the five men now convicted of the crime and awaiting sentence. He stated the reason he had kept silent about what he knew in relation to the suspects was because he "was afraid for his life." Only after all the members of the gang were safely behind bars did he feel he could tell what he knew without fear of reprisal from one or more of the suspects.[19]

Thus ended the testimony of Frank H. Buckles in the case of the *Territory of Arizona vs. John Heath*. As in the first instance of his testifying, during the trial of Dowd, Delaney, Kelly, Sample, and Howard, Buckles' evidence amounted to little more than hearsay. By his own admission, no one overheard his conversation with Dowd, in which the former teamster supposedly told Buckles of their plans to rob Castaneda's. No one overheard Delaney, Dowd, and Kelly, announcing they were going to Bisbee to rob a store as they left his ranch on the 7th. And no one overheard the words that supposedly passed between Buckles and Heath in the Tombstone jail, as the jailor was out of the room "getting a newspaper." The defense attorney was right to question Buckles' motivation for coming forth with this testimony as he did. Was he testifying to save his own hide? Had the prosecuting attorney threatened to indict Buckles as a conspirator if he did not testify against Heath and the others?

Buckles' entire testimony seems suspect. Why would the outlaws confide in Buckles in the first place? It seems odd these men would take the elaborate precaution of going up to the old mine to discuss their plans in secret and then return to the ranch immediately afterwards and tell Buckles exactly what they were up to. Further, why would Heath trust Buckles—a man he barely knew—enough to ask him to "get Pardee out of the way" after he had been incarcerated? Did these men really believe they had a confederate in Frank Buckles and, if so, why would they believe this? Being that Buckles testified during the preliminary examinations of each of the men, would they not have known when he visited them in jail that he had double-crossed them? Why then would Heath have asked him such a heavy favor as to "take care" of Pardee?

Frank Buckles was replaced on the stand by his neighbor, Lucien Pardee, the very man Heath supposedly asked Buckles to take "out of the way." Pardee was sworn in and testified to knowing Dowd, Kelly, Sample, and Howard, and said that Dowd, Kelly and Sample had stayed with him from November 27 until December 5. Pardee insisted the men also told him of their plans to rob a store in Bisbee. He said he was acquainted with a man calling himself Johnson, who would later turn out to be William Delaney. "Dowd told me that Johnny Heith was their partner," stated the witness. "[I] heard a conversation between Delaney and Kelley; Kelley asked Delaney if he had seen Heith. Delaney said; 'No, but they are down there.' Kelley then said; 'Do you know how this thing is fixed up?' Delaney said; 'I have an idea Johnny Heith will be left outside the robbery; we want him to attend business when we are gone.'"

Lubien Pardee then explained how he travelled over to Inman's ranch for some tobacco and a wedge. When he returned, the men asked him if there were any news. He told them of the Gage train robbery and he "suspected two men who had eaten at his place of being the robbers. Dowd said: 'No, those men [Heath and Howard] are two of our friends, who are going to help us rob a store on the 8th of the month.'" At this juncture, the prosecution left off and the witness was cross-examined by the defense attorney. The defense obviously wanted some clarification as to the conversation Pardee claimed he overheard. Pardee responded, "On the 8th of December I heard Red, Kelly, and Dowd talking about Johnny Heith. The first conversation I heard was on the 1st day of December, pretty late in the afternoon. The second conversation was on the 4th, and the third conversation was also on the 4th; all of the conversations on the 4th occurred at night; don't know the exact time, nor the length of time between the conversations; I was inside a tent."

The defense continued to question the witness and Pardee said, "First heard of Heith on the 1st of December; Red told me that Heith and Tex were going to Bisbee. I wanted Red and Dowd to leave my place—was afraid they would be arrested as train robbers." The defense attorney then asked Pardee about his reason for not coming forward sooner with the information he possessed. Pardee replied, "[I] saw Deputy Sheriff Daniel in the Chiricahua mountains; I did not tell him what I have stated in court; did not state all I knew at Heith's examination; I stated the truth to all I was asked; [I] have had no conversation with Sheriff Ward about the case; may have talked about the case, but don't remember with whom; have had conversations with Messrs. Smith and Robinson [the prosecuting attorneys] about the case; have had no conversation with Kelley, Dowd, or Red since Dec. 5."

Pardee was then re-directed by the prosecuting attorney. In response to the attorney's question, he said, "The reason I did not state all that I knew at Heith's examination was because he was the only man arrested and I was afraid of my life at the hand of the others." The defense attorney, in turn, asked the witness if he had been told which store the men planned to rob. Pardee replied, "The parties did not tell me which store in Bisbee City they intended robbing; said it was the one where the miners' kept their money." With this, the questioning was concluded and the witness was allowed to step down.[20]

The testimony of Lubien Pardee, much like that of Frank Buckles, consisted entirely of hearsay. There was no one who could corroborate or substantiate his account of events. He stated that two men had been fed at his home, but he did not know them. He did not point out Heath, who was sitting in the courtroom as being one of those men (though he was not requested to do so). He suspected they were train robbers on the dodge. Dan Dowd later identified Heath and Howard as "friends" and supposedly told Pardee these men were part of their plan to "rob a store" in Bisbee. Why Dowd would have revealed his intentions to Pardee is unknown. All the other information Pardee knew about Heath was obtained by eavesdropping on the conversations of others. The information had not even been shared with him personally. And, while he was never asked directly, he did admit to speaking to both the County Prosecutor and the Assistant County Prosecutor, which begs the question if he had been coerced into testifying under threat of prosecution for aiding and abetting.

Lubien Pardee's testimony marked the end of the first full day of John Heath's trial. The court was adjourned, the jury sent out, the gallery cleared of spectators, and the defendant removed to his cell on the first floor. The court would reconvene Saturday, February 16, at 9:00 a.m.

After the minutes of the preceding day were read and approved, the proceedings continued with the prosecution re-calling H.M. Hartson to the stand to speak to John Heath's actions during the manhunt. Hartson said, "I was one of the sheriff's posse that went after the Bisbee robbers. Heith was one of the posse; he said he did not think Tex was in the outfit [Tex being the only one who had been positively identified at that juncture], he knew the shoes that were on Tex's horse and would know if Tex's horse was there when he saw the tracks; he did not think Tex was there. Heith, Frost, and Waite left balance of posse about 12 or 15 miles from Bisbee and came over towards Tombstone."

Deputy Sheriff Daniels was then called to the stand to testify about the manhunt. "I organized a posse on the night of December 8th to pursue the robbers…. Heith was the first man who came to me and said he wanted to go along." Daniels recalled Heith saying he was "ready and had his horse saddled." The deputy sheriff stated he sent a party immediately to the custom house and that Heith was among them. "I went to the milk ranch to see about getting horses; Heith's party was to start at once. When I got back I found that Indian Joe, who was to guide them, had gone to bed, so the rest did not go. Heith," he said, "went with me and the others to milk ranch; learned when I went there that the party had passed that place; we got there before daylight."

"Heith," Daniels recollected, "said if Jim [Tex] Howard was along he would know it if for his horse was shod in Texas style. When it was light we examined the tracks. After we examined the tracks, Heith said he didn't think the horse was there. We found tracks answering the description but Heith said that was only a swelled heel and not "the kind of a track." The deputy continued in his testimony saying, "After we got six or seven miles the trail became very dim; Heith pretended to find two that went off to the left and three that turned off to the right; he suggested he would follow one trail and I the other, so Frost, Waite, and himself went in the direction of Tombstone." This ended Deputy Sheriff Daniels' testimony on behalf of the prosecution. Curiously, the law officer was not cross-examined by the defense attorney.[21]

With the testimony of Hartson and Daniels, the prosecution endeavored to prove that Heath purposefully tried to lead the posse astray, first, by stating he did not believe that James "Tex" Howard's horse was among those they were following, and second, by stating he had found a place where the trail diverged. The fact is the robbers *had* split up after the robbery. Delaney and Dowd *had* gone south towards Sonora, Mexico, while the other three continued on in the direction of Clifton. There may not have been any "pretending" involved, as Daniels asserted. It is very probable that Heath did find the point in the trail where the suspects parted company. And, to his credit, Heath did not suggest the entire posse follow one trail or the other, but recommended the force be divided and both trails followed.

As to his identification of the track of "Tex" Howard's horse, Heath may have been trying to throw the posse off the scent as it were, or he may have been legitimately mistaken in his identification of the "Texas-style" track left by Howard's horse. Heath had ridden with Howard for sometime—they traveled from Clifton together—and he may well have thought he would recognize the track but, in the end, was not able to. Furthermore, Frank Buckles stated the outlaws traded their own fatigued horses for fresh mounts at Linderman's. During the first trial, Walter Myers testified to the fact the gray horse which Howard had been seen riding prior to and on the night of the robbery was found abandoned in an arroyo near Buckles' the following morning. The evidence suggests that, after the outlaws stopped over at Linderman's, Howard was riding a different horse. This may explain why Heath did not find the "Texas-style" track he expected to see. Unfortunately, for Heath, combined with the other evidence presented previously in the case, his actions during the search for the Bisbee robbers appeared somewhat suspect—as though he may well have been trying to cover for Howard and the others.

After confirming he was employed at Lockwood's corral and had been in Bisbee on the night of December 8, the next witness for the prosecution, John Hiles, testified that he "recognized Tex as one of the five men who rode out of town" immediately following the robbery. Hiles went on to say that he "had often seen Tex and the defendant together." He recalled, "One day, the gray horse was taken from the stable by Tex" and that he (Howard) and Heith had a long consultation together which lasted an hour." The witness was not cross-examined. Hiles was not asked if he had been privy to the conversation or if he knew what the two men had been discussing that day. Once again, the defense attorney seems to have been negligent in his duty to his client.[22]

Galeyville resident Clem Lamstum was called by the court as the next witness for the prosecution. Lamstum asserted he "saw four men with the defendant" in November of the previous year, on either the 25th or 26th of that month. Lamstum identified the men he saw with Heath as Kelly, Dowd, Sample, and Howard. "They stopped in an old cabin not far from my place," he said. "They went away at 8 or 9 o'clock in the morning." Lamstum continued, "I traded horses with Red; while going up the canyon to see the house. Red told me Heith was his partner, and that they had a cattle ranch in Apache county and were now on their way to Sonora to restock it; said he didn't know who the others were, that they had picked them up the other side of San Simeon." This was all the evidence Clem Lamstum gave before being allowed to step down. All it really proved was that Heath was acquainted with four of the outlaws—Howard, Sample, Dowd, and Kelly—and that he travelled some distance with them.[23]

The testimony of the prosecution's witnesses up this point was mostly hearsay and the evidence against John Heath purely circumstantial. Most of the testimony given has very little bearing on the case against Heath (except to inflame the prejudices of the jury in favor of the prosecution). There was no direct evidence which linked Heath to the crime or indicated he had had any part in the planning thereof. By this point, District Attorney Smith, if he were to "make his case" against John Heath, needed a ringer. Smith needed someone who could definitively state Heath conspired with Dowd, Delaney, Sample, Kelly, and Howard in planning the assault on Castaneda's mercantile. The prosecutor found his "ringer" in the person of Sergeant L.D. Lawrence of the 3rd Cavalry.

Sergeant Lemuel D. Lawrence was the next witness for the prosecution to be called on the second day of Heath's trial. He was summarily sworn and stated for the record that his place of residence since November 27 had been the Cochise County jail. Upon being questioned, Lawrence replied, "[I] have heard conversation between the defendants, and have had conversation with them myself; Heith said, in my presence, if Howard had done what they agreed to do neither of them would be in jail now, or suspicioned [sic] of being in the Bisbee murder." According to inmate Lawrence, "The agreement was that Howard was to meet Dan Dowd, Delaney, Kelly, and Red Sample and give them the information they had picked up in Bisbee; then Howard was to go on to Clifton on the night of the robbery, so that neither Heith nor Howard would be suspicioned [sic] at all."

The Sergeant continued, "But in place of all that, because Howard had heard Daniel making some talk in Bisbee that they were train robbers, Howard changed his mind and went with the men to rob the store. Heith blames Howard for his arrest and Howard blames Heith for his arrest. One time, Heith said if old man Pardee told what he knew, they would all hang. Dan Dowd said the same after his trial. [I] have heard Heith had gone to Bisbee to open a dance-hall; the other claim is that Heith put up the job." And thus concluded his statements on behalf of the prosecution. Lawrence was then subject to cross-examination by the defense attorney, Colonel Herring. Herring sought to call into question the validity of the inmate's testimony by calling into question his character and his reasons for appearing before the court.

In answer to the questions put to him by Heath's counsel, Lawrence affirmed, "[I] have been in the army since 1879; have been stationed at different places in Arizona; [I] have been in jail since the 27th of November last for some trouble that occurred in Willcox; never said anything about this case until Mr. Robinson came into the jail yesterday and said I would be subpoenaed as a witness; I told him I would tell what I knew; [I] had no promise from the district attorney whatever." Colonel Herring further questioned him about what Lawrence claimed to have heard. The Sergeant replied,

> Dowd, when he came down, made the remark to Heith; "If Pardee tells what he knows, we will all hang." I have never said I heard Heith say he had nothing to do with this affair—on the contrary, he admitted to me that he was connected with it.
>
> One time, we were talking about breaking jail and Heith showed me a saw, which was afterwards rigged up by Kelly. At that time, Heith told me that he was one of the parties that put up the job— he and Howard together—and if Howard had done what he agreed to, neither he nor Howard would be there now. On leaving Clifton, Howard and himself had put up the job. They were coming to Bisbee to get some items and then Howard was going back to meet these parties on the way from Clifton to Bisbee; the parties Howard was to meet were Delaney, Dowd, Kelly, and Red Sample. One time, when talking about breaking jail, he admitted the same thing, and said, "If Pardee swears to what he knows I will be in the same box with the other men."
>
> Conversations were passing continually between all six of the defendants; after the other five were convicted they were put in separate cells, and I used to carry conversations from one to the other.

The cross-examination by Colonel Herring then turned to the alleged escape plot. Lawrence described how "Heith brought two small saws in jail with him; one was broken [the saw was presented, shown to the witness and then placed in evidence]. I recognize this as the other; they proposed to saw the bars and break jail; I saw Heith give Burns $40 to get the tools for this purpose—three case knives; string was let out the window in rear of the jail; the knives were to be tied on to it and pulled up; I told about the effort to break jail."[24]

Sergeant Lemuel D. Lawrence of the 3rd Cavalry had been indicted by the grand jury for first degree murder in the deaths of W.M. Hill and a fellow soldier, identified only as Sergeant Duffy, during a brawl in I.H. Rose's saloon in the town of Willcox. According to a report published in *The Arizona Weekly Citizen*, Lawrence was deep in his cups and had become "very quarrelsome." When Sgt. Duffy intervened, Lawrence shot him, wounding him fatally. Hill also tried "to quiet Lawrence" and was summarily shot to death by Lawrence. The newspaper noted that Hill was not armed at the time of the shooting. "After shooting Hill, [Lawrence] struck Albert Porter with an empty whisky bottle, fracturing his skull above the eye." Lawrence was subsequently arrested by the authorities. "A coroner's inquest was held, and rendered a verdict in accordance with the above facts." Lawrence was remanded to the Cochise County Jail to await trial.[25]

Sergeant Lawrence flatly denied that he had been offered anything by the Cochise County District Attorney in exchange for his testimony against Heath, but Lawrence was also facing the noose or life imprisonment if convicted for the murders of W.M. Hill and Sergeant Duffy. He had much to lose and everything to gain by informing on his cellmates. Lawrence readily admitted the Assistant District Attorney visited with him and told him he would be subpoenaed. The question then is how would the District Attorney have known to call Lawrence as a witness for the prosecution unless Lawrence had made some entreaty to the District Attorney indicating he was willing to testify against Heath

Willcox, Arizona Territory, where Sergeant Lemuel Lawrence killed two men—one a fellow officer—during a drunken altercation in a local saloon (Arizona Historical Society, 48669).

and the others? Or, perhaps, realizing the case against Heath was weak, the Assistant District Attorney Robinson had approached him. And why would Lawrence be so willing to betray his fellow prisoners? Even in that day and age, being a jailhouse snitch could get a man killed. It was a very dangerous game to be playing. Where was the profit to the man in doing so? One must wonder, in spite of his statement to the contrary, Sergeant Lawrence had not entered in to some kind of deal with the District Attorney in exchange for giving testimony against Heath.

Aside from this, three parts of Sergeant Lawrence's testimonies appear to be questionable. First, Lawrence stated that Heath said, "If old man Pardee told what he knew, they would all hang." The question this statement gives rise to is how would Heath know what Pardee knew, if anything at all? Heath never stayed at Pardee's and could not have known what Pardee knew and did not know, unless the others told him that they told Pardee all the details about the robbery. And, if Dowd and the others had told Heath about spilling the beans to Pardee, why would they not have told Heath that they had also revealed their intentions to Frank Buckles? Heath most likely would not have attempted to have Buckles eliminate Pardee if he had known Buckles knew all about their plans as well. This assumes Heath actually never asked Buckles to do such a thing, which seems all the more doubtful in light of Sergeant Lawrence's testimony.

Second, the Sergeant testified that Heath told him that "on leaving Clifton, Howard and himself put up the job." How could Heath and Howard or any of the others known about the Copper Queen payroll deposits being delivered by the 10th of each month and that these monies were kept in the safe in Castaneda's store if they were residing in Clifton. While it is possible they heard about the safe and the deposits from some third party, possibly even Dowd who had lived in Cochise County previously (though not in Bisbee), it still seems unlikely they would have planned the entire job based on unfounded rumors and back-room anecdotes. They might have travelled to Bisbee to verify what they had heard about the payroll deliveries, but it is very doubtful they would have planned the robbery without first doing some reconnaissance.

And finally, Lawrence asserted that Heath brought two saws into the jail with him. This statement also seems rather suspect. This implies that Heath had known in advance he was to be arrested in connection with the robbery. Only then would the defendant have had the foresight to arm himself with a pair of saws. And, if he knew he was to be arrested, why did he not just run? This would seem to be the more logical option as opposed to letting oneself be arrested and incarcerated and then try to escape. Certainly, someone could have brought Heath the saws once he was jailed, but the idea he had hidden the saws on his person prior to being arrested—indicating that he knew he was to be arrested beforehand—seems extremely implausible. In the end, Lawrence's testimony comes across as extremely dubious. Later developments and his own trial make his testimony against Heath even more suspect.

After Sergeant Lawrence stepped down, William Clancy was called before the court. Clancy was the owner of the distinctively monogrammed time-piece which had been part of the spoils taken from Goldwater and Castaneda's store the night of the robbery. "The watch, marked 'W.C.', and offered in evidence by the prosecution, was upon motion of the Dist. Atty. And by order of the Court returned to W. Clancy, its proper owner." Why the watch was entered into evidence during Heath's trial when the defendant was never in possession of the timepiece is unknown. Why Colonel Herring, as Heath's attorney, did not challenge this piece of evidence being presented or challenge the rather inappropriate returning of the watch to its rightful owner during an active trial and in full view of the jury—a gesture which could only prejudice the members of said jury in favor of the prosecution is also unknown.[26]

James S. Robinson, Cochise County Deputy District Attorney, who agreed to represent Sgt. Lawrence at his trial in exchange for the sergeant's testifying against John Heath on behalf of the prosecution (author's collection).

After Mr. Clancy's watch was returned to him, the court took a recess, reconvening at 1:30 p.m. The first witness to testify that Saturday afternoon was Walter Bush, recalled by the District Attorney. "[I] have previously testified to knowing Heith, Tex, Red, Dowd, Kelly, and Delaney," he said. "On the night of the 12th or 13th of December [I] saw Tex and Red in Clifton." Here the witness was presented with a pocket watch, which he instantly identified, saying, "have seen this watch before; saw it in Red Sample's possession in Clifton; I afterwards got it from Sample after his arrest; he told me he got it from a safe in Bisbee at the time of the raid; Tex was present at the time of the conversation; Red said they had had trouble in Bisbee; had killed one man and probably more; Red said he knew he had killed one man who claimed to be a deputy; he told him to stop; and he refused, he then shot him."

The prosecution witness was then duly cross-examined by the defense. The bartender responded to the question put to him by Colonel Herring, saying, "I was in Maud Elby's room at Clifton at the time of the conversation mentioned; I was not in her employ, she was in mine. The house belongs to the Arizona Copper company." Returning to the subject of the watch, Bush said, "[I] think it was about 2 o'clock at night; did not have the watch on that occasion but a few minutes; gave it back to Red; after the time of Red's arrest," he said, "I had the watch until I turned it over to Deputy Sheriff Hoovey [sic]." This ended the testimony of the witness and, again, there is a discrepancy. If, as Richard Rundle testified, "Red" Sample was one of the men inside robbing the store, how could he have been outside shooting Deputy Sheriff Smith in the forehead? Either Richard Rundle or Walter W. Bush was mistaken in his account of what occurred or was lying outright before the court.[27]

The prosecution had called yet again another witness who knew nothing of Heath's actual involvement in the robbery or the planning thereof. The testimony of Walter Bush had no bearing on the case against John Heath whatsoever. The only possible motive for the recalling of Bush to the stand was to sway the attitude of the jurymen against the defendant, by reminding them that two of the men with whom Heath was acquainted were convicted thieves and murderers. In point of fact, except in the spurious testimony given by Sergeant Lawrence, not one of the witnesses had been able to definitively tie Heath to the crime, but only indicated he was acquainted with the men who had been convicted of carrying out the robbery. All the evidence given against the defendant was either hearsay or purely circumstantial. The prosecution had given the jury nothing of substance.

After the prosecution announced it had finished with its case and rested, "Colonel Herring, defendant's counsel, asked the court for a continuation," reported *The Daily Epitaph*, "on the grounds that he had been taken by surprise by evidence introduced by the prosecution which had not been before the grand jury [most likely the testimony of Sergeant Lawrence]." Judge Pinney denied the motion of the defense counsel, and the trial proceeded. The defense then "asked that subpoenas be issued for Dowd, Delaney, Kelly, Sample, Howard, Patsy Halpin, and Mankins." This request was granted by the court.[28]

Immediately afterwards, the defense began the presentation of its case. *The Tombstone Republican* reported that Colonel Herring, Heath's lawyer, "addressed the jury, and outlined in a forcible and graphic manner the line of defense. Unfortunately, the Colonel's diatribe was not recorded in an extant source. The defense then called its first witness, Thomas R. Sorin. Sorin's testimony was brief. He stated he lived in Tombstone and had, until "about the 1st of December" been in possession of a certain horse. He stated the horse had been left with him by Joseph Dyer. Sorin went on to say the horse was a bay and its name was "Frank." This ended his testimony.

Sorin was followed on the stand by John Montgomery, the owner of the stable which had been referred to numerous times during the trial of Daniel Dowd and his compatriots. Montgomery stated that he too lived in Tombstone and confirmed that he kept a "feed and livery" in the aforementioned burg. The stable owner went on to say that "about the 1st of December" he received from Thomas R. Sorin one bay horse named "Frank." This ended his testimony.

Montgomery was in turn followed on the stand by Joseph D. Dyer, who after he was sworn, stated he was a resident of Bisbee and had been in Tombstone "on December last." Dyer stated he "knew a man named Waite" and that he had "known him about a year." The witness also said he was acquainted with Sorin and Montgomery, the two previous witnesses. "In December last," Dyer said, "I received a bay horse named Frank from Sorin through John Montgomery; [I] sent the horse over to Bisbee by Heath, to whom I had been introduced by Waite." This, Dyer said, all happened on Friday, December 7.[29]

After Joseph Dyer stepped down, Heath's business partner and friend, Nathan W. Waite was called to the witness stand. Waite stated he was residing in Bisbee in December of 1883, and "had been in the saloon business" in that town for approximately 15 months. Waite recalled how he first met John Heath in Bisbee on November 30, when Heath and Howard had come in to the saloon where he was employed. They were introduced by one Frank Corey. Waite recalled that Heath said, "[H]e wanted to meet me after I went off watch." Waite consented to meet with Heath later in the evening after his shift ended.

[Heath] stated he had lived in Clifton, was tired of the place, and also sick; that he thought of going into business in Bisbee; at the time mentioned no business arrangement had been made between Heith and me; made arrangement the following morning to go in to the saloon and dance-hall business.

[I] came to Tombstone on the first of December. On 2d examined goods; remained on the night of 2d; returned to Bisbee on night of 3d. On the 4th was in Heith's company all day; [I] have seen Howard in Bisbee; did not see him with Heith on the 4th; saw Heith on the night of the 4th; did not see him with Howard. On the morning of the 5th, Heith, a Mexican, and myself came to Tombstone with a team; [We] arrived about 8:30; on the 6th bought goods, and got ready to leave for Bisbee; on the 7th saw Joseph Dyer; he asked me to ride a horse for him to Bisbee; introduced Heith to Dyer and he rode the horse out to Bisbee; that night drove out nine miles; on the 8th reached Bisbee at 5 p.m.; first man I saw at saloon was Heith; team was unloaded and effects put in the saloon; saw Heith in the saloon of Dave Lynch; he remained with me in the saloon.

John Heath's Defense Attorney Colonel William Herring, who did an admirable job defending his client in spite of the public's prejudice against his client (Arizona Historical Society).

Waite remembered they "heard the shooting on the night of the 8th" and "when the firing began, Heith asked for his revolver, and I gave it to him." He did not say what Heath did with the gun, but explained that "after the shooting [we] went out on the street and saw several dead bodies." Waite said he and Heath "offered our services to Deputy Sheriff Daniel [sic], to go after the robbers; Daniel [sic] picked out four of the men at the saloon; Heith and I were of the number; [we] went to the milk ranch, picked up trail; followed it some distance until the trail split; Heith, Frost, and I took trail leading toward Tombstone; followed it to the outskirts of town; put up the horses, and I went to bed."

Nathan Waite continued in his testimony saying he saw Heath the following morning. "I woke him up," Waite remembered, "and confronted him with a description I had seen of him in the Tucson *Star*; he got up and came down town, and we met Deputy Sheriff Hatch; we then came to the Sheriff's office [located on the first floor in the Tombstone courthouse], where we met Under Sheriff Wallace; this was in the middle of the forenoon; we stated to Wallace that we came to town with Daniel's posse, and asked if we should continue the search. Wallace told us not to continue but to return to Bisbee; Heith gave Wallace pointers as to who some of the men described in the *Star* were. Wallace gave us notices of reward to be posted up there, and Heith, Frost, and I went back to Bisbee. [We] had been there but a short time when Heith was arrested by some citizens of Bisbee."[30]

Unfortunately, there are no extant copies of the *Arizona Daily Star* for the week following the robbery. *The Arizona Weekly Star* of December 13 contained only one article entitled "The Bisbee Raid," with no mention made of Heath. Neither is there any mention of him in *The Weekly Star* of December 20. It can only be concluded that the article Frost referred to in his testimony was in the daily edition of the Tucson newspaper, probably December 10 or 11. As previously mentioned, *The Star's* rival in Tucson, *The Arizona Weekly Citizen* did make mention of "Joe Heath" on December 15. In a dispatch from Lordsburg, N,M., dated December 12, it was reported that "three rustlers with black masks" had robbed R.H. Porter's saloon. The newspaper asserted that "Joe Heath, who was the leader in the late train wreck near Gage station on the 24th ultimo, is the leader of the party." Could this have been the same article which Frost confronted Heath with on the morning after they arrived in Tombstone? Or was the article which appeared in *The Daily Star* more damning? And was it this article which turned the attention of the county in Heath's direction resulting in his arrest and indictment. Again, not knowing what the article actually said, one can only speculate.[31]

Concluding his statement for the defense, Nathan Waite was cross-examined by the District Attorney. The prosecution first sought clarification in regards to the business, to which Waite replied, "[I] first met Heith on 30th day of November; entered into a partnership the following day; Heith suggested the partnership in the dance house business; on the 1st of December I was broke; raised $150 from Chisholm, on David Lynch's note and my own. We opened the dance house on the night of the 8th. I told Heith the mines paid off on the 10th, and I wanted to get the dance house open by that time." The prosecution then asked about "Tex" Howard. Waite stated he did not know where Howard was from the 30th of November to the 4th of December. He was then asked about Heath's actions the night of the robbery. Waite said, "When Heath got his pistol, he stooped down behind the bar, put the pistol across his knee and remained there until the shooting was over."

Waite admitted he "had not known Heith an hour when I told him about the Copper

Queen paying off on the 10th." The business partner was then asked what he knew of Heath's past. "Heith," he said, "told me he came from Clifton to Bisbee; I never lived in Clifton. I got letters for Heith in envelopes addressed to me from Clifton; I broke them open. Letters came from Cronin to Emma Mortimer [Heath's woman], which I did not open—think I brought the letters to Tombstone and gave them to her." The questions from the District Attorney then turned to the manhunt. Waite stated that Heath knew the horse Tex Howard had rode into Bisbee on. Heath, he asserted, "was the first man to call attention to the split in the trail." The final question during the cross-examination returned to the subject of the letters. Waite said he had known John Heath about "five or six days when I received the letters spoken of."[32]

One of the more preposterous stories circulated about the Bisbee Massacre and Heath's involvement therein was that Heath had a full crowd in the dance hall on the night of the robbery and that, while the robbery was taking place, Heath "danced a jig on the floor of the saloon, cracking his heals together each time he heard a shot." Research traces the source of this story back to Harriet Hankin and her manuscript, "The Bisbee Hold-Up and Its Aftermath"—a manuscript many authors have cited in later works. Whether Hankin invented this story or it was fed to her by one of the "old-timers" in Bisbee (perhaps James Krigbaum, who according to Hankin had a part in every scene of the Bisbee drama) is unknown, but the truth could easily be verified in reading Waite's testimony from the transcript of Heath's trial.[33]

Waite's testimony does give rise to questions—questions that cast some further doubt as to Heath's guilt. For instance, why would a man who was masterminding what would most likely be a very lucrative robbery put so much effort into establishing a business in the very town where the crime was to be committed, even going as far to invest his own money in the enterprise and to bring in a partner who was not privy to the crime? Would it not have been safer and easier just to go through the motions of starting a business—giving him an excuse to be scouting about town—than actually establishing a business as he did? Did Heath really plan to collect his ill-gotten gains from the others then return to Bisbee to continue running his business? Or was he planning to just disappear a few weeks later after the commotion subsided? Taking on a partner and opening a new business seems like a lot of effort to put forth in order to provide oneself with an alibi.

Heath's behavior during the robbery and subsequent manhunt also begs questions. When the shooting started, Waite said Heath asked him for his pistol, but he did not immediately rush outside to intervene. Instead he hid behind the bar and waited. Was this because he knew who was out there and what was going on or was it because Heath was at heart a coward and did not want to get involved and, perhaps, get shot? Waite never says whether either of them looked outside to ascertain the situation. It may be imagined that, since the gunmen in front of the store were firing up and down the street, Heath and Waite could hear the reports of the guns inside the building and judge that they were quite close—literally a few yards away from the entrance to the dance hall. Stepping out the front door of the dance-hall with a pistol while two men are firing rifles at anything that moves would give anyone pause.

And once the shooting was over, Heath and Waite volunteered to ride with the posse. Daniels testified that Heath was the first man to approach him, but according to Waite, he and Heath approached the Deputy Sheriff together. Again the testimony of the witnesses—specifically Deputy Daniels and Nathan Waite—is contrary and the defense counsel missed an opportunity to exploit it. Once on the trail, Heath either did not recognize

Howard's horse's track or pretended not to. This is suspicious and could be interpreted as Heath trying to lead the posse astray. However, Waite said Heath recognized the party they were tracking had split up—Heath was the first to realize this—and suggested the posse split up to follow both trails. If Heath had wanted to cover for the men the posse was chasing, would he have pointed out the divergent paths or would he have simply allowed the Deputy and his men to continue as they had been on the singular trail of the outlaw gang until it finally petered out?

Heath, Frost, and Waite followed the trail they discovered to Tombstone, where they gave up the pursuit for the evening. However, the men had not given up in their efforts to track the bandits altogether as some have suggested. In fact, the following morning Heath and Waite met Deputy Sheriff Hatch and Undersheriff Wallace and asked if they should continue in their pursuit. The lawmen instructed them not to. Rather, they were told to return to Bisbee with circulars announcing the reward. It must be remembered that after spending the night at Soldier's Hole and a good portion of the next day cutting for sign, the Tombstone contingency riding with Daniels gave up the pursuit and returned to that burg. Deputy Sheriff Daniels and the Bisbee men were out a few days longer, mostly questioning local ranchers and prospectors, but eventually they too conceded that the trail had been lost and they returned home to Bisbee, arriving on Friday the 14th.

The testimony of Nathan Waite directly challenged the testimony of one of the prosecution's star witnesses, Deputy Sheriff Daniels, and should have aided the defense's case immensely by raising doubt in the minds of the jurors. It was hoped that Henry Frost, the next to be called to the stand by the defense, would increase significantly the reasonable doubt in the minds of the men sitting in the jury box on the far side of the courtroom. After being sworn, Frost identified himself as a resident of Charleston, but confirmed he was living in Bisbee in December of 1883. He stated he worked as an "adobe mason and plasterer" and had been residing in the Arizona Territory since 1873 and in Cochise County about four years.

"When in Bisbee," Frost said, "[I] stopped at Bob Robert's lodging house. Was in Bisbee the night of the 8th; know of the time of the shooting of parties there; [I] was in a dance-house there, said to belong to Heith, Waite, and Lynch; [I] had known Heith four or five days; I had a stud poker game in the house on the night of the shooting." When questioned about Heath's behaviors during the evening, Frost stated, "At the time of the shooting Heith was in the saloon; most of the people ran out; Heith went to the end of the bar; he raised a six-shooter at the end of the bar." The questioning then turned to Heath's actions during the subsequent manhunt. Frost replied, "After the shooting, Deputy Sheriff Daniel [sic] organized a posse to go after the robbers; Heith and I were of that party; we went to milk ranch and found tracks of five horses, which we followed until we lost the trail; Heith was the one to first discover we had lost the trail. [At this point, both *The Tombstone Republican* and *The Tombstone Daily Epitaph* leave off with their recording of Henry Frost's testimony, stating 'Balance of the witness' testimony has reference to the finding of the trail and the incidents testified to by witness Waite.]" Why the newspapers did not print the testimony of this defense witness in its entirety is a matter open to conjecture and interpretation. The newspapers resumed with the cross-examination of Frost by the prosecution.[34]

The prosecution began the cross-examination of Henry Frost with questions about the manhunt. Frost described what happened: "We followed the trail spoken of about fifteen miles in a north-easterly direction; [there] were two horsemen ahead of Heith and

I when he discovered the trail had split; Heith was the man who proposed the party should separate." Frost continued, "From where we separated it was a mile to where we struck the trail that Heath, Waite, and I followed to Tombstone; I found the trail and called Heith's attention to it; he said he had also found it." The prosecution then asked about the track that Heath said was peculiar to Howard's horse. Frost explained that Heath said, "Tex's horse was shod wide behind like a mule."

The next questions from the prosecutor concerned Heath's behavior in the dance house on the night of the robbery. Frost said he did not see Waite give Heath a pistol and that he believed "Heith raised it himself from the end of the bar." He said he heard Heith state that "Tex used to work for him." "Heith," Frost said, "stood a little inside of the end of the bar; he was leaning with one hand on the bar." While the prosecution concluded their questioning of the witness, the defense attorney felt further explanation was in order and proceeded to re-examine the witness. In response, Henry Frost stated he had not heard "Heith say anything while he stood at the bar, except, 'Better stand back, there is a Winchester going off.'" Frost also recalled, "When coming in on the trail to Tombstone, Heith said 'If Tex is one of the party, and we find him, we'll have to fight to take him.'" This ended Frost's testimony on behalf of the defense.[35]

As noted by the newspapers (whose choice not to print the entirety of the witnesses testimony may well be construed as evidence of their inherent prejudice against the defendant), Frost essentially reiterated much of what Waite had stated before him. However, this only served to strengthen the case for the defense. Frost verified that it was Heath who first realized the trail of the suspects diverged and brought it to everyone's attention. Heath was also the one to suggest the posse spilt up in order to follow both the leads. Frost noted it was he who initially found the trail leading on towards Tombstone, indicating they weren't just being led blindly along on a wild goose chase by the defendant. However, his recollection of Heath's statement about "Tex" Howard, could be construed either as an attempt to frighten his companions in to giving up the search or as Heath recognized the fact they might have to fight a man he was well-acquainted with and indicated a willingness on his part to do just that.

Frost in his testimony about how Heath obtained the pistol the night of the robbery contradicted that of Nathan Waite, Henry Frost's remembrance of Heath's admonishment to the others to "stand back" as the street echoed with the sound of a Winchester rifle, makes plausible the suggestion that it was not so much cowardice, but caution and self-preservation which kept Heath from running into the street with a pistol in hand. Of course, his inaction might also be interpreted as the behavior of a person with a stake in what was happening outside in the street. It might also be that Heath armed himself with the revolver in case the violence in the street happened to spill in through the front door of the dance-house he and his friends were holed up in. His position, as described by both Waite and Frost as being near the end of the bar and slightly behind it, would have been a good defensive position given such a scenario.

In an effort to prove Heath did not have any contact with Dowd, Delaney, and the others just prior to the robbery, the defense called Cesario Lucero (the same man who led Deputy Sheriff Daniels into Mexico in search of Dowd and Delaney, and the same man *The Arizona Weekly Citizen* erroneously reported was hanged in a tree and riddled with bullets by friends of Dan Dowd) to the stand. It may be recalled that William Gerstenberg stated during the first trial that he had seen several men, including Dan Dowd, camped about one-half mile below the slaughter house. Lucero, who stated he was living in Bisbee at the time of the robbery and was employed "in the wool business," said he saw Heath in Bisbee on the evening of the shooting. "Heith," he said, "was on horseback. I saw him riding to my house about four or five hundred yards below the corral; he stopped at my house about ten minutes; he returned to town; [I] did not see him ride below my house" in the direction of where Gerstenberg had said he saw the outlaws' camp.

Under cross-examination by the prosecuting attorney, Lucero stated he had seen Heath at three o'clock in the afternoon on December 8. "My place," he said, "is about one-half mile from the slaughter-house." When asked a second time how long Heath had visited with him, Lucero responded "about fifteen minutes." Unfortunately, this testimony may have had the opposite effect of what was intended. The defense did not explain why Heath had ridden out to Lucero's, leaving the reason as a point for open conjecture. Had the defendant been searching for the men William Gerstenberg had seen earlier in the day, or was he on another errand, or was the defendant simply out exercising his horse in the limited warmth of the afternoon sun on that December day? Lucero's testimony did not aid the defense. Instead, it left the jury with more unanswered questions.[36]

This ended the second day of testimony in the trial of John Heath. In their "Local Notes" section the Sunday, February 17, edition of *The Daily Epitaph* reported that Judge Pinney had notified the "jurors not engaged in the Heith case that they were discharged for the term." The newspaper also praised Colonel Herring, Heath's attorney, saying of the barrister, "[He] is making an able fight for his client ... but the evidence is too strong the other way for him to make a winning one." Finally, *The Daily Epitaph* reported that Emma Mortimer, who the paper identified simply as "John Heath's mistress" had "completely broke down under the shock of Lawrence's testimony against her lord, and was too unwell to appear as a witness in his favor yesterday afternoon when called."[37]

Little is known of Ms. Emma Mortimer aside from her mention in local newspapers regarding her connection to John Heath's trial. In the eyes of society at large, she was nothing more than what she was described as by *The Daily Epitaph*—John Heath's mistress. It is not known when or how she arrived in Cochise County or what brought her to that place. It may be surmised she followed Heath west, but from where exactly—Clifton? Dallas? Waite in his testimony indicated she was residing in Tombstone, but received her mail at his residence in Bisbee. By her own admission, Ms. Mortimer was of the demimonde—a prostitute. She also admitted to giving Heath money, so it may be assumed that not only was Heath her lover but also her pimp.

On February 13, *The New York Times*, one of the many newspapers across the country keeping the people informed about the doings in the wild and wooly Arizona Territory, ran a small article from the Associate Press concerning the delay in sentencing for Dowd and his accomplices. "The newspaper reported "[W]hen the Bisbee murders were called in court this morning for sentence their attorney moved for a new trial. This action will cause a delay of a year before the death penalty can be carried out. The general opinion in the community," stated *The Times*, "is that the prisoners have had a fair trial and that the proof against them was overwhelming. It is believed if they are not legally hanged they will be lynched." Variations on this dispatch appeared in *The Chicago Daily Tribune*, *The Sacramento Daily Record-Union*, *The St. Paul Daily Globe*, and others, with the initial report originating in San Francisco.[38]

Under a bold headline of "NO HOPE!" *The Tombstone Republican* recorded the motion of the defense attorneys on behalf of their clients, in their desperate bid for a new trial given before the court on February 18. Setting the scene, the newspaper reported that the courtroom was "filled to its utmost capacity and many ladies in attendance, but "when the prisoners were brought in at 9 o'clock perfect silence prevailed; everyone though anxious to hear sentence, realized the solemnity of the occasion, and perfect order prevailed." Unfortunately, for those expecting to hear the judge pronounce the sentence of death over the defendants, the defense attorneys had one final card to play in the form of an appeal for a new trial for their clients.

George R. Williams, the attorney for "Big" Dan Dowd and James "Tex" Howard began the day with his motion. Dowd, he stated, "had been arrested on Mexican soil and brought here without extradition papers" which made his arrest an "illegal act." Attorney Judge Drum followed suit and on behalf of his clients, O.W. Sample and Daniel Kelly, "made motion for a new trial on the grounds: 1st—that the court misdirected the jury in a matter of law: 2nd—that the verdict is contrary to the law and evidence; 3rd—that the court has no legal jurisdiction over the person of either James Howard or Daniel Dowd, the defendants above named." Similar motions were filed with the court by Judge Southard and Colonel Herring. While the appeal of attorney Drum seems very much like a last-ditch attempt to delay the inevitable, attorney William's appeal on behalf of Dowd might have had some merit.[39]

The day before, on Sunday, February 17, *the Daily Epitaph* reprinted an article which had first appeared in *The Prescott Miner* in which it was reported that "the Mexican authorities have forwarded a circular to the city of Washington [D.C.] to the effect that Dan Dowd was arrested on Mexican soil without proper papers and contrary to the extradition treaty" that existed between the two countries. The article continued, explaining that Arizona Territorial "Governor Trittle, having received instructions from the secretary of state, is now investigating the circumstances [*illegible*] with the affair. This matter," noted the reporter of the Tombstone newspaper, "has been previously mentioned in the Epitaph and if it turns out that all the trouble has been kicked up by the officious Mexican consul at Tombstone. It would be a good idea to send him home for being to d____d officious."[40]

Defense Attorney George R. Williams, co-counsel for defendants Daniel "Big Dan" Dowd and James "Tex" Howard (Arizona Historical Society, 1728 [cropped]).

In response to the motions of the defense counsel, "District Attorney Smith claimed that in regard to the jurisdiction of the court in the case of Dowd, that it was a question between the United States and Mexico as to whether the laws had been infringed upon." Judge Pinney refused to consider the appeal, stating "if the United States and Mexico wished to intervene, that would be a different thing or if this were a case properly brought before him, it was a matter for a judge to decide and would not effect [*sic*] the judgment in this case." That said, the judge overruled the motions brought before the court for a new trial for the five defendants. Colonel Herring then asked that the sentencing of Dowd, Delaney, Sample, Howard, and Kelly be postponed. Even though the attorney had given no reason for the delay, the court granted the request. Sentencing was set for the following day, Tuesday, February 19, at 1:30 p.m. and the prisoners duly remanded to the custody of the Cochise County Sheriff.[41]

The trial of John Heath resumed with the defense presenting the balance of its case that same day. The most damaging testimony presented by the prosecution thus far was that of Sergeant Lemuel Lawrence and it was the intention of defense attorney Colonel Herring to undermine his credibility. To that end, the defense called the Clerk of the Court, W.H. Seamans to the stand. After he was sworn and identified himself, Colonel Herring put a single question to him. In reply, Seamans said, "There is an indictment against L.D. Lawrence." Herring then asked a copy of the indictment be produced and entered in as evidence. This motion elicited an immediate objection from District Attorney Smith. The objection was sustained by Judge Pinney and the document was not entered into the official record. Still, Herring had made his point.[42]

Cochise County Undersheriff Albert Wallace was the next witness to be called to testify. Wallace was duly sworn and in response to the first question put to him by the defense, the lawman confirmed:

> I was a deputy sheriff of this county last December, acting as such after the 1st of December. On the 9th, I saw Heith in Tombstone, in a place known as the Fountain; conversation occurred between Heith and myself; the interview was quite a lengthy one; we held several while the defendant was in town. I received word from a man coming out of the Fountain that the defendant was there and wanted to see me; I went in, made myself known; defendant said he wanted to have a conversation with me—said he went out with Mr. Daniel's party in pursuit of the robbers. When the trail split he [Heith] followed one branch and Daniel the other; the defendant and his party coming toward Tombstone. After this conversation it was arranged that I was to meet him again in the evening. I do not think I gave him any directions at that time—did afterwards.
>
> I know that shortly after the interview the defendant went to the stable and procured another horse and took a ride around the town; [I] saw him in the evening when he said he had been unsuccessful in finding the trail of the parties; saw Mr. Waite and Frost with him; afterwards saw him at the sheriff's office; next morning [10th], defendant said he was going back to Bisbee; told him I would like him take [sic] with him some circulars that had been issued as to the reward; he took them; Waite was with him. The first visit to the sheriff's office was on Monday; he came again in the evening. I do not know whether these visits were in connection with Mr. Daniel; I should judge they were in connection with the Bisbee murder.

The prosecution declined to cross-examine the witness, and Undersheriff Wallace was allowed to step down.[43]

James "Tex" Howard was escorted in to the courtroom under armed guard and was still manacled when he was asked to take the stand. Howard acknowledged he had been brought directly from the county jail downstairs to the courtroom. Howard further stated he had been incarcerated for a period of about two months and was "one of the parties charged with the killing of D.T. Smith." The outlaw said he knew Heath and had "seen Lawrence." Howard stated emphatically he had not heard any conversation between the defendant and Heath. When pressed, Howard elaborated on this point, "I have been on the south side of the jail; Heith was on the other side of the jail; there is a partition of bars between the cells [and] in the open space above the cells."

The defense attorney then produced the saw which had been entered in to evidence and questioned Howard about it. Howard said, "I have never seen this before; never handed this to Lawrence." When asked about statements he was said to have made about the defendant, Howard replied. "I never said that Heith was the man who organized the plan of the Bisbee murders." At this, the defense rested and the prosecuting attorney came from behind the table to cross-examine the outlaw. To the District Attorney's questions about Heath's alleged conversations with Lawrence, "Tex" Howard replied, "I have not stated to anyone that I have heard any conversation; never heard any talk with Lawrence about it; I am on the left side of the jail as we go in; Heith is on the right side; the cells are back to back; bars on top." The District Attorney then asked Howard about his relationship with the defendant. Howard replied, "[I] have known Heith since 1879; seen him many times in the territory since I knew him; he is an acquaintance of mine, not particularly a friend; he never asked me to testify for him; I never had any talk with any one about this case except Mr. Herring, and what I said to him I have stated here in court today."[44]

The testimony of James "Tex" Howard on behalf of the defense was a two-pronged attack on the prosecution's case. First, Howard, who at this point had been tried and convicted and was either facing a life sentence or the noose the next day, stated for the record that Heath had not been the mastermind behind the robbery. The outlaw said he had known Heath for sometime, but did not consider the man a friend—merely an acquaintance. Howard also repudiated the entire testimony of Sergeant Lawrence. Howard said he had never heard Heath converse with Lawrence. He then described the surroundings in the jailhouse, which gave proof that it would have been nearly impossible for the two men to have a conversation without his overhearing their exchange.

One might wonder if the prosecuting attorney, Colonel Herring, might have made some offer to Howard in exchange for his testimony. The question then is what could Herring really have offered the outlaw? That very morning, Howard and his confederates had been summarily denied a new trial by Judge Pinney. The following morning, the five men would either be sentenced to life in the Yuma Territorial Prison or death on the gallows. The most Herring could promise was to have a word with Judge Pinney and recommend leniency in the sentencing, but in the end, the decision of their fate rested entirely with the magistrate. This being the situation, what motivation did Howard have to perjure himself in defense of Heath—the very man Sergeant Lawrence said blamed him for the robbery going poorly and their all being apprehended? Either James "Tex" Howard had a very strong and completely misplaced sense of loyalty towards Heath or he was telling the truth, the whole truth, and nothing but the truth while on the witness stand.

Not content to simply counter the testimony of a suspected criminal—Sergeant Lawrence—along with the testimony of a convicted criminal—James "Tex" Howard—Colonel Herring called Daniel "York" Kelly as the next witness for the defense. Kelly admitted he had been in the Cochise County jail since December 17, though he did not speak to the reason he was incarcerated. When questioned about Heath and Lawrence, he confirmed he knew Heath and had seen Lawrence in the jailhouse. "Lawrence and I had no conversation about the Bisbee murderers," he stated flatly. "I didn't say to Lawrence defendant [sic] was the man who put up the job." The questioning then turned to the saw. Again Kelly refuted the statements of Lawrence, "I never had any conversation about a saw. I did not say to Lawrence if the defendant was on the outside, I would have no trouble in getting out of jail; didn't say that if Tex, Red Sample, and the defendant had stuck to our agreement that none of us would be in jail now."

When the saw was shown to Kelly and he was again asked about it, he affirmed, "I never have seen this saw before; I had nothing to do with the making of it." He was then questioned about Lubien Pardee, to which he replied, "I know Mr. Pardee; I camped with him last November or December; I did not say anything to Pardee about robbing a store. One day, Delaney came to Pardee's camp with provisions; I left the defendant the 27th of November. Delaney said the defendant was going to open a saloon in Bisbee or Tombstone." Having finished with his questioning of the witness, Colonel Herring resumed his seat and Kelly was then cross-examined by the prosecution. In answer to their queries, Kelly said he knew the defendant and that he had seen him "at San Simon and Galeyville and saw him with Dan Dowd, Red Sample, Tex, and Delaney" when he was staying with Pardee. He also said he "saw the defendant on the 5th of December at Buckles' ranch [en route to Tombstone with Waite]."

"Heith," said Daniel Kelly, "was gone from the 27th of November to the 5th of December. Delaney told me he that he intended to go to Bavispe, Sonora, if he could get Dowd to go with him." The line of questioning then turned back to Pardee and the conversations that took place at his camp. Kelly described the camp thus: "Pardee's camp is built like an Indian's camp; we slept about 80 feet from Pardee's camp; a conversation could not be heard; I have often called to Pardee at night, and had to call loud to attract his attention." With this, the prosecuting attorney left off questioning him further and Daniel "York" Kelly was then allowed to step down and was returned downstairs to his cell. The next to be escorted upstairs to testify was his cell-mate, William Delaney.[45]

Delaney's testimony was in agreement with that of Daniel Kelly and "Tex" Howard. The outlaw said, "[I] was brought from jail to this courtroom; Know Heith; know Lawrence; have been there [in jail] a month; have not heard the defendant say that Tex was to go back from Bisbee to Clifton; have not heard the defendant say that such was the plan agreed upon. Know Kelly; know Pardee; Kelly was at Pardee's when I went there; Kelly asked me had I seen Heith; I said 'Yes, he has gone to Bisbee to start a saloon or dance hall, don't know which.' I saw the defendant at Buckles' ranch." When he was shown the saw, Delaney said he had never before seen it. His cross-examination was brief, with Delaney answering the attorney, "Do not know what Kelly intended to testify to." There was then a re-direct, to which he replied, "Buckles had a conversation with me about the defendant going in to business. Buckles told Heith that Bisbee was a better place to go in to business than Tombstone."

There was then a re-cross examination by the prosecutor and a second re-direct by the defense. Delaney answered the prosecutor, "I was never in Bisbee in my life." He answered the defense attorney, "I had been in Tombstone before." William Delaney was then allowed to step down and was taken from the courtroom and returned to his cell. Daniel "Big Dan" Dowd was then called upon to testify. The shackled man was brought up the stairs, sworn in, and seated in the witness stand. "[I] have been in jail since the 5th of January," Dowd confirmed, "[I] know Lawrence—a soldier; never have heard the defendant say anything about the plans for the Bisbee murders; when I was taken back to jail after my conviction did not say that 'if Pardee told all he knew we would all hang'; never said this to anyone."[46]

Dowd was then cross-examined by the prosecutor. He was asked how long he had known the defendant, to which he replied, "I have known the defendant some time; have spoken to him in Clifton; met him first on this side of Clifton about four miles, just this side of the big hill." The questioning then turned to conversations between the witness and the defendant. Dowd stated, "Heith said to us: 'I am going to have you all subpoenaed on the Lawrence evidence.' [He] did not say he wanted us to stand by him; didn't say there was no use in giving him away." The questions then returned to their meeting on the road and the journey into Cochise County. Dowd said, "After meeting him first, I travelled down the road with him a little way; we did not stop together that night." This concluded Daniel "Big Dan" Dowd's testimony before the court.[47]

Omer W. "Red" Sample was the last of the five men convicted of the Bisbee murders to be called to the stand by the defense. His testimony mirrored those of the previous witnesses: "[I] was brought from the county jail," he said. "Have been there since the 24th of December last; know Heith; have seen Lawrence in the jail; know of no conversation between the defendant and Lawrence about the Bisbee murders. I have been on the same side of the jail as Tex; have not said if Howard has done as he agreed to we would not be in jail, I never said if the defendant was outside we would stand a show of getting out." When presented with the saw, Sample said, "I never saw this before and don't know what it is now."

The cross-examination of Sample was brief. He responded to the questions from the prosecutor, saying, "I have known defendant since some time in August last; was on good terms with him in Clifton." This answer occasioned a re-direct from the defense. Sample expounded upon his statement about knowing Heath, saying, "I have been in the defendant's saloon in Clifton; [I] have drank there; [I] have been in the saloon business myself there." There were no further questions from either the defense or the prosecution and Omer W. "Red" Sample was excused. He was taken by sheriff's deputies out of the courtroom, and back down the winding staircase to his cell, his chains clanking together with each step he took.[48]

Howard, Kelly, Delaney, Dowd, and Sample had all been in agreement in their testimony before the court and their testimony refuted absolutely all that Sergeant Lawrence had sworn to. The men absolutely denied making the statements attributed to them by Lawrence. They denied hearing any conversations between Heath and Lawrence. They denied hearing Heath make any statements to Lawrence. They all admitted being acquainted with Heath, with Sample going as far as to say he had been "on good terms" with the man, but each in turn denied John Heath had in any way been involved in the planning of the robbery. Colonel Herring had done well in questioning Dowd and establishing the fact that Heath told the men he was going to subpoena them but that he had not asked them to "stand by him." Herring was remiss only in not having the other four witnesses make similar statements while under oath in order to drive the point home with the jury.

Daniel Dowd stated that Heath had not said anything to the effect that "there was no use in giving him away." By the same token, there was really no profit for these men in lying on Heath's behalf. Dowd and the others had nothing to lose either way. Their fate was sealed. They had been convicted and were either going to be imprisoned for life or, more likely, hanged by the neck until dead. There was nothing Herring or Heath could have promised them was going to change this. Further, if Heath had been publicly blaming Howard for their predicament and telling Lawrence all about the plans for the robbery, would these men really have been inclined to come to his defense when asked? It is much more likely, if they believed Heath had betrayed them in such a manner, they would have either refused to testify on his behalf or taken the stand as hostile witnesses.

After Sample was escorted back downstairs to his cell, John Heath took the stand in his own defense. He began by stating,

Hovey's Dance Hall and Saloon, Clifton, which was owned by Graham County Deputy Sheriff John M. Hovey, who had been instrumental in the capture of "Red" Sample and "Tex" Howard (author's collection).

I am the defendant in this case; I was at Bisbee when arrested on this charge; had been in Clifton since the 15th of last April; [I] was in the saloon business there; left there the 23rd of last November, on a Thursday, between 12 and 1 o'clock, on horseback. I know Bush, who has testified. I rode down the main street on leaving Clifton; do not remember having seen Bush on the street; [I] was alone. [I] know Tex; have known him for eight or nine years; knew him in Texas; worked with him for three years; saw him for the first time in this territory about the 7th or 8th of November last, at Clifton; saw him in John Hovey's saloon; saw him next about the 25th of November, 20 miles this side of Clifton; I was coming to Tombstone to go in to the saloon business.

Four miles out of Clifton I was overtaken by Dowd, Sample and a man they called Yorkey. [I] rode on with them to Haxie's ranch, where I stayed overnight; none of the others stayed there that night, but all three came back for breakfast; [I] was eating when they came. They wanted me to wait for them, but I rode on two miles and met Tex; that was the first time in the territory; we rode in to Bisbee together; when I met Tex, he was going to Clifton—I was leaving there.

This was all Heath was permitted to say that morning of the February 18, 1884, as Judge Pinney called for a recess in the middle of Heath's testimony, adjourning the court until the afternoon.

After the recess, Heath was brought back up to the courtroom and there, after being reminded he was still under oath, continued his testimony. He recounted his journey to Cochise County,

Howard asked me where I was going. Told him I was going to Tombstone to go in to the saloon business. If I didn't like it there would go to Prescott; Howard said he would too if he had money; I was feeling unwell, and told him if he would accompany me I would pay his expenses; after this conversation we were overtaken by Dowd, Kelly, and Sample; we all stopped at a stage stand and fed horses; after this we mounted the horses, and rode together until reaching forks in the road; here Dowd, Sample and Kelly left us, saying they were going to Mexico. Howard and I rode along together, and were overtaken again by Dowd, Kelly, and Sample. Nothing was said by them concerning the Bisbee matter; we rode on together about 6 miles and camped. I had known Sample in Clifton when

I was in the saloon business. He was a frequenter of my saloon; had a very slight acquaintance with either Dowd or Kelly.

We remained at Cienega all that night; [the] next day went to a station the other side of Bowie [I mean a railroad station]; we stayed in the section house, and got supper, and breakfast there; got there about 5 p.m.; there were a good many people there; next morning left and travelled together to Galeyville; did not remain in Galeyville but one night; we left together and crossed the Chiricahua Mountains; Dowd, Yorkey and Sample [illegible] the summit of the mountains; said they were going to Mexico; [illegible] on the trail; went about 2 miles and got lost; staid [sic] all night; got out of mountains about 11 o'clock next morning; came to Inman's coal camp; stopped and got dinner.

Heath said he and "Tex" Howard next went to Smith's where they got feed for the horses. "[We] left Smith's and after riding about 4 miles I was taken very sick," recalled Heath.

Went on to Buckles' ranch; there I met Delaney; [I] had known him before in Clifton; we arrived at Buckles' ranch about 4 p.m. Remained all night. [I] went to bed as soon as I got there. Just after I went to bed, Howard came in and said Dowd, Kelly and Sample had arrived. Saw them next in the morning at breakfast; remained there all day. Dowd and Sample left after breakfast. Howard and myself staid [sic] there. [I] told Frank Buckles and Delaney that I was going to Tombstone to enter business. They both told me Tombstone was dead, and Buckles told me to go to Bisbee. After the conversation I went down to a well where there were some teamsters. Sat down and conversed with them.

Left Buckles ranch next morning, November 29th, and went to Soldiers' Hole. Howard was with me. From there went to the milk ranch. Next morning went into Bisbee; up to this time there had been no conversation between any of the parties and myself in regard to the Bisbee crime or any other crime. We put up our horses in the corral. Came up town, met Frank Cory; told him my business. Afterward, looked the town over. Rather liked the place. [I] met Cory again. He said two men were going to open a dance house, and maybe I could get in with them. Saw Waite, one of the two men; this was on November 30th. Saw Waite about 8 p.m. of that day. [I] don't think Howard was with me when I had talk with Waite. Interview happened outside the saloon in which Waite was at work. Afterwards, Howard and I went to bed.

Next morning, December 1st, ate breakfast, found Waite, and arrived at an understanding with him; went and looked at [the] dance house; made some few changes; we then went and got our horses and came to Tombstone; arrived about 7 p.m.; made some inquiries for furniture next day and night, and the following morning returned to Bisbee, getting there on the evening of 3d, about 6 o'clock. [I] went to bed that night about 10 o'clock. After breakfast, [I] gave Howard $7 to pay his expanses back to Clifton, and he left. Spent the remainder of the day in and about the dance house. On the 5th of December, Waite and I got [a] four-horse team and started for Tombstone; got in that night. Next morning, we began loading the wagon; remained until the 7th and left that day, on a horse belonging to Mr. Dyer, who wanted the horse ridden to Bisbee.

[I] got to Bisbee about 8 p.m. Saw Howard on the night of the 7th; [I] was surprised to find him there. [He] told me he did not intend to go to Clifton; said he was going to see some Texans. The conversation occurred in a saloon before a crowd. After I left Howard, I went to Lynch's place and took a drink. There was a man with Howard at the time I spoke to him whom I did not know. On the morning of the 8th, got up, was sick; went to the dance house and stayed about there all day; in the evening rode out to summit of the ridge to see if I could see Waite coming with the team. Went to Lucero's and had a drink; then went to town and stayed at the dance house until Waite came. Afterward, unloaded the wagon and went to supper at the French restaurant. After supper, returned to dance house and remained there.

There was gambling, music and dancing going on. I was gambling when I heard three shots. A crippled man ran into the saloon and said man and wife had had trouble. About this time I heard the report of a Winchester, and went to the bar and asked for my pistol. Waite gave it to me, and I stooped down at the end of the bar and held the pistol across my knee. After the shooting ceased, we went out and heard some parties and been killed. Went on down to Goldwater's saloon and there learned the full particulars. Was asked to go out with Deputy Sheriff Daniels after the robbers and did so. Went to the milk ranch and remained until daylight. Daniels told me he believed Jim Howard was one of the party. Told him I did not believe it. My reason for saying this was that I had known Howard for eight years and never knew anything wrong about him.

We were riding along when I told Daniels that some of the tracks left the road. Daniels said he would follow the ones left; went a little further and I called his attention to the fact there were no tracks in the road at all. Daniels wanted to know what I thought about it. Told him I was positive that party had split and he had better split his party. [I] asked him to let me go with Frost and Waite as I knew them. [Daniels] told me if I found the trail to stay with it. I subsequently found some of the tracks I had seen in the road from the milk ranch. Frost also found the tracks the same time I did. We followed the tracks to the outskirts of town. Waite was worn out, and wanted to know what we were going to do. Told him we would go and get fresh horses. On the road, I told Waite and Frost if Howard really was in it, which I did not believe, we would have to fight.

After reaching Tombstone, we inspected all the public and private stables in town, but found no trace of the animals we had tracked. Afterward, met Under Sheriff Wallace and he told me to come around the next morning. Same night, Frost called my attention to a suspicious looking character he had seen in town, and we shadowed him that night. [I] had a conversation with Wallace concerning the Bisbee murders. I received from him some notices of reward for the Bisbee murderers. Put them in my centenas [sic], and after I left town posted them up in Charleston and Bisbee. When I got to Charleston, I inquired for news of the robbers. [I] heard that five men had been seen on the road from Charleston to Bisbee. After leaving Charleston, went to Bisbee, put my horse up, had something to eat, and started to write a letter to my partner in Clifton. While I was thus engaged, I was arrested by some citizens of Bisbee, was searched, and then brought to the county jail.

Afterward, had an examination before a justice of the peace and was held over to await the action of the grand jury. I was searched three times before I was put in jail. At no time did I plan or know anything about the contemplated Bisbee robbery. While I was in jail, I met one Lawrence, a soldier. Dowd did not say in the presence of Lawrence and myself that if Pardee told what he knew we would all hang. [I] never told Lawrence that I had but [sic] up the Bisbee robbery. Never told him that if Howard had done as we agreed, I would not be here. Never told Lawrence that Howard was to go back to meet parties from Clifton. Never told Lawrence that Howard, Dowd, Kelly, and Sample were parties to that agreement. Never, while lying on top of the jail, did I describe to Lawrence how the Bisbee robbery was committed. [I] never heard Kelly make any statement to Lawrence about the murder.

Heath continued with his denials. "[I] never talked to Lawrence about a saw, and did not ask him to help break jail by means of this saw." When the saw was produced and presented to him, Heath stated, "I have seen this saw before in the hands of Lawrence; he showed them to me and, upon my asking what they were, he explained that [they] were to be used in getting out of jail." Heath then returned to his emphatic denials.

Never gave Burns any money to buy case knives. [I] never hung a string out the window at any time. [I] knew nothing at all about it. Lawrence never brought any messages to me from Dowd, Kelly, Delaney, or others concerning jail breaking. [I] did not have $40 to give Burns to buy knives with. Lawrence was in jail when I was put in. He said he was in jail for murder.[I] never heard anything about knives from anyone.

When I was first put in jail, I was on the right hand side opposite the iron cells. [I] remained there until Lawrence made the statement about me. [I] never had any such conversation with Buckles in the jail as he describes. I had a conversation with Lawrence in which he said that his attorney told him that if he would furnish evidence to convict the five men—Delaney, Kelly, Dowd, Sample, and Tex, he would be allowed to go clear when it came to his trial.

And with these statements, Heath concluded his testimony in his own defense. However, he was still subject to cross-examination and District Attorney Smith began by producing a document signed by Heath on his deposition taken before the committing magistrate. Heath was then questioned about his acquaintance with James "Tex" Howard and the other men who had been convicted of the murders in Bisbee.

Heath replied that he "did not know the names of Tex or Kelly applied to Jim Howard or Kelly." He continued, "[I] went to work on Chisholm's trail in Texas with Howard. I refuse to tell whereabouts in Texas I came from, on account of my people. First knew Tex in San Antonio. First place after seeing him in San Antonio was Clifton; saw him once in my saloon. [I] met Tex 20 miles from Clifton. I was coming to Tombstone, he was going to Clifton. I brought him back with me for company. Tex told me at Bisbee he was going back to Clifton. Talked to him in Lockwood's corral on the morning he left, about 20 minutes. [I] was surprised to see him back again on the 8th; he said he was going to see some Texas men to get a job; he left about 7:30 p.m. [I] had seen Dowd, Kelly, and Sample in Clifton. Tex and I left Buckles' ranch together and went to Bisbee together; we ate together and slept together; we got to Buckles' ranch on the 27th of November; met Delaney there." Heath admitted he knew Delaney "was an escape from justice."

When District Attorney Smith asked about his actions during the manhunt, Heath responded, "[I] did not see Tex [sic] horse's tracks in the trail from the milk ranch; if his track was there he had been shod since I saw his track." The question then turned to Heath and Howard's trip into the territory. Heath said, "[Illegible] made a note of the date I left Clifton. [I] was at Galeyville, either on Sunday or Saturday. Next after leaving Galeyville, we got to Inman's. Got lost in the mountains that same day we left Galeyville; got to Inman's the next day, and Buckles' that same night." The prosecution then broached the subject of the saws, to which Heath replied, "Lawrence was the first man I saw with the saws in the jail. Burns was the last man I saw with them. [I] don't know who rigged the saw. [I] didn't see Lawrence rig it; it was not rigged when I first saw it."[49]

With this, the prosecuting attorney desisted in his questioning of the defendant, and John Heath was allowed to step down and return to his chair at the long oak defense table next to his lawyer. Colonel Herring had been right in letting Heath testify on his own behalf as it allowed Heath to clear up some of the questions about his activities that seemed suspicious to the jury. In his testimony, Heath was able to establish that he and "Tex" Howard had known each other for sometime and that he was acquainted with "Red" Sample, as Sample had been a customer in his saloon in Clifton. Heath was absolutely forthcoming on this point. However, his acquaintance with Delaney, Dowd and Kelly was, by his admission, "slight." In fact, Heath did not seem particularly inclined to keep their company during the journey, as evidenced by the fact he refused to wait for them while they took breakfast at Haxie's ranch, setting out on his own from that place, and leaving them behind.

Several times during the horseback trip across the territory, Dowd, Kelly and Sample showed up suddenly and then departed almost as abruptly. When Heath arrived at Haxie's they were with him, but they rode on while he spent the night at the ranch. The three showed up again in the morning, but Heath left without them. Soon after, Heath met up with Howard on the trail, the three men caught up with him again. The five men rode together to the "forks of the road," where Dowd, Kelly, and Sample took their leave, stating their intention was to travel on to Mexico. A little later, the three horsemen showed up again, and they all rode together to Cienega, where they spent the night. After riding to Bowie the following day and then into the Chiricahua Mountains, Dowd, Kelly and Sample deserted Heath and Howard once more, saying again they planned to ride in to Mexico. However, they reappeared at Buckles' ranch just two days later.

It is hard to know what to make of these frequent comings and goings, but it does seem to indicate that Dowd, Kelly, and Sample were fairly shiftless and not given to any specific intent as was Heath. If these men were involved in a conspiracy with Heath, would they not have been inclined to remain in one another's company throughout the journey? The morning after he arrived at Buckles', Heath had breakfast with Dowd, Delaney, Sample, Kelly, and Howard. This is the only time the six men were known to have been together in the same place. However, immediately after the meal, Dowd and Sample took off. They did not announce where they were going. Heath stayed on at Buckles' ranch with Howard (and presumably Delaney and Kelly) one more night. When Heath left Buckles' ranch on November 29, only Howard—his paid companion—rode out with him. With the exception of "Tex" Howard, John Heath was not seen in the company of any of these men again.

During his testimony, Howard admitted he and Heath were more "acquaintances" than "friends" even though by Heath's estimation had known each other "eight or nine years" and had worked together for three years on the Chisholm Trail, probably as cowboys. Though he does not explicitly say, Heath indicated it had been some time since he had seen Howard. In fact, Heath basically bribed Howard to ride with him to Tombstone, saying he would pay his expenses if Howard would accompany him. The reason he gave for asking Howard along was that he was feeling ill and wanted some "company" on the trail. Upon their arrival in Bisbee, the two men separated. When Heath spoke with Nathan Waite about going in to business together he stated that Howard was not present.

True to his word, Heath paid Howard $7 on the 4th of December, so that Howard might return to Clifton. When he saw Howard again on the night of the 7th, Heath said he was "surprised." On the 30th of November, Heath arrived in Bisbee with Howard. Almost immediately, Heath commenced to setting up his business. He recruited a new partner in Nathan Waite, scouted the property, traveled into Tombstone, first to seek out furniture, and a second time to transport that furniture back to Bisbee. The only time Heath and "Tex" Howard were seen together during this time was when Heath met with Howard at Lockwood's stable to pay him off and send him on his way. Otherwise, Heath's actions would seem the actions of a man legitimately trying to get a new business up and running.

In testifying before the court, Heath was also given the opportunity to explain his behavior during the initial days of the manhunt. He implied that he and Deputy Sheriff Daniels were at loggerheads almost from the beginning, when Daniels suggested to Heath that Howard may well have been among the men they were tracking. By way of defending the man, Heath pointed out that he knew Howards' horses' track and did not see it among the tracks left by the outlaws. Heath did state he could have been mistaken and that Howard may have had his horse re-shod, which would explain the fact that he did not find the "Texas-style" track he thought the horse would be making. Later, when Heath told Deputy Sheriff Daniels he believed the bandits had split up; Daniels seems to have summarily ignored him and continued along the same path.

When it became apparent the posse lost the trail of the bandits' altogether and Heath pointed out the fact to Daniels, the Deputy Sheriff asked him what he "thought about it." When he told Daniels he was certain the men they were chasing had split up and that he believed it would be best for Deputy Sheriff Daniels to split his party accordingly, Heath seems to have met with some resistance from the lawman, though the lawman finally conceded to Heath's suggestion. As it turned out, Heath was correct in his assertion, as both he and Frost discovered the trail of the bandits—most likely that of Dowd and Delaney—soon after they took their leave of Daniels and his men. If, as has been so often asserted, Heath's intention was to throw the posse off the scent and lead them astray, why would he have told the Deputy Sheriff about the separation of the party rather than just letting lawman lose the trail altogether?

Heath may have been mistaken about Howard and the track of his horse and which

Tombstone, Arizona Territory 1880s, taken about the time of the trials of the Bisbee bandits and John Heath (author's collection).

may have raised Deputy Daniels' suspicions about the man, but Heath very much redeemed himself when he discovered the outlaws had separated and informed Daniels of this fact. Further, where Daniels quickly loses the trail of the group he is pursuing, Heath and Frost are able to pick up the trail of the other two bandits and follow it some distance, finally arriving outside of Tombstone. Heath, Waite, and Frost go so far as to make a search of the local stables and corrals in that town for the outlaws horses before reporting back to Undersheriff Wallace. There was nothing in his actions to indicate Heath had any objective other than aiding as best he could in the manhunt for the murderers. Why then does Daniels remain suspicious of Heath?

Is it possible that Heath embarrassed the Deputy on the trail by questioning his authority which, in turn, led Daniels to persecute the man? Daniels was the ranking official in charge of the investigation and, thus being, likely felt a certain amount of pride and responsibility in his role as leader of the expedition. The fact that it was Heath who first noticed the bandits had taken divergent trails—a significant clue which Daniels had missed altogether—might well have caused Daniels to lose face in the eyes of the other posse members and caused them to question his abilities as commander. Even if this was not the case, Daniels might have felt Heath, in discovering the clue he overlooked, had in some way slighted him on a personal level, and had taken umbrage with him for this. Either way, Deputy Sheriff Daniels, when he had taken the stand, accused Heath outright of deceit and trying to mislead the posse. It was a groundless charge—a blatant aspersion against Heath—which was not supported by the testimony of any other witness.

During his testimony, Heath was also able to impugn the testimony of Sergeant Lawrence, who claimed that Heath produced the saws, which had been presented as evidence, in to the jailhouse with him. First, Heath explained he was in the process of writing a letter to his "partner in Clifton" when he was arrested by "some of the citizens of Bisbee." Clearly, he was not expecting to be arrested upon his return to Bisbee and had no reason to be secreting saws upon his person. Second, Heath stated he was searched three times before being placed into a cell. Though there is no way of knowing how thoroughly he was searched, if Heath had been hiding saws upon his person as Lawrence claimed, they would have been found by the men who searched him. If this portion of Lawrence's testimony was fabricated, as indicated by the facts given, one must wonder what else the Sergeant had invented.

Emma Mortimer, the woman identified as John Heath's paramour was the next to take the stand on his behalf. After she was sworn in and seated, the defense attorney began with his questions. Ms. Mortimer stated for the record, "[I] reside in Tombstone. Formerly resided at Clifton. While there [I] knew John Heith. Remember his leaving there in latter part of November. The night before he left, I took some of his clothing to be washed. [I] went the next day at 12:45. [I] took them to Heith's room. Gave them to him, and went to my room. He came shortly afterward. Bade me goodbye, and rode out of town." At the urging of Heath's lawyer, Ms. Mortimer continued, "I knew Tex Howard— he was not with him when he left Clifton. [I] know Bush—he works at George Hill's saloon. [I] saw Heith leave town. Howard was not with him. Next saw Heith in a dance house on the 11th."

At this juncture the defense stood down and the prosecution began their cross-examination of the witness. In answer to the queries of the District Attorney, Ms. Mortimer said, "[I] have known Heith about a year. [I] knew Tex a very short time. He went by the name Tex in Clifton. Never knew any other name for him. While at Clifton I was Heith's mistress. I came to Tombstone because I did not want to live in Bisbee. [I] furnished Heith with money. [I] take lodgers; [I] have no women in the house with me. I keep a house of prostitution. I am a woman on the town, and a friend of Mr. Heith's." The prosecution declared they had no more questions for Ms. Mortimer and she was allowed to step down from the stand and resume her seat in the gallery. Ms. Emma Mortimer would find herself testifying once more with regards to John Heath, and then she would resume the anonymity common to her profession and disappear forever from the historical record.[50]

Considering the times and cultural mores of that era, one wonders if Herring's decision to put Ms. Mortimer on the stand was really the best strategy. Certainly, Ms. Mortimer refuted the sworn testimony of Walter Bush, who claimed he had seen Heath riding in the company of "Tex" Howard when he left Clifton. Unfortunately, Ms. Mortimer was an admitted prostitute, which lowered her standing—and thereby her credibility—in the eyes of the all-male jury. Prostitution was a legal business in the Arizona Territory, but it was still not socially acceptable, and women engaged in this profession were usually marginalized and reviled by society at large. Ms. Mortimer also admitted to being John Heath's mistress, which implied that Heath was a married man (which he was). This fact was also damaging to Heath's reputation as it made him seem less than honorable and upstanding.

In the eyes of a jury, one very likely already prejudiced against the defendant, the knowledge of Heath's illicit relationship with Ms. Mortimer only served to make him more suspect. Not only was he acquainted and kept company with known thieves and murderers, he was now revealed to be something of a miscreant himself—a man of questionable character. As adamantly truthful as he may have been in his testimony, Heath was now seen as a philanderer, a pimp, and a sport—a man who lived on the fringes of polite society catering to its more base impulses and desires. As a defense witness, Ms. Mortimer may have cast a shadow of doubt over the testimony of Walter Bush, but she had been less-than-helpful in her secondary role as a character witness.

The final witness for the defense was John M. Requa, who "testified as to position of the cells in the county jail and to his duties as guard." Unfortunately, *The Tombstone Daily Epitaph* did not record his testimony for the edification of its readers. With Requa's testimony given and recorded, the defense rested. Judge Pinney, in a highly unusual move, but not unheard of, allowed the prosecution to re-open its case against Heath. In rebuttal, presumably to the testimony given by Mr. Requa, the prosecution called James C. Krigbaum, the man who had ridden to Tombstone the night of the murders, and William J. "Billy" Ward, the son of the County Sheriff. Krigbaum, who had been hired on by the Sheriff as a special guard, testified thus "[I] am guard at the county jail. Was in when Heith came down from the court room after the testimony of Lawrence, Saturday noon. He told the boys what Lawrence's testimony was. He then said: 'I have never asked you boys to do anything for me. I want you to go on the stand now and help me out.'" This ended Krigbaum's testimony.

Jailer William Ward, Sheriff Jerome Ward's son, took the stand directly after Krigbaum. He was sworn and summarily questioned by the prosecution. In response, Ward said, "[I] am jailer at the county jail. [I] was present at an interview between Lawrence and his counsel, before the former gave his testimony." The saw that had been placed in evidence was then brought out and shown to the witness. Jailer Ward recognized the article, and stated, "I have seen this before. [I] got it from Lawrence. He passed it out to me in a book." This ended the testimony of Sheriff Ward's son and the prosecution again rested. There was no rebuttal from the defense.[51]

The testimony given by Krigbaum was in agreement with what Daniel Dowd had already stated while on the stand. Dowd claimed Heath said, "I am going to have you all subpoenaed on the Lawrence evidence." Heath, Dowd said, had not said he "wanted us to stand by him," nor had he said there was no use in "giving him away." Heath merely wanted their truthful testimony. However, Krigbaum seems to imply that Heath might have been calling in a favor from Dowd, Howard, and the others. This may have been the strategy of the prosecution—to discredit the defense witnesses by implying they were somehow coerced by or conspired with Heath. Once again, the question arises, if Heath made accusations against Howard and the others as Lawrence asserted, why would these men have been inclined to come to his aid and testify on his behalf?

Jailer Ward's testimony and the evidence of the saw only proved that Lawrence had been the last person—and maybe the only person—in possession of the saw. The fact Lawrence "passed it out" inside a book, seems suspect, but in fact proved nothing. There was no tangible evidence and nothing to lead a jury member to conclude that Heath, Howard, Dowd, Delaney, Sample, or Kelly had ever been in possession of the instrument. In the end, all the questions and testimony about the saws was for naught—what happened to the second saw Lawrence claimed he observed remains a mystery. The saw(s) had no bearing on nor relevance to the case against Heath—except that it served to prejudice the jury against the defendant and his witnesses—and should have been objected to by the defense, disallowed by the judge, and stricken from the record.

Judge Robinson, the Deputy District Attorney, "then addressed the jury for the prosecution," reported *The Daily Epitaph*, "in an argument replete with logic, and conspicuous for its dove-tailing of facts into one homogenous whole which left no doubt in the mind of a reasonable man that the prisoner at the bar was the crafty plotter of the robbery which resulted in the murders at Bisbee." Unfortunately, a recording of this compelling and grandiloquent bit of courtroom oratory has yet to be found, so we must accept the discernment of the editor of *The Epitaph* as to the unmitigated effectiveness of the attorney's soliloquy.

"At the close of Judge Robinson's argument, the court was adjourned," noted the newspaper, to be reconvened at 9:00 a.m. the following day, when Colonel Herring would present his closing remarks. "He will be followed by District Attorney Smith [it is unknown why the prosecution was permitted the luxury of twice addressing the jury] and it is thought that the case will be in the hands of the jury and a verdict rendered before noon." In fact, the prediction of the editor of *The Epitaph* of a swift end to the proceedings would be erroneous. He had not taken into consideration Colonel Herring's ambition to see his client absolved.[52]

Chapter Six

The Lynching

While the District Court in Cochise County was busy with trials of the Bisbee murderers and John Heath, the 3rd District Court in Silver City, New Mexico Territory, was busy preparing for the prosecution of the perpetrators of the Gage train robbery. George Washington Cleveland, Frank Taggart, "Kit" Joy, and Mitch Lee were incarcerated in the county jail in Silver City, waiting patiently for the grand jury to be convened. The four outlaws had been in the calaboose since their capture the previous December. The outlaws knew their chances of being indicted for the robbery of the train and subsequent murder of the engineer were good. In common with their counterparts in Tombstone, if convicted, the men faced either a lifetime in prison or death at the end of a rope. Sitting there behind bars, the four outlaws had nothing but time on their hands—time which was spent in studying their surroundings, observing and learning the routines of their captors, and plotting and planning.

Back in the Cochise County Courthouse in Tombstone, on the morning of February 19, 1884, the closing arguments in the case of the *Territory of Arizona vs. John Heath* were being presented, with Colonel Herring, the counsel for the defense taking the floor. *The Daily Epitaph* observed that the courtroom was "somewhat crowded" with "many ladies being present." A transcript of Herring's soliloquy has not been found and, therefore, cannot be presented herein. However, the editor of *The Epitaph* opined that Herring's argument before the jury was "an able and ingenious one, and received much favorable comment from those in attendance." Colonel Herring began his address about 9:15 a.m., just after the court was called to order by Judge Pinney. "It was expected the morning would witness its termination," reported the newspaper, "but the hand pointed the meridian, and counsel was still addressing the jury."

Judge Pinney finally intervened and called for an adjournment of the court until 1:30 p.m. "and the spectators were met in exit by the advance guard of the vast throng which was present at the hour fixed for the passing of sentence upon Dowd, Delaney, Kelly, Sample, and Howard." *The Daily Epitaph* aptly described the scene inside:

> To say that the court-room was crowded would but idly convey the idea. It was literally packed to suffocation, the crowd even pressing on to the dais leading to the judge's seat. The prisoner's dock was crowded with ladies and [a] large delegation were also present on the main floor. Many of those present were representatives of the wealth, beauty, and culture of this city, and it is fair to presume that a desire to hear the eloquence of Messrs. Herring and Smith was the motive prompting attendance, and not that of morbid curiosity to see five unfortunate victims of their own evil passions sentenced to die an ignominious death on the scaffold.

Soon the clank, clank, clank of manacles was heard and the doors swung open to admit the prisoners, closely guarded by the sheriff and his deputies. Slowly, they advanced up the aisle and took seats facing Judge Pinney. The silence was painful when the latter told the five men to stand up and, questioning each in turn, asked him if he had anything to say why the sentence of death should not be passed on him. Dowd, who was first questioned, responded in loud, clear voice, "No, sir"; Sample responded, "No, sir. Nothing that would influence you"; Howard and Delaney answered with a plain, "No, sir"; while Kelly informed the judge that he had much to say, but nothing that in any probability would influence the mind of his honor. Not a blanched cheek or a dimmed eye was in the party, as the judge, in a solemn and measured tone pronounced the sentence.[1]

The court document relating to the sentencing is surprisingly austere, without unnecessary embellishment or enhancement. It simply reads, "The District Attorney, with the defendants and their counsel, came into Court. The defendants were duly informed by the Court of the nature of the Indictment found against them for the crime of murder, committed on the 1st of February, 1884, of their arraignment and plea of 'Not Guilty as charged in this indictment,' of their trial and the verdict of the jury, on the 11th day of February 1884, 'Guilty as charged in the Indictment,' the defendants were asked if they had any legal cause to show why the judgment should not be pronounced against them, to which they replied that they had none. And no sufficient cause being shown or appearing to the Court, thereupon the Court rendered its judgment: That whereas, the said Dan Kelly, O.W. Sample, Jas. Howard, Dan Dowd, & Wm. Delaney having been duly convicted in this Court of the crime of Murder in the First Degree. It is therefore ordered Adjudged and Decreed, That the said Dan Kelly, O.W. Sample, Jas. Howard, Dan Dowd, & Wm. Delaney be sentenced to be hanged by the neck until dead. The defendants were then remanded to the custody of the Sheriff of Cochise County, to be by him executed on the 28th day of March a.d. 1884."[2]

Judge Daniel Pinney was much more eloquent in his delivery of the verdict to the defendants.

You have all been indicted by the grand jury, tried and convicted of the crime of murder in the first degree. There is but little left for me to do. You have appeared in court and stated you were without means, whereupon I assigned you able counsel for your defense, as the law provides, and as it was my duty to do. An impartial jury was impaneled [sic] to try your case, they have returned a verdict of murder in the first degree. Counsel have done all they could do for you. On the conclusion of the testimony is [sic] was agreed that argument should be waived and the case submitted to the jury upon the instruction of the court. In my judgment, this course was on the part of your counsel was as wise a course as they could follow. The facts and circumstances in this case and the links in the chain have been proved step by step have convinced the jury which tried you that you five men were guilty of the murder of Mr. Smith and the other parties at Bisbee on the 8th of December last.

It would ill become me or anyone in my position to heap anything in the way of abuse upon you, I rather pity you. The facts and circumstances detailed in this case to my mind satisfy me, that the verdict the jury have rendered is proper. It is not a pleasant duty for any man placed in my position to pronounce the sentence which the law imposes, and I repeat that it ill becomes me in my position to heap any word of abuse upon you. I pity any man that so far forgets his duty to his country and his God, and so far forgets the teachings of a christian [sic] mother, that one, if not all of you may have had in your childhood, as to permit himself to be so lost to humanity and society, to become so lost to everything human and decent, that you permit yourself to enter into a plan to commit the crime as charged against you. Nothing that I could say would aid you here. It only involves upon me to perform the last act that can be performed here.

The sentence of this court is that you be taken hence to the county jail and there confined until the 28th day of March, 1884, and on that day, between the hours of 10 o'clock in the forenoon and 5 o'clock in the afternoon each of you be hanged by the neck until you are dead.[3]

Judge Pinney was reportedly "visibly affected" during delivery of the sentence and "a perceptible tremor in his voice" was noticed. The defendants stood silently for a moment "as if trying to realize that the entire proceeding was but a phantasy of a dream." Finally, "the broad features of Red Sample relaxed into a smile, and turning to Kelly made some jocular remark." The grave and heavy atmosphere of that singular moment having been thus dispersed, Tex, Delaney, and Dowd joined their companion in making "light of the proceeding, not exactly in a scoffing manner, but as if they realized that the thing was inevitable, and was to be met like men face misfortune." *The Epitaph* reported that only Kelly "seemed cast down" in his demeanor. The prisoners had only just regained their seats when Judge Pinney "remanded them into the custody of the sheriff, and they were led away to the seclusion of the dungeon, from whence they will never again greet the sunshine nor look upon a blue sky, until they see it for the last time on the morning of their execution."[4]

The sentence passed upon Dowd, Delaney, Sample, Kelly, and Howard was met with general acclaim. *The San Francisco Chronicle* stated "the prompt capture and equally prompt conviction of the Bisbee murderers at Tombstone shows that the Arizona authorities are determined to stamp out the lawlessness which has been a great bar to the development of the territory. The bitter feuds which made Tombstone so dangerous a place of residence when the Earps were in power are not likely to occur again." The new, tougher law enforcement policies "shows too a healthy change of sentiment in the territory and that the age of the cowboy had passed." *The Chronicle* predicted it would take some time for the Easterners to "fully appreciate the change" but noted that the territory was "gaining readily in wealth and population" and seemed to believe a new era—devoid of the "playful pastimes of the cowboy" and the "exploits of the horse thief and murderer"—was soon to dawn for the once wicked and raucous territory.[5]

The Tucson Weekly Citizen was in absolute agreement with *The Chronicle* in their statement that the year 1884 "will be noted in this Territory as the great year for hanging murderers and the result will be of great benefit to the Territory." The newspaper continued on to say that such "hanging bees will prove to the world that there are law abiding people here, and men who dare to do their duty" and "convince people in the East that life and property are safe in the Territory." *The Citizen* predicted that this would result in increased emigration. "The days of the boasting murderous cowboy are over, and there will follow in his wake a people that will fill up the Territory by the thousands and make it flourish as a green bay tree in the heart of a 'desert,' or in other words make the tree flourish in the heart of the Arizona deserts." Of course, the newspapermen could not foresee the brutal and bloody range war that would embroil the Tonto Basin region to the north just three years later.[6]

In a related side bar, *The Daily Epitaph* shared with readers the news Deputy Sheriff John Hovey of Graham County, "the gallant official to whose efforts was the means of the capture of 'Red' Sample and 'Tex' Howard is due" was a "prominent" candidate for the office of Graham County Sheriff in the coming elections. "Hovey'" the newspaper declared, "certainly deserves well of his section, and the office of sheriff is a reward, strictly in his line of business, and it is hoped he may receive it." Alas, it was not to be. Deputy Sheriff Hovey would lose to Democratic candidate Ben M. Crawford in the November elections.[7]

Once Dowd and the others had been escorted from the courtroom, the closing arguments in the trial of John Heath resumed, with Colonel Herring picking up from where he left off before the adjournment. *The Epitaph* reported that the attorney spoke for "a little more than an hour in addition to the time taken up by him in the morning." The "distinguished advocate" met with a round of applause at the conclusion of his argument, "for the very skillful manner in which he had made the worse appear the better cause." The newspaper stated, "It was evident that his cunning sophistries and ingeniously spun themes had made more than a passing impression on some of the jury."[8]

Judge Pinney then allowed District Attorney Smith to make a statement in reply to Herring's address—this in addition to the argument presented the day before by Deputy District Attorney Robinson. *The Weekly Epitaph* noted that Marcus Smith had to work hard to "disabuse the minds" after Herring's argument. "For the space of an hour, he handled the weight of his logic, satire, invective and eloquence [illegible] he legal barriers erected by Colonel Herring in his client's defense, and carried the audience with him as he pictured in glowing color the depth of depravity into which he claimed Heith had fallen. The argument was a universally forcible one, and did much to counteract the impression made by preceding counsel." Upon completion of the District Attorney's presentation, the prosecution rested its case. Judge Pinney then charged the jury, saying:

> That murder is the unlawful killing of a human being with malice aforethought, either [illegible] or implied, the unlawful killing may be affected by any of the various means by which death may be occasioned. Express malice is that deliberate intention, unlawfully to take away the life of a fellow creature, which is manifested by external circumstances capable of proof. Malice may be implied when no considerable provocation appear, or when all the circumstances of the killing show an abandoned and malignant heart. All murder which shall be perpetuated by means of poison, or lying in wait, torture, or by any other kind of willful deliberate and premeditated killing, or which shall be committed in the perpetration or attempt to perpetrate any arson, rape, robbery, or burglary, shall be deemed murder in the first degree and all other kinds of murder shall be deemed murder in the second degree.
>
> The jury are instructed that if the killing of the person mentioned in the indictment is satisfactorily shown by the evidence, beyond a reasonable doubt, to have been the act of the defendants or either of them, then the law pronounces such killing murder, unless it appears by the evidence that circumstances existed excusing or justifying the act.
>
> The court instructs the jury that when unlawful unintentional killing of a human being happens in the commission of an unlawful act, which in its consequences tends to destroy the life of a human being, the offence will be murder.
>
> If the jury believe from the evidence, beyond a reasonable doubt, that at the time of the alleged killing the defendants, Howard, Sample, Kelly, Dowd, and Delaney, or either of them, had entered the store of Castaneda [illegible] for the common purpose of stealing or carrying away any articles of personal property and in the prosecution of that purpose, or, in their efforts to escape with such property the defendants, either of them, shot and killed the deceased, as charged in the indictment, then such killing would be murder and it would be wholly immaterial whether such killing was intentional or not.
>
> If the jury believe from the evidence, beyond a reasonable doubt, that the defendants Howard, Sample, Kelly, Dowd and Delaney—or either of them, at the time of the alleged killing made an attack upon any person or persons in the store of Castaneda or on the street in front of the store for the purpose or with the intent of feloniously taking away from the store, by force and against his will, any money, watch, or other articles of personal property, and in the prosecution of that purpose, either one of the defendants shot and killed the deceased, as charged in the indictment, then such killing would be murder, not only on the part of one who fired the fatal shot, but also on the part of one or more of the defendants who were present or, who not being present, hath aided, assisted, advised, and encouraged the original attempt to take the property of any person or persons by force and against his or their will. If the jury from the evidence, beyond a reasonable doubt, are satisfied that defendant Heath, aiding and assisting, was so present or, not being present, aided, assisted, advised, and encouraged the original attempt and, in such case, it would be immaterial whether the shot was fired with the intention of taking the life of the deceased or only disabling him.
>
> The court instructs the jury that an accessory is one who stands by and aids, abets, or assists, or assisting hath advised and encouraged perpetration of the crime. He who thus aids, abets, or encourages shall be deemed and considered as principal and punished accordingly.

The court instructs the jury that the advising or encouraging that may make one an accessory to crime need not be by words. It may be by words, signs, motions, or acts, done or made for the purpose of encouraging the crime.

That, while the law requires in order to find the defendant guilty, that the evidence should prove, beyond a reasonable doubt, that all acted in concert in commission of the crime charged, still it is not necessary that it should be positively proven that they all met together and agreed to commit the crime. Such concert may be proven by circumstances and from all the evidence, the jury are satisfied, beyond a reasonable doubt, that the crime was committed by Howard, Sample, Kelly, Delaney and defendant Heath, and that all acted together in the commission of the crime as charged in the indictment, each aiding in his own way [sic]. This is all the law requires.

And, in passing upon the guilt or innocence of the defendant, the evidence fail to establish, beyond a reasonable doubt, that he was present, taking part in, or aiding and abetting the crime or, if he was not present, that he aided, abetted, assisted advised, or encouraged the same, then the verdict should be not guilty.

The court instructs the jury that before a conviction can rightfully be claimed by the people in this case, the truth of every material averment contained in the indictment must be proved to the satisfaction of the jury, beyond a reasonable doubt. That is a matter of law. The defendant is presumed to be innocent of the crime until such time as the guilt of the Deft. is proved as alleged by competent evidence and beyond a reasonable doubt.

A reasonable doubt [illegible] the meaning of the law is such a doubt as would cause a reasonable, prudent man in the graver and more important affairs of life to pause and hesitate before acting upon the truth of the matter charged.

If the jury believe from the evidence that the defendant made the confession and admissions as alleged and attempted to be proved in this case, the jury should treat and consider such confessions precisely as they would any other testimony, and hence if the jury believe the whole confession to be true, that they should act upon it as true. The jury are to judge of it like other evidence in the case, in [illegible] of all the circumstances of the case, as disclosed by the evidence.

Further, the court instructs the jury that, generally, confessions of a prisoner are of a doubtful species of evidence and to be received with great caution, and the credit and weight to be given to it depend very much upon on what the confessions are, of the crime itself as charged and proved by other testimony, and it is also proven that the person making the confession was so situated that he had an opportunity to commit or assist, aid, or encourage in the commission of the crime, and that his confessions are consistent with such proof and corroborative of it, and that the witness who swears to the confession is apparently truthful, honest, and inteligent [sic] their such confessions so made may be entitled to greater weight.

The court instructs the jury that, although the law makes the defendant in this case a competent witness, still the jury are the judges of the weight to be attached to his testimony and, in consider what weight should be given it, the jury should take into consideration all the facts and circumstances surrounding the case as disclosed by the evidence and give the defendant's testimony such weight as they believe it entitled to in view of all the facts and circumstances proved on the trial and, further, the jury are instructed the credibility of any and all witnesses who have testified in the case is a question exclusively for the jury; they have a right to determine from the appearance of the witnesses on the stand, their manner of testifying, their apparent candor, and fairness. Their apparent intelligence or lack of intelligence, and from all other surrounding circumstances appearing on the trial, which witnesses are the more worthy of credit, and to give credit accordingly. They are not bound to take the testimony of any witness as absolutely true and they should not do so, if they are satisfied from all the circumstances and facts proven on the trial that such witness is mistaken or for any other reason his testimony is untrue or unreliable.

Still if the testimony of a witness or witnesses appears fair—is not unreasonable and is consistent with itself—and the witness or witnesses have not been in any manner impeached, then the jury have no right to disregard the testimony of said witness or witnesses from mere caprice or without cause. It is the duty of the jury to consider the whole of the evidence—and reconcile all the different parts of the testimony if possible, and find a verdict in accordance therewith.

The jury are instructed that the fact that the other defendants named in the indictment have been tried for the same charge will not be considered by the jury in this case. Outside of any trial that has taken place as regards other defendants, the defendant has a right to and should receive a fair and impartial hearing and, if you are satisfied beyond a reasonable doubt from all the facts and circumstances in proof that the defendant is guilt as charged, then you should find him guilty and, if from all the circumstances and facts you are not so satisfied, then you should find him not guilty.

Further the jury are instructed that the fact that the grand jury found an indictment against the defendant is not to be considered as any evidence against him. They will take the evidence and circumstances as proven on the trial and not go outside to look for circumstances or facts not in proof before them.[9]

Colonel Herring, on behalf of his client, also drafted instructions for the jury:

I.

The jury are instructed that where the prosecution rely upon circumstantial evidence to prove the facts necessary to constitute the offence charged in the indictment, the burden is on the prosecution to prove such facts beyond a reasonable doubt. And in such case, any reasonable doubt which arises upon consideration of all the evidence in the case, is the property of the prisoner and the jury should give him the benefit of the same and acquit him.

II.

The prosecution must satisfy the jury beyond a reasonable doubt that the prisoner co-operated with those whom he is indicted in the perpetration of an overt act or overt acts in the execution of a common design to commit the offence alleged in his indictment, and it is not sufficient to show design merely, but it must appear to the satisfaction of the jury that he prisoner acted and assisted or aided, abetted, advised, and encouraged the commission of the felony which resulted in the death of the deceased.

III.

Declarations of the co-defendants in the absence of the defendant are not evidence for any purpose, unless it appears beyond a reasonable doubt, from all the evidence, that he was directly connected with the principle act, namely, the killing of the deceased, in the perpetuation of the robbery as shown by the evidence in the case—and until the prosecution have made out their case by affirmative proof, (the) defendant is not required to explain mere circumstances showing his acquaintance or association with his co-defendants.

IV.

It is the duty of the jury in considering all the evidence in the case, to determine what is to be regarded as direct evidence of the participation of the prisoner in the crime alleged in the indictment, and what is to be regarded as circumstantial evidence—"Direct evidence is where the proof applies immediately to collateral facts supposed to have a connection, near or remote, with the fact in controversy." In the present case, all the proof which applies immediately to the killing of the deceased is direct evidence, and all the proof which applies to collateral facts connected with the killing of deceased is circumstantial evidence.

The circumstantial evidence, as well as the direct evidence, must be proved to the satisfaction of the jury and it is for them to say whether such facts as are proven by the one class of evidence or by the other classes, establish the guilt of the prisoner. If the proof fails to establish the guilt of the prisoners beyond a reasonable doubt, it is the duty of the jury to acquit.

V.

Upon examination of all the evidence in the case, if the jury should find that no direct testimony connects the prisoner with the crime alleged but that circumstantial testimony alone is to be relied upon, then, in order to convict the defendant of the offence charged in the indictment upon circumstantial evidence alone the circumstances proved must all concur to show that he committed the crime or aided, advised, and encouraged the same and must all be inconsistent with any other rational conclusion, and must exclude to a moral certainty any other hypothesis but the simple one of guilt.

(margin notes: People vs. Dick, 32 Cal. 213)

VI.

In considering the evidence in relation to any fact in form of the innocence of the defendant preponderating proof—necessary to satisfy the jury of the fact is sufficient to establish such fact in his form. He is not bound to show this beyond a reasonable doubt.

(margin notes: People vs. Milgale, 5th Cal. 127)

If the testimony in relation to the defendant is entirely circumstantial and there is nothing which connects the defendant directly with the murder of the deceased the defendant is entitled to what the law means by reasonable doubt.

(margin notes: People vs. Lachurnis, 32 Cal. 433)

VII.

If circumstantial evidence alone is relied upon by the prosecution to establish the guilt of the pris-

oner, such proof ought not only to be entirely consistent with his guilt, but it must be inconsistent with every other reasonable hypothesis—based upon the evidence in the case—of his innocence.
VIII.
If the purpose of the co-defendant was robbery and, if as a means to the perpetuation of the robbery, the deceased was killed by either of the prisoner's co-defendants, the crime of murder is established, but it is not enough for the prosecution to prove the crime alleged in order to permit the declaration of those who directly participated in the crime to affect the prisoner who is surrounded with the presumption of innocence, until it is overthrown by competent testimony, the prosecution must show acts of this defendant, on his own declarations, establishing his intention to unite with his co-defendants in the consummation of the common design to commit the crime charged in the indictment and then all the acts of the prisoner must be proven beyond reasonable doubt to have been performed in carrying such design into execution.[10]

Perhaps not being completely satisfied with the aforementioned set of instructions given to the jury, Colonel Herring drafted yet another set for the men sitting in judgment of his client. The first part of this second set of instructions reads as a thinly veiled attack on the credibility of Sergeant Lemuel Lawrence, the prosecution's star witness. The second part was an outright attack on the testimony of Frank Buckles. These instructions were written in a hand different from the first:

In determining the weight of the testimony of any of the witnesses, the jury have the right to consider all the circumstances which any way affect their credibility and they may ascertain as far as the evidence discloses whether a witness was prompted to give his evidence from motives which in their opinions affect his credibility and it is for them to say how far the credibility of a witness is affected in inducing him to pervert the facts from improper or wrongful motives as disclosed by the testimony.
Evidence of the declaration of the prisoner while in custody concerning the testimony of a witness in another case, cannot be regarded by the jury as connecting the prisoner with the defendants in such case, unless it be first established beyond a reasonable doubt that the prisoner was by his own acts a party in the transaction about which the testimony of such witness in such case had been given, and (*illegible*) the jury believe the statement of the witness Buckles in relation to the conversation detailed by him as occurring while the prisoner was in jail the such conversation (a portion of the document is here crossed out, presumably by the author, with the thread continuing below) must be considered by the jury in connection with the other facts in the case as to whether the alleged statement to Buckles were made simply in relation to the case of the other defendants, or in relation to his own case and give it such weight as they may think it entitled to—from all the facts and circumstances in proof in the case.[11]

There was a third set of instructions given the jury by the defense entitled "Addition Request for Defence [*sic*]." These instructions appear to have been written in haste and in pencil.

1.
if the Jury believe that any witness has knowingly and skillfully sworn falsely to any material fact in the case, then in their discretion they can wholly disregard the whole of such witnesses testimony (illegible) so far as it may have been corroborated by other credible evidence or by facts and circumstances as proved at the trial.
2.
You are further instructed that in considering the weight and effect to be given defendant's evidence in addition to noticing his manner & the probability of his statements, taken in connection with the evidence in the case, you should consider his relation and situation under which he gives the testimony. The consequences relating to him from the result of his trial and all the inducement and temptations which would ordinarily influence a person in his situation.
You should carefully determine the amount of credibility to which his evidence is entitled—if convincing and carrying with it a belief in its truth, act upon it. If not, you have a right to reject it.

On a separate sheet, also headed "Additional Request for Defence [*sic*]" and also written in pencil, was the following:

The fact that the prisoner has not [*illegible*] [*illegible*] any evidence of good character is not to be considered as a circumstance against him by the jury.

It would seem that Colonel Herring was acutely cognizant of the fact that John Heath did not appear as the most upstanding and virtuous of men and sought to ensure against the jury holding his lack of "good character" against him while considering the evidence.

And so, after being thus instructed by both the judge and the defense, the jury retired to "deliberate upon a verdict."[12]

The jury in the case of the *Territory of Arizona vs. John Heath* was out nearly five hours—longer than anyone expected it to be. Finally, at 8:00 p.m., the jurors returned to the courtroom, announcing they had come to an agreement. *The Daily Epitaph* reported the verdict was a "compromise one." On the first ballot, the jurors "stood six for murder in the first degree, four for acquittal, and two for murder in the second degree." The final ballot stood six for murder in the first degree and six for acquittal of the defendant. It is not known how many ballots were taken in the interim. Hopelessly deadlocked, the jury returned to the courtroom and their "compromise" verdict was handed over by the foreman to the clerk of the court. Judge Pinney invited John Heath to stand as the verdict was read—"We, the undersigned jurors in the case of The Territory of Arizona vs. John Heith, find the defendant guilty of murder, as charged in the indictment, in the second degree." The document was signed by jury foreman, G.W. Chapman. *The Daily Epitaph* identified the other jurors as William Whitaker, H.H. Allen F. Ruez, J. Ellikson, J.S. Bogart, J.D. McDougal, S.B. Curtis, O.L. Bashford, John Henck, E. Dees, and J.M. Stump.[13]

As had been expected, Colonel Herring immediately moved for "a new trial and the arrest of judgment" on behalf of his client. Judge Pinney scheduled the motion for a new trial to be heard Thursday, February 21, at 9:30 a.m. On Thursday morning, "the minutes of the preceding day having been read and approved" the "motions for a new trial and arrest of judgment" were heard. Judge Pinney dismissed the motions outright. However, the defense "was allowed until the first day of the next term of [the] Court, or as soon thereafter as the Court may convene, to file his Bill of Exceptions." The defense having waived "time for passing sentence," Judge Pinney ordered the defendant to stand. The sentence was then read. It is not known if Judge Pinney had any words for John Heath before passing sentence as he had for Dowd, Delaney, Sample, Howard, and Kelly.

The minutes for the day simply stated, "[t]he Court thereupon sentenced the said defendant John Heith to be confined and imprisoned in the Territorial prison of the Territory of Arizona for the term of his natural life. And so it was ordered, adjudged, & deemed by the Court." Heath was then remanded to the custody of Sheriff Ward "to be delivered into the custody of the proper officers of said Territorial prison." This final task complete, the trial jury was dismissed and the court was adjourned. John Heath was taken back down stairs to his cell on the first floor. He would never again ascend the stairs to the courtroom. He would never again see his attorney. He would never have his "bill of exceptions" heard.[14]

News of the verdict in the Heath case caused an almost instant uproar throughout Cochise County. For the date of Thursday, February 21, 1884, George W. Parsons of Tombstone wrote in his diary, "Fine weather. Heith sentenced today. Imprisonment for life in Yuma. Pretty cheap. Too much so. Not over yet." Parsons' succinct and somewhat ominous entry reflected the general opinion of the populace in Tombstone and Bisbee and that of the neighboring communities. Public opinion had convicted the man even before his trial had begun—even though the evidence against Heath was scant—and the fact that the verdict did not reflect the public's opinion was cause for a smoldering consternation. *The Daily Epitaph* reported the verdict of the jury "gave almost universal dissatisfaction." The newspaper decreed, "Such a thing as a compromise verdict was not warranted by either the law or the evidence. John Heith was either guilty or not guilty of the crime of murder charged against him."[15]

The Tombstone Republican echoed the sentiments of *The Epitaph*: "there seems to have been little doubt in the minds of jurors as to Heith's guilt, and it being the general impression that, if he was guilty at all, he was guilty of murder in the first degree." *The Republican* also asserted there was further evidence against him that was "not brought out in the proceedings." It was erroneously claimed that, after his arrest, Daniel Kelly told a deputy sheriff in Graham County that Heath "was the prime mover of the affair" and that Heath had been in possession of $1,200 taken from Castaneda's store when he was arrested. "A woman in Clifton," stated the newspaper, "says that Emma Mortimer informed her of the move before Heith left Clifton." Further, *The Republican* alleged that Heath "had come to this territory on account of murdering his father-in-law in Texas."[16]

George Parsons, Tombstone resident and diarist, reflected the general public consensus when he stated John Heath, being convicted of murder in the second degree, got off "pretty cheap" (private collection).

George Parsons wrote in his journal, "It is not over yet," as though he was privy to some terrible secret or plan which he dared only hint to even in his diary—as though he knew the drama of Heath's trial was not concluded. In fact, this was the case. By Hankin's account, most likely derived from statements made by Krigbaum, "Two prominent mining men of Bisbee rode over to Tombstone, and arranged a meeting with some of the leading citizens of the county seat. At that meeting, held that night [February 21, 1884] in a building on Fremont Street, agreement was reached that, since the law would not punish Heith as he deserved, the people of the county would have to take matters into their own hands." However, as with the other remembrances of Krigbaum—which Hankin compiled her manuscript from—this account must be considered with a certain degree of skepticism.[17]

The fact is no one recorded whether that such a meeting was actually held or who attended. Douglas D. Martin, editor of *Tombstone's Epitaph*, wrote in his book, "Here again the researcher is checked by a break in *The Epitaph's* files. This time it is a real loss.

Firehouse, Tombstone, A.T., where the vigilantes from Bisbee and Tombstone met before proceeding to the Cochise County Courthouse to lynch John Heath (author's collection).

For there is no spot news story of the formation of a group of one hundred armed, mounted, and angry men in Bisbee, or of their long night ride through a high pass and over starlit deserts. No one tells what the people of Tombstone thought when they were awakened in the early hours of the morning by a cavalcade riding furiously through the city." It seems Martin was mistaken in his assumption that the men came from Bisbee, but it should be remembered that Martin was relying solely on extant issues of *The Tombstone Epitaph* for his information and probably did not cross-reference with other regional newspapers.[18]

Hankin maintains that mines of Tombstone were closed on the morning of the 22nd at the behest of "prominent mining men of Bisbee" and the "leading citizens" of Tombstone, and the men who worked those mines were instructed to meet with men from the town at the Tombstone firehouse upon receipt of a pre-arranged signal. From there the men would proceed southeast along Toughnut Street to the jail, located on the first floor of the Cochise County Courthouse. The only extant local newspaper report, dated March 1, 1884, found in *The Arizona Weekly Citizen*, seems to agree in the main, if not the particulars, with Hankin's story. The perpetrators were identified as "one hundred men, principally miners from the Contention and Grand Central mines, which had been shut down."[19]

Estimates as to the number of men who descended upon the courthouse that February morning, range between 100 and 200. Of these, seven—all reported as being men from Bisbee—were chosen to go in to the courthouse while the rest remained outside. The seven, with guns drawn, "went to the door leading to the jail and rapped for admittance. It was about the hour when breakfast was brought to the prisoners and Billy Ward, thinking it was a man with food, opened the door without looking to see who his visitors were." This was a serious oversight. "Instantly, he was covered with weapons, and a demand was made of him for the keys of the jail. Seeing that resistance was useless, he quietly gave then up." The party then proceeded into the cell block where Heath, Dowd, Delaney, Sample, Kelly, and "Tex" Howard were housed. The reaction of the prisoners to what they must have immediately assumed was a lynch mob was not recorded by the reporter.[20]

The men unlocked and entered John Heath's cell. They "unshackled him and brought him into the corridor of the jail. It was their first intention to hang him to the banister of the stairs leading to the second story, but this plan was abandoned" and the men led their prisoner out the front doors of the courthouse. As the seven emerged with Heath in their custody, they were met by Sheriff Jerome Ward, "who throwing up his hands, exclaimed with a show of authority, 'Stop this! You have got to stop right here!'" Several men from the crowd laid hold of the Sheriff, "and before he could understand what had happened he was picked up and thrown down the stairs." In recounting the story for its readers, *The New York Times* stated the Sheriff was "picked up and gently removed down the steps out of the way."[21]

John Heath, dressed in a flannel undershirt, broadcloth trousers, and with only socks upon his feet, was tied round with a rope. He was led down the concrete courthouse stairs and out into the street. The crowd proceeded further down Toughnut Street with prisoner before them. Strangely, the short journey to the place chosen for Heath's lynching was made at a run. The newspapers noted that the rope he was secured with never became taut and Heath kept the lead the entire way. *The Chicago Tribune* noted that Heath showed "no signs of the white feather." Finally, the mob stopped beneath a telegraph pole on Toughnut just past First Street—one which would in few hours carry the news of this event to the world outside. S.C. Bogg, the former *Tombstone Epitaph* editor who claimed to have been present at the time, said that Heath "stood in the center of the crowd, the coolest one among them."[22]

Back at the jail, William "Bill" Ward, the sheriff's son, "humiliated by what had occurred," deserted his post and did not return for "several hours." James Krigbaum, who was still employed as a special guard, was left in charge. "The five hold-up men were frantic with fear, and begged for greater security; so Krigbaum did what he could to reassure them." Krigbaum told Hankin he adjusted the heavy steel bar which was fitted across the front of the row of cells and locked it in place. He then proceeded to lock the door to the "narrow hall leading to the jailers' room. Next, he re-locked the door into the outer corridor and its companion wooden door. Returning, he locked the door between the inner hallway and the jailers' room, locking himself into that room. Finally he told Hankin, "he hid the keys, so that if asked, he could truthfully say he did not have them."[23]

Whether this occurred as Krigbaum stated is unknown, there being no other sources to corroborate his story. Krigbaum said that he was in the jailers' room with Bill Ward when the mob entered the building. Upon being let in by the unsuspecting Ward, the men pointed their pistols at Krigbaum and demanded his weapons and his keys. He complied with the order as given. Krigbaum asserted there was a third guard on duty, though he did not give the man's name, who he said was also disarmed by the vigilantes. Krigbaum may have been telling the truth, but the only other primary sources available—the newspapers—make no mention of any other guards in the jail aside from Bill Ward.

Back outside, along Toughnut Street, a block and half from the courthouse, a young boy was shimmying up a telegraph pole, trailing behind him a length of rope with a simple noose tied at one end. Beneath the pole stood Heath in a "most wonderful show of bravery" amid the crowd of vengeance-minded men who would in mere moments become his executioners. Heath was asked if he had anything to say before he was to be hanged. Heath calmly replied, "Boys, you are hanging an innocent man, and you will find it out before those other men are hung." Heath then reached into his pocket and produced a silk handkerchief, and asked that it be tied over his eyes. Other accounts described how Heath tied the blindfold on himself. The prisoner declared he was not afraid to die. "I have one favor to ask," he said, "that you will not mutilate my body by shooting into it after I am hung." His executioners agreed to this last request.[24]

Heath said he was ready. The blindfold had been tied about his eyes and his stocking feet bound together to prevent his kicking and thrashing. The noose was dropped over his head and secured around his neck. John T. Heath was then lynched. The *Weekly Citizen* stated simply that "in a moment the body was dangling at the end of a rope from the crossbar on the telegraph pole." The report picked up by the newspapers around the country was more descriptive, saying, "Countless hands grasped the rope, a run was made, and in a twinkling, John Heith was dangling between heaven and earth." What the newspapers avoided mentioning in their rather declamatory reports is that Heath's death was not instantaneous. John Heath was forcibly lifted in to the air by the mob and suspended thus, he slowly but surely strangled to death.[25]

More specifically, the rope about Heath's neck compressed or crushed the carotid artery, the jugular vein, and vertebral artery, leading to loss of blood to the brain. The tightening of the rope above his Adam's apple would have also forced his tongue back and up inside the throat effectively blocking the nasopharynx and preventing oxygen from being taken into the lungs through nose and mouth. His larynx and trachea may also have been crushed causing internal hemorrhaging as the rope rolled up underneath his jaw. While Heath probably lost consciousness within the first three minutes due to loss of oxygen and restricted blood-flow to the brain, his body would have continued to convulse and twitch for several minutes until finally his heart stopped altogether. It was not a pleasant death.[26]

The crowd below stood and watched the spectacle of John Heath's final agonies. When the body finally came to rest, a placard was placed on the telegraph pole, bearing the following inscription:

> JOHN HEITH
> Was hanged to this pole by the
> CITIZENS OF COCHISE COUNTY
> for participating in the Bisbee massacre
> as a proved accessory
> AT 8:00 A.M., FEBRUARY 22, 1884
> (Washington's Birthday)
> ADVANCE ARIZONA!

The *Chicago Tribune* reported that Heath's body was allowed to hang on the pole for about an hour and a half, before being taken down. The newspaper reported that "an immense crowd of men, women and children had congregated on the scene." Photographer C.S. Fly, the man who had photographed the McLaurey brothers and "Billy' Clanton in their caskets after the O.K. Corral shootings, turned out to take the now infamous photograph of Heath on his makeshift gibbet. George Parsons in his diary entry for Friday, February 22, 1884, wrote, "Fine weather. Heith taken from jail this A.M. about eight and hung to telegraph pole on Toughnut near 1st. Very game. No noise or confusion. Saw his body lowered and carted off. Rush for pieces of rope. Humorous verdict. No dissenters. Humane action. Pity hanging wasn't begun three years ago. Great time collecting rewards."

This was also the first time the sanguine events of December 8, 1883, would be referred to as the "Bisbee Massacre."[27]

After it was taken down, Heath's body was conveyed to the coroner's office for an autopsy. A crime having been committed—specifically a murder—such was the official procedure. The body was given over to the Cochise County Coroner, Patrick "Pat" Holland. The attending physician was Dr. George Emory Goodfellow, the same man who had examined the bodies of Frank and Tom McLaurey and William "Billy" Clanton after the O.K. Corral shootings as well as the body of Charlie Storms after he was shot by Earp-ally Luke Short outside the Oriental Saloon in February of 1881. Dr. Goodfellow had also been involved in the manhunt for the Bisbee outlaws, being one of the members of U.S. Deputy Marshal C.B. Sanders' posse which was involved in the running gun battle with the robbers on Cherry Creek, near the town of Galeyville.[28]

The lynching of John Heath (author's collection).

Dr. Goodfellow was born in Downieville California, on December 23, 1855, to Milton J. and Amanda Goodfellow. He was educated at the California Military Academy in Oakland and the University of California at Berkeley where he studied Civil Engineering. He successfully applied to the United States Naval Academy, but was dismissed shortly thereafter following a racially motivated attack on another student. Goodfellow then attended Wooster University Medical School where, on February 23, 1876, he graduated with honors. In November 1876, he married Katherine Colt. The couple conceived a daughter, Edith, and a son who unfortunately died soon after his birth.

Goodfellow began his medical career in Oakland, California, but soon joined his father in Prescott where he worked as the company physician for Peck, Mine and Mill, a mining company, and for the U.S. Army as acting assistant surgeon at Fort Whipple. In 1880, Goodfellow cancelled his contract with the U.S. Army and moved his family to the burgeoning mining camp of Tombstone. Once settled, he hung out his shingle and began his career as a general practitioner. The doctor would come to find himself doing everything from delivering babies to treating gunshot wounds, but it was the latter for which he would become renown. Goodfellow's first office in Tombstone was located on the second floor above the now-famous Crystal Palace Saloon, which he often patronized when not engaged in his profession.

In the event of death in the Arizona Territory, prior to the establishment of the current judicial system—one which might not have been attributable to natural causes—a coroner's jury, a body of six to 12 men, was summoned to determine the cause of death and rule whether it was the result of foul-play. As explained in the *Encyclopedia Britannica*, "The coroner's jury resembles the grand jury in that it does not try cases, but rather reviews evidence that may be relevant at a trial. The jury's verdict states how, when, and where the deceased died. If the jury concludes that the deceased died by murder or manslaughter, it can name suspects, and the coroner can order arrest and detainment, pending grand jury action." As Heath had not died of natural causes, such a jury was immediately convened to investigate, with Pat Holland, the Cochise County Coroner heading the examination.

After examining the body, Dr. Goodfellow was called to testify regarding his findings. Emma Mortimer was also called on to testify, being the nearest person Heath had to family living in the Territory. A transcript of these interviews as conducted by the County Coroner is still available and is reproduced here:

Territory of Arizona
County of Cochise
In the Matter of John Heith,

Dr. Geo. E. Goodfellow.
Q. Have you examined the body of the deceased?
A. I have.
Q. Make any statement to the jury with reference to the cause of death of the deceased.
A. I find that the deceased died of Emphysima [*sic*] of the lungs, which might have been caused by strangulation, self-inflicted or otherwise.

G.E. Goodfellow
County Physician
Subscribed and sworn before me this 22nd day of February, A.D. 1884.
Pat Holland
Coroner in and for Cochise County, A.T.

Emma Mortimer.
Q. Where do you live?
A. Tombstone.
Q. Age?
A. 23.
Q. What is your occupation?
A. Lodging house owner.
Q. How long have you lived in Tombstone?
A. Two months.
Q. Do you identify the body of the deceased?
A. I do. His name is John Heith, age about 32.
Q. How long have you known him?
A. 2 years.
Q. What nativity?
A. Texas.

Emma Mortimer

Subscribed and sworn before me this 22nd day of February, A.D. 1884.
Pat Holland
Coroner in and for Cochise County, A.T.

Territory of Arizona
County of Cochise
We, the undersigned, a jury of inquest, duly impannelled [sic] and sworn before the Coroner of
Cochise County, to inquire whose the body submitted for our inspection, when, where, and by
what means he came to his death, after viewing the body and hearing such testimony as has been
brought before us find: That his name is John Heith, age 32 and nativity of Texas; and that his
death in Tombstone on the 22nd day of February 1884, arose from the effects of Emphysima [sic],
which might have been caused by strangulation self-inflicted or otherwise, is in accordance with
the Medical evidence.

Clemens E. Eschmann	W.D. Shearer	H.M. Woods
George T. Henderson, M.D.	E.P. Terrill	Pat Degnin
J.B. Lacy	S.W. Clawson	C.C. Warner
S.R. Fanell	S. Tribolet	

Endorsed and filed this 22nd day of February, A.D. 1884.
Pat Holland
Coroner in and for Cochise County, A.T.[29]

Dr. George Emory Goodfellow, the physician to the gunfighters, examined John Heath's remains and authored one of the most darkly humorous coroner's reports in the history of the Old West (author's collection).

Dr. Goodfellow's summation has always been a source for amusement for those reading about the Bisbee Massacre, albeit gallows' humor. Even at the time it was a source of amusement as evidenced by a short editorial in *The Arizona Sentinel* of March 1, which read, "The disease of which Heith died, according to the verdict of the coroner's jury was 'emthysema [sic] of the lungs.' A pessimist friend had suggested that it would be a good thing should the disease become epidemic in some locales." However, one is inclined to feel a certain amount of sympathy for Ms. Emma Mortimer, who probably was present when Dr. Goodfellow was interviewed and when he made his flippant remarks concerning the death of her lover.[30]

The editor of *The Arizona Weekly Star*, Louis C. Hughes, was one of the few who did take offense at Goodfellow's joke and he made his distaste known by reprinting an article which appeared originally in the editorial section of *The Chicago Tribune*:

The people of Tombstone, Arizona, have not only a grim sense of humor, but a profound knowledge of Greek. The name of their town, to say nothing of their local newspaper, the Epitaph, is a ghastly joke, which has raised many a smile before now. [On] Washington's birthday, the Tombstone people hanged a man from a telegraph pole, and the coroner's jury found that the lamented deceased came to his death by "emphysema," which might have been caused by strangulation, self-inflicted or otherwise. Emphysema is a swelling caused by air diffused throughout the cellular tissue. The poor wretch who was lynched in Tombstone, according to local authority, died of this peculiar and heretofore undescribed [sic] disorder. Lynching is bad enough, but when it is accompanied by a philogical [sic] joke, it assumes the proportion of an inexcusable outrage.[31]

Louis Cameron Hughes, the editor of *The Arizona Weekly Star,* took umbrage with Dr. Goodfellow's morbid medical report (Arizona Historical Society, Buehman Collection, B887).

One also may feel some sympathy for John Heath's father, who *The Arizona Weekly Citizen* reported had recently arrived in Fairbanks and was en route to Tombstone to visit his son, not knowing what fate had befallen his namesake. While in Fairbanks he was apprised of his son's demise at the hands of the Tombstone mob and "having doubts as to the manner in which he would be received" in Tombstone and "with a heavy heart stricken with grief at the fate of his wayward son," the "old gentleman ... at once turned about and took the next train for his home in Texas." The newspaper continued, "Though the people of Tombstone and vicinity shed no tears over the dead body of John Heath, still they will all feel deeply for the heartbroken father, and pray to heaven that the erring one has not a mother living to mourn the lamentable fate of her son."[32]

While Ms. Mortimer, Nathan Waite, the Heath family and possibly a handful of others might have mourned the death of John Heath, the "universal expression" and general consensus, as reported by *The Chicago Tribune* and others, was "served him right." In fact, some newspapers went as far as to attempt to further justify the lynching of Heath by recounting some of the misdeeds from his past. *The Arizona Silver Belt,* quoting from *The St Louis Republican,* said about Heath, "There have been upwards of twenty cases of burglary, theft, cattle and horse stealing against him in Dallas. Heith is a notorious Dallas county criminal and fled from this county about a year ago." *The Dallas Weekly Herald* went even further in condoning the actions of the Tombstone mob and the vilifying of Heath.[33]

Heath's record is well known here, and on the criminal records of the courts of this county his name appears very frequently, yet by some hook or crook, perhaps shrewdness on his part, he managed to escape the meshes of the law in every instance. Suave in manner and glib of tongue, he paved his way well for one in his position and character, and the officers themselves, who knew full well his true character always credited him with being an exemplary prisoner in his deportment and were tempted to like him better than perhaps he deserved. He never made any breaks against officials here for he knew them personally and was fully aware of what he would have to contend with, yet not withstanding they all knew the man and regarded him as a desperate character.

His old father, who is a farmer of Kaufman County, is acknowledged by all who know him to be an honest man and they sympathize heartily with him. The son John, it appears, was ever of a way-ward disposition, as his record will show. Outside of being arraignment [*sic*] for the theft of stock and on divers [*sic*] other charges, he fell so low that he was running a bawdy house here known as the Long Branch. At one time he drove a hack and was recognized as a bad man. Texas Red, who left here with him, is of the same ilk, and is also in the Tombstone jail, where Heath was under sentence of death. Texas Red was the presiding spirit of the Red Light, a bawdy house here.

After briefly recounting the story of the robbery and killing of "D.T. Smith," *The Weekly Herald* concluded the article saying, "Arizona justice is perhaps rather abrupt and sudden, and not dished out by the legal ladle, yet is very sure."[34]

There were some dissenting voices as well, though they were not specifically in defense of John Heath. An editorial in *The El Paso Lone Star* (reprinted by *The Daily Epitaph*) declared that "the influence of this cool administration of law is far more effective in surprising crime than the violent and unlawful vengeance of an infuriated crowd." The author cited the case of "Greenfield, in New York, who was on three trials convicted of murder in the first degree, and who, after fighting for his life for years, and having every chance to establish his innocence," was finally and legally hanged. This "impressed the public mind with a sense of the power of the law that a century cannot efface." The author concluded, "Lynch law, while in some cases justifiable, always weakens the respect for order and justice."[35]

Camillus Sydney Fly, photographer, took the now infamous photograph of John Heath's lynching and later sold prints of the photograph (author's collection).

The Denver Republican also questioned the necessity of the lynching of Heath: "An Arizona mob lynched a man who had been sentenced by the courts to imprisonment for life. Was this done because the Court refused to do its duty?" *The Arizona Weekly Citizen* fired back, "No sir. The Court did its duty according to the evidence and verdict of the jury rendering a verdict of murder in the second degree. During the fearful trial for murder where five men were sentenced by the court to be hanged, and one man for life, as accessory to the murdering, Judge Pinney did his whole duty, not only to the satisfaction of all, but discharged such duty in a manner as to win praises from every one who passed through the terrible trial." *The Weekly Citizen* defended Pinney and the court with aplomb, but did not answer the question posed by the Denver newspaper: If the court did its duty, why did the citizenry feel it necessary to lynch Heath? Obviously one of the two bodies was in the wrong.[36]

Responsibility for the lynching of Heath would finally fall upon Sheriff Jerome Ward. *The Chicago Tribune* reported that, "although people think Heath deserved hanging, the sentiment of conservative people is loudly censuring Sheriff Ward, for had he had a sufficient guard at the jail, it would have been impossible to have obtained entrance. The only way it could have been done was by using a battering ram and breaking in the walls. It has been subsequently learned that last night [February 21] was the time set for the lynching, but at the time there was a guard who was an ex-policemen, and who the mob knew would die before turning over the keys, so they wisely waited until he had been relieved." The newspaper concluded, "Sheriff Ward, knowing the sentiment of the people, showed a lack of judgment or great carelessness in leaving but two men in charge of the jail." In the end, despite his tireless and determined work in capturing the Bisbee bandits, Ward would be held liable for the actions of the mob.[37]

Camillus S. Fly was a famed Tombstone photographer who visually documented the historic meeting between the Apache chieftain Naiche, Geronimo and General George Crook, and who also took the only known photographs of the Apache while they were still at war with the United States. Fly also captured on film the bodies of the victims of Wyatt Earp and his brothers, who were killed at the O.K. Corral. And so, bolstered by his growing expertise and reputation for being in the right place at the right time, he took advantage of the public's appetite for photographic drama and made a tidy sum selling reprints of his picture of John Heath dangling from the telegraph pole. On March 1, *The Arizona Silver Belt* reported that Mr. Fly, made "large number of copies" of his photo of Heath, but "the demand far exceeded the supply" and an additional lot had to be printed. The photograph, like others Mr. Fly took during that period, has

Cenotaph for John Heath in Boothill Cemetery, Tombstone. John Heath is not buried here. His remains lie in an unmarked grave in the family plot in Terrell, Texas (author's collection).

become a priceless historical artifact, even though it was originally little more than a grisly souvenir sold for profit to the morbidly fascinated.[38]

On a windswept hill just off Highway 80 lies Tombstone's famous Boothill Graveyard, advertised to tourists as the final resting place of some of the most notorious outlaws and wicked criminals of the Old West. If one walks in to the cemetery and strolls down Row 3, there one will find a headstone for John Heath. The inscription, which is painted on the ochre-colored marker in black, reads: "John Heath: Taken from the County Jail & LYNCHED By Bisbee Mob, Feb 22, 1884." Though Heath's name is spelled correctly on the marker, both it and the grave below are fraudulent. In fact, the mortal remains of John Heath lie in an unmarked grave in the Oakland Cemetery in Terrell, Texas. *The Kaufman Sun* on February 28, 1884, reported, "John Heath, the notorious gambler, burglar and horse and cattle thief, who murdered a man in Tombstone, Arizona, while breaking into a bank, and was tried and sentenced to hang, was taken from jail by a mob a few nights ago and hung. The telegrams state that he protested his innocence of the murder until the last, but seeing he was doomed, he asked the mob not to shoot him as he did not wish his body mutilated. His remains were brought to Terrell and interred. He has a noble mother living there."[39]

It is doubtful there was but the most simple of services for John Heath when he was finally interred in the Oakland Cemetery in Terrell. The few, unrecorded words that might have been said over John Heath's earthly remains would have come from his immediate family members, if there were any at all. He was survived by his mother, his father, and his wife, Jennie. Certainly the citizens of Bisbee and Tombstone did not mourn his loss. The only eulogy John Heath received was in the form of a short poem, composed by his comrade Daniel "York" Kelly written on the day Heath was lynched. It is reprinted here in its entirely:

THE HANGING OF JOHN HEATH

As I awoke this morning at eight
I heard a knock at the outside gate
The jailer went to open the door,
And there beheld a hundred or more.

Kreigbaum [sic] came to Ward's relief,
And the jailer left on account of his belief.
The Stranglers came to have some fun;
They roped John Heath and away they run.

The mob went out four by four,
And met the sheriff at the door.
They gave a howl and a roar;
And throwed the old man on the floor.

Harry Solan, brave and true
Entered the door to see what he could do;
But found it was of no avail,
For the mob had taken Heath from the jail.

They went down Toughnut, crossed the main,
And then came back to Toughnut again;

They marched Heath down to the bend,
And here they said the fun would end.

The valiant Heath, for nerve he had no lack,
He told the mob he had one request to make,
Said he, "My boys, when I am dead,
Do not pierce my body with your lead."

They placed brave Heath beneath the wire,
And pulled him up six feet or higher,
The way he died, it was a shame,
But Sheriff Ward was not to blame.

Oh, Stranglers, prepare, for the day will come,
That you will have to meet your doom.
You will curse the hour you were born,
The morning that Gabriel toots his horn.[40]

Daniel "York" Kelly and the others would go to the gallows all the while maintaining the innocence of John Heath.

CHAPTER SEVEN

The Hanging

Immediately after he and his four accomplices were convicted by the court for the murders of John C. Tappenier, Deputy Sheriff D. Thomas Smith, J.A. "Tex" Nolly, and Mrs. Annie Roberts in Bisbee, *The Tombstone Daily Epitaph* recorded "a terrible change" in the countenance of Daniel "Big Dan" Dowd. "The certainty of his execution has forced itself into his mind [and] a most marked change has taken place in him. Upon being brought into court yesterday to testify in the Heith case he was hardly recognizable, so wan and haggard had he become in a few short days. Not only had he changed in appearance, but also in manner, his devil-may-care reckless demeanor having given way to that of a man who hears the rush of Azrael's wings and knows that his eyelids will soon be brushed by them."[1]

The author of the article obviously hoped that "Big Dan" and his cohorts were overcome with feelings of anguish and remorse over their crimes but if in fact they were actually experiencing emotions of this kind, they were not letting it show. It was revealed a few days later—the very day of his sentencing—that Dowd's "wan and haggard appearance" was not due to overwhelming emotions or "dread of impending doom," but rather at having had a portion of one of his fingers amputated. *The Epitaph* did not reveal the cause of the infection which made this operation necessary, only that it explained Dowd's pasty and peaked pallor.[2]

Dowd, Delaney, Kelly, Sample, and Howard were sentenced to be hanged by Judge Pinney on February 19. Their execution was scheduled for March 28, which meant the five men would spend over a month sitting in their cells on the first floor of the Cochise County Courthouse mulling over their fate. All they had was time until the fateful day arrived. Meals were brought to the men at 8:00 a.m., at noon, and again in the evening, care of local dairy rancher J.J. Chandler, who contracted with the County for the feeding of prisoners housed in the jail (at the rate of 62½ cents a day). *The Tucson Weekly Citizen* reported that Sheriff Ward had allowed the men "extra rations" beyond "the usual food allowed the county prisoners." He also supplied the men with "fruits, cigars, and liquor" though it was noted "their allowance in this respect was three drinks of whisky a day." According to the newspaper, the only complaint from the inmates was that the Sheriff "covered them with too many irons."[3]

The Arizona Sentinel reported on March 8, that the construction of the gallows was underway and noted "the drop is sufficiently large to accommodate the whole crowd, and they will be launched into the great unknown at the same instant." Though the inmates were not permitted to venture outside—they took their exercise in the corridors of the cellblock—there were two windows on the first floor of the courthouse which faced out upon the courtyard where the gallows were being built. This meant the prisoners, if they looked out at an angle, could witness the steady construction of the five-man gallows at the rear of the building from the comfort of their cell block windows. Even if they were not peering out the windows, they could hear the sawing and hammering and planing being done on the wooden structure from their cells inside the building.[4]

Unfortunately, there is very little information available about the men who committed the murders and robbery in Bisbee. William E. Delaney seems to have been the black sheep of a fairly respectable Pennsylvania family. He stated he was born July 11, in Scranton. He was the second of three children born to James and Jane Delaney. In the Census of 1860, William is said to have been four years of age, indicating he was born in 1856. His brother, John Carroll Delaney, was reported to be 12. At 14, John Carroll ran away from home to join the Union Army. He would come to be awarded the Congressional Medal of Honor for saving a wounded comrade who would have otherwise burned to death. After the war, John Delaney would find employment as the Librarian for the Pennsylvania State Senate.

By 1870, William Delaney would have been about 14 years of age. There are two young men named "William Delaney" listed as living in Pennsylvania in the 1870 Census, one age 13 and one age 15, but neither would seem to be the son of James and Jane and the brother of John C. Delaney. Had William Delaney followed in his brother's footsteps and left home at an early age? It is impossible to say. After his arrest, *The Arizona Sentinel* explained that Delaney "bore a somewhat unsavory reputation" in his hometown of Harrisburg and was "sent to this country by his relatives to escape arrest for theft." The newspaper neglected to give their source for this information. Delaney indicated it might well have been another murder charge which he had fled from.

The Clifton Clarion reported that Delaney "turned outlaw after the killing of a man named Sawyer in Clifton in August." When he was arrested in Minas Prietas, Delaney had admitted as much to Deputy Sheriff Bob Hatch, saying, "I expect you want me for the Clifton business; I had some trouble in Clifton and had to kill a man there." The shooting scrape between Delaney and Henry Sawyer was duly noted by *The Weekly Phoenix Herald*. The outlaw later stated that the trouble between he and Sawyer began when the latter "interfered with a quarrel" between Delaney and a Mexican woman. It seems Delaney pulled his revolver and shot Sawyer through the heart, killing him outright. The young shootist was subsequently lodged in the city jail. Sawyer's friends threatened to lynch Delaney, but nothing came of it. William Delaney was twenty eight years old at the time of the Bisbee robbery.[5]

During his trial, John Heath stated he first met James "Tex" Howard in San Antonio, Texas, and had "known him for eight or nine years." Heath also said he had worked with Howard for three years" including a period of laboring together as cowboys, on "Chisholm's trail." Howard testified at Heath's trial that he had known the defendant since 1879. Unfortunately, the Federal Census information does not provide any further clues to James Howard's origins or his life before the robbery. A search of the 1880 Census for the state of Texas returned numerous entries for men between the ages of 25 and 35 known as "James Howard" or some variation thereof. However, none of these men were listed as living in San Antonio, though some resided in neighboring counties. Several of the men were described as being single with their occupation listed simply as "laborer," but without more substantial information, it is impossible to say if any of these are the man known as James "Tex" Howard. Prophetically, on the eve of his execution, James "Tex" Howard had told an interviewer from *The Arizona Weekly Citizen* that "his family did not know where he was and would never know."[6]

Omer W. Sample appeared in the United States Census of 1860, the child of William K. and Louiza Sample. The boy was three months of age. The record indicates he was born in Jennings Township, Indiana, and his father's occupation listed as "farmer." Omer W. Sample also appeared in the Census of 1870. He is listed as being ten years of age with no siblings. At the time of the 1870 Census, he was living with his parents Wea Township, Kansas. The youth's occupation was described as "farm laborer." He could not be found in the Census of 1880. Assuming this is the same young man, Omer W. Sample would have been 23 at the time of the robbery in Bisbee.

When Omer W. Sample entered in to a life of crime is unknown. At the time of the assault on Goldwater and Castaneda's store, "Red" Sample had several true bills against him waiting in Clifton. *The Clifton Clarion*, which called Sample the "most notorious" of the five outlaws, stated he had been indicted for the robbery of the Detroit Copper Company's offices the previous summer and that of an "old Mormon rancher" in August 1883. James Patton, in his book *History of Clifton*, asserted it was the Kid Louis gang which was responsible for the Detroit Copper Company robbery. If Sample was indeed running with Kid Lewis and his gang, he was involved with a pretty rough crowd and would have been well-versed in the business of armed robbery.[7]

In an interview given to a reporter shortly before his death, Daniel "York" Kelly asserted he had family in the "old country," perhaps meaning Ireland. His moniker, "York" or "Yorkey," may well be a clue to his origins. Beyond this, the information about the man is scant. *The Clifton Clarion* said only that Kelly had "not been considered a shining light in this community" though the newspaper had nothing specific with which to back this assessment. Kelly obviously had some education as he was able to write as evidenced by the poem he composed after Heath was lynched. Also, in the files relating to the case held at the Arizona State Library, Archives and Public Records is a short note which looks to have been scrawled in pencil. It reads:

> pleasures of no one—
> Shoud [*sic*] be happy
> Home—Friend—Family
> Oh does not sotes [?] by
> Sinner unhappy
> down-heart
> longing
> Yes I am
> No not
> Unhappy in Bondage in chains

The note is not signed or dated. It is impossible to verify the author of the piece, though, being that Kelly was known as something of a writer, it may well be his composition. It is also known that Daniel "York" Kelly converted (or possibly reverted) to the Catholic faith shortly before he was executed.[8]

Daniel "Big Dan" Dowd was even less forthcoming about himself and his past. When questioned by a reporter as to his true identity and asked if Dowd was his real name, the outlaw replied, "Well, that's what I am known by here, and no one will know any other while I live." Having worked for a brief time as a freighter in the Territory prior to the robbery, Dowd seems to have been known and generally liked, as indicated by a brief article which appeared in *The Tombstone Republican*. "A good many citizens of Tombstone were acquainted with him before he became implicated in his present trouble. He was known as a large-hearted, generous man, and was regarded as one the 'gamiest' men in the community."

However, *The Clifton Clarion* had a far different opinion of Dowd. The newspaper described him as "a worthless fellow" suspected of being involved in the attack on a "wagon-load of Chinamen at the Big Hill" which left "two of the Mongolians" dead. On August 29, 1883, three mounted gunmen chased down the stagecoach from Clifton which was being followed by a wagon with several Chinese men. The coach had already crested the hill and was about 200 yards ahead, while the wagon was forced to stop at the top of the hill when "one of the tugs of the wheel horses became detached." It was then the three horsemen descended upon them. "They ordered the Chinamen to throw up their hands and commenced firing, simultaneously, the fire being instantly returned by one of the Chinamen with a Winchester rifle."

The engagement was brief and when the smoke cleared "a ghastly scene presented itself." Two of the Chinamen, Ah Chong and Sam Ting were mortally wounded and lay on the ground "writhing in pain." Ah Lin had been shot through the arm and Ah Hoyt had been shot through the calf. One of the horsemen was also wounded in the melee, a ball from Sam Ting's Winchester tearing into his "left breast and lodging just beneath the skin in the back." However, this did not stop the robbers. "The Chinaman having been overpowered, it was but the work of a few minutes to go through them, the highwaymen obtaining between $250 and $300, four watches, six railroad tickets, four pistols, and a rifle." The gunmen then fled the scene, one heading toward Clifton and the others toward the Gila River.

The Chinamen were loaded back on the wagon and they proceeded six miles on to Lordsburg. Ah Chong and Sam Ting both died from their wounds before noon the following day. A small posse was formed by Deputy Sheriff John M. Hovey (the same man who would be instrumental in the capture of "Red" Sample and "Tex" Howard a few months later) and the robbers pursued, but they were unable to "strike the trail of the escaping parties" and returned that same evening. The following day, Deputy Sheriff Hovey set out again and was able to locate the wounded outlaw at a ranch on the Gila River. Unfortunately, the unidentified outlaw was too badly wounded to make a statement of any kind or identify his partners-in-crime. The outlaw would eventually expire and, though a large reward was offered by the Governor and the County, the other two bandits were never apprehended.

Of course, the newspaper's indictment of "Big Dan" Dowd for the attack on the Chinese was not based on any specific evidence or eyewitness testimony, at least none was revealed in the article. Dowd may have been involved in the robbery and, then again, he may not. If he was, it would certainly set a precedent for what would occur less than four months later on the night of December 8 in Bisbee. It was very well established during the trial that Dan Dowd, the man the residents of Tombstone called "a large-hearted, generous man," was the same man who had stood outside Goldwater and Castaneda's firing indiscriminately at people on the street.[9]

On March 10th, Christopher "Kit" Joy, Mitch Lee, Frank Taggart, George W. Cleveland—the men suspected of planning and implementing the Gage train robbery—in addition to a murderer named Carlos Chavez and a horse and cattle thief named Charles

Spencer, broke out of the county jail in Silver City, New Mexico Territory around 9 o'clock in the morning. The suspects affected their escape by "overpowering the guards and locking them in the cells." The outlaws then took the guards' guns and made good their get away. Almost immediately, a posse of law officers and citizens formed to go in pursuit of the escapees. The lawmen followed the outlaws "to the foothills of the Pinos Altos range … some six miles north of the town, where they overtook them." A firefight ensued "in which Chavez was shot through the head and instantly killed."

The chase continued, until "the fleeing criminals availed themselves of a rocky ridge, thickly covered with brush and grass" where they chose to make a stand. During the subsequent gun battle, George W. Cleveland was shot and killed as was Silver City citizen Joseph W. Laffer. Mitch Lee was mortally wounded. As "the citizens closed in upon them, Taggart proposed a surrender. Deputy Sheriff Hall then ordered him to throw up his hands and come out of the brush, the sheriff keeping him covered with his gun while he approached." Taggart was searched by posse member Charles M. Shannon, who found he had no weapons upon his person. The outlaw confessed that he had surrendered only because he had run out of ammunition. Taggart's emptied pistol was found in the brush nearby.

The posse quickly decided the captured men should pay for the life of J.W. Laffer. Frank Taggart and the mortally-wounded Mitch Lee were summarily hanged by the citizens from a tree not far from the place where they were apprehended. After the life had been choked out of the two outlaws, their bodies were cut down, placed in a wagon with those of George W. Cleveland and Carlos Chavez, and returned to Silver City. According to *The Arizona Silver Belt*, the mortal remains of the men "became the undivided property of the coroner, who, having no use for them, generously presented them to the gravedigger, and who, in turn, gave them as food for worms." Upon examination it was determined his gun had not been fired, and for this reason alone, Charles Spencer avoided the fate of his fellow escapees. He was "returned to his quarters in the jail."[10]

Christopher C. "Kit" Joy was the only one of the prisoners to avoid the posse and make good his escape. *The Mohave County Miner* reported on March 16 that "a party of three started in pursuit of Joy, and it was believed he was overtaken and killed, as his pursuers are very reticent about the matter. In any event he is badly wounded and his escape is simply impossible." However, on March 22, *The Arizona Silver Belt* reported "Kit" Joy was still at large "and when last heard of was in Arizona." The latter newspaper also stated that Joy "had received money from some person in Lordsburg, N.M., who, if discovered, should be lynched for assisting a murderer to escape." "Kit" Joy was described as being 23 years of age with brown hair and gray eyes. He was of fair complexion and had two of his upper teeth broken off.[11]

Six days later, "E. Smith, Sterling Ashley, and Mike McGuire were working about 200 yards above Slayback's ranch, on the upper Gila River when they "noticed a man moving along through the weeds further up the river, and noticed also that he was evidently anxious to avoid observation. Upon catching sight of the men he dropped into the weeds." Smith, Ashley, and McGuire walked down to within 30 feet of the place the man hid himself. After ascertaining his exact position, "Smith and his companions then went off and arming themselves with long range guns" returned to the site and called to the man to surrender himself. The man was armed with a shotgun, but was out of range to use it effectively. He decided then to make a run "for the brush and was shot at but missed."

Christopher Carson "Kit" Joy, one of the Gage Station robbers and only surviving member of the gang (private collection).

For an unknown reason, the fleeing man stopped abruptly, allowing Smith time to draw a bead upon him and shoot him through the left leg below the knee, shattering the bone within. The young man crumpled to the ground and the three pursuers were soon upon him. He surrendered and was disarmed. Though they suspected it from the beginning, Smith and his confederates realized that this was indeed "Kit" Joy, the train robber and escapee from the county jail. "A courier was at once sent to notify Tom Hall, and the latter went out … to meet the party coming in with prisoner." Under escort, "Kit" Joy was returned to the county jail. That evening, a doctor was brought in to examine the wounded outlaw. It was determined that his limb was too badly damaged by the bullet to be saved and, the following morning, "Kit" Joy was separated from his lower left leg.[12]

While "Kit" Joy was on the run in New Mexico, Dowd, Delaney, Howard, Kelly, and Sample were securely confined behind bars on the first floor of the Tombstone Courthouse wiling away the hours and days leading up to the date of their execution. They were not completely without entertainment though. John L. Sullivan, the undefeated boxing champion of the United States, paid the condemned men a visit during his stop-over in Tombstone. In September of 1883, the legendary "knock-out specialist" had begun a promotional, coast-to-coast, railway tour of the United States with five other well-known pugilists. The tour began in Sullivan's hometown of Boston and traveled westward. To help promote the tour, Sullivan announced that he would box anyone at any time during the tour under the Queensberry Rules. The "Boston Strong Boy" offered as much as $1,000 to any man who could enter the ring with him and simply remain standing after four three-minute rounds.[13]

Sullivan and his combination were returning eastward from an engagement in San Francisco, where he defeated renowned local pugilist George Robinson (in what may well be considered one of the strangest fights of Sullivan's career), when they stopped in the Arizona Territory's most infamous town. The night before they visited Tombstone, Sullivan and his crew stopped in Tucson, where the pugilists had given an exhibition at the Park Theatre of the "manly art of self-defense." *The Tucson Weekly Citizen* recorded that Sullivan fought two exhibition bouts that evening. The first with Peter McCoy and the second with Mich Gillespie. None of the rounds lasted more than two minutes. In between, McCoy and Gillespie had a bout of their own. The entire exhibition lasted no more than 45 minutes and was augmented before and aft by performances from local talents including singers Trixie Vernon, Clara Edwards, and "crusher" Rosita de Corase.[14]

The following evening, Saturday, March 23rd, Sullivan and his troupe of pugilists gave a performance in Tombstone. Unfortunately, there are no extant records relating to the evening's entertainments. Most likely it did not differ too much from the performance given in Tucson. As Sullivan's biographer, Michael Isenberg, asserted, at this point in the tour, "the fighters were loafing ... merely going through the motions. The act was badly cribbed." In spite of their lackluster performances, Sullivan and his combination was quite the draw in small towns and burgeoning cities across the United States. *The Tucson Weekly Citizen* noted that a week after the exhibition, L.G. Gifford attended the masquerade ball given at D.H. Armstrong's Opera House attired as the champion. It seemed the wild and wooly town of Tombstone was not immune to the infection of having a renowned national celebrity in their midst either.[15]

The morning after their performance, John L. Sullivan and his entourage visited the infamous Bisbee murderers in their cells at the Cochise County Courthouse. Without a doubt, the outlaws were as star-struck as the rest of the male population of the town. Though most details of the encounter between the champion and the outlaws were not captured, one incident from that Sunday morning was recorded for posterity. It seems that after "scanning the champion closely," James "Tex" Howard said to the Boston slugger, "You are not as big a man as I had imagined, Sullivan. They tell me you can knock anyone in the world out in four rounds; is that so?" Sullivan responded that he believed he could, whereupon "Tex" said:

"Well, I reckon I will have to take your word on it, for chances are I shall never have the opportunity to see whether you can or not."

"But, *there* is a little man who can beat you," said the outlaw, motioning to the diminutive, 54-year-old County Sheriff Jerome Ward.

"How is that?" asked Sullivan, observing that Ward didn't "look like a fighter."

"Tex" smiled. "Well, he ain't, but he'll knock five of us out in one round next Friday morning, all the same."

This witticism elicited laughter from both the visitors and the inmates.

A short time later, as Sullivan and his entourage were readying to depart, the champion turned back to "Tex" and complimented him on his "good looks," to which "Tex" replied, "Well, you're not the prettiest man I ever saw, but I'd take your mug if I had your liberty." This comment provoked another round of laughter in the cellblock. The champion then took his leave of the condemned. John L. Sullivan did not stay in Tombstone to witness the grisly handiwork of Sheriff Ward. The famed pugilist and his entourage caught the next Southern and Pacific train eastward to Deming in the New Mexico Territory, the next scheduled stop on their national tour.[16]

In spite of their bravado, the condemned men must have been subject to an increasing feeling of trepidation as the date of their execution approached. This is evidenced by the more regular visits of two other local personages, Nellie Cashman and Father Patrick J. Gallagher, both of whom seemed intent on saving the immortal souls of the condemned men by facilitating their conversion to Catholicism. *The Tombstone Epitaph* reported that "as the dread day which was to be their last on earth approached more serious thoughts appeared to harass their minds. Father Gallagher was a frequent visitor in the cells of the condemned.... Delaney, Sample and Kelley [*sic*] were the first to listen to the holy counsel of the reverend [father], they having previously received the ordinance of baptism in the Catholic church." Dan Dowd and "Tex" Howard, the newspaper reported, "[r]emained somewhat obdurate."[17]

John L. Sullivan, champion heavyweight pugilist, who visited the Bisbee bandits during his tour of the Arizona Territory (author's collection).

Father Patrick J. Gallagher served as pastor to the Catholic contingency in Tombstone from 1882 to 1884 (possibly 1886), and was replaced by Father Augustine Morin soon after the execution of the Bisbee murderers. The condemned men's other regular visitor was very well-known in Tombstone and points west. Ellen "Nellie" Cashman was often called "The Miner's Angel" and for good reason. Nellie Cashman was born to Patrick and Fanny (nee Cronin) O'Kissane of Middleton, Ireland, a farming community few miles from Queenstown (now Cobh) in County Cork, in 1845. Having been either widowed or deserted, Mrs. Cashman (anglicized from O'Kissane) immigrated to the United States with her two daughters Nellie and Frances (better known as Fanny) around 1850. The family settled in Boston, Massachusetts, with thousands of other Irish immigrants. In 1865, at the close of the Civil War, the Cashman family, like so many others, migrated west, finally settling in San Francisco, California. By 1872, Mrs. Cashman and her eldest daughter were residing in the short-lived silver camp of Pioche in Lincoln County, Nevada.

When the silver in Pioche played out, Nellie Cashman accompanied some of the Nevada miners northward to a new strike in the remote Cassiar District in British Columbia, Canada. It was there she opened her first boarding house and restaurant and it was there she earned her reputation as "The Miner's Angel." The story goes that Ms. Cashman heard of a group of miners who had chosen to winter in the Cassiar District after the mining season had come to an end. That particular winter was exceedingly harsh and the miners were soon stranded and starving as well as suffering from scurvy. News of miners' plight eventually reached Ms. Cashman, who promptly organized a party to go to their aid. After traveling hundreds of miles by foot through the snow and across the ice, Ms. Cashman and the rescue party finally arrived at the camp and saved the snow-bound sourdoughs.

In 1876, Nellie Cashman returned to San Francisco to care for her aging mother. Then, in the fall of 1878, Ms. Cashman moved to the town of Tucson, trading the cold of the northern territories for the heat of the Sonoran desert. Upon her arrival, Ms. Cashman opened a restaurant, which she dubbed Delmonico's, and advertised as "Having the Best Meals in the City." After the death of her husband, Tom Cunningham, in February of 1881, her sister Fanny and her five children moved to Tucson as well. However, Nellie had already moved on, re-locating 80 miles to the southeast to the raucous mining town of Tombstone. There she opened both a boarding house and another restaurant. Fanny helped as best she was able with her sister's various businesses, but she was stricken with tuberculosis and would finally succumb to the disease in July 1884. Francis "Fanny" Cunningham's children would become wards of their Aunt Nellie.

A devout Catholic, Nellie Cashman was always willing to help those down on their luck and regularly fed, clothed, and grubstaked members of the mining community and others who had fallen on hard times. Ms. Cashman also collected donations for and gave to numerous charitable institutions, including the Sisters of St. Anne in Victoria, British Columbia, the Sisters of St. Joseph in Tucson, and the Salvation Army. She is also credited with raising the funds necessary to build the Sacred Heart Catholic Church in Tombstone. Given her compassionate and caring nature, it is not surprising that Nellie Cashman would take an interest in the condemned men languishing in the Cochise County jail and soon be found administering aid, both spiritual and temporal. Even though they were known murderers and thieves, she treated them humanely and with kindness. And in their final hours, Nellie Cashman would be the one protecting their dignity.[18]

Ellen "Nellie" Cashman, the Miner's Angel, protected the dignity of the condemned outlaws by disallowing others to profit from their death (author's collection).

What was to be the simultaneous hanging of five men in Tombstone was of great interest to the populace of the Territory. It also sparked some debate among the citizens about the nature of executions in the county and whether they should be private or public affairs. Sheriff Ward had announced that he would have 1,000 invitations printed for the hanging, which would be distributed to various personages in town. This caused a great uproar among the majority of the population, who felt they were to be deprived of the opportunity to witness such a momentous event for themselves. A reporter for *The Arizona Weekly Citizen* noted that the Sheriff, prior to distribution of the invitations, was being "bothered continually by applicants for passes to the jail yard." The reporter noted, "If closely packed the jail yard will hold 1,400 people."

Still the reporter (who would be one of those fortunate persons admitted inside the walls of the courthouse to view the event) stopped short of advancing the idea that the hanging of Dowd, Delaney, Howard, Sample and Kelly be a public execution. "There is a desire among certain class of people to have the hanging public, in open view of everybody whose morbid curiosity, or other interests, might tempt them to attend. This, certainly under the circumstances, would be wrong." However, it was not concern for the dignity of the condemned that he argues for a "private" execution, but because the "criminals have friends in this vicinity—they assert they have plenty—and if it became known to such parties, they would be liable to create bloodshed, in attempting in a body, and by a sudden attack to rescue the murderers." "Such men," the reporter emphatically stated, "must be kept away from the scene by high, strong walls."[19]

The Weekly Phoenix Herald weighed in on the argument early on, with an editorial on March 6, condemning outright the very idea of public executions. The editorial began: "The press and people of Cochise county are discussing the propriety of public execution of the Bisbee murderers. It seems at least a portion of the public demands a public execution, 'proposes to sup full of horror.' The violent death of a human being at any time and under any circumstances is a terrible scene to witness. No matter if the person be the very incarnation of hell itself, the scene of death, instantly blotting out and casting away the being into the eternal depth of time."

Unfortunately, the balance of the article has been destroyed, but the sentiment is not lost. The author of the article firmly stood in opposition to the proposal of public execution as being an affront to the sensibilities of a civilized people.[20]

On March 22, *The Tombstone Republican* printed a letter received by the editor which argued in favor of public executions from a very self-serving (and rather callous) position:

Editor Republican:

In the recent discussion between your correspondent "One who Paid the Fiddler," and the editor of your esteemed contemporary regarding the hanging of the Bisbee murderers, neither of the disputants ever suggested to Sheriff Ward that he consult the wishes of this community in the matter and govern himself accordingly. I am constantly traveling through this territory, and I have yet to meet a man in it who does not favor public execution of these criminals. It is true that a great many who hold this opinion will not assert it on the house top, nor even give it till [sic] it is asked for, but it was generally known that the private execution was rapidly assuming the shape of a select entertainment for Sheriff Ward's friends, I think there would be a demonstration of opinion that Mr. Ward would not dare to disregard.

A hanging is a hanging, perform it as you will; and its horrors are no less when witnessed by a hundred people than be a hundred thousand. Some regard a public execution as a disgusting spectacle, while others consider it a sublime warning to the evilly disposed, and each class is equally honest in its convictions; but the local champion of the former class will, notwithstanding his protest in Sunday's issue, undoubtedly regale his readers the morning after the execution with a narrative of the occurrence that will be, in attention to detail and accuracy of portraiture, far more disgusting to the average person than the sight itself. But I advocate the public execution of these men from a standpoint entirely different from any yet made public, and I make it known only after consulting some of the largest firms in the city as to its advisability, and receiving their hearty approval of the idea. Should these assassins be executed publicly, people would flock here from all parts of the territory to witness their doom. It is safe to say that 2,000 visitors would be in Tombstone on the 28th of March, and presuming each one would spend ten dollars in the city, we have the handsome sum of $20,000 left with various business houses of the place, and out trade stimulated accordingly. This may not appear to the highly sensitive scribe as a very elevated base on which to rest a plea for a public execution, but our businessmen may be made of sterner stuff, and will try to endure the moral shock of the open hanging may occasion, for the sake of the activity in business, the flux of spectators would create.

There is no sentiment in business and our merchants look upon the inevitable in a very practical way. If the opinion or actions would materially alter the day's occurrence, they would be found to act with the due reserve and consideration; but the occasion does not call for such behavior and realizing the fact that the county has been in a large expense on account of the Bisbee affair and that ultimately this debt must be borne by the people they manifest no reluctance in turning the final act of the tragedy to profitable account and thus become the better able to meet the bills that the tax collector will surely present them next fall. Sheriff Ward should take the hint herein given for the merchants of this community constitute an important factor in an election and tenacious office holders can hardly deem it to their advantage to ignore the wishes of such an element.

Yours, etc.

Mercadero.[21]

One individual seemingly took Mercadero's maxim "there is no sentiment in business" to heart and did his utmost to realize at least some profit from the spectacle of the hanging of the Bisbee murderers. That man was W.M. Constable. *The Arizona Citizen* reported the "speculative citizen" was building a grandstand "on private ground within a few feet of the walls" surrounding the jail yard. The newspaper continued to explain that Constable expected to "seat 600 people" in his bleachers and "intends to charge them a big fee for a seat." The reporter did not condemn Constable's enterprise, but rather observed that "the walls surrounding the jail yard are 13 feet high, and in order to support his six hundred at that elevation and higher too, he must use some very strong supports." The only concern in the reporter's mind was the possibility of a "fatal crash." However, there were others in town, who felt profiteering from the deaths of the Bisbee bandits was an affront to common decency.[22]

In common with Mr. Constable's grandstand, the construction of the gallows was quite the engineering feat. Built almost entirely of wood, the gibbet on which Delaney, Dowd, Kelly, Sample, and Howard were to be hanged was described by *The Weekly Citizen* as "the strongest and surest ever erected in the Territory." A wooden staircase lead eight feet up to the platform, that was 20 feet long and 14 feet wide, upon which the men would stand. The platform stood on four large posts, one at each corner of the structure. The platform area was ringed in on the sides and in front by a single rail. Eight feet above the platform and running the entire length was a single, large eight by six crossbeam, supported by a thick eight by six pillar on either end. It was over this crossbar the ropes would be tied. Cut in the middle of the platform was a large trapdoor which, when activated, would allow all five men to drop through the floor simultaneously.

The Tombstone Republican described in greater detail the mechanism which operated the trapped doors. "The drop," reported the newspaper, "will be supported by several triggers or bolts. These triggers are attached to a through brace, and will be drawn back together be means of a heavy weight that will be let drop from the platform. The five men will drop together, and the drop will be sufficient to insure instantaneous and painless death." The distance of the drop was actually only five feet. Among the designers of the gallows was Pima County Sheriff Robert H. "Bob" Paul. *The Republican* said of the Sheriff,

"What Bob don't know about 'working off' a man neatly and artistically wouldn't make a very large book." *The Arizona Weekly Citizen* said of the structure: "[I]t should excite the admiration of the most experienced hangman."[23]

On the evening of March 26, as Tombstone was preparing for one of the most momentous events in the town's sordid history, the town of Bisbee was awakened from its slumbers by yet more violence. In a dispatch from *The Arizona Daily Star*, it was reported that Deputy Sheriff Daniels had closed up his saloon for the night and gone to bed, when he "was awakened by a noise of some one in the house. Watching, he saw a man with his boots off cautiously approach the safe and attempt to open it." Deputy Daniels picked up his shotgun and called upon the man to desist, whereupon the thief made a desperate dash toward the rear door of the saloon—the same door by which he had entered the building. "Daniels discharged the contents of the shotgun, containing nineteen buckshot, into him. The man fell dead."

The man Deputy Daniels killed was a miner named John Hiles. Harriet Hankin would state in her manuscript that Hiles was "suspected in complicity in the hold up." She also implies that Hiles was the man who took shots at James Krigbaum from the lumberyard during the robbery (if this indeed happened at all). Again, there is no evidence at all to support this assertion. It is very likely this was yet another fanciful tale told her by Krigbaum. A coroner's jury was convened and, after a short deliberation, "returned a verdict in accordance with the above facts, and also justifying the officer."[24]

Why, just a week before Dowd, Delaney, York, Kelly, and Howard were to be hanged, the editor of *The Arizona Daily Star* chose to publish in his columns a short opinion on the lynching of John Heath is unknown, but on March 21, the following editorial appeared within their pages: "The fact as to whether Heith was or was not accessory to the Bisbee outrages is probably known to the five men who are to hang on next Friday. Should they declare him innocent of any knowledge of the affair who has the power to restore Heith to life, and who will answer for his murder? Is a question which the future will have to answer."[25]

This first challenge by *The Daily Star's* editor to public opinion would go unheeded, in contrast to later editorials condemning the vigilante actions of the citizens of Tombstone and Bisbee. Louis Cameron "L.C." Hughes, editor and proprietor of *The Arizona Daily Star*, would be the only dissenting voice to be heard for over a century and a half.

As previously observed, the imminent hanging of five men in Tombstone was a popular subject among the populace and in the newspapers. Those privileged individuals who had received one of Sheriff Ward's exclusive invitations were the envy of their peers. The editor of *The Mohave County Miner* was pleased to acknowledge "the receipt of an invitation from Sheriff Ward" and *The Arizona Daily Star* reported Sheriff Bob Paul "had a ticket for a reserved seat" as well. Diarist George Parsons stated that he too had received an invitation, though he was not in town to attend the event. Still, the lack of a formal invitation did not deter many people. *The Daily Star* reported in the same column that "[q]uite a number of Tucsonites have gone to Tombstone to witness the slaughter of the Bisbee criminals."[26]

During the time they were awaiting execution, the Bisbee bandits no doubt had numerous conversations among themselves, with their jailors, and with their many visitors including Father Gallagher and Nellie Cashman. Unfortunately, none of these conversations were transcribed or recorded for posterity. Throughout the period of their incarceration, Dowd, Delaney, York, Kelly, and Howard steadfastly refused to speak with representatives from the local press. That is, until their final evening on earth. Reporters from *The Tucson Weekly Citizen* and *The Arizona Daily Star*, both Tucson-based newspapers, succeeded in obtaining interviews with the condemned men. The man from *The Citizen* was the first to interview the prisoners, doing so just two days before their scheduled execution.

Initially, Sheriff Ward told the reporter that he had his permission to talk with the men, saying, "Why, certainly, but it is no use. They won't speak to reporters. You will not get a word out of them." When the reporter persisted, the Sheriff led him to the "outer iron girdled door" and entrance to the cellblock. A rapping on the door "brought the question, 'Who is there?' The reply, 'Ward,' caused the inner door in the same cell to open an inch. The eye of a keeper peeped through. Recognizing the sheriff, both doors were opened and the officer and the interviewer passed within. Another grated barrier was unlocked before a look could be had into the corridor to which the cells of the doomed men opened."

The reporter was made to wait in the corridor while the Sheriff went in to talk with the inmates. A moment later the order was given and "a lever from without was turned, a cell door flew open, and out stepped two strongly built, broad shouldered, and ruddy-faced men. Neither could have been over thirty years old, and neither was less than five feet ten in height." The men were identified as William Delaney and James "Tex" Howard. "Stepping into the corridor they laughingly asked; 'Well. What is it?'" The sheriff introduced the reporter to Delaney and Howard, saying he had come to talk with them. The reporter, "fearing the immediate retreat of the desperadoes, quickly said: 'Boys, I am from Tucson, not Tombstone. I would like to publish what you have to say in the CITIZEN there, and promise you faithfully not to misrepresent your remarks in any manner; and also that nothing will be printed until after Friday.'"

This seemed to satisfy the two outlaws and they consented to being interviewed. The reporter began by asking Delaney his opinion of the lynching of John Heath. Delaney replied, saying, "I don't know anything about Heith. I tell you I never saw him until November 27th, until he came to jail. He oughtn't been hung anyhow." The reporter then asked Delaney about himself. Delaney sidestepped the question, saying, "I can say we hadn't a square trial. If we had we wouldn't be here. I am innocent." Delaney continued, saying, "You remember that Castaneda stated he lost something like $1000 from his safe. That money has never been found. Do you wish to tell where it is? Don't know anything about the money." At this point, "Tex" Howard interrupted Delaney, "The man that's got the money knows where it is."

Delaney was asked how he felt about his impending execution. "No man will stand up better than I," he said. Delaney then digressed, and asked the reporter if he had been in Clifton the previous August. When the reporter replied he had not, Delaney said, "Well, some CITIZEN fellow was, and I subscribed for the paper." Delaney was again interrupted, this time by Daniel Kelly, who was still in his cell. Kelly shouted out to his partner, "Tell him how the lawyers defended us." Howard exclaimed, "Didn't defend us at all." The interviewer then asked Howard about his family, to which he replied, they "did not know where he was and would never know."

The conversation returned to the subject of the trial. Delaney said, "if everything was as fair in the proceeding as Judge Pinney's charge, they would have been all right."

"He might have done better," said Howard.

"By the way," said Delaney, "the jury had a lot of Mormons on it. How many? Six, anyhow, and you bet, when some witness said I had a horse with a Mormon brand on, that hung me sure. Why, I don't even know how to steal a horse."

"Yes! Nary a witness told the truth," claimed Howard, "The whole evidence was false, and the jury was no better."

The interview with Delaney and Howard ended thus. The reporter observed that "the men were not ready to make any honest confession as to the part they took in the Bisbee affair. If they had been on a spring picnic they could not have been more contented. Laughing and joking continually, it seemed incomprehensible that the two men were on the verge of the grave. They seemed as reckless of death as they were proven to be of the law. Before the reporter had been with them five minutes, they took advantage of what they considered their condescension to be interviewed by calling on the Sheriff for whiskey." The order was given and Daniel Kelly, Omer Sample, and "Big Dan" Dowd were released into the corridor to join Delaney and Howard to speak with the man from *The Weekly Citizen*.

The reporter noted that "[a]ll excepting Dowd wanted to engage in irrelevant talk at one time. Trying to get some information from the laconic outlaw, the reporter asked if Dowd was in fact his real name. Dowd replied, tersely, "Well, that's what I am known by here, and no one will know any other while I live."

By contrast, Kelly was "quite talkative." When asked, he too said Heath was "wrongfully hung." He explained how he left Heath in the Chiricahua Mountains on November 26. When asked about his impending demise, Kelly reframed the question: "How will I hang? Well. I will walk up. The sheriff will not have to carry me, and if I hang as brave as I walk, I'm all right." When asked about his family, Kelly initially said he "had no relations." When pressed on the subject of his kin, the young desperado admitted "he had some in the old country" and that he "only left there two years ago." At this, Sheriff Ward reportedly laughed.

Kelly said he "believed Judge Pinney appointed as able counsel as could be procured." At this, Howard retorted, "But the jury?" All the prisoners then "expressed contempt for the jury." Delaney summarized his belief, saying, "If the jury had not hung us, they would have been hung." Finally, "Red" Sample spoke up. When asked about Heath, he replied, "No. I believe Heith was hung wrong. He never put up a job with me to rob Bisbee. The fact is Howard and I were together, and if the court had given us time we could have procured two witnesses to prove that we were many miles from Bisbee from 7 o'clock of December 8th to 9 o'clock the next day." The reporter concluded that "what was said of the manners and appearance of Delaney and Howard will also describe the last three interviewed. They were boisterous and apparently little in earnest."

At this point, the reporter concluded that "further questions would not bring facts" and closed the interview. He told the prisoners he would call again the following evening—the eve of their scheduled execution—but the prisoners refused. "No! no! Come to-morrow morning. We don't want to see you at night." The reporter thanked the men and took his leave of the cellblock. As he left the sheriff's office, Sheriff Ward, "Well, young man, you are the first reporter they have allowed to interview them since they were sentenced." Not sure how to respond, the reporter thanked the Sheriff and left the courthouse. There is no evidence that he returned the following morning.[27]

"Advices from Tombstone yesterday," reported *The Daily Star*, "state that the town was fast filling up with people to witness the hanging of the Bisbee murderers." The newspaper estimated that as many as 500 people had made the trip to that burg in anticipation of the big event. There was some concern among the officials of the town that there seemed "a disposition among many to create trouble on account of the execution being within the jail yard and not public." It was reported that the condemned were showing "no fear" in the face of death, "but laugh and joke with each other and assert they will die game. No confessions have been made, and all maintain their innocence." It was expected that the town of Tombstone would, on the day of the hanging, "bear the appearance of a holiday, as all the mines will shout [*sic*] down and many business houses will close their doors during the legal tragedy."[28]

The Arizona Daily Star also reported that Father Antonio Jouvenceau of Tucson had joined Father Gallagher in Tombstone and at noon on the eve of their execution went in to visit the men. *The Tucson Citizen* noted that Father Gallagher had been visiting the men daily since they were sentenced. When Father Jouvenceau arrived in the jail, he was recognized immediately by Dowd and Sample. According to the newspaper, Father Jouvenceau visited Clifton in June of the previous year. "While there he was told by a friend that some of the boys were going to hold him up on his way back to Tucson." This had not dissuaded the priest from making the journey and he arrived at his destination unmolested. Father Jouvenceau told Dowd and Sample this story after he was recognized and the two outlaws said they recalled seeing him at Garcia's ranch where they were staying at the time "but had no intention of disturbing him."[29]

As to their religious affiliation, *The Citizen* reported that Delaney and Kelly were both Catholic, having been raised in the faith. Howard and Sample both expressed the desire to be baptized in the faith before they were hanged. Only Daniel Dowd demurred. One wonders, in those final hours, what they said to the priests regarding their actions and their lives. Did they confess? Were they repentant? Were they regretful? Did they admit their guilt or maintain their innocence as they made their final confessions? Being that the Seal of the Confessional of the Catholic Church absolutely forbids the confessor from betraying in any way the penitent in words or in any manner and for any reason under penalty of excommunication, the priests were under obligation to keep the confessions of Delaney, Kelly, Sample, and Howard in strict confidence. Therefore, it will never be known whether the condemned men

Father Antonio Jouvenceau, who provided spiritual comfort to the condemned in their final hours (Arizona Historical Society, 1812).

admitted their guilt to Father Jouvenceau and Father Gallagher or if they continued with their charade of innocence.

The final twenty-four hours of the five men's existence on this mortal plane was dutifully chronicled by several local newspapers. In keeping with tradition, the doomed men were served a final meal of their choosing. *The Tombstone Republican* recorded that the condemned "regaled themselves with a hearty supper of oysters and other delicacies, furnished by the sheriff." *The Arizona Weekly Citizen* reported Father Jouvenceau and Father Gallagher remained through the evening with the men providing them with spiritual comfort. Nellie Cashman was present as well. A representative from *The Republican*, who was admitted to the cellblock around midnight, later reported he "found the doomed men restless and uneasy, being unable to sleep, which they attributed to the hearty supper they had eaten. The remainder of the evening was passed in a similar manner, the horror of their situation evidently being fully realized, and only occasionally relieved by short periods of slumber."[30]

While Delaney, Dowd, Kelly, Sample, and Howard were attempting to get some shut-eye on the eve of their execution, a righteous drama was unfolding on the other side of the jail yard wall. A few days before the scheduled hanging, the indefatigable Mr. Constable had finally completed construction of his high-rise grandstand abutting the walled courtyard and had sold out all the seats available on his make-shift structure at a cost of $1.50 a head. However, as Hankin observed, many citizens of the town "strongly disapproved of the man's intention of commercializing the sufferings of the condemned prisoners." Chief among the dissenters was Nellie Cashman, "who decided to put a stop to the disgraceful enterprise." As Hankin noted, being she was held in high regard by the local miners and others in the community, it was easy for Ms. Cashman "to find any number of willing hands to assist when she wanted something."

According to an article published in *The Arizona Weekly Citizen*, at half-past four on the morning of the execution, a group of 150 miners, described by the newspaper as being predominantly Irishmen, descended on the courthouse with the intention of dismantling Mr. Constable's grandstand. The mining men secured several heavy ropes around the "great timber supports" and as a body pulled them out from under the wooden bleachers. The entire scaffolding swayed in the air for a moment and then came tumbling to the ground "with a crash that shook Tombstone." *The San Francisco Bulletin* reported that six or seven persons were injured during its destruction, "one man having a leg broken and another an arm." *The Weekly Citizen* also reported that "several shots were fired to frighten the guards around the courthouse, but no one was injured." Mr. Constable's reaction to the vandalism was not recorded, nor whether he was obliged to return the monies which he had collected in advance from the townspeople who had sought to view the hanging from atop his contrivance.[31]

A few hours later, James Howard and Omer W. Sample, under the auspices of Father Jouvenceau and Father Gallagher, underwent the sacred rite of baptism and were received into the Catholic faith. *The Republican* reported that the rite was conferred upon them in the presence of a number of invited ladies and gentlemen in the jail. A short time later, Will Baron, a local barber, arrived "with his shaving utensils [and] was admitted to the jail." Each man in turn "submitted to his tonsorial manipulations. They were then dressed in neat suits of black furnished for the occasion by Sheriff Ward." The newspaperman reported, "As they were being attired in grave clothes an occasional grim joke at the appearance of some of their comrades was indulged in by the bandits."[32]

At 9:00 a.m., the prisoners received a visit from A.S. Dungan, a correspondent associated with *The Arizona Daily Star*. Dungan was accompanied into the cellblock by Sheriff Ward, Pima County Sheriff "Bob" Paul, and a stenographer by the name of Arthur A. Smith. The reporter first interviewed William Delaney. Delaney was particularly forthcoming with the reporter:

> I have no particular objection to talking. I might as well occupy my time now, as I will not have much opportunity in the future. I was born on July 11, 1856, in Scranton, Pa. But I am supposed to have left Harrisburg under suspicion of a murder, of which I am innocent. I have lived in this territory for four years, prospecting and mining. I have been indicted in Graham county for shooting a man through the heart, who interfered in a quarrel between a Mexican woman and myself, but I am entirely innocent of this crime, and we are victims of men who procured our arrest on account of our bad reputations, in order to receive the reward offered. This is an unfortunate circumstance and I am no more guilty than you are.
>
> I was not a particular friend of John Heith and only knew him a few months. He never put up a job with me to raid Bisbee, and as far as I know, had nothing to do with the affair. I believe he was hanged in the wrong. I have been told that the public expect us to weaken on the scaffold. You see how we act now, and at the last we will die brave. Although our knees may buck a little, I think we will not make a speech on the scaffold.
>
> I am glad the miners tore down the platform outside the jail yard that was to give so many people a free exhibition. Five hundred men sitting up in there, in addition to the eight hundred in the yard would make us a little shaky.

The newspaper reported that with "considerable animation" Delaney remarked, "We had a good breakfast this morning, and we got away with it!" At this, "Red" Sample chimed in, saying, "Yea, you bet we filled ourselves, but we are liable to back when we get there."

The correspondent went on to describe William Delaney as "a short, well-built man about five feet four inches in height [quite a difference from the description of the outlaw given by the correspondent from *The Tucson Weekly Citizen*], he has clear, intelligent eyes, black hair, and expresses himself in gentlemanly language." He described Daniel Kelly as "25 years of age, five feet six inches in height, and of a very dark complexion." The reporter added that Kelly would not give the name of the town or state in which he was born. "Omer W. Sample is a native of Missouri, is 24 years old, six feet one inch in height, and is a splendid specimen of physical manhood, but of brutal countenance." He also revealed that he had "been suffering from a gunshot wound in the side." Not surprisingly, "Tex" Howard claimed to be from Texas. He told the reporter that his was an assumed name, and he was often called "Handsome Tex." He gave his age as 24 years and was described by the reporter as having an "intelligent, manly face."

Dan Dowd was with whom the last the reporter spoke with. He asserted he was 27 years old and weighed in at 180 pounds. He explained he lived in Arizona "and was born, to use his own words, 'not far from this place.'" The reporter described Dowd as being "apathetic" and said he "showed traces of great suffering, although he endeavored to bear himself quietly." Unfortunately, the newspaper did not print the entirety of each of the statements of the condemned men. Dungan did report, "Each of the men endorsed in almost identical language the statement of Delaney, that they knew very little about Heith, and believed that he was lynched for a crime of which he was as innocent as themselves."[33]

The Republican noted, "The reverend fathers and Miss Nellie Cashman were in constant attendance and the forenoon gradually wore away." The condemned men were said to have been "bearing up bravely and conversing upon ordinary topics with greatest nonchalance." A little before 1:00 p.m., "at the request of the condemned the dath [*sic*] warrant was read in the cell by Sheriff Ward and was listened to attentively by the unfortunate men.

The reading was commenced in a clear, firm voice, but when that portion was reached commanding him to hang until they were dead the men standing before him, it is no discredit to the sheriff to say that his voice became tremulous and husky with emotion."

The document which Sheriff Ward read is reprinted here:

> Territory of Arizona against Daniel Kelly, Omer W. Sample, indicted as W.B. Sample, James Howard, Daniel Dowd, & William Delaney.
> The Territory of Arizona to the Sheriff of the County of Cochise,
> Greeting:
> Whereas, on the 11th day of February, A.D. 1884, the jury in the above entitled action returned a verdict of guilty of Murder in the first degree against the defendants, Daniel Kelly, Omer W. Sample, indicted as W.B. Sample, James Howard, Daniel Dowd, and William Delaney; and whereas on the 19th day of February A.D. 1884, the defendants Daniel Kelly, Omer W. Sample, indicted as W.B. Sample, James Howard, Daniel Dowd, & William Delaney being there and then present before said Court and each of them then and there asked by the Court if they or either of them had any legal cause to show why sentence should not be pronounced against and upon each of them, and there appearing no legal cause by their replies, the Hon. D.H. Pinney, Associate Justice, presiding in the Second Judicial District of said Territory and Judge of said Court pronounced sentence against and upon the said defendants, Daniel Kelly, Omer W. Sample, indicted as W.B. Sample, James Howard, Daniel Dowd, & William Delaney, in the words following, to wit:
> "The sentence of the Court is that you be taken hence to the County jail and there confined until the 28th day of March A,D, 1884, and on that day between the hours of 10 o'clock in the forenoon and 5 o'clock in the afternoon, that you and each of you be hanged by the neck until you are dead.
> Now you, the said sheriff, are hereby required, directed and commanded to execute the said sentence in the manner and at the time herein set forth, and this shall be your sufficient warrant thereafter."
> Witness, Hon. D.H. Pinney Associate Justice presiding in the Second Judicial District of the Territory of Arizona at the Court House in the County of Cochise, this 21st day of February 1884.
> (The document was signed, "D.H. Pinney, Judge Presiding" and witnessed the same date by W.H. Seamans, the Clerk of the Court.)[34]

The reading of the Death Warrant by Sheriff Ward was concluded at 12:55 p.m. The Sheriff then turned to the inmates and told them, "Boys, you have asked the privilege of going to the scaffold free from straps and manacles. This privilege I grant you, but each of you will be taken by the arm of an officer." Sample retorted, "I would rather be strapped than packed up to the scaffold." The other four concurred. Sheriff Ward there and then decided to allow them "to walk from the jail to the death-trap free and untrammeled." After the decision was made, the five men were served a final cup of "strong coffee, stronger stimulants being refused."[35]

"Promptly at one o'clock p.m. the procession to the scaffold moved from the condemned cell, headed by Rev. Fathers Antonio Jouvenceau and Gallagher, and Sheriff Ward. Each prisoner was attended to the gallows by an officer of the law." Omer Sample was escorted by Sheriff "Bob" Paul, James Howard by Deputy Sheriff William Corbett, Daniel Dowd by Deputy Sheriff Bob Hatch, William Delaney by Deputy Sheriff Crowley of Willcox, and Daniel Kelly was last, escorted by Deputy Sheriff Fred Ward. The solemn procession walked out of the back door of the cell block, down the short flight of stairs, and into the courtyard thronged by humanity. *The Tombstone Republican* reported that the gates to the jail yard were "thrown open at 12 o'clock and in a few minutes the waiting multitudes were inside." *The Weekly Citizen* reported that over 2,000 people turned out to witness the execution, "one half being within the jail yard and the others on housetops in the vicinity."[36]

Mrs. Martha Swain, wife of Judge George Washington Swain, arrived in Tombstone in 1882 and moved into the house which abutted the courthouse. In an interview printed years later in *The Tombstone Epitaph*, Mrs. Swain recalled the day of the hanging rather vividly. "After Nellie Cashman and her miner friends had destroyed the bleachers which were to seat uninvited guests to the hanging of the five holdup men and slayers on March 28, 1884, the curious began to climb any tree or roof nearby which they could overlook the hag-pit below. So many of them climbed atop the Swain roof that the entire building threatened to collapse under the weight and the Swain family was forced to hire a couple of special policemen to keep the crowd from the roof."[37]

Meanwhile, inside the jail yard, the law officers slowly escorted their black-clad charges through the dense crowd of onlookers to the foot of the gallows and up the nine steps leading to the platform. *The San Francisco Bulletin* noted that the five outlaws marched "to their doom with light, springing steps, their countenances beaming with smiles." *The Daily Star* observed that "Tex Howard and Wm. Delaney were cool and composed and smiling greeted their numerous acquaintances in the jail yard." By contrast, "Red Sample and Dan Kelly faltered and showed a little nervousness, the former almost losing his muscular control." The stairs to the gallows were "ascended in silence" and each took a seat on one of the five chairs which "were awaiting their reception." Next, "the broad brimmed sombreros with which the doomed and daring rustlers were wont to shield themselves from the inclimencies of weather while scouring the mountains and mesas" were removed and "exchanged for the horrible black caps."

While seated on the platform, the five outlaws were seen to glance "anxiously around, first at the crowd surrounding them and then at the dangling nooses and other ghastly paraphernalia of death." Surveying the crowd, Delaney, Kelly, and Omer Sample "recognized some familiar faces" and shouted out their last "Goodbyes!" to those persons. "A series of handshakes followed between the men standing on the very threshold of death and the attending officers and priests." Directly after, the attendant officers strapped down the arms and legs of the condemned men with heavy leather belts. This task being completed, Sheriff Ward turned to his charges and said, "Stand up, boys." This order was quickly complied with and the five chairs in which the men had been seated were removed from the platform. The five men were then given the opportunity to voice their final remarks.

Omer W. Sample, standing on the far west side of the platform, spoke first. He said in a loud firm tone of voice, "Gentlemen, before I die I wish to say a few words. I die innocent of the murders and robbery committed in Bisbee on the 8th of December last, and, so far as I know, John Heith had nothing to do with the affair. He never put up any such job with me. I die in a firm belief in the Catholic church and request a Christian burial."

James "Tex" Howard, who stood directly beside Sample was the next to speak. Unfortunately his final words were not recorded. *The Tombstone Republican* only stated that he had "asserted his innocence of nay complicity in the affair and also his belief in the innocence of Heith." Neither was recorded the final declaration of Dan Dowd, standing in the middle of the platform between Howard and Delaney. The newspaper simply said Dowd "reiterated the statements already made and also requested a Christian burial."

William E. Delaney was next to speak, "Gentlemen, I expect in a few minutes to meet my God. I am entirely innocent of the crime of which I was convicted and if I had had a fair trial I would not be here today. I request a Christian burial and hope that Father Gallagher will conduct the services and look after our bodies."

Daniel "York" Kelly, who occupied the final spot on the far east side of the scaffold

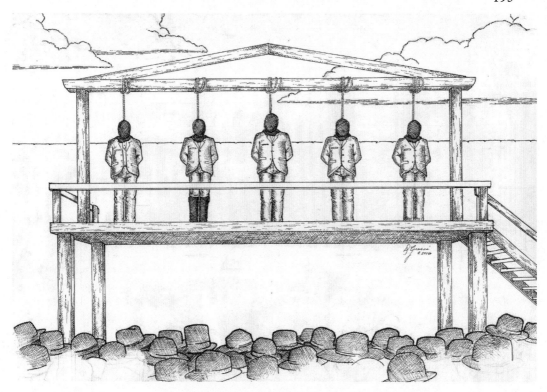

"On the Scaffold" (author's illustration).

was silent for a moment, his face was described as "already as pallid as that of a corpse." Then isolated voices within the crowd called to him by name—"Kelly! Kelly!"—and he found his tongue again. "Well, my friends, I bid you goodbye. I am innocent of the murders committed at Bisbee on the evening of December 8th," he said. "I never yet murdered a human being. I have only one request to make and that is a Christian burial." Kelly then again fell silent.

Sheriff Ward asked the men if they had anything further to say, to which they all replied, "No."

"The nooses were then adjusted to their necks by the attending officials, the priests meanwhile whispered words of consolation in the ears of the doomed murderers, who each stood firm as adamant throughout the trying ordeal." As the noose was pulled down over his head, Dan Dowd was heard to exclaim, "This is a regular choking machine." The black caps were then pulled down over their faces and the long hemp ropes were adjusted for proper placement and tightened around each man's throat. There the five men stood for a moment as the Sheriff took up his position near the cord which secured the trapdoor. It was then Daniel Kelly, his voice muffled by the hood which covered his features, said, "Let her go!"[38]

The time was 1:18 p.m.

Death by what is termed "standard drop" or "judicial" hanging is caused by several factors. In theory, the hangman or hangmen will calculate the drop distance required to break or dislocate the bones in the man's neck based on his weight, height, and build. As the body is dropped through the trapdoor, it begins to pick up speed as the forces of gravity pull it downward. By the time the man's body reaches the end of the rope and the rope pulls taut, it is exerting upwards of 1,000 pounds of torque pressure on the vertebrae in the neck. The sudden stop that occurs when the slack in the rope has played out causes the bones in the neck to break or come apart and in doing so sever the upper cervical or spinal cord. To achieve this result the actual length of the drop need only be five to nine feet.

When the bones in the neck, specifically the second and third or third and fourth cervical vertebra are fractured and the spinal cord is torn or severed, the blood pressure in the body drops to nearly undetectable levels in less than a second. The man almost immediately loses consciousness. But apoplexy [bleeding into an organ or loss of blood flow to an organ] rarely kills suddenly and the subject invariably succumbs to asphyxiation. The heartbeat and limited respiratory functions may continue for 15 to 20 minutes. Additionally, muscular spasms and convulsion may occur during this period and the body may be seen to jerk and twitch. Secondary trauma in the region of the neck usually includes crushing of the pharynx and severing or tearing of the carotid arteries. However, it is commonly held that the man feels little or no pain during the process.[39]

It was only a fraction of a moment between Kelly's final utterance and Sheriff Ward's cutting of the cord "by which the 250-pound weight was suspended." The "ponderous" trapdoor beneath the men's feet fell away "with a swish and resounding bang as it struck the framework of the scaffold. The five stalwart forms shot suddenly downward, and the ropes became taut and the framework quivered with the descending weight" of the bodies of the men. "Every joint in the timbers" which comprised the gallows was heard to creak and moan. "The suspended forms of Sample, Howard, Delaney, and Kelly" turned slowly at the ends of the ropes. None of the four was seen to have "moved a muscle after the fatal drop."

However, the form of Dan Dowd was seen to struggle and jerk about uncontrollably in the space beneath the platform, the drop not having been sufficient to cause the vertebrae in his neck to be broken. The crowd convened in the jail yard and those persons on the rooftops and within the trees outside the walls watched with grim fascination as Dowd's legs were "drawn up convulsively several times, and his whole body was shaken as with the mortal agony of suffocation." Dowd continued to hang there, writhing and bucking, until he finally asphyxiated. Then there was a general silence beneath the gibbet.

The Tombstone Republican reported that "pulsation" continued to be "perceptible [*sic*]" in Howard at seven minutes, in Dowd at seven and a half minutes, in Sample at five and a half minutes, Delaney at seven and a half minutes, and in Kelly at nine minutes after their drop through the trapdoor. The bodies of the Bisbee bandits were allowed to hang there in the early spring air for a full half hour before they were officially pronounced to be dead. Then, at 1:45 p.m., the quintet of corpses was cut down and "placed in neat but plain coffins"

Grave of James "Tex" Howard, Boothill Cemetery, Tombstone (author's collection).

Top, left: Grave of William "Billy" Delaney, Boothill Cemetery, Tombstone. *Top, right:* Grave of Daniel "York" Kelly, Boothill Cemetery, Tombstone. *Bottom, left:* Grave of Daniel "Big Dan" Dowd, Boothill Cemetery, Tombstone. *Bottom, right:* Grave of Omer W. "Red" Sample, Boothill Cemetery, Tombstone (author's collection).

and conveyed to the city morgue, where they were each identified in turn by Father Gallagher. A cursory autopsy was subsequently performed and it was concluded by the physicians in attendance "that with the exception of Sample, the necks of all the executed felons had not been dislocated." *The Republican* stated that remaining four had died of strangulation.[40]

A dispatch exclusive to *The Arizona Weekly Citizen* corrected the report circulated by *The Republican*, stating. "the necks of all were broken but Dowd's. He was strangled." The Tucson-based newspaper revealed that, after the autopsy was performed, the bodies of the Bisbee bandits were put on display at the morgue, "where hundreds are now thronging to obtain a view of the dead faces." It is curious the absence of Camillus Fly, the photographer who photographed the mortal remains of the Billy Clanton and Frank and Tom McLaurey after the O.K. Corral street fight and who captured for posterity the image of the body of John Heath suspended by a rope from the arm of a telegraph pole, who was not on hand to record the spectacle that was the hanging of Delaney, Dowd, Sample, Kelly, and Howard.[41]

News of the quintuple hanging in Tombstone was quickly disseminated across the country via telegraph. *The San Francisco Bulletin* reprinted the full account on the first page of their March 29 edition. *The Chicago Tribune* also included the story, along with the stories of William R. McDonald, hanged in San Bernardino, California, for the murder of his mistress, Maggie O'Bryan; Joe Howard, hanged in Sumter, North Carolina, for the murder of Simon Gaskins, the man who had married Howard's step-daughter with whom Howard was having "criminal relations"; and Francisco Perez, hanged in Placerville, California, for the murders of William and Jacob Wirges. The eight hangings were covered by *The New York Times* as well in their edition of March 29. Of course, the majority of the newspapers in the Arizona Territory carried news of the hanging too, including *The Weekly Phoenix Herald* and *The Arizona Silver Belt*. Each devoted several column inches to the story, the latter going so far as to employ the vernacular in a flippant headline, "A Daisy Drop."[42]

The hanging of the Bisbee bandits was also noted in the diaries of many local residents. George W. Parsons stated that on March 26 he "received an invitation today to be present at the hanging of Dowd, Sample, Kelly, Delaney, and Howard." Unfortunately, he was visiting relatives in California at the time of the hanging and was unable to attend. Under the date of March 28, Tucson saloon-keeper George Hand, wrote in his journal: "The last of the Bisbee murderers, 5 in number, were hung [*sic*] at 1:18 today in the City of Tombstone, Cochise Co, by Sheriff Ward. Three of them were baptized in the Catholic church and made Christians. The other two must necessarily go to hell."[43]

The day after the hanging—after the crowds had glutted themselves with staring into the faces of the deceased on display in the morgue—the mortal remains of the Bisbee bandits were turned over to Father Gallagher at the Catholic Church for burial. No one came to claim the bodies of any of the five men. The five wooden caskets were unceremoniously sealed then driven by horse and wagon out to the windswept piece of desert that was commonly referred to as "Boothill"—a makeshift graveyard in use since the town of Tombstone was first founded. There, five holes were excavated and it was there, on that lonely hill strewn with prickly pear cacti and creosote bushes, William E. Delaney, Omer W. "Red" Sample, James "Handsome Tex" Howard, Daniel "Big Dan" Dowd, and Daniel "York" Kelly—the men convicted and executed for their roles in the Bisbee Massacre—were finally laid to rest.[44]

Chapter Eight

The Aftermath

The day after the hanging of Delaney, Dowd, Howard, Kelly, and Sample, the editor of *The Arizona Daily Star*, Louis C. Hughes, printed the following editorial:

> Yesterday was hangman's day in Tombstone. Five men, charged with the crime of murder, tried, convicted and sentenced, were executed according to the form of law. Whether mankind or the community has, or will be benefited by the slaughter of the criminal's remains to be seen. No reflective person can well consider execution of human beings in any other light than that of barbarism. It is revolting to every sense of human nature, and contrary to moral and inspired teaching. The death penalty has a tendency to cheapen human life, inspires less fear of death, and cultivates brutal, bloodthirsty spirit among the more depraved class. It is not in the least creditable to those who show the morbid curiosity of witnessing an execution of a human being, of looking on while the cold decree of law murders a brother man. No matter how great the criminal or how great the crime, none but a depraved nature can look on with any other feeling than that of horror. This fact alone is sufficient proof that the death penalty is contrary to human nature, as certainly as it is contrary to divine law. If a man slay his brother in anger, for lucre or other cause, it does not mend matters for the law to commit a second crime. The murdered cannot be restored by such an act of the law. If it is to mete out revenge that the law executes its victim, then it is in direct violation of the divine precept, "Vengeance is mine, I will repay saith the Lord." The crime of murder is generally committed by the reckless or insane; those who have no fear of death or possess no control over their passion. In either case, there should be some other punishment than execution. Far better make the punishment imprisonment for life at hard labor, thus inflicting a punishment which would afford at least an opportunity for the criminal to reform, if he have a family that he may be compelled by his prison labor to support them, and should there exist any doubt of his guilt time must unfold his innocence, To make such a punishment effective, however, there should be no power to pardon, either by the governor or legislature. Imprisonment should be absolute except in case of newly discovered evidence, and of such a character that there was no doubt of its genuineness, This is a question well worth considering by our coming legislature. Such a law would make the punishment of crime more certan [*sic*] and its effect upon the community could not be other than good. Crime should be punished, but some other remedy than that of strangling the criminal should be adopted.[1]

It was a bold and progressive editorial, albeit probably not a very popular one with the citizenry of the Arizona Territory. While Hughes' argument against the death penalty was sound and the editor even offered a viable alternative to execution, it was not a position readily embraced by the general populace, who held to an older divine precept—the Lex Talionis, or "life for life, eye for eye, tooth for tooth, hand for hand, foot for foot." This was amply demonstrated by the extralegal lynching of John Heath who, even though he had been convicted and sentenced to life imprisonment by the court, was seen by the people to be deserving of greater punishment and was dealt with by the people accordingly, in a manner they thought more befitting the crime.[2]

Hughes, who had formerly served as both a probate judge and as county attorney and would go on to be appointed as the Territorial Governor in 1893 by president Grover Cleveland, took it upon himself to address what he felt was a grave injustice perpetuated by the people of Tombstone and Bisbee, specifically Heath's lynching. In the same edition that featured his editorial on the death penalty, Hughes took the vigilantes to task, writing, "Acts committed in passion are generally regretted. Such is the experience of the mob which hung Heith." Further in the column, Hughes expounded upon the subject, "Red Sample on the scaffold declared Heith had nothing to do with the Bisbee robbery and murder. How will the Tombstone mob who murdered him settle the matter with there conscience?" These were comments meant to provoke response and provoke a response they did.[3]

However, it was not the Tombstone newspapers which were found to be defending the actions of their citizenry, but B.A. Stephens, the editor of the rival Tucson newspaper, *The Arizona Daily Citizen*. In response to Hughes' editorial comments, Stephens wrote,

> The Star seems to think that the testimony of hanged murderers is conclusive as to the evidence of Heith. We have the same testimony to prove the innocence of the men who were legally hanged. They died solemnly protesting their own innocence of the terrible crime of which they had been duly convicted. If such evidence is to be taken to prove that Heith's hanging was a mob murder, why does it not prove that five legal murders were committed yesterday? That is the logical sequence of the Star's reasoning. Lynching is to be deprecated on general principles, as showing a belief in the community that the law and its methods are inadequate in certain emergencies. There is no evidence to show that an innocent man was the victim in the late Tombstone lynching. However, this is not the first time that the Star has posed as the defender and apologist of Cochise county outlaws.[4]

Hughes presented the challenge and, in response, Stevens had come out swinging. He argued that if one was to believe "Red" Sample's assertion about John Heath's innocence, one must necessarily believe his assertion about his own innocence, which would make both the lynching of Heath and the hanging of the Bisbee quintet murder. This is a common fallacy of logic, known as "denying the antecedent." In with his final sentence, Stephens threw what must be considered a low blow and attacked the rival newspaper's reputation. To Hughes' credit, he did not respond in kind to the provocation in Stephen's diatribe. *The Star's* editor instead remained focused on the subject of the argument, writing in reply:

> Our evening contemporary does not quote us right when it says that "the STAR seems to think that the testimony of the hanged murderers is conclusive evidence to the innocence of Heith." We do not think any such thing, but do, without hesitation say that all of the evidence, taken in connection with the last words of the criminals, is about as conclusive as the evidence can be that Heith was an innocent man, so far as the Bisbee outrage is concerned. A jury of twelve men heard all of the evidence, and six of them stood for acquittal, six for conviction, and they finally agreed on murder in the second degree, knowing full well, that if innocent, time would reveal the fact. This jury was made up of men all strangers to Heith. The feeling in Tombstone and especially around the court

Grave of Louis C. Hughes, territorial governor and editor of the *Arizona Star* newspaper, one of the few men brave enough to publicly condemn the lynching of John Heath.

during the trial was very strong. He had no friend, no sympathizers, no one to sway public opinion in his favor. Yet, in the face of all this, the jury found him guilty of the second grade of the crime. The mob believed him guilty, rushed into the jail, took him out and hung [sic] him without a moment's warning. Heith stated to them he was innocent, and that when the five men in jail were hung [sic] they would find out their mistake. These men went to the scaffold last Friday and declared Heith was an innocent man. Had he been living, this statement could have saved his life; but Heith and been hung [sic] and buried. The words of these criminals could not restore him to life. The evidence of his innocence is strong. The near future may throw new light upon the real facts. Some one is responsible. Some one will have to answer. The majesty of law will assert itself.[5]

Hughes' counter attack was brilliant. It raised a reasonable doubt as to Heath's guilt while implying that those who participated in the lynching as murderers, all without ever casting aspersions on or questioning the inherent integrity of his rival at *The Weekly Citizen*. Only in his assumption that the "near future" might "throw new light upon the real facts" of the case, did Hughes let his own optimism override his common sense. He could not really have expected anyone to agree with him, for to agree with his argument would have been to admit that the citizens of Tombstone who participated in the lynching were common murderers—no different from the men who they had just a week before convicted and hanged. The mob was not about to begin to question their own righteousness in this regard. Hughes had basically lost even before he had begun.

The editor of *The Citizen* was not about to allow his rival to have the last word on the subject either. Stephens, by way of response, would publish two separate editorials in the same edition. In the first part of his retort, Stephens returned to the argument he employed before—an argument based on a faulty logic—and followed this up with a Red Herring fallacy (specifically, *argumentum ad consequentiam* or an appeal to consequences):

Our morning contemporary thinks we quoted it wrong when we said that that paper seems to think that the testimony of the hanged murderers is conclusive as to the innocence of Heith. If we had had any doubt in the first instance that the editor of the paper believed as stated above heretofore, we now think that he believes entirely in the innocence of Heith—believes the assertion of the murderers; if he believes them in the case of Heith, he must believe them in the case of all the rest; for in the next breath in which they declared their own innocence they declared Heith's innocence; if they were truthful in one instance, they were truthful in the other. If our contemporary is not careful, it will become the defender of outlaws, and we should be sorry if it did this. The outlaw class of this Territory has got such a "back-set" in the last few months that, if followed up vigorously, it will never regain. There is not a Territory or State in this Union freer of crime to-day than Arizona; there is not a State or Territory where murderers receive punishment as quickly as in Arizona. Every lover of law and order should endeavor to strengthen the arm of the law and the law abiding people rather than weaken it. It is not a question of Heith's innocence now. He has been tried, convicted, found guilty, and hanged, and it is encouragement to the lawless to defend him or, at this stage of the game, throw doubt upon his guilt. Heith was assuredly guilty, and should have perished on the scaffold with the rest, not hanged by a mob. We deprecate such acts, and hope it may not occur again. The law in this Territory to-day is ample, and the judges and people are in favor of carrying out the spirit and letter of the law, and all attempts at mobocracy are wrong and should be resisted by the law-abiding people.

This first editorial was followed up with a second, more pointed article. However, not having the capacity to argue logically against Hughes' assertions, Stephens chose to simply stand with the mob, defend their actions as being beneficial in helping to deter crime in the Territory, and chastise Hughes for not doing the same.

The Star in order to defend itself for posing as the defender of Heith, the leader of the Bisbee murderers attempts to do something he will materially fail at. The CITIZEN does not need to be heralded as in favor of the law as opposed to mob law. It was the first paper in the territory to deprecate the hanging of the Florence and Tombstone men. But we are glad to have stirred up the matter, even at the expense of misrepresentation by our morning contemporary, which however is no new thing for that journal to do when cornered. He does not deny but that he believes that Heith was innocent and should not have perished. If our neighbor has not been able to understand us, we will say further: that the murderers were tried, convicted, and hanged "by law." Heith was tried, convicted, and hanged by a "mob"; they are both gone and to now attempt to make it appear they or any part of them are innocent, is encouragement to the lawless element in the Territory. In so far as that extends, so far is the Star posing as an enemy of law and order. The majesty of law is what has been the effort of the courts and the best part of the people to establish and to make crime odious even to criminals— not to make that class fearful of mob law, but the penalty of law of the people, and if the Star will use its influence in that direction it will accomplish some good.[6]

If Hughes thought to reply to Stephens, he must have thought the better of it. Perhaps the editor came to realize the futility of his position—the mob which hanged Heath and its representative at *The Weekly Citizen* were not going to concede to wrongdoing. Whatever his reason, Hughes chose to disengage and there were no further articles concerning the lynching of John Heath within the pages of *The Arizona Daily Star*. Interpreting Hughes' silence as being indicative of abdication, the editor of *The Arizona Weekly Citizen* also let the matter go. And so the subject of John Heath's lynching was unceremoniously laid to rest—just as he had been after he was hanged—to be summarily forgotten as other news came to the fore and the attentions of the public diverted elsewhere.

William Delaney's brother, John Carroll Delaney, also spoke out publicly in defense of his sibling. In a special dispatch to *The Boston Herald*, the Congressional Medal of Honor winner declared his brother innocent and had been the victim of a conspiracy intended to wrest away his interest in a potentially lucrative mining property. From the April 7, 1884, edition, the article is reprinted here in its entirety.

A strange story is told in connection with the arrest, trial, and execution of William E. Delaney, librarian of the Pennsylvania state Senate. Delaney was recently hanged at Tombstone, Ariz., with four others, for the murder of the Bisbee family on Dec. 8. Capt. Delaney is thoroughly convinced that his brother was innocent of the crime for which he suffered death. As soon as he learned that his brother was to be executed, he made every possible effort to save him from the gallows. He claims to have secured positive proof that his brother had never been at the place of the murder, and that when the Bisbee family was murdered, he had been in Mexico, over 200 miles distant. Delaney is said to have been convicted on the testimony of one Daniels, who swore he saw Delaney a few minutes before commission of the crime. Efforts to get Delaney a new trail were unsuccessful. Capt. John C. Delaney placed $1000 in the hands of Fr. McBride of this city, with instructions to forward the money to the Catholic priest at Tombstone, Ari., to pay a lawyer to take charge of Delaney's case. A reply was received from Fr. P.J. Gallagher that $10,000 could not secure the services of a lawyer for the intended purpose, owing to the desperation of the men who want to see Delaney hanged. On March 22, Fr. Gallagher wrote to Capt. Delaney thus: "The lawyers still refuse to take the appeal, because of the dread of the community. Sentiment has changed very much, however, in your brother's favor. As you are informed, there is no direct proof against him. Yet I can do nothing unless I can get an appeal taken. I have done all I can." An unsuccessful effort was made to have President Arthur stay the execution, and Delaney was executed protesting his innocence. On the day before that hanging, Delaney wrote his brother that Daniels, the principle witness against him, had on the previous night shot and killed a man. It was claimed that Delaney's life was sacrificed by men in pursuit of revenge and gain, and that the men whose evidence convicted him received a reward of nearly $1700. Besides, Delaney had incurred the hatred of lawless men. Delaney is alleged to have located three valuable copper claims in Arizona. He was offered $6000 for the claims, which proposition Capt. Delaney told his brother to reject. The bid was increased to $10,000, but again refused at the request of his brother. The man who offered these sums became young Delaney's enemy, and involved him in a quarrel with a drunken Mexican woman. While wresting a revolver from the woman, the man fired at Delaney, who, returned the fire, wounded his adversary. A few days later, the men met in a cabin, when Delaney was assailed again. This time he badly wounded his enemy. Delaney was arrested, but acquitted, the evidence showing that he acted in self-defense. Threats were then made by the wounded man that he would have Delaney's life. Delaney thought it advisable to leave for Mexico.

During his absence the plot concocted to implicate him in the Bisbee murder. Delaney's copper claims had been located and perfected under law, and when he realized he would hang, he made a deed of them to his brother John, which was mailed, but has not reached its destination. It is believed the deed was stolen from the mail through the instrumentality of those in pursuit of the claims.

Was Delaney innocent or was the report in the Boston newspaper simply a reprint of falsehoods that William Delaney and foisted upon his older sibling in an effort to gain his brother's sympathy and garner his brother's aid in trying to save himself from the hangman's noose? In fact, aside from the evidence on which John Heath was convicted, the evidence against Delaney was the weakest link in the prosecution's case. Notwithstanding, Deputy Daniels' identification of Delaney as the man who came in to his saloon just prior to the robbery, there were no other witnesses to definitively put Delaney at the scene of the crime. Even Daniels was unable to say for certain that the man who had entered his saloon that evening was the same man who stood on the porch of Goldwater and Castaneda's store and fired on innocent by-standers. William Delaney had been convicted wholly on circumstantial evidence, but the evidence was pretty convincing, at least to the members of the jury. Had the deeds to the mining claims ever surfaced, it would give some credence to John Delaney's story. However, an inspection of mining claims of Graham County uncovered nothing which would serve to substantiate the story. There was no mention in the extant record books of any property belonging to William Delaney.

The rewards which distributed among the various officers who aided in the apprehension of the bandits did aggregate to a rather tidy sum—far more than Delaney had claimed. The Cochise County Treasurer awarded County Sheriff Jerome Ward $500 each for the "arrest and conviction" of "York" Kelly and William Delaney (although it was actually Deputy Sheriffs Daniels and Hatch who apprehended Delaney in Mexico), A. G Hill received $500 each for the arrest and conviction of James "Tex" Howard and "Red" Sample, and Deputy Sheriff Daniels was given $500 for bringing in Dan Dowd. Altogether this added up to $2500. In addition there were the reward monies paid by the Copper Queen Mining Company to these individuals for their assistance in the capture of the Bisbee bandits. Why William Delaney claimed the men who convicted him "received a reward of nearly $1700" is unknown.[7]

The editor of *The Arizona Citizen* did make the effort to acknowledge some the "officials of Cochise county" with whom he had the opportunity to meet and interact during his stay in Tombstone, especially Sheriff Ward and his deputies. "The sheriff," he said, "never failed to grant any reasonable request made by the reporter, although at times rushed with business." He called Undersheriff Albert Wallace "an efficient officer and affable gentleman" who "aided materially in preventing any unpleasant interruption in the tragic ceremony of Friday." Stephens acknowledged the "courtesy" of the Clerk of the Court, Captain W.H. Seamans, and the "kindly favors bestowed by Henry J. Howe, the United States deputy surveyor." The editor also made mention of Cochise County Recorder Albert T. Jones, who was "unremitting in his efforts towards assisting the visiting correspondents" and "the always genial coroner, Pat Holland."

The editor went further still in "bestowing deserved praise," singling out Pima County Sheriff R.H. "Bob" Paul for a "complimentary word." Sheriff Paul, the editor explained, had "escorted 'Red' Sample to the scaffold, and had full charge of the doomed man until the trap fell." He even "adjusted the noose" about Sample's throat. Sheriff Paul, asserted the newspaperman, "did his work better than those in charge of the other prisoners" and "evinced more coolness and tact in the arrangements." He noted that the Sheriff, "[i]nstead of placing the knot at the side or the back of the neck, drew it under the chin, and kept it there notwithstanding repeated calls from the crowd to change it." The editor concluded that, when it came to executing a man, Sheriff Paul "knew his business."[8]

Sheriff Robert H. "Bob" Paul would go on to enjoy a long, prosperous career in law enforcement. He would seek re-election to the office of Pima County Sheriff later that year and win. He served as Pima County Sheriff until 1886. He then went to work as a detective for the Southern and Pacific Railroad, hunting down the perpetrators of the infamous Cienega Creek train robberies. Paul remained employed with the S.P.R.&R. until 1889, when he took a position with the Los Angeles Police Department. Due to his reputation as a stalwart and efficient lawman, Paul was appointed by President Benjamin Harrison as U.S. Marshal for the Arizona Territory, replacing William Kidder Meade, a post he held until 1893, when Mead was appointed for a second term by incoming president Grover Cleveland. In 1899, Bob Paul was appointed Under Sheriff of Pima County. He served until January of 1901 in that capacity. Just three months later, on March 26, 1901, Robert H. "Bob" Paul succumbed to nephritis or kidney failure. He was 70 years old.[9]

Cochise County Sheriff Jerome Lemuel Ward was not so fortunate. He too would seek re-election in November of 1884, and it was then that the ghost of John Heath would return to haunt him. The sheriff was held to blame for allowing the mob to storm the jail and take Heath out of his custody, even though it was reported at the time that Sheriff Ward had attempted to stop the actions and, for all his efforts, had been physically thrown aside. In addition, in June of 1884, there was an incident at the Hadson & Co. Bank, which "had been placed in the charge of Sheriff Ward by the Grand Jury, with instructions to let no one, even the assignee, take anything from." According to *The Mohave County Miner*, a shortage of $6823.05 was discovered by the committee charged with investigating the failure of the bank. County Treasurer Ben Goodrich, Under Sheriff A.O. Wallace, Sheriff Ward and his son, Fred, were among those who were found to have received "county funds on special deposit." The monies were returned and nothing further came of the matter, but Ward would not even garner the nomination of his party in the primary election.[10]

Jerome Lemuel Ward, former sheriff of Cochise County and guard at the Arizona Territorial Prison in Yuma, later in life (author's collection).

Out of a job, Ward first tried his hand at cattle ranching in the Salt River

Valley, then he opened a livery stable in Tombstone. By 1885, the former sheriff was working in Phoenix, where he opened a "livery business on South Third street below the old Lemon Hotel." By August of 1886, the former lawman had deserted Tombstone altogether. Three years later, Ward's home in Phoenix would burn to the ground. His monetary loss was said to be $5000. Still, Jerome Ward was a determined man. In April 1887, *The Daily Tombstone Epitaph* reported that Ward was "building the finest livery stable that has ever been built in Arizona" and called the proprietor "a first-class livery man."[11]

The following year, the former sheriff and Ward family patriarch would throw his hat in the ring and announce himself as a candidate for the Maricopa County shrievalty. *The Weekly Tombstone Epitaph* scoffed at the idea. "The fact that he had allowed a prisoner to be taken from under his charge and lynched, while he was Sheriff of the county, ought to be sufficient reason for his overwhelming defeat." In spite, of the Tombstone newspaper's condemnation, Ward would receive the Republican Party's nomination but would lose in his bid to become sheriff to the Democratic contender, W.T. "Bud" Gray. It was a very close race, but in the end, Ward lost by a single vote in the November election.[12]

Even though he had been unsuccessful in his election bid, Jerome Ward was not one to remain idle, and his persistence and tenacity were finally rewarded in the summer of 1891, when he was appointed Board of Prisons Commissioner, replacing J.S. Robbins. In response to news of his appointment, *The Arizona Sentinel* said of Ward, "[he] is highly spoken of where he is known, has an excellent record as a public officer, and is said to be a man of sterling character, and possessed of a fine executive ability." In December of 1891, just a few weeks after his appointment, the former sheriff's sons, Fred W. and "Frank" Ward, were appointed by the commission as guards in the territorial prison at Yuma with a quarterly salary of $300.[13]

Jerome Ward was also very involved in the local community. A veteran of the Civil War, he was a member of the local chapter of the Grand Army of the Republic. He was also president of the Jockey Club and a member of the Peach Pickers' Club, a semi-secret fraternal organization. In July, of 1894, he was reportedly teaching a U.S. history class to the locals, which was, by all accounts, well-attended and "receipts for tuition were satisfactory." However, one might wonder if the flurry of community involvement was Ward's assuage in response to the death of his wife and son. On November 12, the previous year, *The Arizona Republic* reported that Mrs. J.L. Ward was "quite ill" and that "there was little hope for her recovery." Three days later, *The Tombstone Epitaph* reported, Mrs. Ward had succumbed to her illness of "several weeks," adding, "She had many friends in Tombstone who will be pained to hear of her death."[14]

In April 1894, death again visited the Ward family, taking Fred W. Ward, who "died at the residence of his brother Frank Ward on Jones street [in Phoenix], in the presence of his relatives and friends." *The Arizona Sentinel* reported that Fred Ward had been "sick nearly four months" and that his death was "not unexpected." The newspaper said during his tenure as a Deputy Sheriff in Tombstone, he had proved "himself a worthy and efficient officer." Fred W. Ward was survived by his wife, "an estimable young lady of this village" and his daughter, age seven, who would become the ward of her grandfather.

The Yuma-based newspaper went on to say that "[h]is father, ex-commissioner of the Territorial prison, and one of Arizona's most prominent men, has been at his son's bedside for the past 13 weeks, and the sad affair occurring so soon after the death of his wife, which our readers will remember occurred last November, has all but prostrated him." But Jerome Ward was not given to capitulation. In August of that same year, he again announced his candidacy for the office of Sheriff for Maricopa County. *The Arizona Weekly Journal-Miner* recommended him as being a "good man" and stated he "would make our sister county a good sheriff." Unfortunately, Ward did not receive his party's nomination, running last among the various nominees in the ballots taken at the convention. Still, the aging ex-lawman had his other business ventures to occupy him, including his livery, a shuttle service from Phoenix to Prescott, and various real estate investments.[15]

In 1897, *The Arizona Sentinel* reported that Jerome Ward had accepted a position as a guard at the Territorial Prison in Yuma. He was 64 years of age at the time of the appointment. A year later, *The Arizona Republican* noted that Ward "who tread the walls of the pen as a guard" was in Tucson. "He formerly lived in Phoenix and now registers from Willcox." The reason for his short tenure as a corrections officer and his decision to move to the town of Willcox are unknown. Only a year later, tragedy would again touch the life of Jerome Ward.[16]

In November of 1899, Jerome Ward's son William J., who was employed as a deputy sheriff in San Diego County, California, was attacked by a convict named Russ who he was escorting to San Quentin prison. According to the article which appeared in *The Arizona Sentinel*, the younger Ward was aboard the steamer *Santa Rosa* with the convict when the attack occurred. "[T]hinking there was no chance of escape [Deputy Ward] had gone to sleep, but in the meantime the steamer put in to a small harbor and Russ, thinking to escape, pounded him over the head with a heavy water bottle, fracturing the skull." Russ was unsuccessful in his attempt and William J. Ward, despite early predictions for his recovery, succumbed to his injuries, and died a few days afterward in San Luis Obispo.[17]

Following the death of his son, Jerome Ward again donned the distinctive blue officer's uniform and returned to work at the Territorial Prison in Yuma. A decade later, *The Arizona Republican* would make note of one of the elder Ward's frequent visits to Phoenix, saying "the oldest guard, in point of service, at the territorial prison, is in town today." "Mr. Ward," the newspaper stated, "became a penitentiary guard thirteen years ago and has attended so many hangings that he has earned the sobriquet of 'Hangman.'" Jerome Ward would remain an officer with the department until the "removal of the prison to Florence ... after the admission of the territory to statehood."

In 1912, the year Arizona was finally admitted to the Union, the former sheriff of Cochise County, Prison Commissioner, and member of the Grand Army of the Republic moved to San Diego. *The Arizona Republican* said of the man, "Notwithstanding his age, he was in vigorous health." Indeed, it was not old age which would finally claim him, but an accident. On September 26, during "the course of a parade, he was struck by an auto truck, receiving injuries from which he died that night." *The Bisbee Daily* review eulogized him thus: "As an early day frontier officer he was widely famed. As sheriff of this county he hung four [sic] men who made the famous Bisbee hold-up raid." In fact, Ward died just three months prior to the 30th anniversary of the robbery. Jerome Lemuel Ward was 80 years old at the time of his demise.[18]

Among those seeking to unseat Sheriff Ward in the election of 1884 was his own Deputy Sheriff, William Daniels. Daniels would run as a Democrat after receiving the nomination from his party, but would lose to the Republican candidate and another of Sheriff Ward's former deputies, Robert "Bob" Hatch, for the position in the general election. Daniels subsequently took a job as a mounted U.S. Customs Inspector. Then, on June 8, 1885, while traveling with Milton Gilliam between Tombstone and Bisbee, the men found a fresh trail indicating there were Apache in the area. The tracks led in the direction of the ranch of Sandy Bob. The pair took their intelligence to Bisbee, arriving that evening. After telling Sandy Bob of their discovery, it was decided that a posse would be sent out in pursuit of the renegades.

The following morning Daniels and Gilliam set out for Forrester's ranch to secure horses for the men, only to find that there were none available, as they had all been turned out to pasture. Forrester's 14-year-old son offered to go out with Daniels and Gilliam in search of the horses, much to the chagrin of the boy's mother. Daniels and Gilliam promised the woman no harm would come to her son and that the three of them would return by nightfall. Only then did Mrs. Forrester consent, and the three rode out towards Dixie Canyon in search of the livestock. Daniels, Gilliam, and Mrs. Forrester's son "had ridden out about 10 miles when they struck on no less than 50 different trails which were very fresh. Daniels said he felt sure the Indians were in Dixie canon, and they rode a piece in that direction."

Gilliam soon saw several Apache

Grave of Cochise County Deputy Sheriff William "Billy" Daniels, killed by Apaches in 1885. Evergreen Cemetery, Bisbee (author's collection).

and the smoke of their campfires up the canyon. He called Daniels' attention to what he saw. Daniels took up his field glasses in order to get a better look, then turned to Gilliam saying, "Milt, there's a thousand of them up there! Let's get out of here!" The three riders immediately wheeled their horses about and began to flee, "but were cut off by 7 or 8 Indians they had not seen before. Daniels fired two shots at them with his revolver and Gilliam fired 4 shots from his Winchester, the Indians meanwhile keeping up a regular fusillade." It was then one of the Apaches' shots found its mark tearing through Daniels' saddle scabbard and hitting his horse. The horse leaped in to the air and fell breaking its neck." The Forrester boy, who had expended all the ammunition in his rifle, and Gilliam, continued in their flight from the Apache. Gilliam recalled that as soon as Daniels went down, one of the Apache was upon him and shot him seven times in the head. The warrior then proceeded to stove in his skull with the butt of his gun.

"Gilliam and the boy rode down the road until they met three teamsters with their wagon who were hauling lumber to Bisbee and three horsemen coming from Bisbee. Upon seeing these men, the Apache gave up their quarry and rode back in the direction of their camp. The group returned to the scene of the killing, but the Apache had departed. Daniels' mutilated body had been stripped of coat and vest as well as his guns and saddle." The men packed Daniels' remains on to the wagon and continued on their way to Bisbee. "Gilliam and the boy had a very narrow escape," stated the Tombstone newspaper, "and

[Gilliam] attributed the saving of his life to the boy, Forrester." *The Arizona Champion* reported that, upon receiving the news of Daniels' death, "an armed force of men [from Bisbee] started in pursuit of the Indians."

William A. Daniels was initially buried in the Bisbee Cemetery. However, his remains were moved to the Evergreen Cemetery in Lowell, Arizona, in 1908, when the Bisbee Cemetery was converted to a city park. The inscription on his marble headstone reads, "He was always found battling for the right." The Apaches who killed him were never apprehended.[19]

Deputy Sheriff Robert "Bob" Hatch, who had accompanied Deputy Sheriff Daniels into Mexico in pursuit of William Delaney, was elected to the office of Cochise County Sheriff in 1884. His tenure in that office was not nearly as newsworthy as either of his predecessors in the position, John Behan or Jerome L. Ward. Though he did have to contend with some criminals, Hatch's duties were mostly confined to the more mundane, such as conducting sheriff's sales, collecting tax and licensing fees, and serving subpoenas. Hatch would run as incumbent again in 1886, and would be supported by *The Daily Tombstone*. The sheriff, the newspaper praised, "has been a faithful officer" and "has won the friendship and esteem of the citizens of this county." In spite of the recommendation, Hatch would lose the election to the challenger, John Slaughter.[20]

Bob Hatch would remain in Tombstone until 1890, working as a city policeman. That year, the former sheriff took a job as the assistant superintendent at the territorial prison, under Frank S. Ingalls, who had been appointed in July of that year by Territorial Governor Lewis Wolfley to replace John Behan, the former Cochise County Sheriff. *The Tombstone Daily Prospector*, with respect to Hatch's extensive experience in law enforcement and seeming disregard for his superior, Ingalls, called it a "case of placing the top rail at the bottom of the fence." Hatch's wife would join him in Yuma in September after selling their furnished house in Tombstone. "Bob" Hatch would also join J.H. Taggart, F.W. Ewing, and several other gentlemen in forming the Yuma Building and Loan Association the following year.[21]

Bob Hatch would have a long and varied career in law enforcement, working as a City Marshal in the town of Yuma, as well as a Deputy U.S. Marshal for the territory under U.S. Marshal William Kidder Meade. A lifelong Republican, Hatch also ran for the position of assemblyman in his adopted city in 1896. By 1900, he was back in the County Sheriff's office, working as Under Sheriff to J.M. Speese. Hatch also worked for a brief period as a census enumerator on the Fort Yuma Indian Reservation. When incumbent Speese lost out to Gus Livingston in his re-election bid, Hatch was retained by the incoming officer as the county jailor.[22]

On June 3rd, 1904, Robert S. "Bob" Hatch died at his home in Yuma. *The Arizona Republican* said of him, "[He] was one of the best known men of the southern part of the territory. He lived in Yuma many years. He was at one time connected with the office of the sheriff and at another was the assistant superintendent of the penitentiary. He was for a long time active in the affairs of the Republican party of the territory."[23]

Judge Pinney would serve only one more year on the Supreme Bench of the Arizona Territory. As an independent, who did not affiliate himself with either of the major political parties, it was expected that Pinney would retain his position as Associate Justice even with a changing of the political landscape in Washington. However, this was not to be the case. After Democrat Grover Cleveland took office in 1885, he had Pinney removed from the bench and replaced him with William W. Porter. *The Daily Tombstone* insinuated it was due to Pinney's decision in "Mack vs. The Phenix [sic] Mine, the latter being owned by Seymour, who contributed $30,000 to the Democratic campaign fund." The disappointed Pinney wired the President, saying, "I know you do not wish to do me a wrong. Can I have a hearing?"[24]

The judge would file suit citing "based on the asserted lack of power of removal of Territorial judges by the President." It was to no avail. *The Epitaph* reported that Judge Pinney continued to hold court until the arrival of his replacement. Finding himself out of a job, Pinney, his wife Mary, and their children, Harry, Sidney, and Nannie, pulled up stakes and moved on to Napa City, California, staying only a year before returning to Chicago, Illinois, where Pinney resumed his practice as an attorney. His eldest son William stayed behind in Arizona Territory, having business interests in Phoenix. Judge Pinney and the family would return to the territory in 1900, taking up residence in the bustling burg of Phoenix, where the Judge still retained some properties.

Pinney was instrumental in the fight against the Arizona and New Mexico Territories being brought in to the union as a single state, traveling to Washington, D.C., at the behest of the Territorial Bar association of Arizona. In 1907, Judge Pinney partnered in a new law firm with J.H. Langston, probate judge for Maricopa County. Twice more, the judge would ask to be re-appointed to the Arizona Supreme Court. Both times he was refused. Judge Pinney eventually retired and moved to Lawrence, Michigan, where he resided on a small farm. Ill health eventually forced him to move back to Chicago. Judge Daniel H. Pinney died May 13, 1921, in Joliet, Illinois.[25]

In the obituary for John Heath's erstwhile attorney, Colonel William Herring, *The Phoenix Republican* lauded, "Few Arizonans have had as much to do with political and judicial history of the territory" and *The Tombstone Epitaph* was in full agreement, calling Col. Herring a "loyal Arizonan, public spirited, big hearted pioneer, eminent and able jurist"—a man who "indeed helped make history for the state he loved so well." *The Tucson Citizen* stated simply that Arizona had lost "one of her most able lawyers and one of her most illustrious citizens"—a man "known all over the state and loved wherever known."[26]

Even before he had taken John Heath's case, Colonel Herring was well-known throughout southern Arizona, both as a formidable attorney and as a mining man. In spite of the lynching of his client, for whom he was preparing an appeal, the Colonel would persevere. Herring acted as county prosecutor in the *Territory vs. Fry* in 1886 and the *Territory vs. Barton* in 1887, and also defended the men indicted for the Pantano train robbery in 1888. In 1891, he was appointed Attorney General of the Arizona Territory by Governor John N. Irwin and was instrumental in drafting the first constitution of the state. Herring was unwavering in his support of the Free Silver movement and wrote this into the constitution. However, he was opposed state control of rivers and canals and fought to have women's suffrage excluded from the proposed charter. He resigned the convention when it was not. Col. Herring would remain Attorney General until Governor Irwin was replaced by Democrat Louis C. Hughes, the former editor of *The Arizona Daily Star*, in April of 1893.[27]

The Colonel returned to private practice, but was not long out of the public arena. He took a position as chief counsel for the Copper Queen Company and the Phelps Dodge Corporation, defending their interests when needed. He also continued to take criminal cases, sometimes as the defense attorney and sometimes, as in the case of the *Territory of Arizona vs. Joe Curby*, in aid of the prosecution. In 1894, Herring helped to found the

Territorial Bar Association and was chosen as its president. In spite of his opposition to the inclusion of an article addressing women's suffrage in the state constitution, Col. Herring was firm supporter of women's rights, which often made him the target of local newspapers.[28]

Though he enjoyed much success as an attorney and was financially solvent, Herring continued to invest in various mining ventures. In 1890, the Colonel sold the Neptune group of mines to the Copper Queen Company for $80,001. He also had an interest in the Guiding Star mine in Tombstone, and maintained an interest in the Bonanza and two other claims in the same area—claims which according to *The Bisbee Daily Review* he had received a "number of good offers" for.[29]

In 1891, Herring's son died of a cocaine overdose during a dental procedure. The Colonel's daughter, Sarah Herring Sorin, decided to carry on the family tradition and, after being admitted to the bar in the Arizona Territory, she returned to New York City to study the law. She graduated fourth in her class from the University of New York,

Sarah Herring, daughter of Colonel Herring, and the first woman to present a case before the United States Supreme Court (Arizona Historical Society, 17431).

School of Law in 1894, and returned to Tombstone. Perhaps sensing Tombstone was beginning its decline, Col. Herring moved his family and his law firm to Tucson in January of 1896, and established new offices in the Radulovich building with his daughter under the name of Herring and Sorin. The father-daughter team was instrumental in the obtaining a decision in favor of their clients, in the famous *United States vs. Copper Queen Consolidated Mining Company* case of 1898. According to *The Coconino Sun* "Miss Herring's argument was quite the attraction."[30]

In 1898, the 65-year-old litigator was appointed chancellor of the board of regents of the University of Arizona by Governor Nathan Oakes Murphy. During his tenure in that position, Herring secured donations and gifts from various companies, including $5,000 from the Copper Queen Mining Company, to build Herring Hall, the school's first gymnasium. In 1903, the firm of Herring and Sorin, which was at the time representing "at least a dozen corporations" including the Copper Queen Mining Company, Phelps, Dodge & Co., the El Paso and Southwestern Railroad, and the Detroit Company would take on a new partner, Thomas Mitchell. In May of the following year, Mrs. Mary I. Herring, the Colonel's devoted wife, died after a brief illness in her home in Tucson. In January of the following year, Col. Herring would be attendance when his daughter became the first woman to argue before the U.S. Supreme Court in the case of *Charles M. Taylor vs. Thomas Burns*.[31]

In 1906, the firm of Herring and Sorin hired former Yavapai County District Attorney E.E. Ellinwood and opened "a new office in Bisbee." In response to the news, *The Tucson*

Left: United States Senator Marcus Aurelius Smith, the former Cochise County district attorney (author's collection). *Right:* Grave of Colonel William Herring, John Heath's lawyer, enjoyed a long and prosperous career as an attorney—Evergreen Cemetery, Tucson.

Citizen (formerly *The Arizona Weekly Citizen*) reported that "Col. Herring is advancing in years. He will soon be 74 years of age, and believes he is entitled to moderation in his labors. He has no idea of giving up work entirely, but feels that he does not desire to work as hard and persistently as he has in the past." By this time, Herring had been chief counsel for Phelps, Dodge & Co. for a quarter of a century as well as conducting a "lucrative and important private business in association with his daughter, Sarah." Still in 1908, the aging attorney was reported as being involved in the case of the *Territory of Arizona vs. The Copper Queen Mining Company* over taxes owed by the company, with the Colonel representing that defendant.[32]

Three years later, on July 10, at the age of 79, Colonel William Herring would succumb to apoplexy, dying in his home in Tucson. He was interred beside his wife Mary Herring, and his daughter Bertha in Evergreen Cemetery. Colonel Herring's other daughter, Sarah Herring Sorin, died in 1914 in Globe, Arizona, of bronchial pneumonia, but was buried in Tucson just a few yards from her father, mother, and sister.

District Attorney Marcus Aurelius "Mark" Smith would also be favored with a long and prosperous career. Smith concluded his term as Cochise County District Attorney in 1885 and returned to private practice. The following year, Smith was unanimously elected as the Arizona Territorial delegate to the U.S. Congress, handily beating out Republican Curtis C. Bean. Smith was re-elected to the post in 1888, this time defeating Republican candidate Thomas F. Wilson. During this period, Smith also bought an interest in *The Phoenix Gazette* newspaper and teamed up with attorneys Ben Goodrich and

Webster Street to form the law firm of Goodrich, Smith, and Webster. Smith and Goodrich were retained by the defendants in the Wham Paymaster Robbery case, one of the most celebrated trials of the territorial period. Attorneys Smith and Goodrich were successful in getting their clients acquitted of all the charges brought against them.

While in Washington, Smith labored hard on behalf of the territory authoring numerous proposals to aid in bolstering the economy and to encourage investment. In 1890, Smith set forth his first statehood proposal. He would introduce several more before the Congress during his tenure. That same year, Smith, despite being held up in Washington tending to his official duties which led to a significant delay in his campaign for reelection, trounced his Republican rival, George W. Cheyney. In January 1892, Smith returned to the nation's capitol with a new resolution to admit Arizona to the Union, backed by a new constitution proposal, the charter having been overwhelmingly passed by voters in December of the previous year. Though the House readily passed Smith's bill, the Senate allowed it to die in committee.

Delegate Smith was elected a fourth time in late 1892, beating the Republican challenger, Flagstaff attorney and rancher William Stewart. As before, Smith's primary focus was achieving statehood for the Arizona Territory. In 1894, Smith decided against running again, citing the poor health of his wife, Elizabeth Rathbone Smith. The former county prosecutor did serve as the Assistant United States Attorney for the Arizona Territory from October 1895 until October 1896, when he decided to once again seek the office of Territorial Delegate to the U.S. Congress. Securing the Democratic nomination, he went on to defeat both the Republican nominee, Andrew J. Doran and the Populist nominee, William Owen "Buckey" O'Neil in the general election. He would introduce 22 bills during his term, including yet another statehood proposal. Though the passage of a statehood bill continued to elude him, Smith did obtain the authorization to build a permanent capital building in the city of Phoenix, which had usurped the designation as the capitol of the territory from Prescott in 1889.

The former Cochise County Attorney had moved his residence from Tombstone to Tucson in 1896, where he would continue to reside until his demise. Though he intended to run for office again in 1898, his wife Elizabeth became severely ill on the eve of the Democratic Convention. Smith withdrew his name from consideration and returned to private practice so he might stay near his ailing wife. Elizabeth Rathbone Smith would die just over a year later on October 16, 1899. The following year, Smith decided to again run for the office of delegate. However, this time his most significant opposition would come from fellow Democrat, John F. Wilson, who received the nomination in 1898 after Smith withdrew, and who was subsequently elected to the post. At one point, the Democratic Convention in Phoenix was host to two sets of convention officers and nominees, and witnessed a riot after a fight broke out between the opposing groups. Finally, on October 12, 1899, Wilson withdrew from the race. Smith beat out the Republican nominee and was once again sent to Washington as the representative from the territory.

Again, the majority of Smith's efforts were on behalf of Arizona's continuing campaign for statehood. Such was his zeal, that when the representative from Indiana introduced an amendment to a bill that would have the Arizona and New Mexico Territories added as one single state, the delegate argued so vehemently in opposition he over-exerted himself and collapsed on the floor of the House. Doctors at first feared he suffered a stroke, but the delegate's collapse was finally determined to have been caused by lack of sleep. After recuperating for two weeks in Washington, Smith took his leave for Kentucky, his home state. Certainly the collapse gave him pause, and when asked if he would run again in 1902, Smith demurred. Former rival John F. Wilson would receive the nomination and go on to win the election, while Smith returned to Tucson and his private legal practice.

When Wilson declared he would not seek re-election in 1904, Smith ran once more and was elected. Smith continued to fight against the joint-statehood proposal. This would be the platform on which he would again be elected to the office of Territorial Delegate in the 1907 election. Though his Republican challenger also opposed joint-statehood, voters believed Smith had done more to further the cause of an independent Arizona during his tenure in office. In 1908, Smith introduced his last bill in favor of Arizona statehood. This bill, like those he had introduced previously, was a failure. In February 1909, Smith decided to quite the House of Representatives and the office of Territorial delegate for good. However, the 57-year-old attorney was not yet through in the nation's capitol.

President William Taft had partially run his campaign on a promise of finally bringing both the New Mexico and Arizona territories into the Union. The Arizona statehood bill was introduced in January of 1910 and by June that year had passed through both the house and the Senate and been duly signed in to law. Smith attended the Arizona Constitutional Convention in October, and though he disapproved of the new state constitution, he chose to support it anyway. Then, in September of 1911, Marcus A. Smith announced his intention to seek one of the two seats for the office of State Senator of Arizona. Smith also changed his party allegiance, abandoning the old Democratic Party for the new Progressive Party. Henry F. Amherst and Smith beat out the other Democratic contenders in the primaries and then swept the November ballot. Amherst reportedly received more votes than did Smith, much to the latter man's chagrin. Still, Smith would have the honor, after so many years of fighting for statehood, of being one of the men chosen to represent the new state in the U.S. Senate.

Smith was sworn in on April 2, 1912. As senator, Smith avoided party rivalries, especially the one which had arisen between President Taft and former President Theodore "T.R." Roosevelt, and, instead, fought for appropriations for Arizona projects. He also served on a number of Senate committees including those for the Conservation of Natural Resources, the Geological Survey, Public Lands, and Railroads. When President Woodrow Wilson took office in 1914, Smith became a supporter of Wilson's "New Freedom" initiatives. In November of that year, with support of Wilson and Arizona Governor George W.P. Hunt, Senator Smith was elected to his second term. Initially, he supported Wilson's neutrality stance in regard to the war in Europe, However, though he was absent when the Senate voted to send troops to the continent, he came out in support of the action. Smith also supported some of the more onerous legislation that came with it, including the Espionage Act of 1917, the Selective Service Act of 1917, and the Sedition Act of 1918.

Despite his age—the Senator turned 63 in 1920—Smith ran for the office once more. He was able to win the Democratic primary, but lost to Republican Ralph Cameron in the general election. Many voters seemed upset that Smith had spent more time in his home-state of Kentucky than he did visiting the state he represented in Congress. After the election, Smith found himself in a poor financial position and in need of a job and asked President Wilson for an appointment. Wilson, on his last day in office, appointed Smith to the International Joint Commission. Smith remained in Washington, D.C., taking up residence in the Occidental Hotel. He still made occasional trips to Kentucky to visit his family, and he did receive occasional visits from his niece. In his old age, he developed arthritis and his health began to fail. Marcus Aurelius "Mark" Smith died on April 7, 1924, of heart disease and was taken to Kentucky to be buried in Cynthiana, at the Battle Grove Cemetery. His epitaph speaks to his Congressional service though Smith had wanted it to read, "Here lies a good man—a lover of fast horses, pretty women and good whiskey."[33]

The Cochise County Deputy County Attorney, Judge James S. Robinson, would continue to practice law for the remainder of his life. Two years after he helped secure the convictions of John Heath and the Bisbee bandits, the man who also represented the notorious Tombstone outlaws Isaac "Ike" Clanton and John Peters "Johnny" Ringo, was recommended by *The Daily Tombstone* as a candidate for the office of territorial representative to the U.S. Congress. The newspaper stated, "Judge Robinson is one of the most learned men in Arizona, and his former experience in Congress make [*sic*] him one of the best men that could be sent as a delegate, and we are positive he could be elected by a larger majority than any other man who ever run [*sic*] for office in this Territory." However, as *The Daily Tombstone Epitaph* reported, "Judge Robinson could not be induced to accept an office."

Though they had come out in his favor initially, *The Daily Epitaph* began to deride

Grave of senator and former Tombstone district attorney Marcus A. Smith, Battle Grove Cemetery, Cynthiana, Kentucky (private collection).

Robinson for his membership in the Anti-Chinese League and for his support of the boycotting of "all who employ or patronize Chinamen." In the April 9 edition, *The Epitaph* identified Robison as one of the "boss bollycotters" and observed that he and Judge Reilly were "fully imbued with a sense of their own importance." The following day the newspaper remarked cynically, "Judge Robison's work in this anti–Nash-Boycotting business is due to pure philanthropy." In spite of these criticisms, Robinson continued with his efforts on behalf of the Anti-Chinese League, lecturing in Tombstone, Wilcox, and other local towns on "the evils caused by the Chinese ... and the reasons why they should be removed."[34]

In July of 1886, the attorney, who had long suffered from a variety of debilitating illnesses (one of which compelled him to step down from his appointment as a judge for the United States District Court in Arkansas), found it necessary to retire to convalesce in Walter's Springs in Napa County, California, to recuperate. However, by September, Robinson had returned to Tombstone to tend to his work and his mining interests. That same month, *The Daily Tombstone* noted "workmen in the Little Giant mine, owned by Judge Robinson of this city, encountered large body of very rich ore yesterday in the shaft." In November, the newspaper reported that the jurist had had "an offer of $20,000 for his Little Giant mine." In the same column it was revealed that Robinson was "still confined to bed by illness." Robinson would take the offer on his property and then relocate with his wife, Sarah J., to California.[35]

Judge Robinson "resided in San Diego and San Bernardino, California, and afterward went to Los Angeles, where he was associated with John Robarts, removing from that city to Oakland, California, where he became the partner of Judge Glodsby." According to a biographer, "Wherever he was located, Judge Robinson enjoyed an important and distinctively representative clientage and his professional associated were ever eminent lawyers." It was during this period that Robinson changed his political affiliation. In a letter published by *The Tombstone Prospector*, Robinson stated, "I have been a faithful and ardent Republican ... until the most recent Republican convention, held in St. Louis, inserted in the platform of principles the single gold standard doctrine, which read out of the party thousands of Republicans, including myself." By the time he returned to the Arizona Territory in the fall of 1898, Robinson was declaring himself a full-fledged Democrat.

"Judge James S. Robinson," wrote a reporter for *The Bisbee Orb*, "and wife, father and mother of Mrs. J.J. Patton, arrived on the train this morning from Oakland, Cal. Judge Robinson was a resident of Tombstone in the early eighties, and was a member of the bar in this county when it included some of the brightest minds on the coast, and was assistant district attorney at the time of the execution of the Bisbee murderers, and was, on account of the position he held, one of their prosecutors and largely instrumental in their conviction, He is an able jurist, and faithful counselor. The judge and his estimable wife will make their home in Bisbee."[36]

Three years later, Robinson would throw his hat in the political ring, running as a Democrat for the position of Bisbee City Councilman. *The Tombstone Epitaph*, which had formerly maligned Robinson, said of the candidate, "Everybody knows the Judge to be thoroughly capable and peculiarly fitted for the important duties to come before the legislature." Unfortunately, Robinson would lose the election to Republican candidate C.C. Warner. Then, in December, *The Epitaph* reported that the judge was again "on the sick list and obliged to remain at home undergoing treatment." For the next two years the county newspapers would continue to report on the former attorney's failing health. It was during this time the judge relocated to the site of his greatest triumph— Tombstone.[37]

In August of 1902, *The Bisbee Daily Review* noted, "Mrs. J.J. Patton and two daughters left yesterday for Tombstone in response to a telegram that her father, Judge Robinson, is dangerously ill." Finally, on May 22, 1903, *The Bisbee Daily Review* reported, "Another of Cochise county's pioneers has passed away. At Tombstone, Wednesday evening, Judge James S. Robinson breathed his last after long period of illness." The newspaper continued, "About eighteen months ago the deceased was made the victim of a severe attack of paralysis and since that time had been gradually growing weaker. Every effort to save his life was made, but medical skill could not cope with the disease." *The Review* went on to speak to the man's life and his accomplishments, saying of the former barrister, "as a lawyer he strove at all times to see that right and not might prevailed." The newspaper concluded, "Tombstone was selected as the burial place. It was there that Judge Robinson lived the most active part of his life." In November of the same year, Mrs. Sarah Robinson followed her husband to the grave.[38]

Sergeant Lemuel D. Lawrence, M Company, 6th Cavalry, who had been the county's key witness in the Heath case, would be brought to trial just a month after the hanging of the Bisbee bandits, for the murders of W.M. Hill and Sergeant Duffy in I.H. Rose's saloon in Willcox. He would be represented by the firm of Smith, Robinson, and Goodrich—the private practice of Cochise County District Attorney Marcus A. Smith and Deputy District Attorney Robinson. On May 17, 1884, *The Arizona Weekly Citizen* reported that Lawrence had been tried with the "jury rendering a verdict of manslaughter." On June 14, *The Arizona Champion* reported that having been "convicted of manslaughter, for killing of a fellow soldier at Willcox some months ago," Lawrence was sentenced by Judge Pinney to 18 months confinement in the Territorial Penitentiary in Yuma.[39]

Lawrence would appeal the verdict and sentence through his attorneys at the firm of Smith, Robinson, and Goodrich. The motion for appeal was continued to the November 1884 term of the court, and then continued to the November 1885 term. However, in August 1885, Ben Goodrich, the attorney of record for L.D. Lawrence, had applied to the Board of Pardons for clemency for his client. It must have been summarily denied, as Lawrence was back in court in November. By this juncture, Lawrence was being represented by W.H. Lavage. He appeared before Judge Barnes. *The Daily Tombstone* reported that in the case of the "Territory vs. L.D. Lawrence—Jury trial, bringing in verdict of not guilty; there being no evidence by prosecution, whereupon defendant was discharged."[40]

Nothing was heard of Sergeant Lemuel D. Lawrence again.

The very fact that Lawrence was not found guilty of murder in the first degree and sentenced to life imprisonment or to be hanged for the killing of an unarmed man, namely W.M. Hill, gives credence to the argument that he had cut a deal with the District Attorney, Marcus A. Smith, offering his testimony against Heath in exchange for leniency. The fact that is was Ben Goodrich, Smith's partner in the law firm of Smith, Robinson, and Goodrich, who represented Lawrence during the appeal process gives further credence to the argument. Did Lawrence, fearing he might share the fate of the Bisbee bandits, approach Smith with the proposition or did the District Attorney, knowing his case against John Heath was weak, approach Lawrence? Was there a deal made for Lawrence to render assistance in Heath's trial in return for a lighter sentence when he finally came to trial? It can't be proved conclusively, but the circumstantial evidence makes it seem quite probable that this is what occurred. And it may well have cost an innocent man—John Heath—his life.

Tombstone City Cemetery, final resting place of Judge James Robinson (author's collection).

Even with Lawrence's testimony, the jury could not come to a consensus about Heath's guilt. Without Lawrence's testimony, Heath may well have been acquitted.

Heath's friend, Nathan W. Waite, did not leave southern Arizona, but he does seem to have distanced himself from the towns of Tombstone and Bisbee. In December of 1884, *The Arizona Weekly Citizen* reported that Dr. T.W. Seawell had died at Waite's ranch in Babocamori Valley. The newspaper reported that Dr. Seawell "had been ailing for some time, and thinking a change would benefit him, concluded to pay his friend Waite a visit, but he gradually sank and passed away." In February 1886, the delinquent tax notice published in *The Daily Tombstone* indicates that Waite was still residing in "Barbacomrie" and was partnered with a man by the name of Readf. Their tax bill, with penalties and fees was $17.26.

By April 1886, Nathan Waite was residing in the town of Patagonia and serving as the post master. In August 1887, *The Tombstone Epitaph*, gave notice that a letter addressed to N.W. Wait remained at the post office unclaimed. In August of 1889, *The Tombstone Daily Epitaph* made a similar announcement. And so, John Heath's friend, Nathan W. Waite fades from history.[41]

Walter W. Bush, the Clifton bartender who testified against Heath as well as "Tex" Howard and "Red" Sample, returned to Clifton, Arizona, after the trial. By February of 1885, Bush had partnered with G.N. Gentry, forming the firm of Bush & Gentry Real Estate and Live Stock Brokers. In their advertisements, Bush & Gentry asserted they had for sale "several fine ranches" and would "contract for delivery of any number or class of cattle at any point in New Mexico or Arizona." However, by October, W.W. Bush and his partner were being sued by Betterton, Son, & Co in Civil Court. The case was continued for the term.[42]

A W.W. Bush is reported to have sold a property to H.G. Pecks in the October 22, 1910, edition of *The Arizona Republican*. However, neither Walter W. Bush nor W.W. Bush appear anywhere in the 1900 or the 1910 Federal Census of the Territory (the Federal Census of 1890 is lost to history). A W.W. Bush is also reported to have been staying at the Commercial Hotel according to the April 6 and November 4, 1911, editions of the aforementioned newspaper. *The Republican* reported in September 1913 that "Walter Bush has sold his Chandler ranch and will move to Bakersfield, California." Yet, five months later, one W.W. Bush was advertising "40 acres, 7 miles from Phoenix" at $145 an acre replete with "good alfalfa, fine soil, good fence, double ditched. Class A water." The advertisement directed the interested party to contact "W.W. Bush with D.W. Hall & Co." at 21 N. 1st Street in Phoenix. This same advertisement would appear along with three other properties in the March 4, 1914, edition of *The Republican*. The contact person for all the properties was listed as W.W. Bush.[43]

Walter W. Bush could not be found in the 1920 Federal Census for Arizona either and it cannot be ascertained with any certainty that the newspaper articles previously mentioned are referring to the man who formerly testified in the trial of the Bisbee bandits. In fact, another by the name of W.W. Bush begins to appear in the newspapers of southern Arizona in 1903. In September of that year, a W.W. Bush was reportedly arraigned before Justice McDonald on the charge of carrying a concealed weapon. *The Bisbee Daily Review* noted that "W.H. Bush, the father of the young man who was arrested came up from Douglas" to witness the proceedings and pay his son's fine. This same W.W. Bush would be mentioned several times over the next several years in the newspapers of southern Arizona in connection with all manner of legal infractions including the shooting of one Walter Dale during an attempted burglary of the Coney Island Saloon in Douglas, which Bush owned.[44]

The fact that the W.W. Bush mentioned in the Bisbee newspapers of the early 20th century shared a common occupation—saloon owner—with the Walter W. Bush who testified in the Bisbee murder trials might lead one to believe they were one and the same person. However, the mention of a father coming to the aid of "young man" in his time of trouble indicates it was probably another person altogether. Assuming Walter W. Bush was between the ages of 20 and 30 at the time of the Bisbee trials, he would have been well into his 40s by the early 1900s—not exactly a "young man."

What finally became of Walter W. Bush, the former Clifton bartender and real estate agent, remains unknown.

Emma Mortimer, John Heath's mistress, also disappears into the annals of history without leaving the scantest trace. As a known prostitute and a member of what was commonly known as demimonde, Ms. Mortimer would have been very much marginalized by society in general. Her comings and goings and social activities would not have been published in the local newspapers, unless, of course, she ran afoul of the law. She may well have moved from Tombstone as soon as she had the means and settled somewhere else. Still, she had very few options open to her. Once a woman was relegated to the profession it was nearly impossible for her to get out.

The census records of 1890, 1900, and 1910, list a number of women living in the western United States named "Emma Mortimer." Perhaps one of these women was formerly the lover of John Heath. Then again, none of them may be. There is also the possibility she changed her name, either by marrying or adopting an alias. "Emma Mortimer" may well have been an alias. The death records and obituaries available also list a number of women by the name of "Emma Mortimer" but, again, it is almost impossible to say with any certainty that one of these was the same woman who was John Heath's companion. In the end, the mystery of who Emma Mortimer was, where she came from, and where she ended up is just that—a mystery.

Heath's long-suffering wife, Virginia Tennessee "Jennie" Ferrell, would live of the rest of her days in Texas. She never remarried. She never bore any children. She continued to reside with John Heath's parents. Heath's father, John Heath, died September 26, 1895, and his mother, Sarah A. Heath, died in September 9, 1910. They were buried beside the unmarked grave of their only son in the family plot in the Oakland Memorial Park in Terrell, Texas. By 1900, the 43-year-old Jennie Heath was living in the Dallas Ward, Dallas, Texas, with her sister Alice Ferrell, working as a dressmaker. Virginia Tennessee "Jennie" Ferrell would die of "coronary occlusion" in Dallas of February 16, 1950, at the age of 92.[45]

Nellie Cashman, the woman who provided spiritual comfort to the outlaws in their final days, would continue on in the Arizona Territory, spending her time overseeing her business ventures, raising her sister's children, and traveling back and forth across the deserts between Tombstone, Tucson, Prescott, and Jerome. In 1888, she became involved with mining operations in the Harqua Hala Mountains about 80 miles west of Phoenix, Arizona, with Bob Stein, Henry Watton, and Mike Sullivan. In February of the following year, it was reported in *The Phoenix Daily Herald* that Cashman and Sullivan were to marry, but, if there was a romance between the partners, nothing ever came of it. Soon Cashman was back in Tombstone, tending to her businesses and her nieces and nephews. However, by November of 1897, Nellie Cashman had had enough of the Arizona Territory. Lured by the reports of rich gold strikes in the land of the midnight sun, Cashman was reported to have begun outfitting for an expedition to the Yukon Territory.

The 54-year-old Cashman reached the town of Dawson in the Yukon, in April of 1898, and promptly opened a restaurant. She also engaged in prospecting, eventually staking a claim that sold for $100.000. Cashman remained in Dawson until 1904, when she relocated to Fairbanks in the Alaska Territory and opened a grocery store in that burg. She was also involved in several mining ventures and the raising of funds for the Episcopalian St. Matthews Hospital. Legend has it that Cashman would bankroll the gamblers of that city in return for a percentage of their winnings. However, it wasn't long before her wanderlust overtook her once more, and in 1907, at the age of 60, Nellie Cashman relocated once more to the Koyukuk mining district, in the foothills of the Brooks Mountain Range, about 300 miles west of Fairbanks. She wound live out the remainder of her life as a resident of Koyukuk, though during the winters she would travel south to visit her family in the lower 48 states,

Ellen "Nellie" Cashman, the woman who administered comfort to the Bisbee bandits in their final days, in her later years (Arizona Historical Society, 1924).

including her nephew Nike Cunningham, who had become a successful banker in Bisbee, Arizona.

By the summer of 1924, Cashman's health was failing. She traveled first to St. Ann's Mission in Nulato, Alaska. From there she traveled to her former home of Fairbanks, where she was admitted to St. Josephs Hospital. From St. Joseph's Cashman was sent to Providence Hospital in Seattle, Washington, but did not remain there long. In early October, Nellie Cashman packed her gear one more time and took a ship northward to Victoria, British Columbia. Upon arrival, she was admitted to St. Ann's Hospital, the building of which she had helped to finance. Nellie Cashman died there on January 4, 1925, in the company of Dr. W.T. Barrett and Sister Mary Mark of the Alaska Sisters of St. Anne. The official cause of death was determined to be "unresolved pneumonia." Ellen "Nellie" Cashman, the woman known as the "Miner's Angel" and the women who administered comfort to the Bisbee bandits in their final days, was laid to rest in the Ross Bay Cemetery in Victoria, British Columbia. She was 80 years old.[46]

The droll physician who authored one of the most flippant coroner's reports ever recorded, Dr. George Goodfellow, would remain a resident of Tombstone for many years after the trial and hangings of the Bisbee bandits. In January of 1885, several prominent citizens recommended Goodfellow to the Board of Supervisors as the official physician for the county, which would put him in charge of the County Hospital system. The board rejected the idea of contracting Goodfellow, settling on Dr. George C. Willis instead. Still, Dr. Goodfellow was regularly requested to consult on autopsies and as an expert witness in court cases. He also had a lucrative private practice which included providing medical services for the local mines and mining companies and patching up the victims of gunshot wounds. Dr. Goodfellow would come to treat so many bullet wounds during his career—and in doing so, develop a number of pioneering treatments (he performed the first known laparotomy surgery on a gut-shot patient)—he would eventually earn the sobriquet "Physician to the Gunfighters."

Though a married man with a young daughter named Edith, Goodfellow was known to be a hard-drinker, a gambler, and philanderer. He was also give to violence. On August 8, 1889, Goodfellow stabbed a man named Frank White in the back with a dagger during a melee on Allen Street in Tombstone. Apparently, the night before, while under the influence, Dr. Goodfellow had lost a large sum of money while gambling with Mr. White. Goodfellow was arrested and fined for carrying a concealed weapon. By 1889, his wife, Katherine, was living with relatives in to Oakland, California. His daughter spent her time shuttling back and forth between Tombstone and Oakland. Katherine Goodfellow nee Colt would succumb to consumption in August of 1891.

For all his personal faults, Goodfellow was a man of science and retained an unquenchable thirst for knowledge. After the Bavispe earthquake struck Sonora, Mexico, on May 3, 1887, Goodfellow, who was bilingual, traveled there to treat the survivors. Fascinated by the seismological event, the doctor made two more trips into the Mexican interior to study and record the effects of the quake. His subsequent report was highly praised by the U.S. Geographical Service and was considered a pioneering achievement in the study of earthquakes on the North American continent. Goodfellow also immersed himself in the study of local reptiles including rattlesnakes and Gila monsters and published articles about the creatures in the *Scientific American* and the *Southern California Practitioner*.

When his friend and fellow doctor, John Handy, was killed in 1891 by Mrs. Handy's lawyer in the culmination of a rather messy divorce proceeding, Dr. Goodfellow re-located to Tucson to assume Handy's practice. Goodfellow ran his practice out of the Orndorff Hotel and worked at St. Mary's hospital. It was a good time for Goodfellow. In addition to his private practice, Goodfellow was employed by the Southern Pacific Railroad as chief physician and, in 1892, Territorial Governor Louis C.

Dr. George Emory Goodfellow, the physician to the gunfighters, later in life (author's collection).

San Francisco Earthquake of 1906, which ruined Dr. Goodfellow's fortunes and destroyed most of his writings and research notes (author's collection).

Hughes appointed Goodfellow to the post of Arizona Territorial Health Officer, a position he held until 1896. Goodfellow was also appointed surgeon of the First Regiment of the Arizona National Guard with the rank of Major. When not at school in the East or visiting relatives in Oakland, Goodfellow's daughter Edith lived with him in the hotel on Pennington Street.

Dr. Goodfellow finally decided to quit the Arizona Territory in 1897 and moved on to Los Angeles, California. When the Spanish-American War erupted in 1898, Goodfellow was "drafted" by his friend General William Shafter, the commander of all land forces in Cuba, to serve as his personal physician. Reports concerning Goodfellow's role in the conflict are convoluted at best, but he was recognized by the United States Congress for "especially meritorious services" during the campaign. After he mustered out, Dr. Goodfellow returned to Tucson, and then traveled to Los Angeles. By 1899, Goodfellow was residing in San Francisco and employed as chief physician for the Atchison, Topeka and Santa Fe Railroad.

There is some indication that Dr. Goodfellow remarried during the period, taking a wife known to history only as Mary Elizabeth. Very little is known about her. Though married, Goodfellow continued to play the role of man-about-town, with memberships in the Claremount Country Club, the California Club, the University Club, and the famed Bohemian Club. He continued to make a good living with his medical practice (with fewer bullet wounds to contend with on a regular basis) and submitting articles to various medical journals, many on diseases of the prostrate. He also began speculating in real estate as he had in Tucson. However, his good fortune came to an abrupt end on the morning of April 18, 1906, with the Great San Francisco earthquake and subsequent fire.

Goodfellow, who was living in the St. Francis Hotel at the time, lost everything, including all his private journals, drafts of articles, and personal records. He also saw his numerous real estate investments go up in smoke, quite literally. After the quake, Dr. Goodfellow attempted to re-establish his practice, but was unsuccessful. The following year, Dr. Goodfellow went back to work for the Southern Pacific Railroad as the Chief Physician in Mexico as the company expanded its operations south of the international border. Based out of Guaymas, Goodfellow continued to work for the Southern Pacific until his health began to take a downward turn. In March of 1910, Goodfellow was stricken with some form of neuritis which paralyzed his arms. He traveled to Los Angeles for treatment with his sister's husband, Dr. George W. Fish, but to no avail. His condition continued to deteriorate until the morning of December 7, 1910, when Dr. George Emory Goodfellow finally succumbed.[47]

After the trial, Frank H. Buckles, one of the chief witnesses called by the prosecution against Tex Howard, "Big Dan" Dowd, Daniel Kelly, William Delaney, and "Red" Sample, returned to his ranch and his former life. Occasionally, his name would appear in the local papers. In November of 1891, *The Tombstone Epitaph* reported Buckles serving on the Grand Jury. The following month, Frank Buckles was again mentioned, this time in *The Arizona Weekly Citizen*, as being the recipient of a "homestead patent" on his Sulpher Springs ranch. His discovery in May of 1892 of a blood-bespattered saddle and canteen, along with a government-issue blanket, bridle, rifle scabbard, and broken gunstock near the Swisshelm Mountains also made the newspapers. Buckles tracked the horse "which had been carrying the outfit," but was unable to locate the rider. A few months later, a pair of overalls containing a leg bone and some letters in the pocket would be discovered in the vicinity. However, the mystery of the missing rider would never be resolved.[48]

In June of that year, *The Epitaph* noted the birth of a son in the Buckles household. On January 29, 1893, the newspaper reported that Frank Buckles was in Durango, Colorado and stated, "His family will move there next week." A cursory review of the Colorado newspapers of the era revealed nothing about the Buckles family or its patriarch. However, Frank H. Buckles does appear in the 1900 Federal Census. The family, including his wife Ida R., and children Rose, Harry, Gertrude, and Roy, along with an Abby R. Randall, Robert Edwards, and Henry Sloan, were said to be living in West Pagosa Springs, in the county of Archuleta, Colorado. Buckles' age is listed as 41. His occupation is given as "merchant."

In 1907, the Buckles name would again appear in the Southern Arizona newspapers. On January 16, *The Bisbee Daily Review* would report that Buckles, "a guest of the Goldman Hotel [in Douglas], was found drawing his last breath when the proprietor of the hotel reached him." Buckles, the newspaper explained, had "arrived in Douglas on Friday morning with H.E. Williamson from Pagosa Springs, Colorado, a little town near Durango. Friday and Saturday he looked up some old friends here." The newspaper went on to say that Buckles "announced his desire to take a bath, stating that he had been invited to dinner with his friend, C.A. Overlock." Mrs. Fisher, wife of the hotel's operator, "conducted Mr. Buckles to the bath room and going in turned on the gas of the instantaneous heater and filled the tub about half full with water; when she left the bath room, Mr. Buckles entered it and shut the door."

About ten minutes later, A.A. Fisher, the proprietor was alerted to the smell of gas emanating from the bath room. Upon investigating, Fisher found the door of the room locked. A boy was lifted up, put through the transom window, and unlocked the door.

Mr. Buckles was found lying on the floor gasping his last. He was immediately removed to another room and a doctor was called, but it was too late. A coroner's jury was convened and concluded that the "deceased was 47 years old and that he met his death by being asphyxiated by gas, accidently." On his person was found over $1,100 and it was later revealed that he had told friends he intended "going into business of some kind which he would determine after looking over the conditions and opportunities" in the area.

The body of Frank Henry Buckles was shipped back to his wife in Pagosa Springs and was buried in Hilltop Cemetery.[49]

Frank Buckles' former neighbor, Lubien Pardee, with whom the Bisbee bandits stayed prior to the robbery, also disappears completely from historical records after the trial. His name does not appear in any of the extant Arizona newspapers after the trial, nor is his existence, under this name, recorded in U.S. Census reports. For all intents and purposes, the man simply disappears. It may well be, having testified against the Bisbee bandits, Pardee felt he might be a target for retribution from their friends and confederates who lived outside the law. Or, perhaps, having admitted to giving shelter to the outlaws, Pardee, like Henry Frost, became a *persona non grata* among the citizenry in Bisbee and Tombstone. No longer feeling safe or welcome in Cochise County, Mr. Pardee may have moved from the territory after the trial, changed his name, and lived out the rest of his life in another locale under an assumed identity. It is impossible to say with any certainty what became of Lubien Pardee.

Nickolas Olguin, who had been instrumental in the capture of "Tex" Howard and Omer "Red" Sample, was arrested, along with his crew, in connection with the shooting deaths of L.M. Clements and his partner, William Wryscarber. Olguin and eight others were brought before the Probate Judge Hyatt in Solomonville to answer for the murders. *The Arizona Weekly Citizen* predicted on January 5, 1884, that Olguin and his co-defendants would "be released on a writ of habeas corpus. Indeed, after a brief examination, Judge Hyatt ordered the men discharged." Both *The Tombstone Republican* and *The Arizona Weekly Citizen* expressed concern that, if the men were not made to answer for the killing, a race war between the Mexicans and Anglos would erupt in Graham County.

"The Clifton Clarion, while deploring the death of the unfortunate men, disclaims any criminal intent on the part of Olguin and his posse," wrote *The Republican*. *The Clarion*, seeming to ignore the fact that Olguin and his crew had killed two innocent men, defended Olguin's vigilantism, saying, "To come right down to hard facts, the officers of this county either would not or could not do their duty by the murdering gang who have infected this locality, and so Nicholas and his men were called upon. They started in by killing Kid Lewis [the outlaw who Omer 'Red' Sample was believed to have ridden with], for which act a considerable portion of the people of Clifton desired to have them indicted, but the grand jury ignored the matter. Now comes up the killing of these two men. The same persons who wanted to have Nicholas indicted for killing Kid come to the front to throw mud upon him and his posse for this last act. This time they are reinforced by some good citizens, who allowed their prejudice against Mexicans to get the better of them."

In the end it all came to naught. There were no race riots or civil unrest in Graham County and Olguin was freed to go about his business. It was the officers of Graham County who finally apprehended the outlaws Olguin had initially gone in search of. *The Arizona Weekly Citizen* reported on February 23, that "Tommy the Kid" was arrested "for an attempt made by him and Doc Baker to murder Nicholas Olguin some time since in that county." The law officers were of the opinion the subsequent conviction of the outlaw for attempted murder would be a "sure thing." The newspaper reminded its readers that "it was while hunting Baker and Tommy, for an attempt on his life, that Olguin and posse killed two prospectors whom they mistook for them."[50]

Ironically, the manhunt, during which Olguin and his posse killed L.M. Clements and William Wryscarber and aided in the capture of "Tex" Howard and "Red" Sample, became Olguin's shining moment. On January 26, 1884, *The Arizona Champion* reported that "William Church, Esq., the president of the Detroit Copper Company, last week presented Nicholas Olguin with a costly saddle, which he purchased in Denver for him." The newspaper went on to report that Henry C. Hooker, owner of the Sierra Bonita ranch and one of the most powerful cattlemen in the Arizona Territory, "sent word to Olguin that he desired to present him with two blooded saddle horses."[51]

Things did not go quite so well for some of Olguin's posse members. In March of 1886, Catalino Martinez, who *The Clifton Clarion* identified as "one of the Olguin gang, who is charged with the murder of two prospectors two years ago, and who was released by writ of habeas corpus" had been arrested in Morenci the previous Friday and "securely domiciled in the County jail, where he will be kept until called for." Olguin himself was not doing well either. What became of Martinez is a mystery. In January of 1885, Olguin was listed among those on the Delinquent Tax List, owing $7.72 for "improvements of ranch, Middle Gila." After this, mentions of Nicholas Olguin in the newspapers and other historical documents are sparse.[52]

The Rio Grande Republican reported in October of 1897, the District Court of New Mexico had found Jesus Enriquez, Maxamiliano Romero and one *Nicolas* Olguin, who had been indicted by a grand jury for assault with intent to kill, not guilty. In a separate action, the court dismissed the case of *The Territory of New Mexico vs.* Nicolas *Olguin*, for assault with intent to kill. No other documentation about the cases has been found. Seven years later, on October 14, *Nicolas* Olguin took for his bride a young woman by the name of Teresa Relles. The couple was married in Morenci, in Graham County, Arizona Territory. However, the 1880 Federal Census for Grant County, New Mexico, indicates that Nicolas Olguin, age 27, was married to one Romana C. Olguin and had four children with her, so this is probably not the same man. Then, in March of 1919, *The Copper Era* newspaper of Clifton reported that Nicholas Olguin had sold a house located in Morenci to Ms. Ramona Padella, realizing $180 from the sale.[53]

In 1910, the name *Nicolas* Olguin begins to appear in *The El Paso Herald*. The first mention of him is in June that year in connection with the filing of a deed for "40 acres one mile northwest of Vinton. Tex.; consideration $1800." In September, Olguin was put on notice for failing to pay the 30 cent per acre assessment for water use to the El Paso Valley Water Users' Association. Nicolas Olguin was said to owe for the usage on one acre. The following year, *The Herald* reported that Nicolas Olguin purchased two lots in "Lincoln Park, Manzana street, between Martinez street and Boone avenue" from Rafael Barela for $1,500. Then, in March 1912, "Nicolas Olguin and wife" sold a 5 acre property in Socorro, Texas, to Seth B. Orndorff for a consideration of $10. Orndorff then sold Olguin a 10.55 acre lot for $1,050.

Finally, on February 4, 1922, *The Bisbee Daily Review* reported that "Nicholas Olguin, 79, proprietor of a small grocery store" in El Paso, was "found murdered" in his store at about 7 o'clock the evening before. The newspaper reported that Olguin had been shot twice, his body "pierced by two bullet wounds. Coins from a sack in which the grocer kept his day's receipts were found scattered on the floor." *The Review* stated there had been "no witnesses to the tragedy." It is not known if the Nicholas Olguin who was murdered by thieves inside the grocery store in El Paso was the same Nicholas Olguin who led the posse which murdered L.M. Clements and William Wryscarber and was instrumental in the capture of "Tex" Howard and "Red" Sample, though it seems quite possible.[54]

The 23-year-old Christopher "Kit" Joy, the last of the Gage train robbers, had been languishing in the county jail in Silver City, New Mexico, since March 1884. Finally, in August, the one-legged outlaw came to trial to answer for his part in the hold-up of November 1883, "which resulted in the death of Theopholus C. Webster." *The Arizona Silver Belt* reported that his trial was "set for August 18th, in the 3rd Judicial Court, at Silver City." The Pinal County newspaper reported that "Alexander Campbell, of Tucson, is there on behalf of Wells Fargo & Co. and the Southern Pacific R.R., for the purpose of assisting in the prosecution of the case." *The Silver Belt* continued, "Joy's lease on life is short. It is said the proof of his complicity in the robbery and murder is conclusive."[55]

In July, "Kit" Joy was indicted by the Grand Jury, on two counts of murder, in the death of engineer Theopholus C. Webster and posse member Joseph L. Laffner, and on two counts of armed robbery. Joy's counsel, Fielder & Fielder, attempted several evasive legal maneuvers, including an Affidavit for Change of Venue, filed August 8, 1884, a Motion for Continuance, filed August 14, 1884, and a Motion to Quash the Indictment, filed November 17, 1884, all in an effort to delay the trial and secure their client's freedom. In spite of the legal wrangling and the inability of the court to settle on a jury, "Kit" Joy was arraigned for his crimes and, after pleading "not guilty" to the murder indictments, given a trial. After hearing the evidence presented and giving the matter due deliberation, the jury in the case of the *Territory of New Mexico vs. "Kit" Joy* found the defendant guilty of murder in the second degree.

On November 20, 1884, "Kit" Joy was sentenced by District Judge S.F. Wilson to spend the remainder of his "natural life … in such penitentiary as is or may be provided by law for the imprisonment of Territorial convicts, whose punishment shall have been assessed as imprisonment in the Territorial prison" and to pay the costs for his prosecution. *The Arizona Silver Belt* noted that Joy "maintained a cool and unruffled demeanor during the trial." Upon hearing sentence passed, Joy declared openly, "I am not guilty. The evidence against me was false and manufactured by the railroad officials, but I believe the jury acted honestly. I will go to the penitentiary and try to perform whatever duty may be assigned to me, and I hope by an honorable course to regain my liberty through the pardon of the governor."[56]

In June of the following year, "Kit" Joy appears on the New Mexico Territorial Census as residing in Santa Fe. His profession is listed as "convict." In actuality, Joy was employed. He was among the 18 prisoners brought in from Grant and Sierra Counties to aid in the construction of the new Territorial prison. Over the years, Joy would receive some notoriety for his criminal deeds. In August 1887, in an article from *The Southwest Sentinel* detailing some of the more recent train robberies in the Arizona and New Mexico Territories, Joy was mentioned by name. He also received mention in *The San Francisco Call*, in October 1897, in an exposé on infamous stagecoach and train robbers. Oddly, the article did not elaborate on his crimes but focused on his escape from the Silver City jail. The periodical explained that Joy, having avoiding the fate of Mitch Lee and Frank Taggart, had been captured and brought to trial in New Mexico, and "in consideration of his crippled condition and in deference to the prayers of his aged father and mother" had been "let off" with a verdict of murder in the second degree. The California newspaper "believed" "Kit" Joy was "serving his time at the prison in Santa Fe."[57]

In spite of his predicament, "Kit" Joy had not given up. In May 1893, *The Western Liberal* reported that "a worthy gentleman is now, in the goodness of his heart, circulating a petition which prays for the release of the fiend, and the same old arguments about his lost leg and his poor old mother are again being used to gain signatures." Obviously, the editor of the newspaper opposed the idea of executive clemency for Joy. "It is sincerely hoped," he wrote, "that those who are asked to sign the position, will stop, think, and refuse." The editor reasoned that, "if the law is to be a terror to evil doers, and a protection to life and property, murderers and robbers must know that they will receive the lawful punishment for their crimes. They must not have cause to think that they can violate the law, with the strong chance they will escape punishment altogether, and that even if they receive a sentence in some degree adequate to their crime, it will not be enforced."

The author of the article must have felt very strongly about his position with regards to clemency for "Kit" Joy, as he continued his harangue against Joy and the notion of a pardon in a separate article on the next page of the same edition. The voice of the editor of *The Liberal* was not the only one to be raised in opposition to the idea of clemency for the former train robber and convicted murderer. The editor of *The Southwest Sentinel* also came out against Joy, saying, "It is hoped that the Governor will not pardon Kit Joy, the man who murdered Engineer Webster and robbed a train in the Southern Pacific about ten years ago. The list of pardoned murderers is long enough now and it is time it came to a halt."

However, Territorial Governor Edmund G. Ross agreed to commute "Kit" Joy's sentence, with good time allowed, to 20 years. Still, the aging outlaw was adamant in seeking a full pardon, petitioning Governor Ross once more, in September of 1889 and petitioning, Ross' successor, Governor Lebaron Bradford Prince in January of 1891. Unfortunately for Joy, Edward C. Wade, who served as the prosecutor at Joy's trial, was very much opposed to the idea of the outlaw's sentence being commuted and wrote Governor Prince in protest. Governor Prince refused "Kit" Joy's appeal. Joy would serve five more years in the Territorial Penitentiary, finally being pardoned in April of 1896 by Governor William Taylor Thornton and released by prison superintendent Colonel Edward C. Bergman.[58]

From Santa Fe, "Kit" Joy moved to the Arizona Territory. By 1910, the 49-year-old Pennsylvania native was residing in Huachuca City (then part of the U.S. military reserve or fort) with his mother, Mary A. Joy, and opened his own tailoring business. The following year, "Kit" Joy's mother died and the one-legged tailor moved to the town of Buena, Arizona Territory. However, after World War I, the town of Buena collapsed and "Kit" Joy was forced to move on. He chose the town of Garden Canyon as his new home. He attempted to open a new shop, but business was not what it had been. So, the elderly Joy decided to supplement his meager earnings by going in to the bootlegging business, bringing wine and other liquors in to the state from Mexico. In May 1926, Joy and his partner-in-crime, Warren Mimms, were arrested by federal agents and charged with violation of the Volstead Act. Joy and Mimms appeared before Judge William Sawtelle in Tucson, pled guilty and were fined a dollar a piece and sentenced to five months in jail.

Joy returned to the town of Garden Canyon after his release and quietly lived out the next ten years in that burg. Christopher Carson "Kit" Joy would finally die of pneumonia, at the Cochise County Hospital, in the town of Douglas, on April 14, 1936, at the age of 74 years. His mortal remains would be interred in the Evergreen Cemetery in Bisbee, Arizona.[59]

Joseph Goldwater, who allegedly attempted to sell the men who robbed him new overcoats, would continue on in the mercantile business after the robbery. *The Daily Tombstone*, in an exposé on the fledgling town of Bisbee from November of 1885, made mention of the entrepreneur and his business, "J. Goldwater & Co. have a large general merchandise store and do a big business their principle trade being with merchants from Sonora who annually spend many thousands of dollars." Strangely, the newspaper made no mention of his partner, Jose M. Castaneda, in whose wife's name the business remained under.

Goldwater was doing a fair amount of traveling throughout the region in connection with his business as evidenced by reports in the various local newspapers. The week after the aforementioned article appeared in *The Daily Tombstone*, Goldwater was reported to be a guest at the Occidental

Evergreen Cemetery, Bisbee, Arizona, the final resting place of John Tappenier, Annie Smith, J.A. "Tex" Nolly, three of the victims of the Bisbee Massacre, and the infamous Christopher "Kit" Joy (alas, their exact gravesites have been lost) (author's collection).

Hotel there. His name also appeared in many of the other regional journals during this period. However, trouble seemed to haunt Goldwater's every endeavor. *The Daily Tombstone* noted in their edition of February 10, 1886, that Charleston customs inspector Samuel Katzenstein had seized "another haul of contraband goods near Fairbanks." The goods were said to "belong to a Charleston man" but were "consigned to Joe Goldwater." The purpose of smuggling was to avoid paying duties on imported goods coming in to the country. Though smugglers were arrested and their horses, wagon, and goods seized, the incident had negligible repercussions for Goldwater.[60]

In fact, in spite of his possible involvement in smuggling operations, Goldwater was reported in September that year to have been one of the securities on an undisclosed bond. But by then, Goldwater and his partner, Castaneda, were very much among the moneyed elite of Bisbee. *The Tombstone Epitaph* reported in August of 1887 that the Board of Equalization of Cochise County had raised the tax assessment on Goldwater & Co. merchandise to $1,500. Then, in July of the following year, the Goldwater & Co. assessment was raised again to $2,000. Obviously, Goldwater and Castaneda were doing very well for themselves with both the mercantile business and their supplementary investments.[61]

An odd and unexplained note appeared in the December 3, 1887, edition of *The Tombstone Epitaph*. The Cochise County Board of Supervisors agreed to pay J. Goldwater & Co. $12 for "burying L. Torres." *The Arizona Daily Citizen* reported in July that "Prefect Torres, of Oposura, a brother of Col. Torres of the Mexican army" had been killed while traveling from Lampasas to Oposura, after encountering what was described as a "large band" of Apache. Four of the 15 soldiers who were accompanying Prefect Torres, were also killed in the fight. It seems doubtful, seeing that the skirmish which took the life of Prefect Torres occurred in Mexico that Goldwater & Co. would be subsidizing his burial in Bisbee. Who L. Torres was and why Goldwater & Co. were subsidizing his burial remains a mystery.[62]

In March of 1888, *The Epitaph* reported that Goldwater was part of a committee which "was appointed with power to dispose of" properties deeded to the "bondsmen of A.J. Ritter, late County Treasurer" as security. Upon quarterly examination of the books of the County Treasurer by the Board of Supervisors in January, it was found that "the aggregate sum of $6,599.47 was missing from the coffers of the County. County Treasurer Ritter was accused of "illegally" appropriating the funds "without any warrant of [the] Board or other authority of law." The Board demanded Ritter replace the funds to which "said A.J. Ritter replied that he had nothing to replace." The Board, not satisfied with this answer, "resolved and ordered ... that A.J. Ritter,[be] suspended from the discharge of nay official act as ... County Treasurer and ex-officio Tax Collector, until such defalcation shall be adjudicated." The matter of the missing monies was heard before the District Court in February, with Col. William Herring and Ben Goodrich appearing as counsel for the defense. In spite of his employing such fine legal counsel, the judge found in favor of the County and ordered that A.J. Ritter "pay the money over to the county." Ritter, of course appealed the court's decision, but that did not stop the judgment and his properties were subsequently auctioned off.[63]

While *The Epitaph* covered the scandal involving former County Treasurer Ritter and Goldwater's involvement therein, the newspaper made no mention of the marriage of Goldwater in July of that year to Manuela Arvisa. In fact, none of the newspapers of the territory made any mention of the nuptials at all even though the ceremony took place in Tombstone. It is possible that the marriage, though officially recorded by the County, was not given recognition in the press due to the fact that Goldwater, a Caucasian of Jewish ancestry, was marrying a woman of Hispanic descent, which, at the time, was not considered proper. Marriages that did not adhere to prevailing social mores—which dictated that one did not marry outside one's own ethnic group—though recognized officially, were not generally celebrated by the community at large.[64]

For the six months, Goldwater's name did not appear in any of the social pages in any of the local newspapers. When his name does resurface, in early 1889, it is in a notice "Dissolution of Partnership" in *The Tombstone Daily Prospector*. According to the advertisement, "A.A. Castaneda, of the firm of J. Goldwater & Co., has sold all her right, title and interest to Lemuel Goldwater [Joseph's eldest son], who will in future become a full partner in the firm's business houses." The notice went on to state that the firm of J. Goldwater & Co. was comprised of J. Goldwater, A. Guidani, and Lemuel Goldwater, "who will collect all accounts due the late firm and who will pay all liabilities of said firm." The reason for Castaneda's decision to quit that partnership and to quit Bisbee is unknown, though one source claims a devastating fire had caused him to reconsider the partnership and sell his share of the company. However, no record of such said fire could be found.

Even though they were no longer business partners, Goldwater and Castaneda remained close. Their names were still linked, as evidenced by an article which appeared in *The Arizona Silver Belt* in August 1889, in connection with an anti-statehood movement in Benson. J. Goldwater, Lemuel, and Castaneda's son, along with 14 others, were named by *The Arizona Silver Belt* as being part of a grassroots coalition which came out against the Territory's bid for statehood. Also, in August, *The Tombstone Daily Epitaph* reported that the Cochise County Board of Supervisors had "ordered that the Treasurer receive the taxes and penalty of 1888 from J. Goldwater, on lot in Fairbank assessed to Rogers Bros. in 1888, but owned by J. Goldwater."[65]

Castaneda's name would be mentioned one final time in connection with that of Joseph Goldwater, when *The Tombstone Daily Epitaph* reported on September 3, 1889, that Don Castaneda had been in Tombstone the day before to "attend the funeral of J. Goldwater." Joseph Goldwater died Saturday August 31, 1889, in Tombstone after a "brief illness." *The Arizona Sentinel* eulogized him thus:

> Joseph Goldwater, one of Arizona's pioneers, died in [Tombstone] Saturday afternoon after a brief illness. He occupied a place in Arizona's history which few men can claim. He came to the Territory early in the sixties and began business at La Paz on the Colorado River. There were a number of well-known citizens of Arizona at that place at the time among which may be mentioned Sam Drachman, of Tucson, Charles Granville Johoston [sic], of [Tombstone], and his brother, M. Goldwater, now of Prescott.
> Mr. Goldwater came to Yuma from La Paz, where he lived some time, after which he visited and did some business in nearly every mining camp in the Territory of any size. His life was full of hardship and bitter experience. He was not a man who courted the friendship of everyone, but those whom he counted on as his friends were true as steel. He braved the dangers of Indian outbreaks. Outlaws, time and again, had robbed him of the fruits of his toil, but he never uttered a word of complaint. He had many faults as all mortals have, but his many acts of charity and kindness toward those who were in need of assistance, are monuments to his memory which are lasting. He leaves two grown up sons and one daughter by his first wife. He was married about a year ago. His widow survives him. He had a lucrative business at Fairbank, which will be carried on by his sons who have managed his affairs so successfully during the past few years.

The Arizona Weekly Citizen reported that Goldwater left an estate valued at $89,961. In accordance with his wishes and the tenants of his faith, the remains of Joseph Goldwater were shipped over to San Francisco by locomotive and he was buried in a Jewish cemetery therein. However, sometime after the Earthquake of 1906, Goldwater's mortal remains were disinterred and moved to the Hills of Eternity Memorial Park Congregation, in Colma, California.[66]

As noted earlier, Joseph Goldwater's partner in the mercantile, Don Jose Miguel Castaneda, finally quit the mercantile business and the town of Bisbee in 1889. However, Castaneda was not retiring altogether. He moved to the town of Benson, which had become a major rail stop on the Southern Pacific Railroad line, and there he opened a new, luxury hotel, which he christened The Virginia. Castaneda's lodging house very quickly established a reputation as one of the finest in the territory and the proprietor became equally well-known. "At Benson," wrote a reporter for *The Arizona Weekly Enterprise*, "the railroad time schedule renders it necessary to remain overnight and one is at first inclined to find fault with the traveling accommodations. But this ungracious mood is soon dispelled by the genial treatment of landlord A.A. Castaneda, of the hotel."

The Florence newspaper went on to say, "Here one can get as good a meal and as clean and comfortable a bed as one could desire, and the accommodations are all good. Mr. Castaneda is one of Arizona's oldest pioneers; his hair is whitening with autumnal frosts

Don Castaneda's Virginia Hotel, Benson A.T., which Castaneda opened after dissolving his partnership with Joe Goldwater and leaving Bisbee (Arizona Historical Society, 78332).

of life, but his energy and vigor are still unimpaired." A correspondent from *The Arizona Weekly Citizen*, while traveling across the state, also stopped over in "the thriving town of Benson, altitude about 5,300 ft., and population something less than 500. Here the passengers are met by A.A. Castaneda, the suave host of the Virginia Hotel, the popularity of which may be more correctly gauged than otherwise by a reference to the register, which shows for the past month an average daily arrival of from 10 to 20 guests. The house," wrote the reporter, "contains 25 well furnished rooms, a good table, and those who indulge say Cas. is the boss mixer of toothsome beverages." Obviously, the former mercantile owner had found his niche.[67]

In 1891, when U.S. President Benjamin Harrison visited the southern portion of the Arizona Territory during a cross-country, whistle-stop tour, it was Don Castaneda who was on hand to play the role of host for the chief executive and his entourage. *The Tombstone Epitaph* reported, "The train containing the presidential party arrived at 5:15 this afternoon. Great preparations had been made for their reception. The troops from [Fort] Huachuca had been drawn up and fired a salute as the train drew in. A break was made for the Virginia hotel by the presidential party as soon as the train was brought to a standstill. Mine host Castaneda had expected them and after regaling themselves upon one of the justly celebrated dinners they returned to the depot." President Harrison made a short speech to the troops before re-boarding the train and continuing his journey west.[68]

Of course, serving the President in his hotel, only added to Castaneda's reputation. In August of the following year, the "gracious" hotelier was given mention in a special business edition of *The Arizona Republican*. Beneath a re-print of his photograph, the Phoenix newspaper gave both the man and the hotel a stellar review. The author of the piece wrote,

> As a central point between El Paso and Yuma, Benson commands a position that calls for first-class accommodations. It is the terminus of the New Mexico, Arizona & Sonora Railway. As the trains

reach here at such hours as to render in necessary to stop over night, a good hotel is very requisite. All who may have, in the emergencies of travel, to stop over at Benson, may be confidently directed to the Virginia Hotel, as being the only first-class hotel in the town.

This hotel was opened three years ago on the American plan. It contains twenty-five light and airy sleeping rooms. With a capacity for the accommodation of thirty people at a time, and has an elegantly furnished parlor for the convenience of the lady guests. Mr. J.M. Castaneda is the genial host of this hotel. He had several large and elegantly fitted up sample rooms for commercial men, and they will find home-like comfort staying at this house. The dimensions of the house are 50 × 100 feet. The proprietor has had considerable experience in business, having kept this house for several years, and has been in business in the territory twenty-nine years. He has an extensive acquaintance, and knows exactly what his guests want. Everything about the house is in the latest improved style, and of the very first class. Every attention is given to the comfort of the traveling public, and we predict for Mr. Castaneda a successful career, for there is nothing that impresses the traveler as good attention and the evidences of a desire to please, all if which qualities are possessed, in a marked degree, by Mr. Castaneda.[69]

Don Castaneda, as he was known locally, was also mentioned frequently in the local "society pages" as the century was coming to its close. On June 14, 1894, Castaneda's name appeared four times within the pages of *The Oasis*, a newspaper based out of Arizola. The newspaper reported that on "Tuesday, Mr. J.M. Castaneda went to Tucson on business" and returned Wednesday morning. The newspaper also reported that Castaneda's 15-year-old son Rudolph, who was attending St. Michael's College in Santa Fe, New Mexico Territory, had received a "very credible" report card from the college. *The Oasis* also made mention of the whirl-wind which "swept through Mr. Castaneda's store, breaking all the glasses in the front doors." The reporter noted that "after the dust settled the clerks' hair could be seen standing straight."

Finally, in the same edition, on a slightly comical note, the newspaper printed the following anecdote: "It is related that at Benson, not long ago, an eastern tenderfoot was invited to dinner 'a la Mexicana' by mine host Castaneda, of the Virginia hotel. The piece de resistance of really excellent repast consisted of tamales, made in a delicious way for which Mr. Castaneda is noted. Afterward, in reply to an inquiry how he like the dinner, the tenderfoot replied that 'he liked it very much, but there was something wrong about the bananas.'"[70]

The Oasis continued to relate for its readers news about Don Castaneda for the next several years. In August of 1894, the newspaper noted that the hotelier had given a total of $55 "toward completion of the Catholic Church structure at Benson." In September, it was revealed that "Mine host Castaneda of the Virginia hotel has received a couple of cases of fine 'Purity' whisky" which had taken first prize at the World's Fair in Chicago the previous year. And, in December of 1896, *The Oasis* noted that Mr. Castaneda was "building an addition" to his hotel "which will include several rooms and water pipes" running throughout. A Mr. H. Gerwein was said to be the contractor employed "for the carpenter work."[71]

By all reports, Don Castaneda was doing quite well in his various enterprises. *The Tombstone Epitaph* in their official Property Assessment estimated the furniture in the hotel's addition to be valued at $200. In fact, Don Castaneda was perceived as being so affluent, he became a target for thieves. *The St. John's Herald* reported in August of 1898, A.A. Castaneda's store—a mercantile he had opened in 1894 in Benson featuring "dry good, boots, shoes, clothing, hats & caps, hardware, dress goods, groceries, provisions, etc."—"was burglarized a few nights ago, the thieves offecting [sic] an enterance [sic] by the front door." The Apache County newspaper reported that the burglars had "secured obout [sic] $250 worth of watches, razors, etc. and $5 in change from the cash register." The thieves were apprehended soon afterwards in Deming, New Mexico, when they attempted to sell several of the stolen items to "a rail road man there."[72]

While it must have been disconcerting for Castaneda to once again find himself a victim of a crime, in comparison to what he had endured during the Bisbee robbery, this must have been much more bearable. It certainly did not have a noticeable effect on Castaneda's business ambitions. Two years later, the hotelier and merchant joined with a group of like-minded investors in financing the Arizona Clay Manufacturing Co. which produced pressed brick for construction, as well as "drain and sewer pipe, irrigating pipe, roofing, tiles, glazed tiles for floors, hollow building blocks, and terra cotta work of all kinds." *The Oasis* reported that "the company is capitalized at $60,000 and already nearly one-half of the stock has been subscribed." The president and director of the new company was named as J. M Castaneda.

Unfortunately, Don Castaneda would not be able to see the new company established. On September 28, 1901, Don Jose Miguel Castaneda died. *The Oasis* newspaper, which had followed the doings of the Castaneda family for years, eulogized the man with a full front-page tribute in both English and Spanish.

It was undoubtedly that hard work attendant upon organizing and setting into operation the affairs of [the Arizona Clay Manufacturing Co] and getting installed it big machinery plant, that [sic] brought on the fatal illness. He had been very busily engaged with the affairs of the company for many weeks and was considerably run down. About two weeks before his decease he was attacked with dysentery, but would not give up, going to Bisbee, on business of the company. There he became much worse, and returned home, being confined to his bed until Friday, September 27th, growing gradually weaker and weaker. Upon that day he was taken with attacks of heart failure. He was removed to Tucson to the Sisters' Hospital, where he died Saturday morning, the 28th.

The remains were returned to Benson Sunday, and Monday morning, September 30th, the obsequies were attended by a large concourse of citizens from all parts of Cochise county, with many sorrowing friends from adjoining counties. The funeral services were conducted by Right Reverend Bishop Granjon of the diocese of Arizona, assisted by Reverend Father Juan Chacon and Reverend Father J. Gjeldof, the two senior prelates coming to Benson for the special purpose.

Don Jose Miguel Castaneda—"a strong, fearless and picturesque personality, with the freedom of the great plains in mind and action, and possessing a spit of adventure, reckless daring, and unbounded good

The grave of Don Jose Miguel Castaneda, Seventh Street Cemetery, Benson (author's collection).

fellowship"—was survived by his wife, Amparo Arvizo Castaneda, and nine children. He is interred in the Seventh Street Cemetery in Benson, Arizona.[73]

As to the town of Bisbee, the daring and brutal robbery of Goldwater and Castaneda's General Merchandise Emporium would be the final hurrah of the "wild west days" in that burg. As evidenced by the lynching of John Heath, a man who's only proven offense while residing in the Arizona Territory was his tenuous association with some of the men who committed the crime, the residents of Bisbee were not going to allow their community to be overrun, as so many other frontier towns and camps had been prior, by lawless, recusant elements. The community might tolerate a certain amount of vice—gambling, prostitution, opium dens, and the like—but they were not going to tolerate outright criminal behavior or those persons who might involve themselves in such activities. Fortunately, for the town of Bisbee, subsequent advancements and circumstance were favorable to the community's designs.

Metallurgist James A. Douglas had counseled Martin and Ballard and Reilly and, later, his employers at Phelps, Dodge & Co. to purchase the Atlanta mining claim which abutted

Dr. James S. Douglas eventually became president of Copper Queen Consolidated Mining Company and, later C.E.O., at the behest of Phelps, Dodge & Co. and remained in that position until his death in 1918 (author's collection).

the Copper Queen. Phelps and Dodge had taken Douglas' advice and purchased the claim. According to Douglas, the company then proceeded to spend two years and over $60,000 "on exploration that had not yielded a carload of ore." Meanwhile, the owners of the Copper Queen were experiencing hardships as well, as the large ore body they had been a successfully mining, which had been netting about 12 percent copper, was almost "pinched out." The owners of the Copper Queen were "drifting east along [the Atlanta]" and drifting west along the Copper King claim "in search of another ore body."

"Mr. James and Mr. Dodge had become thoroughly disheartened" with the Atlanta mine, but agreed to offer up another $15,000 to Douglas in order to sink one final shaft in the area where a "narrow vein" from the lucrative Copper Queen ore body crossed over on to Atlanta claim. The investment would pay off spectacularly. As Douglas recalled, in July of 1884, "at 210 feet from the surface the shaft penetrated a very rich ore body, which almost simultaneously was entered by the level being driven east" from the Copper Queen claim. Basically, both companies had struck the same enormous ore body of copper-rich malachite at the same time. Douglas had tapped in to the vein from above and the Copper Queen Mining Company had struck it from the east. At this point, Ballard and Reilly, the owners of the Copper Queen claim, and D. Willis James and William Dodge, Jr., the owners of the Atlanta claim, found themselves at an impasse.

The law of the apex, which was universally recognized, stated that the owner of one claim could follow a newly discovered vein into an adjoining claim owned by another. As both companies could claim rights under this law, it seemed as if there might be a protracted legal battle. As neither the owners of the Atlanta claim nor the owners of the Copper Queen wanted to engage in such litigation, the two companies began a series of negotiations. Finally, according to Douglas, a "consolidation was made of the two companies and their holdings" and, of this merger, the Copper Queen Consolidated Mining Company was born. Not long after, James and Dodge bought out Mr. Martin and Mr. Reilly, increasing their ownership in the company from two-sevenths to nine-tenths. Phelps, Dodge & Co. also bought out a number of the surrounding claims, including the Dividend and the Neptune, owned by Holbrook and Cave.

James Douglas, who had initially been given 10 percent ownership in the Atlanta as remuneration for his consulting work for Phelps, Dodge & Co. was made president of the new Copper Queen Consolidated Mining Company. Over the next few years Phelps, Dodge & Co. would buy up the majority of the other outstanding claims in Mule Pass, including the Copper King, the Baxter, the Hendricks, the Rucker, and the remaining holdings of the Holbrook and Cave Company. Before long the majority of the properties in the area were under the auspices of the Copper Queen Consolidated Mining Company. By 1887, the company had upgraded its operations in Bisbee by building a new smelter with four state-of-the-art furnaces, capable of producing well over a million pounds of copper a month.

In 1888, after Thomas Nickerson, president of the Atchison, Topeka, and Santa Fe Railroad refused to build a line into Bisbee, Phelps, Dodge & Co. began work on the Arizona and South Eastern Railroad, connecting Bisbee directly to the Santa Fe line in Fairbank. The railway project, completed in February of the following year, not only allowed the Copper Queen Consolidated Mining Company to more easily and cost-effectively freight in needed equipment and materials and freight out its product, it also allowed for an influx of consumer goods and sundries, which prior to then had been nearly unattainable to the majority of the community. Ironically, even after the line had been completed, people traveling to and from Bisbee were still obliged to make the journey by stagecoach or other horse-drawn conveyances.[74]

In 1902, the town of Bisbee was incorporated. In his book about Bisbee, Carlos A. Schwantes asserts that "Bisbee was never a company town in the strictest sense," but, in fact, Phelps, Dodge & Co. (which dispensed with the Copper Queen Consolidated Mining Company name after the company re-structured in 1908) exerted considerable control over everything which it did not own outright. Schwantes explained that Bisbee "established a municipal government, police and fire departments, and chamber of commerce" which he concedes were "more or less independent of the company." In an exposé about the town, published in July of 1891 by *The Arizona Weekly Citizen*, the author writes of how "everything is conducted on a gigantic and most systematic plan" conceived of and implemented by Phelps, Dodge & Co. Of the 2,000 residents residing in Bisbee, the reporter estimated that about 600 worked in the Copper Queen mine (at an average wage of $3.50 a day). Yet even those persons whose livelihoods were not directly under the control of the company were still obliged to submit to the company's direction.

Bisbee, Arizona Territory, circa 1903, the year after the town was incorporated. In 1929, the town became the county seat (Arizona Historical Society, 27800).

The Citizen's correspondent exuberantly described the new two-story company store being constructed—replete with elevators, telephones, speaking tubes, and electric light— to replace the existing one. He described the store which was to be replaced as "one of the most general trading establishments in Southern Arizona, always having on hand a stock of about everything needed by anyone." He also made mention of the hospital with its "friendly shelter, and services of physicians [partially maintained by a $1 deduction from the monthly wages of each man] and the local library, which held about "1,000 volumes comprising standard authors … many of the best periodicals, magazines, and large newspapers of America and Europe, and all of the local organs"—all of which were constructed and operated at the behest of Phelps, Dodge & Co.

The author of the article did give mention to some of the local, independent businesses and business owners, such as S. Berkowitz, who "conducts the most extensive trade outside the company's store," as well as B. Carlitto and V.G. Medigovich, who sold groceries and other provisions. Also noted were I.W. Wallace's cigar store, the Can-Can Restaurant, Muhein and Dubacher's Mountain Brewery, Abraham Fribolet's butcher's shop, Perkins & Co. Drugstore, and the O.K. Stable, for those needing a horse or a wheeled conveyance. Additionally, construction was under way on the new Catholic Church. Not surprisingly, the author makes no mention of the numerous saloons and brothels operating

Oldest known photograph of Brewery Gulch, Bisbee, where the red light district and gambling halls were relegated to before they were finally closed down forever (Arizona Historical Society, 52976).

up and down Brewery Gulch. As author and historian Patrick Murphin asserted, "The professional class was just as dependent on the company as the underground miners. Only the bars, whorehouses, and opium dens were truly independent."[75]

However, even these businesses—the brothels, saloons, gambling houses, and other "vice dens"—were forcibly regulated by the city fathers, who were in turn beholden to Phelps, Dodge & Co. These more prurient enterprises were relegated to a certain zone within the town—specifically, an area at the upper end of Brewery Gulch—and were systematically licensed and taxed by the county and the city. Those businesses or persons who defied the authority of powers-that-be—those who flagrantly flaunted or broke the law—were arrested by peace officers and fined by local magistrates. In more extreme cases, the offending business or persons were simply chased out of town. The fact was, from the upstanding, legitimate businesses to the more bawdy and salacious enterprises, everything was being operated under the auspices and with the sanction of Phelps, Dodge & Co.

In its early years, the population of Bisbee was overwhelmingly male. Those who governed and controlled the town understood that the men who were employed in the mines needed some form of amusement in their off-hours, whether it be drinking, gambling, or visits to the brothels. In order to keep the men placated, Phelps, Dodge & Co. and the local government were willing to allow those businesses which catered to the men's baser desires and needs. However, the city fathers were equally determined not to allow Bisbee to become a wild frontier town like Tombstone or Clifton, where criminality

Top: Bisbee's Main Street, where the robbery took place, in the early 1900s. Most of the original buildings, including Castaneda's General Merchandise Emporium, had been lost to fire or flood or torn down. *Bottom:* Bisbee's Main Street today (2016) (author's collection).

and lawlessness were accepted and murder and theft were common occurrences. To this end, they put in place laws which served to keep the town from being overrun by the so-called "sporting crowd" and other undesirable elements.

To further combat the possible ascendancy of lawlessness and wickedness in Bisbee, the mining interests, specifically Phelps, Dodge & Co., began actively recruiting and employing married men and their families, as opposed to the transient or "tramp" miners, who would drift from camp to camp, had few, if any, ties to the community, and had little regard for the prevailing social order. Married men—men with familial responsibilities and obligations—were considered to be more reliable workers and more likely to settle in town and engage in community building. Married men were also thought to be more likely to re-invest their hard-earned wages in the enterprises and endeavors, such as churches, schools, and other public works projects, which benefited the community at large, as opposed to further financing the saloons and brothels and gambling houses.

As the years passed, city ordinances were introduced to further curtail and control vice operations within the town. By way of example, in February of 1902, immediately after the town was incorporated, the Bisbee City Council passed a resolution that forbade women from frequenting saloons altogether. Women were not allowed "to sing, dance, recite, or play on any musical instrument, give any theatrical performance [or] serve as waitress or barmaid or take part … in any game of chance or amusement played in a saloon."

Reproduction of the woodcut of hanging that appeared in the *Arizona Citizen*. The original wood block from which the print was taken has been lost (reproduction by author).

Boothill Cemetery, Tombstone, Arizona, where lie the remains of the Bisbee bandits (though it is uncertain exactly where the five outlaws are buried) (author's collection).

Though the ordinance did not state so specifically, its purpose was to keep the prostitutes from plying their trade outside of the red light district. Just eight years later, the City Council had garnered enough support to pass Ordinance No. 153 which finally closed the brothels and cribs at the top of Brewery Gulch forever.

This is not to say crime was completely eradicated in the town of Bisbee. As evidenced by police records and court dockets from 1884 onward, the town still had its fair share of misdeeds and malfeasance. Between the day of the robbery in 1883 and 1902, the year the town was incorporated, there were a number of murders committed, but the majority of these, if not all, were the result of domestic disputes, arguments over unpaid debts, over-reactions to perceived slights, or any number of other petty disagreements. The town would never again see a crime comparable in its brazenness, recklessness, and murderousness to the Bisbee Massacre.

In 1912, just 12 days before Arizona would officially be welcomed into the union that was the United States of America, *The Coconino Sun* reported that a singular relic of the old territorial days had been discovered in Tombstone. The wooden scaffold on which Dan "Big Dan" Dowd, William Delaney, Omer W. "Red" Sample, Daniel "York" Kelly, and James "Tex" Howard were hanged, as well as Messrs. William and Thomas Halderman, convicted of murdering Constable Ainsworth in 1899, was found in the County Courthouse, where it had been stored after being dismantled for the last time in 1905.

Unfortunately, as the Flagstaff newspaper reported, the old scaffold was "no more. The last of it was cut up to furnish kindling wood for the fires in the county jail" just the week before.[76]

Then, in January of 1952, a woodcut made at the time of the hanging of Dowd, Delaney, Sample, Kelly, and Howard was found in the archives at the Acme Printing Company in Tucson. The printing block was quite primitive, having been whittled with a jackknife into the surface of an ordinary piece of hardwood by some "enterprising and imaginative printer." The block was originally used by *The Arizona Weekly Citizen* as an accompanying illustration to the article they published about the hanging in the edition of March 15, 1884. At the time the illustration was published, it was lambasted by the editor of the rival newspaper, *The Arizona Daily Star*, who said, "it was fortunate ... that the cut was not published before the hanging, for if the gang had seen it they would have certainly committed suicide to have escaped such a representation after death." While the editor of *The Star* went on to sarcastically praise the illustration as "very credible for our evening contemporary," today, it is something very special: that small wooden printing block is the only remaining artifact from that fateful day, aside from the graves of the deceased out along Interstate 80 in the Boothill Cemetery.[77]

Chapter Notes

Prologue

1. Douglas D. Martin, *Tombstone's Epitaph* (Albuquerque: University of New Mexico Press, 1951), pp. 245–246. Thus far, a typescript of Bogg's account of the lynching of John Heath which Martin cites in his book has not been found.

2. Carl Chafin, ed., *The Private Journal of George Whitwall Parsons Volume II: The Tombstone Years 1879–1887* (Tombstone, AZ: Cochise Classics, 1997), p. 176.

3. Harriet Hankin, "*The Bisbee Hold Up and Its Aftermath,*" Unpublished, undated manuscript. A longtime Bisbee resident, Ms. Hankin was fortunate enough to be able to interview several witnesses to the events surrounding the Bisbee Massacre, including James Krigbaum, H.M. Woods, and Mrs. H.M. Woods. Ms. Haskin's typescript, may have been published in the December 14, 1927, edition of *The Bisbee Evening Ore* newspaper, of which there are no extant copies.

Chapter One

1. Returns from Regular Cavalry Regiments, 1833–1916, 6th Cavalry, 1875–1880, roll 63, National Archives Microfilm, University of Arizona Library, Tucson.

2. James F. Duncan, "Stories of the Early Days of Cochise County," *The Bisbee Daily Review*, 19 November 1911, p. 9.

3. "Notice of Location Rucker Mine," Records of Pima County, book B, p. 693, transcribed Records Book 1, p. 100, Arizona State Library, Archives and Public Records, Record Group 101, SG 5, Office of the Cochise County Recorders (includes deeds of mines transcripted from Pima County), 1866–1881.

4. "George Warren," *The Arizona Weekly Enterprise*, 11 July 1901, Hayden File 1835—, The Arizona Historical Society; James Hart, *History of George Warren* (Biofile, 1926, Unpublished typeset held by The Arizona Historical Society).

5. "Mercey [*sic*] Notice of Location," Records of Pima County, Book B, p. 719, transcribed Records Book 1, p. 113 (The Arizona State Library, Archives and Public Records list the Book as B and the page as 705, but the original document is not extant); James F. Duncan, "Stories of the Early Days of Cochise County," *The Bisbee Daily Review*, 19 November 1911, p. 9.

6. Mining claims which George Warren staked himself or witnessed for others may be found in the Arizona State Library, Archives and Public Records. Record Group 101, SG 5, Office of the Cochise County Recorders, 1866–1881; James F. Duncan, "Stories of the Early Days of Cochise County," *The Bisbee Daily Review*, 19 November 1911, p. 9.

7. "Copper Queen Mine Notice of Location," Records of Pima County, Book B, p. 574. Transcribed Records Book 6, p. 627; Lynn R. Bailey, *Bisbee: Queen of the Copper Camps* (Tucson, AZ: Westernlore Press, 1983), pp. 15–16.

8. "Halero, et al. to George H. Eddleman, et al.," Cochise County Deed of Mines, Book 6, p. 662, and "Marcus F. Herring to George Klein and G.H. Anshurtz," Book 5, pp. 123–125, Arizona State Library, Archives and Public Records, Record Group 101, SG 5, Office of the Cochise County Recorders, 1866–1881; "Copper King Mine" and "Copper Queen Mine," Location Notices, Pima County Recorder's Office Record Books, Record Group 101, SG 5. Book K, pp. 271–271, 2745, Arizona State Library, Archives and Public Records; James F. Duncan, "Stories of the Early Days of Cochise County," *The Bisbee Daily Review*, 19 November 1911, p. 9.

9. Annie M. Cox, *History of Bisbee 1877 to 1937* (Tucson: Dissertation, Graduate College, University of Arizona, 1938), pp. 8–9; "George Warren to George Atkins," Records of Deeds to Mines, Pima County, Book 1, pp. 631–636, and Book 6, p. 774, Arizona State Library, Archives and Public Records, Record Group 101, SG 5, Office of the Cochise County Recorders, 1866–1881.

10. Cox, pp. 21–22; Bailey, p. 51; James F. Duncan, "First Restaurant," *The Bisbee Daily Review*, 3 August 1931, p. 7.

11. James F. Duncan, "Stories of the Early Days of Cochise County," *The Bisbee Daily Review*, 12 November 1911, p. 9.

12. "Bisbee City," *The Arizona Weekly Citizen*, 16 October 1880, p. 1; "Bisbee City," *The Arizona Weekly Citizen*, 18 September 1880, p. 1.

13. Bailey, p. 23. "Neptune Mine & Excelsior Mine," Pima County Recorders Office Record Books, Book C, pp. 117–118, Arizona State Library, Archives and Public Records, Record Group101, SG 5, Office of the Cochise County Recorders, 1866–1881.

14. "Col. Herring Passes Away Full of Days," *The Arizona Republic*, 11 July 1912, p. 1; John S. Goff, *Arizona Territorial Officials V: The Adjuncts General, Attorneys General, Auditors, Superintendents of Public Instruction, and Treasurers* (Swannanoa, NC: Black Mountain Press, 1975), pp. 72–73; "Final Disposition of the Earp Case," *The Tombstone Daily Epitaph*, 20 February 1882, p. 2; "Leslie's Luck," *The Tombstone Weekly Epitaph*, 18 November 1882, p. 1.

15. Cox, pp. 16–21; "Marcus F. Herring, et al. to Edward Reilly" and "George W. Atkins, et al. to Edward Reilly," Cochise County Deed of Mines, Book 4, pp. 523–526, 530–536. Transcribed Records Book 1, p. 15. Arizona State Library, Archives and Public Records, Record Group 101, SG 5, Office of the Cochise County Recorders, 1866–1881.

16. Bailey, p. 19.

17. William B. Elper, *Bisbee Vignettes* (Bisbee, AZ: Copper Queen Publishing Company, 1978).

18. "Death of D.W.F. Bisbee," *The Evening Bulletin*, 9 May 1885, p. 2; James F. Duncan, "Rush to Camp," *The Bisbee Daily Review*, 3 August 1931, p. 7; Larry D. Ball, *Desert Lawman: The High Sheriffs of New Mexico and Arizona, 1846–1912* (Albuquerque: University of New Mexico Press, 1992), p. 351.

19. James Douglas, *Notes on the Development of Phelps, Dodge & Co.'s Copper and Railroad Interests* (Bisbee, AZ: Frontera House Press, 1906). Reprinted in 1995.

20. Sylvio Leblond, "Douglas, James (1800–86)," in *Dictionary of Canadian Biography* 11 (Toronto: University of Toronto/Université Laval, 2003), accessed December 22, 2013, http://www.biographi.ca/en/bio/douglas_james_1800_86_11E.html.

21. Bailey, pp. 85–86; "Murder Most Foul," *The Weekly Arizona Citizen*, 9 October 1880, p. 2.

22. Henry P. Walker and Don Bufkin, *Historical Atlas of Arizona, 2nd Ed* (Norman: University of Oklahoma Press, 1986), p. 32; "Eleventh Legislative Assembly," *The Weekly Arizona Miner*, 18 February 1881, p. 2.

23. "Dividends," *Engineering and Mining Journal, Vol. 32* (Chicago: University of Chicago Press, 1881), p. 16; Bailey, pp. 26–27.

24. Phelps Dodge Corporation History, *International Directory of Company Histories, Vol. 28* (St. James, MO: St. James Press, 1990). Retrieved December 10, 2011 from www.funduniverse.com.company histories.Phelps-Dodge-Corporation-Company-History.html.

25. Cox, pp. 32–33; "Territorial News Notes," *The Arizona Weekly Citizen*, 22 January 1881, p. 3; "Charleston to Bisbee," *The Arizona Weekly Citizen*, 13 March 1881, p. 1; "Tombstone Topics," *The Arizona Weekly Citizen*, 28 August 1881, p. 4.

26. *The Arizona Weekly Citizen*, 6 March, 1881, p. 2. Reprinted from *The Tombstone Daily Epitaph*. Bailey, pp. 86–87. Bailey, quoting James Duncan, identified the men involved in the February 26, 1881, shooting as "A. Jordan and Peter Hogan" while the *Arizona Weekly Citizen* identified them as "James Jourdan and Ben Hogan,"

27. "Atlanta," Location Notice, Pima County Recorder's Office Record Books, Book G, p. 227, Arizona State Library, Archives and Public Records, Record Group 101, SG 5, Office of the Cochise County Recorders, 1866–1881; "G.A. Atkins, et al. to A.A. White, et al.," Records of Deeds to Mines, Pima County, Book 3, pp. 133–136, Arizona State Library, Archives and Public Records, Record Group 101, SG 5, Office of the Cochise County Recorders, 1866–1881; Charles K. Hyde, *Copper for America: The United States Copper Industry from Colonial Times to the 1990s* (Tucson: University of Arizona Press, 1998), pp. 125–126.

28. "J.B. Smithham, et al. to G.E. Dodge, Jr., et al.," Records of Deeds to Mines, Pima County. Book 3, pp. 220–225, Arizona State Library, Archives and Public Records, Record Group 101, SG 5, Office of the Cochise County Recorders, 1866–1881, Office of the Cochise County Recorders, 1866–1881; James F. Duncan, "Some Interesting and Important Happenings During the First Year," *The Bisbee Daily Review*, 3 December 1911, pp. 1, 5–6.

29. "The Vote of Cochise County by Precincts," *The Tombstone Weekly Epitaph*, 11 November 1882, p. 3; James F. Duncan, "Unfought Duel," *The Bisbee Daily Review*, 3 August 1931, p. 7.

30. "Arizona-Bisbee-Camp-Thomas," *McKenney's 1883 Business Directory of the Principle Towns of Central and Southern California, Arizona, New Mexico, Southern Colorado, and Kansas* (Oakland, CA: Pacific Press Publishers), p. 268; Opie Rundle-Burgess, *Bisbee Not so Long Ago* (San Antonio, TX: The Naylor Company, 1967), p. 58.

31. "Bisbee," *The Tombstone Republican*, 6 October 1883, p. 1, 3–4.

32. Cox, pp. 87–95; James F. Duncan, *The Bisbee Daily Review*, 3 August 1931, p. 7; Bailey, p. 23.

33. "Bullets at Bisbee," *The Arizona Daily Citizen*, 21 January 1883, p. 1.

34. *The Arizona Weekly Citizen*, 21 May 1882, p. 1; "Cow-boys," *The Arizona Weekly Citizen*, 11 December 2012, p. 4. Re-printed from the *Prescott Democrat*.

35. "Relief for Arizona," *The Arizona Weekly Citizen*, 12 February 1882, p. 2; "Pencil Points," *The Arizona Weekly Citizen*, 30 July 1882, p. 4.

36. *The Arizona Weekly Citizen* carried numerous reports of the continuation of cowboy depredations throughout southern Arizona after the exit of the

Earp brother. For specific incidents see the issues of 15 May, 19 May, 14 July, 28 July, and 8 September 1883; "Telegraph," *The Arizona Weekly Citizen*, 4 August 1883, p. 1; "A Yankee Odyssey," *Journal of Arizona History* 30, no. 1 (1989): 80; "Telegraph," *The Arizona Weekly Citizen*, 1 December 1883, p. 1; "The Situation in Clifton," *The Arizona Weekly Citizen*, 1 December 1883, p. 4.

37. Information on the town of Clifton, Arizona, primarily derived from: James M. Patton, *History of Clifton* (Clifton, AZ: Greenlee Historical Society, 2008).

38. John Boessenecker, *When Law Was in the Holster* (Norman: University of Oklahoma Press, 2012), pp. 261–262.

39. Dean Smith, *The Goldwaters of Arizona* (Flagstaff, AZ: Northland Press, 1986), pp. 71–87.

40. "Joseph Goldwater & The Goldwater Affair," *The Arizona Weekly Citizen*, 20 February 1881, pp. 1–2; "The Truth," *The Weekly Arizona Miner*, 25 February 1881, p. 4; "Discharge of Goldwater," *The Arizona Weekly Citizen*, 5 April 1881, p. 3; Smith, pp. 71–87; "Bad Joseph Goldwater," *The San Francisco Examiner*, 29 January 1881, p. 1.

41. "Jose Miguel Castaneda," *Portrait and Biographical Record of Arizona* (Chicago: Chapman Publishing, 1904), pp. 902–907; Audrey Mac Hunter and Randall Henderson, "Boom Days in Old La Paz," *Desert Magazine*, 1958.

42. "From Ehrenberg," *The Arizona Citizen*, 9 August 1873, p. 3; "Recapitulation," *The Arizona Sentinel*, 21 November 1874, p. 2; "Letter from Colonel Hodge," *The Arizona Sentinel*, 27 May 1876, p. 2.

43. "McCrackin and Signal," *The Arizona Sentinel*, 6 July 1878, p. 1; "Freight Arrivals," *The Arizona Sentinel*, 25 May 1878, p. 3; "Local Matters," *The Arizona Sentinel*, p. 3; "Freight Arrivals," *The Arizona Sentinel*, 8 May 1879, p. 3 and 24 May 1879, p. 3.

44. Nathan W. Waite, *Tenth Census of the United States, 1880* (NARA microfilm publication T9, 1,454 rolls), Records of the Bureau of the Census, Record Group 29, National Archives, Washington, D.C., Census Place: *Wash District Pat'A Mountains, Pima, Arizona*, roll 36, Family History Film: 1254036, p. 240C, Enumeration District 004, image 0495; Boessenecker, p. 261; James F. Duncan, "Setting the Scene," *The Bisbee Daily Review*, November 1911, p. 9.

Chapter Two

1. "Delaney 'Dead to Rights,'" *The Tombstone Republican*, January 1884, p. 3; "William Gerstenberg," *The Tombstone Daily Epitaph*, 12 February 1884, p. 4. During the subsequent trial, statements were made by Deputy Sheriff Daniels and William Gerstenberg which indicated that two of the robbers, William Delaney and Daniel "York" Kelly were seen in town just prior to the robbery, probably on a reconnaissance mission. However, most eyewitnesses agreed the outlaws all rode in together. It may then be assumed that, after reconnoitering the town, De-

laney and Kelly rode back out to meet their confederates and then rode back into town with them.

2. Harriet W. Hankin, "*The Bisbee Holdup and Its Aftermath*" (Unpublished, undated manuscript), MS. 0329, Harriet Warning File, Arizona Historical Society. (This manuscript may have been published previously in *The Bisbee Evening Ore*, 14 December 1927, but the author has hereto been unable to locate an extant copy of this newspaper); James F. Duncan, "Some of the Murders and Other Crimes Committed during the Early History of the Warren District," *Bisbee Daily Review*, 26 November 1911, p. 1.

3. "Richard Rundle," *The Tombstone Republican*, February 1884, p. 1.

4. "H.M. Hartson," *The Tombstone Republican*, February 1884, p. 1; Raiding Rustlers, *The Tombstone Republican*, December 1883, p. 1; "Joe Goldwater," *The Tombstone Republican*, February 1884, p. 1; Smith, pp. 81–82.

5. "Richard Rundle," *The Tombstone Daily Epitaph*, 10 February 1884, p. 4; "H.M. Hartson," *The Tombstone Republican*, February 1884, p. 1; "Raiding Rustlers," *The Tombstone Republican*, December 1883, p. 1; "Telegraph," *The Arizona Weekly Citizen*, 15 December 1883, p. 1.

6. "Joe Goldwater in the Hands of the Philistines," *The Tombstone Republican*, December 1883, p. 3. Whether or not this exchange actually occurred is open to debate, but it is entertaining and so was included by the author in the narrative.

7. "H.M. Hartson," *The Tombstone Republican*, February 1884, p. 1; "Richard Rundle," *The Tombstone Republican*, February 1884, p. 1.

8. Harkin, p. 6; Cox, p. 55; "H.M. Hartson," *The Tombstone Republican*, February 1884, p. 1; Scott Brown (Ranger), *Collection of Arizona Historical Articles* (Buckskin Mountains, AZ: Arizona Print, 1890), p. 2.

9. "Raiding Rustlers," *The Tombstone Republican*, December 1883, p. 1; "In the Matter of the Estate of D.T. Smith, deceased, January Term 1884," Cochise County District Court Probate Minutes, p. 532; "H.M. Hartson," *The Tombstone Republican*, February 1884, p. 1; Harkin, p. 8; "J.W. Howell," *The Tombstone Republican*, February 1884, p. 1; "Walter Bush," *The Tombstone Daily Epitaph*, 10 February 1884, p. 4; Brown, pp. 2–3.

10. "Raiding Rustlers," *The Tombstone Republican*, December 1883, p. 1; "Telegraph," *The Arizona Weekly Citizen*, 15 December 1883, p. 1.

11. "Deputy Sheriff W.A. Daniels," *The Tombstone Republican*, February 1884, p. 1; "The Bisbee Banditti," *The Tombstone Republican*, December 1883, p. 3.

12. "Will Hang!," *The Tombstone Daily Epitaph*, 17 February 1884; "The Loop!," *The Tombstone Daily Epitaph*, 19 February 1884, p. 4.

13. "No Hope!," *The Tombstone Republican*, February 1884, p. 1; "The Loop!," *The Tombstone Daily Epitaph*, 19 February 1884, p. 4.

14. Harkin, pp. 3–4; "Telegraph," *The Arizona*

Weekly Citizen, 15 December 1883, p. 1. It has been suggested that Mrs. Annie Roberts was not a target, but rather was hit by a bullet intended either for Indian Joe or Deputy Sheriff William Daniels.

15. Harkin, pp. 5, 9.

16. "Deputy Sheriff W.A. Daniels," *The Tombstone Republican*, February 1884, p. 1; "The Bisbee Banditti," *The Tombstone Republican*, December 1883, p. 3; "Richard Rundle," *The Tombstone Republican*, February 1884, p. 1; "John Hiles," *The Tombstone Republican*, February 1884, p. 1.

17. "William Gerstenberg," *The Tombstone Daily Epitaph*, 12 February 1884, p. 4; "William Gerstenberg," *The Tombstone Republican*, February 1994, p. 1.

18. "Deputy Sheriff W.A. Daniels," *The Tombstone Republican*, February 1884, p. 1; Harkins, p. 9; "Raiding Rustlers," *The Tombstone Republican*, December 1883, p. 1.

19. Brown, p. 3; "Mr. Rundle," *The Tombstone Republican*, February 1884, p. 1; "H.M. Hartson," *The Tombstone Republican*, February 1884, p. 1; "Telegraph," *The Arizona Weekly Citizen*, 15 December 1883, p. 1; Hankin, pp. 11–12.

20. Brown, p. 5.

21. Tombstone Inquest Record, Territory of Arizona Vs. John Heath, Carl Chafin Research Collection, MS. 1274, F. 67, held by the Arizona Historical Society, Tucson.

22. *Ibid.*

23. *Ibid.*

24. *Ibid.*

25. "Raiding Rustlers," *The Tombstone Republican*, December 1883, p. 1.

26. *Ibid.*

27. Edward C. Godnig, "Vision and Shooting," *The Police Policies Study Council*, 2004. Retrieved 5 July 2014, from http://www.theppsc.org/Staff_Views/Godnig/vision_and_shooting.htm.

28. "H.M. Hartson," *The Tombstone Republican*, February 1884, p. 1.

Chapter Three

1. "Telegraph," *The Arizona Weekly Citizen*, 15 December 1883, p. 1.

2. *Ibid*; "Raiding Rustlers," *The Tombstone Republican*, p. 1.

3. "Will Hang!," *The Tombstone Daily Epitaph*, 17 February 1884, p. 4; "The Loop!," *The Tombstone Daily Epitaph*, 19 February 1884, p. 4; "Relic Brings to Light Something New About John Heath," John Heath Vertical File, Arizona State Library, Archives and Public Records.

4. "Raiding Rustlers," *The Tombstone Republican*, p. 1; Clay Thompson, "Soldier's Hole: Old West Pit Stop," *The Arizona Republic*, 21 July 2008. Retrieved on 13 January 2014 from http://www.azcentral.com/arizonarepublic/arizonaliving/articles/2008/07/21/20080721azhist0721.html.

5. "Raiding Rustlers," *The Tombstone Republi-can*; "Raided by Mounted Men," *New York Times*, 10 December 1883.

6. "News by Wire," *The Weekly Arizona Miner*, 30 November 1883, pp. 2–3.

7. "Local Matters," *The Arizona Sentinel*, 1 December 1883, p. 3.

8. "The Gage Station Train Robbers," *Sacramento Daily Record Union*, 13 December 1883, p. 2; "Telegraph," *Arizona Weekly Citizen*, 15 December 1883, p. 2.

9. "Telegraph," *Arizona Weekly Citizen*, 15 December 1883, p. 2.

10. *Ibid.*

11. "Return of the Posse," *The Tombstone Republican*, December 1883, p. 2.

12. William A. Daniels, Find-A-Grave, Memorial # 38777593, created by Alice Daniels, record added 26 June 2009. Retrieved 28 December 2014 from http://www.findagrave.com/cgi-bin/fg.cgi?page=gr&GRid=38777593; William B. Daniels, *Tenth Census of the United States, 1880* (NARA microfilm publication T9, 1,454 rolls), Records of the Bureau of the Census, Record Group 29, National Archives, Washington, D.C., Census Place: Baracomari Valley, Pima, Arizona; Roll: 36; Family History Film: 1254036; p. 236D; Enumeration District: 004; Image: 0488.

13. "$5000 Reward (advertisement)," *The Tombstone Republican*, December 1883, p. 2.

14. Anton Mazzanovich, *Trailing Geronimo* (Los Angeles, CA: Haynes Corp., 1931); Anton Mazzanovich, "The Bisbee Store Hold-Up," *Progressive Arizona*, August 1926, pp. 11, 33, and continued in September 1926, pp. 27–28. In the article, Mazzanovich, who was a writer later in life, puts himself at the center of the action and paints himself as the hero of the tale. It is likely that much of his story is romanticized. It is hard to determine what his level of involvement in the arrest of Daniel Kelly truly was.

15. "Telegraph," *The Arizona Weekly Citizen*, 15 December 1883, p. 1; "Return of the Posse," *The Tombstone Republican*, December 1883, p. 2.

16. Hankin, p. 18.

17. "Arrested on Suspicion," *The Tombstone Republican*, December 1883, p. 3; "Telegraph," *The Arizona Weekly Citizen*, 15 December 1883, p. 2.

18. "Telegraph," *The Arizona Weekly Citizen*, 15 December 1883, p. 2; "The Train Robbers," *The Tombstone Republican*, December 1883, p. 2; "Arrested on Suspicion," *The Tombstone Republican*, December 1883, p. 3.

19. "Telegraph," *The Arizona Weekly Citizen*, 22 December 1883, p. 1.

20. "The Robbers' Trail," *The Arizona Weekly Citizen*, 22 December 1883, p. 3.

21. *Ibid.*

22. "Telegraph," *The Arizona Weekly Citizen*, 22 December 1883, p. 1; "Sheriff Ward," *The Arizona Champion*, 1 December 1883, p. 2.

23. "Bisbee Murderer Caught," *The Arizona Weekly Champion*, 22 December 1883, p. 2; "Telegraph," *The Arizona Weekly Citizen*, 22 December 1883, p. 1.

24. "Telegraph," *The Arizona Weekly Citizen*, 25 February 1883, p. 2; George M. Ellis, "Sheriff Jerome L. Ward and the Bisbee Massacre of 1883," *The Journal of Arizona History* 35, no. 3 (1994): 317–318; "We understand…," *The Tombstone Weekly Epitaph*, p. 2; Seymour and Christine Rose, Jerome L Ward, Biofile, Arizona Historical Society, 1963.

25. Ellis, pp. 317–319. There are a number of good books about the Earp/cowboy feud. The author recommends Paula Mitchell Marks, *And Die in the West: The Story of the O.K. Corral Gunfight* (Norman: University of Oklahoma Press, 1989). *The Arizona Weekly Citizen* ran a number of articles concerning Jerome Ward's tenure as Cochise County Sheriff including January 21 and 26, April 1, May 19, October 27, November 10, December 8, 1883.

26. "Telegraph," *The Arizona Weekly Citizen*, 22 December 1883, p. 1; "Bisbee's 45–60s," *The Tombstone Republican*, January 1884, p. 3.

27. "Telegraph," *The Arizona Weekly Citizen*, 15 December 1883, p. 2.

28. "Telegraph," *The Arizona Weekly Citizen*, 29 December 1883, p. 2.

29. "Telegraph," *The Arizona Weekly Citizen*, 22 December 1883, p. 2.

30. *Ibid.*

31. "Well Done," *The Arizona Weekly Citizen*, 22 December 1883, p. 2.

32. "Graham County Troubles," *The Tombstone Republican*, December 1883, p. 3.

33. "Big Red Sample," *The Tombstone Republican*, December 1883, p. 2.

34. "The Train Robbers," *The Arizona Weekly Citizen*, 29 December 1883, p. 4.

35. "Return of the Posse," *The Tombstone Republican*, December 1883, p. 2; "Dowd and Delaney," *The Arizona Silverbelt*, 5 January 1884, p. 3.

36. "In the Toils," *The Tombstone Republican*, January 1884, p. 1; "Telegraph," *The Arizona Weekly Citizen*, 12 January 1884, p. 1.

37. "In the Toils," *The Tombstone Republican*, January 1884, p. 1; "A Dishonorable Assassin," *The Tombstone Republican*, December 1883, p. 2.

38. "The Train Robbers," *The Tombstone Republican*, January 1884, p. 1; "A negro by the name…," *The Arizona Silver Belt*, 12 January 1884, p. 4.

39. "Republican Echoes," *The Tombstone Republican*, January 1884, p. 2; *The Arizona Champion*, 19 January 1884, p. 2.

40. "Telegraph," *The Arizona Weekly Citizen*, 12 January 1884, p. 3; "Sample and Howard Arraigned," *The Tombstone Republican*, December 1883, p. 1.

41. "Big Dan in the Prisoner's Dock," *The Tombstone Republican*, January 1884, p. 3.

42. "Telegraph," *The Arizona Weekly Citizen*, 12 January 1884, p. 3.

43. William M. Breckenridge, *Helldorado: Bringing Law to the Mesquite* (Boston: Houghton Mifflin, 1928), p. 197.

44. "Delaney Caught," *The Arizona Weekly Citizen*, 19 January 1883, p. 3.

45. "Is Delaney Captured?," *The Tombstone Republican*, January 1884, p. 3.

46. "Is Delaney Captured," *The Tombstone Republican*, January 1884, p. 3; "Telegraph," *The Arizona Weekly Citizen*, 19 January 1884, p. 1.

47. "Delaney 'Dead to Rights,'" *The Tombstone Republican*, January 1884, p. 3.

48. "Telegraph," *The Arizona Weekly Citizen*, 19 January 1884, p. 2.

49. "A Faithful Officer Rewarded," *The Tombstone Republican*, February 1884, p. 1; "Telegraph," *The Arizona Weekly Citizen*, 12 January 1884, p. 1.

50. "Billy Delaney," *The Tombstone Republican*, January 1884, p. 1; "Bill Delaney," *The Arizona Sentinel*, 26 January 1884, p. 2.

Chapter Four

1. "Telegraph," *The Arizona Weekly Citizen*, 2 February 1884, p. 1.

2. John S. Goff, *Arizona Territorial Officials I: The Supreme Court Justices* (Swannanoa, NC: Black Mountain Press, 1975), pp. 84–87.

3. "The Bisbee Bandits To Be Tried," *New York Times*, 27 December 1883, p. 1; Arizona Statewide Archival and Records Project (1941), *The District Courts of the Territory of Arizona* (Phoenix, AZ: Arizona Statewide Archival and Records Project, held by Arizona State Library, Archives and Public Records), LA 11.2:D 47, p. 25.

4. Coles Bashford, *The Compiled Laws of the Territory of Arizona, Including the Howell Code and the Session Laws from 1864 to 1871* (Albany, NY: Weed, Parsons and Co., 1871), pp. 117–125; "Territory of Arizona vs. Daniel Kelly, et al.," 7 February 1884, The Arizona Historical Society, MS 180, F. 1060, Reel 67; "The Territory of Arizona vs. Dan'l. Dowd, et al.," Criminal Subpoenas, Nos. 165, 166, 167, 168, 6, 9, 11 February 1884, RG 101, SG 4, held by Arizona State Library, Archives and Public Records.

5. "Telegraph," *The Arizona Weekly Citizen*, 16 February 1884, p. 1; "Territory of Arizona vs. Daniel Kelly, et al.," 7 February 1884, The Arizona Historical Society, MS 180, F. 1060, Reel 67; "Territory of Arizona against Daniel Kelly, et al.," Crime of Robbery Indictment, RG 101, SG 4, held by Arizona State Library, Archives and Public Records.

6. "Grand Jury Report," *The Tombstone Republican*, February 1884, p. 1.

7. "Hard Game," *The Tombstone Republican*, January 1884, p. 2.

8. "The Bar of Justice," *The Tombstone Republican*, February 1884, p. 2.

9. Linda Weiland, "Tombstone Courthouse State Historic Park," *The Tombstone Times, 2003–2010* (Tombstone, AZ: Goose Flats Graphics), retrieved 18 May 2015 from www.tombstonetimes.com/stories, courthouse10.html.

10. "Territory of Arizona vs. Dan Dowd," W.B. Sample, J. Howard, D. Kelly, W. Delaney, and John Heith, 7 February, 1884, Minutes of the District Court,

Cochise County, 1882–1887, Books 2 & 3, Case 165, pp. 599–600, Film File 90.5.86, held at Arizona State Library, Archives and Public Records; "The Bar of Justice," *The Tombstone Republican*, February 1884, p. 2.

11. Nathan W. Waite to John Heath (undated), RG 101, SG 4, held by Arizona State Library, Archives and Public Records.

12. Robert Austin to John Heath, 14 January 1884, RG 101, SG 4, held by Arizona State Library, Archives and Public Records.

13. Nathan W. Waite to John Heath, RG 101, SG 4, held by Arizona State Library, Archives and Public Records. John Heath's saddle (#1399), saddlebags (#1397), and pearl-handled, engraved revolver (#1916) are the property of the Arizona Historical Society. Around 1940, the saddle and saddlebags were donated to A.H.S. as a long-term loan by Dr. and Mrs. N.M. Shaw of Cochise Stronghold. The loan was later converted to a gift by Mrs. James B. Shaw, also of Cochise, AZ. The Shaw family received the saddle from Thomas Sorin, who was the son-in-law of William Herring. Thomas Sorin married Sarah Herring in 1898. The Colt Frontier model revolver is said to have come from Selim Franklin, probably Jr., the grandson of William Herring. His mother was Henrietta Herring (another of William's daughters) who married his father, Selim Franklin Sr. in 1898. The A.H.S. records suggest that the pistol was donated by Franklin, Jr., in 1955. Since Selim Franklin, Sr., died in 1927, it must actually have come from Selim, Jr., who was born in 1908. The photographs, which were taken by the author, are used herein with express permission of the Arizona Historical Society.

14. "The Bar of Justice," *The Tombstone Republican*, February 1884, p. 2.

15. "Telegraph," *The Arizona Weekly Citizen*, 16 February 1884, p. 1.

16. "The Bar of Justice," *The Tombstone Republican*, February 1884, p. 2; "Telegraph," *The Arizona Weekly Citizen*, 16 February 1884, p. 1; "Verdict," Territory of Arizona vs. Daniel Kelly, O.W. Sample, James Howard, Dan Dowd, Wm Delaney, 11 February 1884, #165, RG 101, SG 4, held by Arizona State Library, Archives and Public Records.

17. "Affidavit for Continuance," Territory of Arizona vs. Dan'l Kelly, et al., filed 8 February 1884, RG 101, SG 4, held by Arizona State Library, Archives and Public Records.

18. "Affidavit for Continuance," Territory of Arizona vs. O.W. Sample, et al., 8 February 1884, RG 101, SG 4, held by Arizona State Library, Archives and Public Records.

19. "Affidavit of Howard," Territory of Arizona vs. Dowd, Kelly, et al., 8 February 1884, Case 165, RG 101, SG 4, held by Arizona State Library, Archives and Public Records.

20. "The Bar of Justice," *The Tombstone Republican*, February 1884, p. 2.

21. "The Bar of Justice," *The Tombstone Republican*, February 1884, p. 2; Territory of Arizona vs. Dan Dowd, Omer W. Sample, J. Howard, D. Kelly, W. Delaney, and John Heith, February 8 1884, Minutes of the District Court, Cochise County, 1882–1887, Case 165, Books 2 and 3, p. 106, Film File 90.5.86, held at Arizona State Library, Archives and Public Records.

22. "Behind the Bars," *The Arizona Weekly Citizen*, 2 February 1884, p. 2; "One of the Gage Train Robbers," *The Arizona Champion*, 26 January 1884, p 1.

23. "Behind the Bars," *The Arizona Weekly Citizen*, 2 February 1884, p. 2.

24. "The Gage Gang," *The Tombstone Republican*, February 1884, p. 1.

25. *The Arizona Champion* (reprinted from *The Tombstone Daily Epitaph*), 1 March 1884, p. 3.

26. "Trial of the Banditti," *The Tombstone Republican*, February 1884, p. 1.

27. "Doomed: The Shadow of Death Envelopes the Bisbee Murderers," *The Tombstone Daily Epitaph*, 10 February 2014, p. 4.

28. *Ibid.*

29. *Ibid.*

30. "An Act, No 70," *Laws of the Territory of Arizona, Twelfth Legislative Assembly: Also Memorials and Resolutions* (Prescott, AZ: Arizona Miner Steam-Printing Office, 1883), p. 135; John P. Hoyt (compiler), *The Compiled Laws of the Territory of Arizona, 1864–1877: Compiled and Arranged by Authority of an Act of the Legislative Assembly, Approved February 9, 1877* (Detroit; Richmond, Backus & Company, 1887), p. 72.

31. "Doomed: The Shadow of Death Envelopes the Bisbee Murderers," *The Tombstone Daily Epitaph*, 10 February 2014, p. 4.

32. *Ibid.*

33. *Ibid.*

34. *Ibid.*

35. *Ibid.*

36. *Ibid.*

37. *Ibid.*

38. *Ibid.*

39. Hankin, pp. 5, 9; In his book, *Tombstone's Epitaph* (Albuquerque: University of New Mexico Press, 1951), author Douglas D. Martin identified the robbers inside the store as James Howard, Omer W, Sample, and "York" Kelly. Evidence suggests he was correct in this assertion.

40. "An Act, No 70," *Laws of the Territory of Arizona, Twelfth Legislative Assembly: Also Memorials and Resolutions* (Prescott, AZ: Arizona Miner Steam-Printing Office, 1883), p. 135.

41. "Doomed: The Shadow of Death Envelopes the Bisbee Murderers," *The Tombstone Daily Epitaph*, 10 February 2014, p. 4.

42. "Murder," *The Tombstone Daily Epitaph*, 12 February 1884, p. 4; "Found Guilty," *The Tombstone Republican*, February 1884, p. 1. At this time, the two newspapers were published separately by Epitaph Printing and Publishing Co. and W.D. Crow & Co., respectfully. However, both newspapers were under the auspices of editor, Charles Reppy. The newspa-

pers would merge before the end of the year, becoming *Tombstone Daily Epitaph and Republican,* with Reppy and Crowe as the owners. The proceedings of the trial from February 11, 1884, appeared in both newspapers. However, only *the Epitaph* printed the case for the defense.

43. "Found Guilty," *The Tombstone Republican,* February 1884, p. 1.

44. "Murder," *The Tombstone Daily Epitaph,* 12 February 1884, p. 4.

45. "Found Guilty," *The Tombstone Republican,* February 1884, p. 1.

46. "A Dishonorable Assassin," *The Tombstone Republican,* December 1883, p. 2. The more conspiracy-minded among us (such as those who believe Johnny Ringo was killed by someone other than Johnny Ringo) might suggest the aforementioned article was planted by law enforcement in an attempt to divide the loyalties of the gang. I decided against entertaining such notions in this volume.

47. "Murder," *The Tombstone Daily Epitaph,* 12 February 1884, p. 4.

48. *Ibid.*

49. "Trial of the Banditti," *The Tombstone Republican,* February 1884, p. 1.

50. *Ibid.*

51. Territory of Arizona vs. Dan Dowd, W.B. Sample, J. Howard, D. Kelly, W. Delaney, 11th February, 1884, Minutes of the District Court, Cochise County, 1882–1887, Books 2 & 3, Case 165, pp. 609–611, Film File 90.5.86, held at Arizona State Library, Archives and Public Records; "Trial of the Banditti," *The Tombstone Republican,* February 1884, p. 1; "Murder," *The Tombstone Daily Epitaph,* 12 February 1884, p. 4.

52. "Murder," *The Tombstone Daily Epitaph,* 12 February 1884, p. 4.

53. *Ibid.*

54. *Ibid.*

55. *Ibid.*

56. *Ibid.*

57. *Ibid.*

58. *Ibid.*

59. "Murder," *The Tombstone Daily Epitaph,* 12 February 1884, p. 4; Instructions to the Jury from Judge Pinney, RG 101, SG 4, held by Arizona State Library, Archives and Public Records.

60. "Instructions asked by Prosecution," Territory of Arizona vs. Daniel Dowd, et al., RG 101, SG 4, held by Arizona State Library, Archives and Public Records; "Murder," *The Tombstone Daily Epitaph,* 12 February 1884, p. 4.

61. Territory of Arizona vs. Dan Dowd, W.B. Sample, J. Howard, D. Kelly, and W. Delaney, 11 February 1884, Minutes of the District Court, Cochise County, 1882–1887, Case 165, Books 2 & 3, pp. 609–610, Film File 90.5.86, held at Arizona State Library, Archives and Public Records; "Notes," *The Tombstone Daily Epitaph,* 12 February 1884, p. 4; "Law Abiding," *Weekly Phoenix Herald,* 21 February 1884, p. 1.

62. "Notes," *The Tombstone Daily Epitaph,* 12 February 1884, p. 4.

63. "The Bisbee Tragedies," *The Chicago Daily Tribune,* 12 February 1884; "Arizona—The Bisbee Murder Case," The Sacrament Daily Record-Union, 13 February 1884, p. 2; "Telegraphic Briefs," *The Las Vegas Daily Gazette,* 12 February 1884.

64. "The Bisbee Bandits," *The Arizona Silver Belt,* 16 February 1884, p. 2.

65. "Telegraph," *The Arizona Weekly Citizen,* 16 February 1884, p. 2.

Chapter Five

1. Territory of Arizona vs. John Heith. 12th February, 1884, Minutes of the District Court, Cochise County, 1882–1887, Case 165, Books 2 & 3, p. 618, Film File 90.5.86, held at Arizona State Library, Archives and Public Records; "Heith the Accomplice," *The Tombstone Republican,* February 1884, p. 1. In almost all the documents from the court in the various newspapers that covered the proceedings, John Heath's name was spelled incorrectly, as "Heith." Why they persisted in this error is unknown, but family history documents conclusively prove that this latter spelling is incorrect. However, to preserve the integrity of and remain in agreement with the original documents and newspapers, the author has chosen to retain the incorrect spelling (wherever it appeared) in transcribing them. In all other cases, the correct spelling of John Heath's name has been employed.

2. 1850 U.S. Federal Census, Marshall, Harrison, Texas, Roll: M432-911 p. 57B, image 119; 1860 U.S. Federal Census, Keatchie, De Soto, Louisiana, Film Roll M653-410, p. 901, image 477; 1870 U.S. Federal Census, Shreveport, Caddo, Louisiana, Film Roll: M593-508, p. 556A, image 525; Census of the United States, 1850, 1860, 1870, Records of the Bureau of the Census, Record Group 29, National Archives, Washington D.C.; Marriage certificate of J.T. Heath and Miss J. Farrell, Marion County, 7 February 1875, State of Texas; "At His Rows' End," *The Kaufman Sun,* 21 February 1884; "Court of Appeals," *The Weekly Democratic Statesman,* 25 December 1879, p. 3.

3. "John T. Heath v. The State," Jackson & Jackson, Argued and Adjudged in the Court of appeals of the State of Texas during The Tyler Term, 1879, and *The Early Part of Galveston Term, 1880, Vol. VIL* (St. Louis, MO: F.H. Thompson and Company, 1880), pp. 464–467.

4. "John Heath Captured," *The Dallas Daily Herald,* 7 April 1880, p. 4.

5. "Heath is Here," *The Dallas Daily Herald,* 23 April 1880, p. 5; "Attached Witnesses," *The Dallas Daily Herald,* 23 April 1880, p. 5; "John Heath Acquitted," *The Dallas Daily Herald,* 24 April 1880, p. 5.

6. "John Heath on Trial," *The Dallas Daily Herald,* 8 May 1880, p. 4; "John Heath Cleared," *The Dallas Daily Herald,* 11 May 1880, p. 8.

7. "A Man Robbed at the Long Branch," *The Dallas Daily Herald,* 1 June 1881, p. 5.

8. "Threatened her Life," *The Dallas Daily Herald*, 4 June 1881, p. 4; "Under Bond," *The Dallas Daily Herald*, 4 June 1881, p. 5; "City Chips," *The Dallas Daily Herald*, 4 June 1881, p. 5.

9. "Out on Bond," *The Dallas Daily Herald*, 4 June 1881, p. 5; "Their Case Continued," *The Dallas Daily Herald*, 4 June 1881, p. 5.

10. Joice Heth (c.1756–February 19, 1836[11]) was an African-American slave who was exhibited by circus promoter Phineas Taylor "P. T." Barnum with the false claim that she was the 161-year-old nursing "mammy" of George Washington; "John Heath," *The Dallas Daily Herald*, 21 March 1882, p. 4.

11. State of Texas v. John Heath, cause no. 5624, Minutes, 14th District Court, Dallas County, Texas, vol. N, p. 628; State of Texas v. John Heath and Georgia Morgan, cause no. 5888, Minutes, 14th District Court, Dallas County, Texas, vol. O, p. 218; State of Texas v. John Heath, cause no. 5624, Minutes, 14th District Court, Dallas County, Texas, vol. O, p. 400; State of Texas v. John Heath, J.K. Hall, and John Heath Sr., cause no. 3973, and State of Texas v. John Heath and J.A. Lindsey, cause no. 3945, Minutes, 14th District Court, Dallas County, Texas, vol. O, pp. 55–56, Texas and Dallas History Collection, Dallas Public Library.

12. State of Texas v. John Heath and D.A. Moore, cause no. 3997, State of Texas v. John Heath cause no. 3936, and State of Texas v. John Heath, cause no. 5078, Minutes, 14th District Court, Dallas County, Texas, vol. P, p. 442, Texas and Dallas History Collection, Dallas Public Library.

13. Territory of Arizona vs. John Heith, 7 February 1884, Case 165, Minutes of the District Court, Cochise County, 1882–1887, Books 2 & 3, pp. 630–631. Film File 90.5.86, held at Arizona State Library, Archives and Public Records; "Will Hang!," *The Tombstone Daily Epitaph*, 17 February 1884, p. 4.

14. "Heith the Accomplice," *The Tombstone Republican*, February 1884, p. 1.

15. *Ibid.*

16. *Ibid.*

17. *Ibid.*

18. *Ibid.*

19. *Ibid.*

20. *Ibid.*

21. *Ibid.*

22. *Ibid.*

23. *Ibid.*

24. *Ibid.*

25. "Later," *The Arizona Weekly Citizen*, 24 November 1883, p. 2.

26. Territory of Arizona vs. John Heith, 16 February 1884, Case 165, Minutes of the District Court, Cochise County, 1882–1887, Books 2 & 3, pp. 632–633, Film File 90.5.86, held at Arizona State Library, Archives and Public Records.

27. "Will Hang!," *The Tombstone Daily Epitaph*, 17 February 1884, p. 4.

28. Territory of Arizona vs. John Heith, 16 February 1884, Minutes of the District Court, Cochise County, 1882–1887, Case 165, Books 2 & 3, pp. 633–634, Film File 90.5.86, held at Arizona State Library, Archives and Public Records; "Will Hang!," *The Tombstone Daily Epitaph*, 17 February 1884, p. 4.

29. *Ibid.*

30. *Ibid.*

31. As noted, there appear to be no extant copies of *The Arizona Daily Star* for the week following the robbery. All that exists is microfilm copies of the run of the Star from that year, all of which leave off on June 30, 1883, and resume the following January. The reason for this loss is explained in a book entitled *Double Fold: Libraries and the Assault on Paper* which was authored by Nicholson Baker and published by Random House in 2001. The author highly recommends this volume to aspiring researchers.

32. "No Hope!," *The Tombstone Republican*, February 1884, p. 1.

33. Hankin, p. 7.

34. "Will Hang!," *The Tombstone Daily Epitaph*, 17 February 1884, p. 4; "No Hope!," *The Tombstone Republican*, February 1884, p. 1.

35. *Ibid.*

36. *Ibid.*

37. "Local Notes," *The Tombstone Daily Epitaph*, 17 February 1884, p. 4.

38. "The Bisbee Murderers," *New York Times*, 14 February 1884, p. 5; "The Bisbee Murderers," *The Chicago Daily Tribune*, 14 February 1884, p. 2; "Sentence of the Bisbee Murderers Delayed," *The Sacrament Daily Record-Union*, 14 February 1884, p. 4; "They Will Lynch Them," *The St. Paul Daily Globe*, 15 February 1884, p. 3.

39. "No Hope!," *The Tombstone Republican*, February 1884, p. 1; "Notice of Motion for a New Trial," Filed 18 February 1884, Territory of Arizona vs. Daniel Dowd, James Howard, et al. RG 101, SG 4, held by Arizona State Library, Archives and Public Records.

40. "Too Officious," *The Tombstone Daily Epitaph*, 17 February 1884, p. 1.

41. "No Hope!," *The Tombstone Republican*, February 1884, p. 1.

42. "The Loop!," *The Tombstone Daily Epitaph*, 19 February 1884, p. 4.

43. *Ibid.*

44. *Ibid.*

45. *Ibid.*

46. *Ibid.*

47. *Ibid.*

48. *Ibid.*

49. *Ibid.*

50. "The Loop!," *The Tombstone Daily Epitaph*, 19 February 1884, p. 4.

51. *Ibid.*

52. *Ibid.*

Chapter Six

1. "The Fatal Day," *The Tombstone Daily Epitaph*, 20 February 1884, p. 4.

2. "Convicted of Murder in the First Degree," The Territory of Arizona against Dan Kelly, et al. Case 165, RG 101, SG 4, held by the History and Archives Division Arizona State Library, Archives and Public Records.

3. "The Fatal Day," The Tombstone Daily Epitaph, 20 February 1884, p. 4.

4. Ibid.

5. "As Others See Us," The Tombstone Daily Epitaph, 20 February 1884, p. 4.

6. "The live Bisbee murders...," The Tucson Weekly Citizen, 23 February 1884, p. 2. For further information on the Tonto Basin Feud, refer to Don Dedera's A Little War of Our Own: The Pleasant Valley Feud Revisited (Flagstaff, AZ: Northland Press, 1988).

7. "A Gallant Officer," The Tombstone Daily Epitaph, 20 February 1884, p. 4.

8. "Heith's Trial Resumed," The Tombstone Daily Epitaph, 20 February 1884, p. 4.

9. The Court Instructions to the Jury, John Heath (Heith), Cochise County Criminal, 1881–1903, RG. 101, SG. 8, Box 1, Folder 1, held at History and Archives Division, Arizona State Library, Archives and Public Records.

10. Instructions Requested on the part of the Defendant, John Heath (Heith), Cochise County Criminal, 1881–1903, RG. 101, SG. 8, Box 1, Folder 1, held at History and Archives Division, Arizona State Library, Archives and Public Records.

11. Additional Request for Defence [sic], John Heath (Heith), Cochise County Criminal, 1881–1903, RG. 101, SG. 8, Box 1, Folder 1, held at History and Archives Division, Arizona State Library, Archives and Public Records.

12. John Heath (Heith), Cochise County Criminal, 1881–1903, RG. 101, SG. 8, Box 1, Folder 1, held at History and Archives Division Arizona State Library, Archives and Public Records; "Heith's Trial Resumed," The Tombstone Daily Epitaph, 20 February 1884, p. 4.

13. "Heith's Trial Resumed," The Tombstone Daily Epitaph, 20 February 1884, p. 4.

14. Territory of Arizona vs. John Heith, 21 February 1884, Minutes of the District Court, Cochise County, 1882–1887, Case 166, Book 3, p. 10, Film File 90.5.86, held at History and Archives Division, Arizona State Library, Archives and Public Records.

15. Carl Chafin, ed., The Private Journal of George Whitwell Parsons: The Tombstone Years 1879–1887, Vol. II (Tombstone, AZ: Cochise Classics, 1997), p. 176; "The Fatal Day," The Tombstone Daily Epitaph, 20 February 1884, p. 4.

16. "Murder in the Second Degree," The Tombstone Republican, February 1884, p. 3.

17. Hankin, p. 25.

18. Douglas D Martin, Tombstone's Epitaph (Albuquerque: University of New Mexico Press, 1951), pp. 245–246.

19. Hankin, pp. 26–27; "Telegraph," The Arizona Weekly Citizen, 1 March 1884, p. 1.

20. "Telegraph," The Arizona Weekly Citizen, 1 March 1884, p. 1.

21. "Telegraph," The Arizona Weekly Citizen, 1 March 1884, p. 1; "The Lynching of John Heith," New York Times, 24 February 1884, p. 3.

22. "Telegraph," The Arizona Weekly Citizen, 1 March 1884, p. 1; "Judge Lynch," The Chicago Tribune, 23 February 1884, p. 3; Martin, p. 246.

23. Hankin, p. 29.

24. "Telegraph," The Arizona Weekly Citizen, 1 March 1884, p. 1; "Judge Lynch," The Chicago Tribune, 23 February 1884, p. 3; Martin, p. 246.

25. Ibid.

26. Jason Payne-James, Anthony Busuttil, and William S. Smock, eds., Forensic Medicine: Clinical and Pathological Aspects (Cambridge, England: Cambridge University Press, 2003), p. 265–269.

27. "Heith's Hanging," The Arizona Weekly Citizen, 1 March 1884, p. 2; "Judge Lynch," The Chicago Tribune, 23 February 1884, p. 3; Martin, p. 246; Chafin, p. 4.

28. Don Chaput, Dr. Goodfellow: Physician to the Gunfighters, Scholar, and Bon Vivant (Tucson, AZ: Westernlore Press, 1996); "Raiding Rustlers," The Tombstone Republican, p. 1.

29. Inquest on the Body of John Heath, Document No. 100, 1st Judicial Dist., County of Cochise, Filed March 5, 1884, Carl Research Collection, Ms. 1274, F. 67, held by the Arizona Historical Society.

30. "The disease...," The Arizona Sentinel, 1 March 1884, p. 2.

31. "The Chicago Tribune...," The Arizona Daily Star, 7 March 1884, p. 2.

32. "The father...," The Arizona Weekly Citizen, 1 March 1884, p. 3.

33. "John Heith," The Arizona Silver Belt, 23 February 1884, p. 2.

34. "Heath Hung by Mob," The Dallas Weekly Herald, 28 February 1884, p. 5.

35. "El Paso Lone Star," The Tombstone Daily Epitaph, 20 February 1884, p. 2.

36. "An Arizona mob...," The Arizona Weekly Citizen, 1 March 1884, p. 2.

37. "Judge Lynch," The Chicago Tribune, 23 February 1884, p. 3.

38. "Before the body...," The Arizona Silver Belt, 1 March 1884, p. 2.

39. "Hanged by a Mob," The Kaufman Sun, 28 February 1884. Unfortunately, there are no extant copies of this newspaper for this date, only a recurring reference to the article that I found in numerous places: 1880 U.S. Federal Census, Terrel, Kaufman, Texas, Roll: 1350, Family History Film: 1255315, p. 115B, Enumeration District: 038.

40. Daniel Kelly, "The Hanging of John Heath" (1884). Transcribed from the Hankin manuscript, pp. 33–34. Hankin indicates Kelly's poem was published in The Tombstone Daily Epitaph, but she neglects to give the date. The author was unable to find the poem in the extant copies of that newspaper.

Chapter Seven

1. "A Terrible Change," *The Tombstone Daily Epitaph*, 17 February 1884, p. 4.

2. "It appears…," *The Tombstone Daily Epitaph*, 20 February 1884, p. 4.

3. "For Feeding of Prisoners," Cochise County, Bisbee, Board of Supervisors Minutes, 1881–1887, File Film # 90.1.1, Index 1, p. 448, held at the Arizona State Library, Archives and Public Records; "Last of the Bisbee Murderers," *The Arizona Weekly Citizen*, 29 March 1884, p. 2.

4. "Drift-Wood," *The Arizona Sentinel*, 8 March 1884, p. 2.

5. "United States Census, 1880," index and images, *FamilySearch* (https://familysearch.org/pal:/MM9.1.1/MWF9-GB9, accessed 13 Jul 2014); John C. Delaney in household of Cordelia A. Murray, Harrisburg, Dauphin, Pennsylvania, United States, citing sheet 158D, NARA microfilm publication T9; "Bill Delaney," *The Arizona Sentinel*, 26 January 1884, p. 2; "Hard Game," *The Tombstone Republican*, January 1884, p. 2; "Murder," *The Tombstone Daily Epitaph*, 12 February 1884, p. 4; "Another Shooting Scrape," *Weekly Phoenix Herald*, 13 September 1883, p. 2; "Death Penalty," *The Arizona Daily Star*, 29 March 1884, p. 1.

6. "The Loop!," *The Tombstone Daily Epitaph*, 19 February 1884, p. 4; "Hard Game," *The Tombstone Republican*, January 1884, p. 2; "Last of the Bisbee Murderers," *The Arizona Weekly Citizen*, 29 March 1884, p. 2.

7. "United States Census, 1860," index, *FamilySearch* (https://familysearch.org/pal:/MM9.1.1/M4FG-JLK, accessed 13 July 2014), Omer W Sample in household of William Sample, Jennings Township, Fayette, Indiana, United States; "1860 U.S. Federal Census—Population," Fold3www; household ID 225, NARA microfilm publication M653, p. 32; FHL microfilm 803256, "United States Census, 1870," index and images, *FamilySearch* (https://familysearch.org/pal:/MM9.1.1/MCJR-GJL, accessed 13 Jul 2014), Omer W Sample in household of William K Sample, Kansas, United States; family 4, NARA microfilm publication M593, FHL microfilm 000545938, p. 1; "Hard Game," *The Tombstone Republican*, January 1884, p. 2; James M. Patton, *History of Clifton*, Greenlee County Chamber of Commerce, 1977, p. 106–108.

8. "Hard Game," *The Tombstone Republican*, January 1884, p. 2; "Pleasures of no one…," Territory of Arizona vs. Dan Dowd, et al., RG 101, SG 4, held by Arizona State Library, Archives and Public Records.

9. "Last of the Bisbee Murderers," *The Arizona Weekly Citizen*, 29 March 1884, p. 2; "The only one…," *The Tombstone Republican,* February 1884, p. 4; "Another Hold Up," *The Arizona Silverbelt*, 8 September 1883, p. 2.

10. "Gage Station Murderers," *Arizona Silver Belt*, 22 March 1884, p. 2; "Silver City," *Mohave County Miner*, 16 March 1884, p. 2.

11. "B.C. Joy alias Kit Joy," Register of Prisoners Confined in the County Jail of Grant County, New Mexico 1877–1895, Grant County, Box 12294, p. 31, held by State Records Center and Archives, New Mexico Commission of Public Records.

12. "Kit Joy Wounded and Taken Prisoner," *The Lincoln County Leader*, p. 1.

13. Christopher Klein, *Strong Boy: The Life and Times of John L. Sullivan, America's First Sports Hero* (Guilford, CT: Lyons Press, 2013).

14. "John L. Sullivan," *The Arizona Weekly Citizen*, 22 March 1884, p. 3.

15. Michael T. Isenberg, *John L. Sullivan and his America* (Chicago: University of Illinois Press, 1994), p. 162; "The Bandaged Baille," *The Tucson Weekly Citizen*, 29 March 1884, p. 1.

16. "Howard and Sullivan," *The Arizona Weekly Citizen*, 29 March 1884, p. 3; "Interviewing the Condemned," *The Arizona Daily Star*, 27 March 1884, p. 4.

17. "Dancing on Air," *The Tombstone Daily Epitaph*, 28 March 1884. An extant copy of the newspaper of this date was not found by the author. Douglas Martin's book *Tombstone's Epitaph* was utilized as the reference. This was cross-referenced with Robert E. Ladd's *Eight Ropes to Eternity* (Tombstone, AZ: Tombstone Epitaph, 1965), pp. 2–9. Both publications re-printed the original article in its entirety.

18. Hoffman Bros, *Hoffman's Catholic Directory, Almanac and Clergy List* (Milwaukee, MN: M.H. Wiltzlus Co., 1886), p. 356; Information about Nellie Cashman was derived from Don Chaput's *I'm Mighty Apt to Make a Million or Two: Nellie Cashman and the North American Mining Frontier* (Tucson, AZ: Westernlore Press, 1995); Ronald Wayne Fischer, *Nellie Cashman: Frontier Angel* (Honolulu, HI: Talei Publishers, 2001).

19. "Last of the Bisbee Murderers," *The Arizona Weekly Citizen*, 29 March 1884, p. 2.

20. "The press and…," *The Weekly Phoenix Herald*, 6 March 1884, p. 2.

21. "Communicated," *The Tombstone Republican*, March 1884, p. 3.

22. "Last of the Bisbee Murderers," *The Arizona Weekly Citizen*, 29 March 1884, p. 2.

23. "Last of the Bisbee Murderers," *The Arizona Weekly Citizen*, 29 March 1884, p. 2; "Dancing on Air," *The Tombstone Republican*, March 1884, p. 1 (does not exist in microfilm, from author's collection of ephemera).

24. "Shot in the Attempt," *The Weekly Phoenix Herald*, 27 March 1884, p. 4; Hankin, pp. 21–22; "Drift-Wood," *The Arizona Sentinel*, 29 March 1884, p. 2.

25. "The fact…," *The Arizona Daily Star*, 21 March 1884, p. 2.

26. "We acknowledge…," *The Mohave County Miner*, 30 March 1884, p. 3; "Quite a number…" and "Sheriff Paul left…," *The Arizona Daily Star*, 28 March 1884, p. 2.

27. "Last of the Bisbee Murderers," *The Arizona*

Weekly Citizen, 29 March 1884, p. 2; "Death Penalty," *The Arizona Daily Star*, 29 March 1884, p. 1.

28. "The Bisbee Murderers," *The Arizona Daily Star*, 28 March 1884, p. 2.

29. "The Bisbee Murderers," *The Arizona Daily Star*, 28 March 1884, p. 2; "Last of the Bisbee Murderers," *The Arizona Weekly Citizen*, 29 March 1884, p. 2.

30. "Dancing on Air," *The Tombstone Republican*, March 1884, p. 1; "Last of the Bisbee Murderers," *The Arizona Weekly Citizen*, 29 March 1884, p. 2.

31. Hankin, pp. 34–35; "Last of the Bisbee Murderers," *The Arizona Weekly Citizen*, 29 March 1884, p. 2; "Five Men Hanged," *San Francisco Bulletin*, 29 March 1884, p. 1. The injuries reported by *The Bulletin* were not mentioned in any extant local newspaper.

32. "Dancing on Air," *The Tombstone Republican*, March 1884, p. 1. *The Republican* identified Dowd and Howard as being the recipients of the rite of baptism as opposed to *The Weekly Citizen* which named Sample and Howard.

33. "Death Penalty," *The Arizona Daily Star*, 29 March 1884, p. 1.

34. "Dancing on Air," *The Tombstone Republican*, March 1884, p. 1; Death Warrant, Territory of Arizona vs. Dan Dowd, et al., District Court, Second Judicial District, County of Cochise, Arizona Territory, Case. 165, Filed 1 April 1884, RG 101, SG 4, held by Arizona State Library, Archives and Public Records.

35. "Dancing on Air," *The Tombstone Republican*, March 1884, p. 1.

36. "Death Penalty," *The Arizona Daily Star*, 29 March 1884, p. 1; "Five Men Hanged," *San Francisco Bulletin*, 29 March 1884, p. 1; "Dancing on Air," *The Tombstone Republican*, March 1884, p. 1.

37. "Mrs. Martha Swain Recalls Arrival in Tombstone," *The Tombstone Daily Epitaph*, 28 January 1943. Retrieved 26 December 2013 from http//www.tombstone1880.com/archives/swain.htm.

38. "Death Penalty," *The Arizona Daily Star*, 29 March 1884, p. 1; "Five Men Hanged," *San Francisco Bulletin*, 29 March 1884, p. 1; "Dancing on Air," *The Tombstone Republican*, March 1884, p. 1; *The Daily Star* recorded Kelly's final words as, "Let her loose."

39. Dr. Dinesh Rao, "Hanging," from *Dr. Dinesh Rao's Forensic Pathology*, 1993. Retrieved on 2 September 2014 from http://www.forensicpathologyonline.com/e-book/asphyxia/hanging; Julia Layton, "How does death by hanging work?," HowStuffWorks.com. Retrieved on 4 January 2007 from http://health.howstuffworks.com/diseases-conditions/death-dying/death-by-hanging.htm; Roger S. Tracy, "The Question of Pain in Hanging," *Popular Science Monthly* 13 (July 1878). Retrieved on 2 September 2014 from http://en.wikisource.org/wiki/Popular_Science_Monthly/Volume_13/July_1878/The_Question_of_Pain_in_Hanging.

40. "Death Penalty," *The Arizona Daily Star*, 29 March 1884, p. 1; "Five Men Hanged," *San Francisco*

Bulletin, 29 March 1884, p. 1; "Dancing on Air," *The Tombstone Republican*, March 1884, p. 1.

41. "View the Dead Bodies," *The Arizona Weekly Citizen*, 29 March 1884, p. 2.

42. "Five Men Hanged," *San Francisco Bulletin*, 29 March 1884, p. 1; "The Gallows," *The Chicago Tribune*, 29 March 1884, p. 3; "The Penalty of Their Crimes," *New York Times*, 29 March 1884, p. 2; "How the Murderers Died," *The Phoenix Weekly Herald*, 3 April 1884, p. 2; "A Daisy Drop," *The Arizona Silver Belt*, 29 March 1884, p. 3.

43. Carl Chafin, ed., *The Private Journal of George Whitwell Parsons: The Tombstone Years, 1879–1887, Volume II* (Tombstone, AZ: Cochise Classics, 1939), p. 186; Neil Carmony, ed., *Whiskey, Sixguns, and Red Light Ladies: George Hand's Saloon Diary, Tucson, 1875–1878* (Silver City, NM: High Lonesome Books, 1994), p. 235.

44. "View the Dead Bodies," *The Arizona Weekly Citizen*, 29 March 1884, p. 2.

Chapter Eight

1. "Yesterday was…," *The Arizona Daily Star*, 29 March 1884, p. 2.

2. "Exodus 21," *The Holy Bible, King James Version*.

3. "An act committed…" and "Red Sample declared…," *The Arizona Daily Star*, 29 March 1884, p. 2.

4. "The Star seem to…," *The Arizona Weekly Citizen*, 5 April 1884, p. 2.

5. "Our evening contemporary…," *The Arizona Daily Star*, 1 April 1884, p. 2.

6. "Our morning contemporary…" and "The Star in order…," *The Arizona Weekly Citizen*, 5 April 1884, p. 2.

7. "Believed Him Innocent," *The Boston Herald*, 7 April 1884, p. 4; Cochise County, Bisbee, Board of Supervisors Minutes, 1881–1887, File Film # 90.1.1, Index 1, held at the Arizona State Library, Archives and Public Records.

8. "Tombstone Officials," *The Arizona Weekly Citizen*, 5 April 1884, p. 2.

9. Information about Robert "Bob" Paul derived primarily from *When Law was in the Holster: The Frontier Life of Bob Paul* by John Boessenecker, a book the author recommends highly.

10. "The Tombstone Bank," *The Mohave County Miner*, 1 June 1884, p. 3. Oddly, neither Sheriff Ward nor the missing monies were given mention in the official report as re-printed in the *Arizona Weekly Citizen* of 7 June 1884.

11. "J.L. Ward…," *The Daily Tombstone Epitaph*, 22 December 1885, p. 3; "The residence…," *The Weekly Journal Miner*, 14 August 1889, p. 2; "Local Notes," *The Daily Tombstone Epitaph*, 14 April 1887, p. 1.

12. "The Phenix papers [*sic*]…," *The Weekly Tombstone Epitaph*, 12 August 1889, p. 3; "Ex-Sheriff 'Bud' Gray has…," *The Arizona Republic*, 7 October 1893, p.1.

13. "New Prison Board," *The Arizona Sentinel*, 22 August 1891, p. 2; "Frank Ward…," *The Tombstone Daily Epitaph*, 27 December 1891, p. 5.

14. "Local Briefs," *The Arizona Republic*, 22 July 1894, p. 1; "Personal," *The Arizona Republic*, 12 November 1893, p. 5; "Mrs. J.L. Ward died…," *The Tombstone Daily Epitaph*, 15 November 1893, p. 3.

15. "Obituary," *The Arizona Sentinel*, 14 April 1894, p. 3; "J.L. Ward is a candidate…," *The Arizona Weekly Journal-Miner*, 22 August 1894, p. 2; "The Real Work," *The Arizona Republic*, 5 September 1894, p. 4.

16. "Local Notes," *The Arizona Sentinel*, 28 August 1897, p. 3; "Pima County," *The Arizona Republic*, 21 June 1898, p. 3

17. "J.L. Ward left…," *The Arizona Sentinel*, 18 November 1899, p. 3.

18. "Of Local Interest," *The Arizona Republic*, 7 December 1910, p. 6; "Former Phoenician Killed at San Diego," *The Arizona Republic*, 30 September 1913, p. 5; "J.L. Ward Dead—First Sheriff of Cochise," *The Bisbee Daily Review*, 5 October 1913, p. 9. The discrepancies—"first sheriff / four men hanged"—in his obituary in the Bisbee newspaper must be put down to poor research on the part of the reporter.

19. "Cochise Democrats," *The Arizona Weekly Citizen*, 9 September 1884, p. 3; "Indian News," *The Tombstone*, 11 June 1885, p. 3; "The Savages," *The Arizona Champion*, 13 June 1885, p. 3. *The Tombstone* of June 10, 1885, reported that Daniels was "killed instantly" by the Apache, but was later found with "the top of his head blown off and his throat cut from ear to ear." There is no reason given for the discrepancy between this and the story of Milton Gilliam given.

20. "For Sheriff…," *The Daily Tombstone*, 28 October 1896, p. 2.

21. "Report of Chief of Police," *The Tombstone Daily Epitaph*, 25 January 1890, p. 3; "An Arizona exchange…," *The Tombstone Prospector*, 15 July 1890, p. 4; "Personal Points," *The Tombstone Daily Prospector*, 19 August 1890, p. 4; "For Sale, Cheap," *The Tombstone Daily Prospector*, 2 September 1890, p. 4; "Notice," *The Arizona Sentinel*, 4 July 1891, p. 4.

22. "Local notes," *The Arizona Sentinel*, 6 July 1894, p. 3; "R.S. Hatch," *The Arizona Sentinel*, 17 October 1896, p. 2; "R.S. Hatch and…," *The Oasis*, 26 May 1900, p. 4; "Official Directory," *The Arizona Sentinel*, 28 November 1900, p. 1; "Official Minutes of Board of Supervisors," *The Arizona Sentinel*, 24 April 1901, p. 1.

23. "Arizona Happenings," *The Coconino Sun*, 11 June 1904, p. 5; "Of Local Interest," *The Arizona Republic*, 6 June 1904, p. 6.

24. Calumet Press, *Album of Genealogy and Biography, Cook County, Illinois with Portraits* (Chicago: Calumet Book and Engraving Co., 1890), pp. 154–155; "When Cleveland…," *The Daily Tombstone*, 9 March 1886, p. 3; John S. Goff, *Arizona Territorial Officials I: The Supreme Court Justices 1863–1912* (Swannanoa, NC: Black Mountain Press, 1985), pp. 84–87.

25. "Much interest…," *The Daily Tombstone Epitaph*, 18 March 1886, p. 2; "Local Notes," *The Daily Tombstone Epitaph*, 13 May 1886, p. 4; "Judge Pinney is now…," *The Daily Tombstone Epitaph*, 28 September 1886, p. 3; John S. Goff, *Arizona Territorial Officials I: The Supreme Court Justices 1863–1912* (Swannanoa, NC: Black Mountain Press, 1985), pp. 84–87.

26. "Col. Herring Passes Away Full of Days," *The Arizona Republic*, 11 July 1912, p. 1; "Renowned Arizonan Goes to His Reward," *The Tombstone Daily Epitaph*, 14 July 1912, p. 4; "In the passing of…," *The Tombstone Daily Epitaph*, 21 July 1912, p. 2.

27. "The Trial of the Train Robbers," *The Arizona Weekly Citizen*, 21 January 1888, p. 3; "The case of the Territory Vs. Fry…," *The Daily Tombstone*, 4 August 1886, p. 3; "Arizona in Brief," *The Arizona Weekly Citizen*, 28 March 1887, p. 3; John S. Goff, *Arizona Territorial Officials V: The Adjuncts General, Attorneys General, Auditors, Superintendents of Public Instruction, and Treasurers* (Swannanoa, NC: Black Mountain Press, 1985), pp. 72–73; " Col. Wm. Herring of Tombstone…," *The Arizona Weekly Journal-Miner*, 4 March 1891, p. 2; "Col. Herring has withdrawn…," *The Tombstone Daily Epitaph*, 4 October 1891, p. 5; "G.W. Cheyney returned…," *The Tombstone Daily Epitaph*, 4 October 1891, p. 3.

28. "Guilty," *The Tombstone Daily Epitaph*, 27 May 1894, p. 4; "Local Notes," *The Tombstone Daily Epitaph*, 11 March 1894, p. 3; "As Col. Herring talked…," *The Arizona Republic*, 12 February 1895, p. 8.

29. "$80,001," *The Tombstone Prospector*, 16 September 1890, p. 1; "Mining Notes," *The Tombstone Daily Epitaph*, 21 August 1892, p. 4; "Tombstone District," *The Bisbee Daily Review*, 8 October 1905, p. 12.

30. "Col. William Herring has…," *The Arizona Republic*, 9 January 1896, p. 5; "Copper Queen Company Wins," *The Coconino Sun*, 18 June 1898, p. 4.

31. Javier Morales, *They Fought Like Wildcats Centennial (1914–2014): Herring Hall—Where it all began* (allsportstucson.com, 2014), retrieved on 26 September 2014 from http://allsportstucson.com/2014/06/08/they-fought-like-wildcats-centennial-1914-2014-herring-hall-where-it-all-began/; "Thomas Mitchell…," *The Arizona Silver Belt*, 10 May 1900, p. 3; "Death of Mrs. Colonel Herring," *The Border Vidette*, 16 May 1903, p. 1.

32. "Goes to Bisbee," *The Coconino Sun*, 24 February 1906, p. 1; "Copper Queen Suit to Begin This Morning," *The Bisbee Daily Review*, 6 May 1908, p. 5.

33. John S. Goff, *Arizona Territorial Officials III: Delegates to Congress, 1863–1912* (Swannanoa, NC: Black Mountain Press, 1985), pp. 130–147.

34. "Delegate to Congress," *The Daily Tombstone*, 16 March 1886, p. 2; "Local Notes," *The Daily Tombstone Epitaph*, 10 April 1886, p. 3; "Local Notes," *The Daily Tombstone Epitaph*, 19 March 1886, p. 3; "Local Notes," *The Daily Tombstone Epitaph*, 9 April 1886, p. 3; "Anti-Chinese Meeting," *The Daily Tombstone*, 28 June 1886, p. 3.

35. "The workmen…," *The Daily Tombstone*, 22 September 1886, p. 3; "The Little Giant Mine," *The Daily Tombstone*, 23 October 1886, p. 3; "Silver Quotations," *The Daily Tombstone*, 10 November 1886, p. 3.

36. *Arizona Biographical, Volume 3* (Chicago: The S.J. Clarke Publishing Co., 1916), pp. 513–514; "Gold and Silver," The *Tombstone Prospector*, 7 August 1896, p. 4; "Judge James. S. Robinson…," *The Arizona Republic*, 11 October 1898, p. 3.

37. "Democratic Ticket," *The Cochise Review*, 2 November 1900, p. 1; "Local Notes," *The Tombstone Daily Epitaph*, 4 November 1900, p. 2; "County Results," *The Cochise Review*, 7 November 1900, p. 1; "Local Notes," *The Tombstone Daily Epitaph*, 30 December 1900, p. 4; "Local Notes," *The Tombstone Daily Epitaph*, 22 December 1900, p. 4.

38. "Mrs. J.J. Patton…," *The Bisbee Daily Review*, 13 August 1902, p. 8; "Death of Judge Jas. S. Robinson," *The Bisbee Daily Review*, 22 May 1903, p. 1; "Gone to Her Mother's Bedside," *The Bisbee Daily Review*, 25 November 1903, p. 2. The author personally searched the Tombstone City Cemetery but was unable to find the final resting place of Judge James Robinson.

39. "The trial of L.B. Lawrence…," *The Arizona Weekly Citizen*, 17 May 1884, p. 2; "Territorial Items," *The Arizona Champion*, 14 June 1884, p. 2.

40. Territory of Arizona vs. L.D. Lawrence, Case 170, Criminal Calendar District Court, held at the Arizona State Library, Archives and Public Records; "Notice," *The Tombstone*, 31 August 1885, p. 2; "District Court," *The Daily Tombstone*, 17 November 1885, p. 3.

41. "Arizona News," *The Arizona Daily Citizen*, 13 December 1884, p. 34; "Read and Waite…," *The Daily Tombstone*, 13 February, p. 6; "Letter from Harshaw," *The Arizona Weekly Citizen*, 10 April 1886, p. 3; "Letter List," *The Tombstone Daily Epitaph*, 27 August 1887, p. 3; "Letter List," *The Tombstone Daily Epitaph*, 11 August 1889, p. 3.

42. "Bush & Gentry," *The Clifton Clarion*, 18 February 1885, p. 4; "Civil Calendar," *The Clifton Clarion*, 28 October 1885, p. 3; "District Court," *The Clifton Clarion*, 18 November 1885, p. 3.

43. "Record of Transfers," *The Arizona Republic*, 22 October 1910, p. 4; "Personal Mention," *The Arizona Republic*, 6 April 1911, p. 2; "Personal Mention," *The Arizona Republic*, 4 November 1911, p. 9; "Walter Bush…," *The Arizona Republic*, 19 September 1913, p. 7; "A Bargain," *The Arizona Republic*, 10 February 1914, p. 3; "For Sale, Bargains" and "Personal Mention," *The Arizona Republic*, 4 March 1914, p. 9.

44. "Bush's Fine is Paid," *The Bisbee Daily Review*, 20 September 1903, p. 5. For more information on W.W. Bush of Douglas: "Nothing New About Escapes," *The Bisbee Daily Review*, 19 December 1903, p. 1. "Bush Discharged," *The Bisbee Daily Review*, 21 August 1904, p. 7; "Shooting at Douglas," *The Bisbee Daily Review*, 19 January 1905, p. 3; "Hayden Happenings," *The Arizona Republic*, 21 April 1916, p. 4.

45. Jennie Heath, 1900, Dallas Ward 9, Dallas, Texas, Roll 1625, p. 3A, Enumeration District 0118, United States of America, Bureau of the Census 12th Census of the United States—1900, Washington D.C. National Archives Records Administration, 1900, T623, 1854 Rolls; Sue Anne Norris (2013), John Heath & Sarah A. Heath, Find A Grave Memorial, #103297837, FindAGrave.com, retrieved on 1 October 2014 from http://www.findagrave.com/cgi-bin/fg.cgi?page=gr&GRid=103297837; Mrs. Virginia Tennessee Heath, State File No. 5987, Certificate of Death, Texas Department of Health, Bureau of Vital Statistics, State of Texas.

46. Here again, the author highly recommends Don Chaput's *I'm Mighty Apt to Make a Million or Two: Nellie Cashman and the North American Mining Frontier* (Tucson, AZ: Westernlore Press, 1995) for more information on Nellie Cashman.

47. Don Chaput, *Dr. Goodfellow: Physician to the Gunfighters, Scholar, and Bon Vivant* (Tucson, AZ: Westernlore Press, 1996). The author is indebted to Don Chaput for the information regarding Dr. George Emory Goodfellow. Another highly recommended book from a highly respected Old West historian and author.

48. "Grand Jurymen," *The Tombstone Daily Epitaph*, 8 November 1891, p. 4; "Homestead Patents," *The Arizona Weekly Citizen*, 5 December 1891, p. 4; "A Mysterious Find," *The Tombstone Daily Epitaph*, 29 May 1892, p. 5; "A Ghastly Find," *The Tombstone Daily Epitaph*, 28 August 1892, p. 6.

49. "Born," *The Tombstone Daily Epitaph*, 12 June 1892, p. 4; "Local Notes," *The Tombstone Daily Epitaph*, 29 January 1893, p. 4; United States of America, Bureau of the Census, Twelfth Census of the United States, 1900, Washington, D.C.: National Archives and Records Administration, 1900, T623, 1854 rolls, Census Place: West Pagosa Springs, Archuleta, Colorado, Roll: 121, p. 5B, Enumeration District: 0001, FHL microfilm: 1240121; "Frank Buckles is Found Dying," *The Bisbee Daily Review*, 16 January 1907, p. 3; "Frank Henry Buckles," findagrave.com. Record created by C. Fahey on December 6, 2009, record #45179758, retrieved 17 November 2014 from http://www.findagrave.com/cgi-bin/fg.cgi?page=mr&MR id=46827298.

50. "Telegraph," *The Arizona Weekly Citizen*, 5 January 1884, p. 1; "The Clifton Clarion says…," *The Arizona Champion*, 12 January 1884, p. 3; "Telegraph," *The Arizona Weekly Citizen*, 5 January 1884, p. 1; "Anticipated Anarchy," *The Tombstone Republican*, January 1884, p. 1; "Telegraph," *The Arizona Weekly Citizen*, 22 February 1884.

51. "The Clifton Clarion says…," *The Arizona Champion*, 26 January 1884, p. 2.

52. "A bench warrant…," *The Clifton Clarion*, 31 March 1886, p. 4; "Delinquent Tax List," *The Clifton Clarion*, 28 January and 11 February 1885, p. 2.

53. "District Court," *The Rio Grande Republican*, 1 October 1897, p. 1, Case numbers 2524 and 2525. The Territory of New Mexico vs. Jesus Enriquez and

Maxamiliano Romero and Nicolas Olguin & The Territory of New Mexico vs. Nicolas Olguin were located in The Records of the U.S. Territorial and New Mexico District Court for Dona Ana Criminal Docket "C" 1896–1910, SN 14434, p. 26, but the actual case files seem to have been lost; Olguin and Relles, Details for Marriage ID#393683, The Western States Marriage Record Index, Graham County, Arizona, vol. C, p. 173. Held at Special Collections & Family History, BYU, Idaho; 1880 Federal Census, Silver City, Grant County, New Mexico Territory, Roll: 802, Family History Film 1254802, p. 342A, Enumeration District: 015, Image: 0690.

54. "Documents Filed for Record," *The Copper Era*, 31 March 1910, p. 1; "Daily Record," *The El Paso Herald*, 13 June 1910, p. 4; "Notice to Water Users," *The El Paso Herald*, 22 September 1910, p. 5; "Daily Record," *The El Paso Herald*, 19 January, p. 3; "Daily Record," *The El Paso Herald*, 7 March 1912, Feature and Society News Section, p. 9; "Proprietor of El Paso Store Slain," *The Bisbee Daily Review*, 4 February 1922, p. 6.

55. "The trial of Kit Joy...," *The Arizona Silver Belt*, 9 August 1884, p. 2; True Bill, The Territory of New Mexico vs. Kit Joy, Criminal Cases #1530, 1531, 1534, 1535, 1884–1885, Sierra County District Court, Box 12294 (90 pages), New Mexico State Records Center and Archives, New Mexico, Commission of Public Records; Motion for Continuance, 14 August 1884; Affidavit for Change of Venue, 8 August 1884; Motion to Quash the Indictment, 17 November 1884, The Territory of New Mexico vs. Kit Joy, Criminal Cases #1530, 1531, 1534, 1535, 1884–1885, Sierra County District Court, Box 12294 (90 pages), New Mexico State Records Center and Archives, New Mexico; Sentence, 20 November 1884, The Territory of New Mexico vs. Kit Joy, Criminal Cases #1530, 1531, 1534, 1535, 1884–1885, Sierra County, District Court, Box 12294 (90 pages), New Mexico State Records Center and Archives, New Mexico; "The trial at Hillsborough...," *The Arizona Silver Belt*, 19 November 1884, p. 3; *The Southwest Sentinel*, 20 November 1884.

56. New Mexico Territory Census of 1885, National Archives and Records Administration (NARA), Washington, D.C.; *Schedules of the New Mexico Territory Census of 1885*, Series: M846, Roll: 5; "More convict labor," *The Las Vegas Daily Gazette*, 8 January 1885, p. 1; "Train Robberies," *The Tombstone Daily Epitaph*, 20 August 1887, p. 3; "Men Who Have Stopped California Stages," *The San Francisco Call*, 10 October 1897, p. 22.

57. "Kit Joy," *The Western Liberal*, 5 May 1893, p. 1; "On the first page...," *The Western Liberal*, 5 May 1893, p. 2; "A Sensible View," *The Southwest Sentinel*, 9 May 1893, p. 2; "It is hoped...," *The Southwest Sentinel*, 23 May 1893, p. 2.

58. United States of America, Bureau of the Census, Thirteenth Census of the United States, 1910 (NARA microfilm publication T624, 1,178 rolls), Records of the Bureau of the Census, Record Group 29, National Archives, Washington, D.C., 1910, Census Place: Huachuca, Cochise, Arizona, roll T624_38, p. 15B, Enumeration District, 0010, FHL microfilm: 1374051; Edgar Beecher Bronson, *Red-Blooded Heroes of the Frontier* (Chicago IL: A.C. McClurg & Co., 1910). Compiled and edited by Kathy Weiser/Legends of America, updated November 2010. The Legends of America website includes the following disclaimer: "The text as it appears here; however, is not verbatim, as it has been heavily edited including truncation in parts and additional information added," retrieved on 22 November 2014 from http://www.legendsofamerica.com/we-kitjoy.html; "Christopher Carson "Kit" Joy," Memorial #76080829, findagrave.com, record created by Alvin Poole on September 6, 2009, retrieved on 20 November 2014 from http://www.findagrave.com/cgi-bin/fg.cgi?page=gr&GRid=76080829&ref=acom.

59. "Bisbee," *The Daily Tombstone*, 21 November 1885, p. 3; "Local Notes," *The Daily Tombstone*, 24 November 1885, p. 3; Local Notes," *The Daily Tombstone*, 10 February 1886, p. 3.

60. "County Records, Local Notes," *The Daily Tombstone*, 10 September 1886, p. 3; "Notice!," *The Tombstone Daily Epitaph*, 13 August 1887, p. 3; "Notice!," *The Tombstone Daily Epitaph*, 28 July 1888, p. 3.

61. "Official Proceedings," *The Tombstone Daily Epitaph*, 3 December 1887, p. 3; "Territorial and General," *The Clifton Clarion*, 28 July 1886, p. 3.

62. "The bondsmen of...," *The Tombstone Daily Epitaph*, 17 March 1888, p. 3; "Official Proceedings," *The Tombstone Daily Epitaph*, 7 January 1888, p. 3; "The County Victorious," *The Tombstone Daily Epitaph*, 11 February 1888, p. 3.

63. "Joseph Goldwater and Manuela Arvisa." This record can be found at the County Courthouse located in Cochise Co. Arizona, vol. 1, p. 45, Upper Snake River Family History Center and Ricks College (Rexburg, Idaho) and Ancestary.com, Arizona Marriage Collection, 1864–1982, Provo, Utah.

64. "Dissolution of Partnership," *The Tombstone Daily Prospector*, 6 February 1889, p. 2; *Portrait & Biographical Record of Arizona* (Chicago: Chapman Publishing Co., 1904), pp. 902–907. This author was unable to find any evidence to support the claim made in the aforementioned book that Castaneda had "...left (Bisbee) because of a devastating fire which destroyed his store and its contents, causing a loss of $85,000"; "The revolt in Benson...," *The Arizona Silver Belt*, 17 August 1889, p. 3; "Official Report," *The Tombstone Daily Epitaph*, 13 August 1889, p. 3.

65. "Local Notes," *The Tombstone Daily Epitaph*, 3 September 1889, p. 3; "Death of Joseph Goldwater," *The Arizona Sentinel*, 7 September 1889, p. 3; "Latest Territorial News," *The Arizona Weekly Citizen*, 12 October 1889, p. 3; "Joseph Goldwater," *JewishGen Online Worldwide Burial Registry,* JewishGen.com (Ancestry.com Operations Inc., Provo, UT, 2008).

66. "Benson," *The Arizona Weekly Enterprise*, 7 December 1889, p. 2; "Benson," *The Arizona Weekly Citizen*, 11 July 1891, p. 1.

67. "A Grand Reception," *The Tombstone Daily Epitaph*, 26 April 1891, p. 4. On a rather comic note, *The Epitaph* reported that at one point during Harrison's speech, "a cowboy with a big hat and a six-shooter came up to get a glimpse of the president. Mrs. Harrison saw him and, pulling the president in to the car, closed the door. (Postmaster General and industrialist John) Wannamaker crawled under a seat. It was ten minutes before the latter could be persuaded to come out from under the bed and it was not until he had been assured that the 'bad man' was the Tombstone agent for his Philadelphia clothing house that he condescended to come to the front."

68. "J.M. Castaneda, of Benson," *The Arizona Republic*, August 1892, Special Resources Edition, p. 42.

69. "Tuesday...," *The Oasis*, 14 June 1894, pp. 5–6.

70. "A Good Showing," *The Oasis*, 9 August 1894, p. 5; "Town and Country," *The Oasis*, 13 September 1894, p. 5; "Personal Items," *The Oasis*, 26 December 1896, p. 4.

71. "Official Report Property assessment," *The Tombstone Daily Epitaph*, 12 July 1897, p. 4; "Prospector...," *The St. John's Herald*, 6 August 1898, p. 1; "A.A. Castaneda & Co," (advertisement), *The Oasis*, 19 July 1894, p. 8.

72. "Brick Factory at Benson," *The Oasis*, 25 May 1901, p. 12; "Jose Miguel Castaneda," *The Oasis*, 26 October 1901, p. 1; "Jose Miguel Castaneda," *Portrait and Biographical Record of Arizona* (Chicago: Chapman Publishing Co., 1904), pp. 902–907.

73. James Douglas, *Notes on the Development of Phelps, Dodge & Co.'s Copper and Railroad Interests* (Bisbee, AZ: Frontera House Press, 1906; reprinted 1995). Further information about the town of Bisbee culled from Carlos A. Schwantes' *Vision and Enterprise: Exploring the History of Phelps Dodge Corporation* (Tucson: University of Arizona Press & Phelps Dodge, 2000).

74. Carlos. A. Schwantes, *Bisbee: Urban Outpost on the Frontier* (Tucson, AZ: University of Arizona Press, 1992); Thomas E. Sheridan, *Arizona: A History, Revised Edition* (Tucson: University of Arizona Press, 2012); "Copper Queen," *The Arizona Weekly Citizen*, 11 July 1891, p. 1; Patrick Murfi, "Bad Day at Bisbee," *Heretic, Rebel, a Thing to Flout* (2014). Retrieved on 25 November 2014 from http://patrick murfin.blogspot.com/2014/07/bad-day-at-bisbee. html.

75. Bailey, pp. 92–98; Cox, pp. 75–81; Schwantes, pp. 64–69.

76. "Famous Old Scaffold Used to Start Fire," *The Coconino Sun*, 2 February 1912, p. 1.

77. "Notable Relic of Arizona's Past Found," *The Tucson Daily Citizen*, 1 January 1932, p. 6; "The Citizen gives...," *The Arizona Daily Star*, 30 March 1884, p. 3. The illustration included herein is an artist's reproduction of the print based on the one that accompanied the 1932 article. The original printing block could not be found at any on the state or local archives, museums, or repositories.

Bibliography

Books

Arizona Biographical, Volume 3. Chicago: S.J. Clarke, 1916.

"Arizona-Bisbee-Camp-Thomas." *McKenney's 1883 Business Directory of the Principle Towns of Central and Southern California, Arizona, New Mexico, Southern Colorado, and Kansas*. Oakland: Pacific Press, 1883.

Ball, Larry D. *Desert Lawman: The High Sheriffs of New Mexico and Arizona 1846–1912*. Albuquerque: University of New Mexico Press, 1992.

Bailey, Lynn R. *Bisbee: Queen of the Copper Camps*. Tucson: Westernlore Press, 1983.

Bashford, Coles. *The Compiled Laws of the Territory of Arizona, Including the Howell Code and the Session Laws from 1864 to 1871*. Albany: Weed, Parsons, and Co., 1871.

Boessenecker, John. *When Law Was in the Holster*. Norman: University of Oklahoma Press, 2012.

Breckenridge, William M. *Helldorado: Bringing Law to the Mesquite*. Boston: Houghton Mifflin, 1928.

Brown, Scott. *Collection of Arizona Historical Articles*. Buckskin Mountains, Arizona, 1890.

Calumet Press. *Album of Genealogy and Biography, Cook County, Illinois with Portraits*. Chicago: Calumet Book and Engraving Co., 1896.

Carmony, Neil, ed. *Whiskey, Sixguns, and Red Light Ladies: George Hand's Saloon Diary, Tucson, 1875–1878*. Silver City: High Lonesome Books, 1994.

Chafin, Carl, ed. *The Private Journal of George Whitwall Parsons Volume II: The Tombstone Years 1879–1887*. Tombstone: Cochise Classics, 1997.

Chaput, Don. *Dr. Goodfellow: Physician to the Gunfighters, Scholar, and Bon Vivant*. Tucson: Westernlore Press, 1996.

Chaput, Don. *I'm Might Apt to Make a Million or Two: Nellie Cashman and the North American Mining Frontier*. Tucson: Westernlore Press, 1995.

Dedra, Don. *A Little War of Our Own: The Pleasant Valley Feud Revisited*. Flagstaff: Northland Press, 1988.

Douglas, James. *Notes on the Development of Phelps,*

Dodge & Co.'s Copper and Railroad Interests. 1906. Reprint, Bisbee: Frontera House Press, 1995.

Fischer, Ronald Wayne. *Nellie Cashman: Frontier Angel*. Honolulu: Talei Publishers, 2000.

Goff, John S. *Arizona Territorial Officials I: The Supreme Court Justices*. Cave Creek: Black Mountain Press, 1975.

Goff, John S. *Arizona Territorial Officials III: Delegates to Congress, 1863–1912*. Cave Creek: Black Mountain Press, 1985.

Goff, John S. *Arizona Territorial Officials V: The Adjuncts General, Attorneys General, Auditors, Superintendents of Public Instruction, and Treasurers*. Cave Creek: Black Mountain Press, 1975.

Hoffman Bros. *Hoffman's Catholic Directory, Almanac and Clergy List*. Milwaukee: Hoffman Bros. Catholic Publishers, 1886.

Hoyt, John P., comp. *The Compiled Laws of the Territory of Arizona, 1864–1877: Compiled and Arranged by Authority of an Act of the Legislative Assembly, Approved February 9, 1877*. Detroit: Richmond, Backus & Company, 1877.

Hyde, Charles K. *Copper for America: The United States Copper Industry from Colonial Times to the 1990s*. Tucson: University of Arizona Press, 1998.

Isenberg, Michael T. *John L. Sullivan and his America*. Urbana: University of Illinois Press, 1994.

"Jose Miguel Castaneda." *Portrait and Biographical Record of Arizona*. Chicago: Chapman, 1904.

Klein, Christopher. *Strong Boy: The Life and Times of John L. Sullivan, America's First Sports Hero*. Guilford: Lyons Press, 2013.

Ladd, Robert E. *Eight Ropes to Eternity*. Tombstone: Tombstone Epitaph, 1965.

Laws of the Territory of Arizona, Twelfth Legislative Assembly: Also Memorials and Resolutions. Prescott: Arizona Miner Stean-Printing Office, 1883.

Leblond, Sylvio. "Douglas, James (1800–86)." In *Dictionary of Canadian Biography*, vol. 11. Toronto: University of Toronto/Université Laval, 2003.

Marks, Paula Mitchell. *And Die in the West: The Story of the O.K. Corral Gunfight*. Norman: University of Oklahoma Press, 1989.

Martin, Douglas D. *Tombstone's Epitaph*. Albuquerque: University of New Mexico Press, 1951.

Mazzanovich, Anton. *Trailing Geronimo*. Los Angeles: Haynes Corp, 1931.

Patton, James M. *History of Clifton*. Greenlee Historical Society, 2008.

Payne-James, Jason, Anthony Busuttil, William S. Smock, eds. *Forensic Medicine: Clinical and Pathological Aspects*. Cambridge: Cambridge University Press, 2003.

Phelps Dodge Corporation History. *International Directory of Company Histories*, Vol. 28. Detroit: St. James Press, 1999.

Rundle-Burgess, Opie. *Bisbee Not So Long Ago*. San Antonio: The Naylor Company, 1967.

Smith, Dean. *The Goldwaters of Arizona*. Flagstaff: Northland Press, 1986.

Walker, Henry P., and Don Bufkin. *Historical Atlas of Arizona*, 2d ed. Norman: University of Oklahoma Press, 1986.

Internet Resources

Bronson, Edgar Beecher. *Red-Blooded Heroes of the Frontier*. Chicago: A.C. McClurg & Co., 1910. Comp. and ed. Kathy Weiser/Legends of America. Updated November 2010. https://books.google.com/books/about/The_Red_Blooded_Heroes_of_the_Frontier.html?id=p91emAEACAAJ.

Godnig, Edward C. "Vision and Shooting." *The Police Policies Study Council*. 2004. Retrieved 5 July 2014. http://www.theppsc.org/Staff_Views/Godnig/vision_and_shooting.htm.

Layton, Julia. "How Does Death by Hanging Work?" HowStuffWorks.com. 4 January 2007. http://health.howstuffworks.com/diseases-conditions/death-dying/death-by-hanging.htm.

Morales, Javier. *They Fought Like Wildcats Centennial (1914–2014): Herring Hall—Where It All Began*. Allsportstucson.com. 2014. Retrieved 26 September 2014. http://allsportstucson.com/2014/06/08/they-fought-like-wildcats-centennial-1914-2014-herring-hall-where-it-all-began/.

Murfi, Patick. "Bad Day at Bisbee." *Heretic, Rebel, a Thing to Flout*. 2014. Retrieved 25 November 2014. http://patrickmurfin.blogspot.com/2014/07/bad-day-at-bisbee.html.

Rao, Dr. Dinesh. "Hanging." *Dr. Dinesh Rao's Forensic Pathology*. 2013. http://www.forensicpathologyonline.com/e-book/asphyxia/hanging.

Tracy, Roger S. "The Question of Pain in Hanging." *Popular Science Monthly* 13 (July 1878). http://en.wikisource.org/wiki/Popular_Science_Monthly/Volume_13/July_1878/The_Question_of_Pain_in_Hanging.

Periodicals and Journals

Ellis, George M. "Sheriff Jerome L. Ward and the Bisbee Massacre of 1883." *The Journal of Arizona History* 35, no. 3 (1994).

Mac Hunter, Audrey, and Randall Henderson. "Boom Days in Old La Paz." *Desert Magazine* 21, no. 9 (1958).

Mazzanovich, Anton. "The Bisbee Store Hold-Up." *Progressive Arizona* 3, no. 2 (August 1926): 27–28.

Titcomb, Edward. "A Yankee Odyssey." *The Journal of Arizona History* 30, no. 1 (1958).

Newspapers

Arizona Champion 1883–1891
Arizona Daily Star 1879–present
Arizona Republican 1890–1930
Arizona Sentinel (Yuma) 1872–1911
Arizona Silver Belt (Globe) 1878–present
Arizona Weekly Citizen 1880–1901
Arizona Weekly Enterprise 1881–1893
Bisbee Daily Review 1901–1971
Boston Herald 1846–1917
Chicago Daily Tribune 1872–1963
Coconino Sun 1891–1896
Copper Era (Clifton) 1899–1911
Daily Tombstone 1885–1886
Dallas Daily Herald 1873–1887
El Paso Herald 1881–1931
Evening Bulletin (San Francisco) 1855–1895
Kaufman Sun 1880–1911
Las Vegas Daily Gazette (New Mexico) 1881–1886
Lincoln County Leader 1882–189?
New York Times 1857–present
Oasis (Arizola) 1893–1920
Rio Grande Republican 1881–1914
Sacramento Daily Record Union 1875–1891
St. John's Herald 1885–1903
St. Paul Daily Globe 1884–1896
San Francisco Call 1895–1913
Southwest Sentinel (Silver City) 1883–189?
Tombstone Daily Epitaph 1885–1887
Tombstone Daily Prospector 1887–1891
Tombstone Epitaph 1887–present
Tombstone Republican 1882–1884
Tombstone Times 2003–present
Tombstone Weekly Epitaph 1882–1887
Weekly Arizona Miner 1877–1885
Weekly Democratic Statesman (Austin) 1871–1883
Weekly Phoenix Herald 1882–1896
Western Liberal (Lordsburg) 1887–1919

Unpublished Manuscripts

Cox, Annie M. *History of Bisbee 1877 to 1937*. Diss., Graduate College, University of Arizona, 1938.

Hankin, Harriet W. "The Bisbee Holdup and Its Aftermath." Unpublished, undated manuscript. MS. 0329, Harriet Warning File. Arizona Historical Society.

Hart, James. "History of George Warren." Biofile. Unpublished typescript. Arizona Historical Society, 1926.

Index

Numbers in **bold italics** indicate pages with photographs.

257